John Adams and the Spirit of Liberty

American Political Thought
edited by
Wilson Carey McWilliams and Lance Banning

John Adams
and the
Spirit of Liberty

C. Bradley Thompson

University Press of Kansas

© 1998 by the University Press of Kansas
All rights reserved

Published by the University Press of Kansas (Lawrence, Kansas 66049),
which was organized by the Kansas Board of Regents and
is operated and funded by Emporia State University, Fort Hays
State University, Kansas State University, Pittsburg State University, the
University of Kansas, and Wichita State University.

Library of Congress Cataloging-in-Publication Data

Thompson, C. Bradley.
     John Adams and the spirit of liberty / C. Bradley Thompson.
        p.   cm. — (American political thought)
     Includes bibliographical references and index.
     ISBN 0-7006-0915-6 (cloth : alk. paper)
     1. Adams, John, 1735–1826—Views on liberty. 2. Adams, John,
    1735–1826—Political and social views. 3. Liberty.
    4. Constitutional history—United States. I. Title. II. Series.
    JC585.T49   1998
    323.44—dc21   98-17730

British Library Cataloguing in Publication Data is available.

Printed in the United States of America

10 9 8 7 6 5 4 3 2 1

The paper used in this publication meets the minimum requirements of the
American National Standard for Permanence of Paper for Printed Library
Materials Z39.48-1984.

To My Mother and Father

CONTENTS

PREFACE

Modern scholars of the American Revolution have produced an avalanche of books and articles on Thomas Jefferson, James Madison, Alexander Hamilton, George Washington, and Benjamin Franklin. John Adams, by comparison, has not fared so well. In recent years he has been the subject of several excellent biographies, but on the whole he remains largely ignored by the scholarly community. Particularly slighted has been the most remarkable and distinguishing feature of a remarkable and distinguished career: his political and constitutional thought. The last monograph devoted exclusively to examining his political thought was published over thirty years ago. His great treatise on government, *A Defence of the Constitutions of Government of the United States of America*, is rarely studied today and almost certainly never taught. In fact, the *Defence* has never been republished in a modern edition, and the last monograph to examine it systematically was published in 1915. Recovering the neglected and often abused political thought of this important Revolutionary and founding statesmen is the purpose of this book. I seek to explicate John Adams's political reasoning through a reexamination of his major political writings from the "Dissertation on the Canon and Feudal Law" to his *Discourses on Davila*.

Central to Adams's political philosophy is the distinction he drew between "principles of liberty" and "principles of political architecture." The first relates to questions of political right and the second to constitutional design. Coincidentally, the historical development of Adams's political thought and the context in which he wrote mirror this theoretical distinction. During the Revolutionary period, Adams debated American Loyalists and English imperial officials over the true nature of justice and the British constitution. In the years after Independence, he debated with French *philosophes* over the best form of government. Following Adams's lead, this book is divided into two parts. The first chronicles Adams's early intellectual development and, more importantly, his conceptualization of moral and political liberty during the years of the imperial crisis. My primary focus here is to illuminate his two most important pre-Revolutionary essays, "A Dissertation on the Canon and Feudal Law" and "The Letters of Novanglus." Part Two presents Adams's theory of political architecture through an extended analysis of his two great treatises, *A Defence of the Constitutions* and the *Discourses on Davila*.

By reexamining Adams's political thought, I have tried to reconstruct the contours and primary influences that helped to shape his mental universe, the prevailing ideas that he challenged and sought to counteract, the questions and problems that he thought central to the theory and process of constitution-making, the method and modes of reasoning that he employed to answer those questions, and the kind of audience that he sought to influence. Ultimately, I have tried to establish the status and integrity of Adams as an independent thinker, one who would not concede the truth to popular opinion as he attempted to secure the American Revolution with a just and lasting constitutional order.

Over the years I have received a great deal of intellectual, moral, and financial support from many friends, colleagues, and private organizations. Friends—Brendan McConville, Richard Vernier, Joyce Chaplin, Peter McNamara, Lenore Thomas Ealy, John Turner, Stephen Presser, Peter W. Schramm, Bradford P. Wilson, and Gary L. McDowell—read sections of the manuscript at various stages of its development, and I am greatly indebted to them for their encouragement and discerning criticisms.

Throughout my career, I have received the good will of many senior scholars. I would like to thank John L. Thomas, Peter Onuf, Joseph J. Ellis, Michael McGiffert, John P. Diggins, Fred Matthews, and Forrest McDonald for their support and guidance. Leonard Liggio, Jeremy Shearmur, and Steven Davies saved me from early blunders and have provided much wise counsel over the years. Lance Banning and Wilson Carey McWilliams supported the project from the beginning and offered searching criticism along the way.

My greatest intellectual debts are to my teachers. This book began as a doctoral dissertation at Brown University under the supervision of Gordon S. Wood. Professor Wood's scholarly example, support of my efforts to pursue an independent path, and unspoken trust in my judgment have guided my work over the years. Indeed, he will never know the many ways in which he inspired and improved this book. In 1989 I attended an extraordinary seminar on "Revolutionary Constitutionalism" at Harvard University, team-taught by Professors Ralph Lerner and Harvey C. Mansfield. The intellectual seriousness and high level of discussion in that course woke me from my dogmatic slumbers. They have since supported my work and career in untold ways, and for that I am deeply appreciative. Finally, Paul Lowdenslager, my first teacher, took a young man destined for a life in athletics and gently turned his soul toward the more permanent things. Though he did not live to see its completion, the genesis of this book began with him.

I should also like to thank those organizations that have supported my work over the years: the Institute for Humane Studies, the Earhart Foundation, the John M. Olin Foundation, and Ashland University. I am grateful for the cooperation and courtesies extended me by the staff of the Massachusetts Historical Society and *The Adams Papers*. A wonderful year spent in England as a John Adams Fellow at the Institute of United States Studies, University of London, allowed me to finish this book in the same city that Adams wrote his *Defence of the Constitutions*. I am greatly indebted to its Director, Gary L. McDowell, for providing a home away from home and for many stimulating conversations on the philosophic origins of American constitutionalism.

I would also like to thank the editors of *The Review of Politics* and the *Journal of the Early Republic* for allowing me to reprint material in Chapter 6 that originally appeared in their pages. Chapter 1 first appeared as "Young John Adams and the New Philosophic Rationalism" in *The William and Mary Quarterly*, 3d Ser., 40 (1998): 259–80. It is reprinted with permission of the Omohundro Institute of Early American History and Culture.

Lastly, I must thank my family. My parents have patiently and lovingly supported my work over the years. My greatest debt is to my wife, Sidney (my Abigail), who read, corrected, and improved the entire manuscript many times over. This she did unfailingly, often with a crying baby in her arm. Her strength and support mean more than she will ever know. I hope that our young sons, Henry and Samuel, will learn the moral integrity of John Adams as they grow into honorable manhood, and with that the obsession of their all-too-delinquent father.

INTRODUCTION

John Adams was America's finest eighteenth-century student of the political sciences. No one, not even Thomas Jefferson or James Madison, read as much or thought as long and hard about questions of human nature, natural right, political organization, and constitutional construction. His friend and Revolutionary compatriot, Benjamin Rush, thought there was a consensus among the founding generation that Adams possessed "more learning probably, both ancient and modern, than any man who subscribed the Declaration of Independence."[1] Modern scholars largely agree with this assessment. Adams's *A Defence of the Constitutions of Government of the United States of America* is often described by political scientists as one of the great tracts in the history of American political thought and is frequently cited by historians as an important guide to understanding American Revolutionary constitutionalism. Thus, in attempting to explain the causes and meaning of the American Revolution, historians have often turned to Adams because he is considered by many as its most thoughtful spokesman. If Samuel Adams or Patrick Henry represent the spirit of the independence movement, John Adams embodied the mind of the American Revolution.[2]

General commentators also attribute to Adams a central role in the American Revolution. He will forever be remembered as an important leader of the radical political movement in Boston; as one of the most thoughtful and principled voices at the Continental Congress; as the author of the "Novanglus" essays, considered by many the best encapsulation of the colonial opposition to English imperial policy, and of "Thoughts on Government," which provided the blueprint for a number of state constitutions; as the principal architect of the Massachusetts Constitution; as the founder of the Revolutionary Navy; and finally, as having played a central role in negotiating a peace treaty with Great Britain. Adams witnessed the Revolution from beginning to end: he assisted James Otis in the Writs of Assistance case in 1761, and he was a participant at the peace ceremonies in Paris in 1783. Adams played so many important roles at such critical points in the movement for independence and in the formation of the national polity that to misunderstand his thought and deeds is to mis-understand the Founding.

Despite all these achievements and accolades, historians have never been quite sure what to make of Adams. In fact, time has not been so kind to Adams's post-Revolutionary reputation. The career of the new nation's first vice president and second president was and has been the object of criticism, ridicule, and ideological ire. It is a now commonly held opinion that Adams's political thought underwent a profound transformation in the years after the end of the War for Independence, that he became increasingly conservative and cynical about the regenerative effects of republican government. In the short space of ten or fifteen years, the ide-alistic revolutionary is said to have become one of America's most noto-rious conservatives. There is a growing consensus among historians today that Adams lost touch with the rapidly changing dynamics of political discourse in America during the post-Revolutionary years, and that his political thought became "anomalous" and "irrelevant" to the newly emerging world of egalitarian politics.[3]

Surely these opinions would have bewildered and troubled Adams. Indeed, we know they did, for they are exactly the same charges that were leveled against him by many of his contemporaries. From the first moment that he heard them, Adams vehemently denied that he had dis-avowed his revolutionary republicanism for the aristocratic forms and for-malities of the British constitution. He bitterly complained that he had deviated not one whit from his revolutionary principles. No contempo-rary statesman, he complained, had more consistently pursued and applied the principles of the Revolution to the task of constitution mak-ing. Adams would have been especially puzzled and hurt to learn that modern scholars have suggested that he did not understand what was hap-pening to the nature of political discourse in the new republic. Adams thought he understood all too well what was happening, and he did not like it. In the end, we must determine whether Adams understood his own principles as well as modern historians claim to understand them.

John Adams has thus always posed a genuine problem for historians. From the moment he entered public life, he always seemed to travel the road not taken. Americans have rarely seen a political leader of such fierce independence and unyielding integrity. Few gave as much or were as uncompromisingly devoted to the Revolutionary cause. In political debate he was intrepid to the verge of temerity, and his political writings reveal an utter contempt for the art of dissimulation. Unable to meet falsehoods halfway and unwilling to stop short of the truth, Adams was in constant battle with the accepted, the conventional, the fashionable, and the popular. He would compromise neither with Thomas Hutchinson nor with the Boston mob. From his defense of English soldiers at the Boston Massacre trial to his treaty with the French in 1800, Adams had a way of shocking and disarming his most ardent supporters and his most partisan opponents. Ever the maverick, he predicted, with a justified degree of bitterness, that "mausoleums, statues, monuments will never be erected to me. . . . Panegyrical romances will never be written, nor flattering orations spoken to transmit me to posterity in brilliant colors."[4] To some, however, the complexity of the man and the problematic nature of interpreting his political thought is the very reason why a figure like Adams is worth studying.

Over the course of the last three decades, historians have most often studied Adams's political thought from the perspective of two very different methodological approaches. One method explains Adams's political thinking as it was shaped by a nonrational "inner" world, while the other explains the meaning of those ideas as they correspond to an "outer" world of social and economic change. Ironically, both approaches were inspired by the writings of the Harvard historian Bernard Bailyn.

The first attempts to explain the motives, sources, content, and limits of Adams's political writings by uncovering the unconscious and nonrational personality characteristics that formed his response to and understanding of the great events that unfolded around him. The psychoanalytic approach to studying Adams was first suggested in Bailyn's review essay of the *Diary and Autobiography of John Adams*, published in 1961.[5] For Bailyn, it was Adams's "sensuous apprehension of experience," his "feelings" and "sensitive reactions to the human realities about him" that shaped and defined the parameters of his political thought. "It is with these central personality characteristics in mind—characteristics formed in a troubled youth, modified and consolidated in maturity," he wrote, "that one can best understand Adams's response to the Revolutionary crisis and the sources of his political theory." Bailyn went so far as to suggest that Adams's "political theory was an effort to express in the constitutional language of his day the implications of this dark, introspective psychology."[6] This suggestive attempt to draw a link between the "inner" and the "outer" life of Adams became the explicit theme of Peter Shaw's illuminating biography, *The Character of John Adams* (1976) and, more recently, of Joseph J. Ellis's *Passionate Sage: The Character and Legacy of*

John Adams (1993). For Shaw, the sources of Adams's political thought were found in the psychic inner world of eighteenth-century Puritan village life. His stated purpose in studying Adams was to "intellectualize his behavior and to personalize his ideas." According to Shaw, Adams's *Defence of the Constitutions* should be studied as a reflection of his disordered personality.[7]

A second method employed in recent years to explain Adams's political thought is often described as the "ideological" approach.[8] Following the lead of anthropologists and sociologists, the ideological historians have attempted to bridge the traditional intellectual dichotomy between rhetoric and reality by explaining the thought of individual thinkers or of entire societies as a response to and a reflection of a socially ordered consciousness. By locating Adams's ideas in the rapidly changing social, economic, and political contexts of eighteenth-century Massachusetts, the ideological historians have sought to explain how and why the content of his political thought was shaped by immediate cultural experiences. John R. Howe's *The Changing Political Thought of John Adams* (1966) contains the fullest expression of this mode of interpretation. Howe's method sought to explain Adams's political thought by examining the "immediate experiences through which he passed." According to one historian of the ideological school, Adams's major work in political theory "grew out of his Massachusetts experience."[9]

There is much to be said for these two different interpretive methods. There is no question that Adams's personality was unique. Benjamin Franklin captured the essence of Shaw's interpretation when he described his Revolutionary colleague as one who "means well for his country, is always an honest man, often a wise one but sometimes, and in some things, absolutely out of his senses."[10] There is also much to be said for the view that Adams's personal experience of mounting social crises in America and Europe had an important effect on the way he conceptualized certain intellectual and political problems. To be sure, he was as attuned to the changing nature of American society and the consequences for political life as any member of the Revolutionary generation. Fortunately, neither Howe nor Shaw succumbs to a simple-minded, single-cause determinism; both incorporate a sophisticated synthetic method that takes account of the multiple forces that influenced, shaped, and determined Adams's thought.

Despite their different approaches, these two modes of interpretation share certain methodological premises and conclusions derived from modern social-science thinking. Both accept the general premise that all thought is and must ultimately be explained by external factors that stimulate, shape, and delimit its boundaries and meaning. Among the various nonrational factors commonly invoked to determine the meaning of a text are social environments, cultural networks, economic structures, linguistic paradigms, psychological parameters, climates of opinion, and ideological signs. But do such methods of interpretation adequately explain the reasons that led Adams to write as he did and what he did? Can they explain how this enormously learned man understood the philosophic character of his own *Defence of the Constitutions* or *Discourses on Davila*, or the perennial human questions they claim to address? Do they provide a sufficient condition for understanding the depth and complexity of a man who claimed to have discovered the "truth" about certain questions of justice and political organization? As enlightening and helpful as these studies have been, they suffer from one serious flaw: they do not attempt to understand Adams as he understood himself; that is, they do not appreciate the highly self-conscious role that Adams pursued as a statesman, as a political thinker, and as a revolutionary constitution-maker. Nor do they sufficiently take into account the purpose and philosophic problems that Adams consciously assigned to himself and then attempted to solve in a systematic and final way. Quite possibly the most distinguishing characteristic of Adams's public career was his status as an *independent* thinker. Our challenge is to reexamine Adams's political thought from a more comprehensive and authentically historical perspective, one sensitive not only to his New England experiences but also to his own understanding of causality and agency.

For these reasons alone, it would be inappropriate to study John Adams from the same methodological perspective that one might use to examine the popular and partisan pamphleteers of the Revolutionary and Founding periods. Ultimately, what I am suggesting is that certain Founders like Adams constitute a class of their own, and must therefore be studied by a different method and judged by different historical standards. It would be ludicrous to superimpose on Adams the same interpretive framework used to examine the editor of a small-town newspaper. Likewise, it would be entirely unfair to contrast for the sake of criticizing or dismissing Adams's political ideas relative to works like *The Federalist*. We should keep in mind that *A Defence* and *The Federalist* were addressed to different kinds or levels of readers, and they were intended to serve very different ends. The language and rhetoric employed by the authors of *The Federalist* were more democratic than they might otherwise have been had Madison or Hamilton written a political treatise solely for statesmen and constitution makers. Furthermore, had Madison or Hamilton written such a treatise before the Constitutional Convention, it is likely that their views would have been much closer to those they expressed behind the closed doors of the Philadelphia Convention than those written for the popular press. Unlike James Madison, Adams did not have to compromise his political ideas in a constitutional convention, nor did he have to pander to the passions, opinions, and interests of a newspaper audience.

In the chapters that follow, I have attempted to study Adams's political and constitutional thought from a new angle of vision. Far from adopting an internal, "textualist" mode of interpretation, I have attempted to provide a better context, one better attuned to the specific circumstances in which Adams wrote, more akin to how he understood his own context, and truer to his principles and presuppositions. His reasons for writing A *Defence of the Constitutions* were many: politically, he was sparked to write by Shays's Rebellion and the calling of the French Assembly of Notables; personally, he was encouraged to write by Thomas Jefferson and Dutch constitutional reformers; ideologically, he was provoked to write in order to counter the ideas of certain French *philosophes* from influencing republican reform in America and France. But to ask *why* he wrote is different than to ask *what* he wrote. Answering this latter question requires that we enter the intellectual world inhabited by John Adams and confront the ultimate context that opens the way to a more satisfying explanation of his thought. In the end, it is by locating the philosophic context— Adams's understanding of and confrontation with the tradition of political philosophy extending from Herodotus and Plato to John Locke and Adam Smith—that we can best understand his political thought. The mode of inquiry that I have applied to the study of John Adams differs from the psychoanalytic and ideological approaches in the following important way: It is precisely the "reading and reasoning" rejected by Howe and Shaw as the essential condition for understanding Adams's political thought that I reexamine and restore as the most important mode of explaining the ideas of this complex man. In the very same way that David Hackett Fischer has recently put Paul Revere back in the saddle, I have studied Adams by returning him to his library.[11]

To enter that world we must first confront naively, openly, even sympathetically, Adams's assumptions, ideas, and intended audiences as he understood them. Lest we assume from the outset that we are more intelligent than John Adams or that we can understand his thought better than he understood it himself, we should begin our study with a recognition that his *Defence of the Constitutions* is a strange and enigmatic book, and that his claim to have discovered the truth might not be simply a rationalization or the fancy of an overheated imagination. More importantly, we must temporarily suspend our modern belief in how ideas ought to be explained and open ourselves to a strange and different world that understood nature and causation, philosophy and history, in ways very different from our own. This means that my starting point in trying to understand and explain Adams's thought has been informed by my sense of how eighteenth-century philosophers and statesmen pursued and conceptualized the moral and political sciences.

Central to my method has been a recognition of the intellectual war of ideas that Adams saw himself engaged in, the allies that he marshaled to his side, and the opponents against whom he was reacting. I have therefore immersed myself in the tradition of political philosophy that Adams stood ready to affirm or deny. This means that I have attempted to read those texts as Adams might have. When a writer claims, as Adams did, that he has discovered the "infallible truth" about the so-called perennial questions of political life, it would be simply negligent for the historian not to take the claim seriously. Thus, I have been less interested in re-presenting or repeating the conclusions of Adams's investigations than in studying the intellectual technique, the modes of reasoning that he brought to bear on the great questions of political organization and constitutional construction. Ultimately, however, I have attempted to go beyond the internal logic of the text to uncover the boundaries of Adams's thought, to seek its depth and range, its starting and its ending points. With that task in mind, it is hoped that a new John Adams, one to be admired more than pitied, will emerge from the pages that follow.[12]

Part I

Principles of Liberty

Chapter 1

Calvin, Locke, and the American Enlightenment

During his retirement years, John Adams was fond of saying that the War for Independence was a consequence of the American Revolution. The real revolution, he declared, had taken place in the minds and hearts of the colonists in the decade or two before 1776. What he meant by this evocative statement and how he understood the sources and nature of America's Revolutionary transformation have long intrigued historians. In an 1818 letter to Hezekiah Niles, Adams left a clue to his meaning. Among other things, he said, there had been a *"radical change"* in the people's "religious sentiments of their duties and obligations." This "great and important alteration" in the colonists' religious and moral character forced them to rethink their duties and obligations to king and Parliament after imperial authorities began to violate "their lives, liberties, and properties."[1] How can historians examine or measure the causes and nature of such a phenomenon? We might begin by looking to Adams himself: his early diary records in remarkable detail a "radical change" in his religious and moral views. If we are to understand how John Adams experienced the coming of the Revolution, we must begin by examining the assumptions and ideas through which he filtered and interpreted events of the day.

Historians have commonly described John Adams as a Puritan or neo-Puritan and have equated his diary with the self-exorcising daybooks of his Calvinist forebears.[2] Two important attempts to examine Adams's early years agree that his behavior and character traits, his knowledge and ideas, and even his response to the Revolutionary crisis were largely shaped by a strict Calvinist heritage and the cultural remnants of Puritan manners and mores. According to Bernard Bailyn, Adams "unconsciously and unquestioningly accepted as his own the exacting behavioral standards of the Bible Commonwealth." For Edmund S. Morgan, the early diary "reveals Adams in full pursuit of the Protestant Ethic."[3] At a time when historians are looking to classical-republican or classical-liberal paradigms to explain the coming of the American Revolution, Bailyn and Morgan usefully remind us that its deepest roots were very much indigenous.

3

The portrait of Adams as Puritan or Calvinist is most often based on two arguments. The first suggests that his early diary sustains the themes and elements characteristic of the Puritan confessional: sin, self-examination, preparation, repentance, self-mastery, the quest for salvation. At first glance, we see a young man facing what Morgan described as the classic Puritan dilemma: the struggle between earthly desires and otherworldly obligations. Inspired by Max Weber's *The Protestant Ethic and the Spirit of Capitalism*, Morgan explained Adams's struggle against vanity, his asceticism, and his search for a calling as a form of secularized Puritanism. For Morgan, it was John Adams and not Benjamin Franklin who best embodied Puritan forms and formalities.[4]

The second argument suggests that Adams adopted a view of human nature and Christian sin that was fundamentally Calvinist. Certainly, since the publication in 1964 of the *Diary and Autobiography of John Adams*, there has been a strong tendency among Adams scholars to interpret his mature political ideas from the perspective of his "dark, introspective psychology," a psychology shaped early in life and within a Puritan mental universe. Adams's views on human nature were, in the words of Bailyn, "more akin to those of his Calvinist forebears . . . than of the eighteenth-century Enlightenment." One scholar has attempted to explain Adams's political philosophy in the light of a "psychology of political behavior derived from Calvinist theology," and another has gone so far as to compare Adams's *Defence of the Constitutions of Government of the United States of America* to Cotton Mather's *Magnalia Christi Americana*.[5]

There can be no doubt that Adams's diary resembles the daybooks of his Puritan ancestors and records struggles very much like theirs. Readers see a young man plunging into the depths of his soul, ferreting out hidden and impure motives, searching for, identifying, and confronting the secret passions that seem to direct his private and public actions. His strict daily regimen and constant self-examination surely owed something to the moral world created in his parents' home. Adams bore signs of the Protestant ethic his whole life: he was always looking inward, assessing the state of his soul, struggling against idleness, vanity, and luxury. In a way, Bailyn and Morgan were right: Adams never quite kicked the Puritan habit. But can we rightly call him a Puritan? Did his social and political thought reflect a Calvinist or even a secularized Calvinist view of human nature? Or are the dominant sources, foundations, and substance of Adams's thinking to be found elsewhere?

A fresh examination of Adams's diary and early correspondence reveals a very different young man than the one hitherto described. Spilling from almost every page is another image: We see the intellectual awakening and maturing of the youthful Adams as he enthusiastically begins to view the world and his fellow man from a position contrary to that of his Puritan ancestors. The diary shows a young man enjoying his liberation from the psychological imperatives and intellectual blinders associated with an inherited culture. Adams obviously delighted in his own flowering ratiocination and the unfolding and empowering of his own mental processes. He was constantly probing, assessing, validating, classifying, and cataloguing the constitution of nature and human nature. Deeply influenced by modern natural philosophy, he searched into nature for its underlying laws; he kept trying to make sense of, and bring order to, the seeming disorder of the natural and social world around him. In all these ways, John Adams's diary is an exemplary document of the eighteenth-century American Enlightenment.

By focusing on Adams's subrational inner world—his "central personality characteristics," his "tormented tossings and turnings," his "sensuous apprehension of experience," and his "sensitive reactions to the realities about him"—scholars have neglected to account for the self-conscious intellectual transformation that takes place in the diary. Paying virtually no attention to Adams's explicit and repeated declarations of the debt he owed to an entirely different intellectual tradition, they have overestimated the role played by Puritan ways in Adams's life and thought, and they have underestimated the influence that modern philosophic rationalism played in revolutionizing his mental and moral universe.[6]

The most remarkable feature of Adams's formative intellectual years was the degree to which he confronted and consciously repudiated the orthodoxies of New England Puritanism. From 1756 to 1760, Adams used his diary to work out a new way of understanding piety, virtue, and right living. This chapter proposes to demonstrate that Adams not only rejected theological Calvinism but also disavowed much of his Puritan past by developing and embracing a view of nature, man, and moral obligation that drew heavily on the enlightened views of Bacon, Newton, and Locke. Most importantly, his confrontation with Locke's *An Essay Concerning Human Understanding* marked the turning point in the young man's intellectual and moral life. The *Essay* was important to Adams's intellectual development because it provided him with a method for thinking. We can never appreciate *what* Adams thought until we know *how* he thought. By examining his youthful mental processes, we can see how he began to transform the New England

Protestant ethos into a distinctly modern form of liberal individualism. In a larger sense, Adams's intellectual biography helps illuminate why and when many American colonials moved consciously away from Puritan orthodoxy and toward Enlightenment rationalism.[7]

The Frigid John Calvin

When John Adams entered Harvard College in 1751 at age fifteen, his father, Deacon John Adams, expected him to study for the ministry.[8] In Cambridge, however, the young man encountered a different intellectual world. He was particularly influenced by John Winthrop, Hollis Professor of mathematics and natural philosophy. Winthrop introduced Adams to the new philosophic rationalism associated with the modern revolution in the natural sciences. His lectures in "Experimental Phylosophy" sought to explain the lawlike regularity of the Newtonian conception of nature. On April 9, 1754, Adams recorded in his diary that "Sir Isaac Newtons three laws of nature" and their application to planetary motion were "proved and illustrated" in Winthrop's lecture. Years later, he would say that his training in the sciences and mathematics gave him a "degree of Patience of Investigation, which I might not otherwise have obtained." Adams soon realized that he could apply the new scientific method to the study of man and society. The concrete and detailed observations of human nature, the sharp and vivid descriptions of those around him, the acute dissection of motives and actions, and the painstaking accumulation and cataloguing of historical actors that fill the diary attest to the importance of Winthrop's method for Adams's intellectual development.[9]

While Adams was studying at Harvard, his home town of Braintree became embroiled in controversy over the religious views of the local Congregational minister, Lemuel Briant. The event had a profound impact on Adams's intellectual development and ultimate career choice. In 1749, Briant had openly challenged Puritan orthodoxy with a sermon on "The Absurdity and Blasphemy of Depreciating Moral Virtue." Braintree soon divided into two warring parties "concerning the five points" of traditional Calvinism: total depravity, unconditional election, limited atonement, irresistibility of grace, and perseverance of the saints. Briant was publicly censured for views that were seen as dangerously close to Arminianism, the doctrine that men by their own free will could achieve faith and through good works win God's saving grace. "Ecclesiastical Councils" called to resolve the issue met in the home of Deacon Adams.

Young John read all the pamphlets of the controversy, for and against, and he attended the council, which he described as more an inquisition than a free and open exchange of ideas.[10]

Disturbed by the "Spirit of Dogmatism and Bigotry" he witnessed in his father's home, Adams concluded "that the Study of Theology and the pursuit of it as a Profession would involve me in endless Altercations and make my life miserable, without any prospect of doing good to my fellow Men." He found troublesome the prospect of constant scrutiny and censorship. At this time, he records, he began to seriously question whether he was cut out for the life of a New England minister. Soon thereafter, he began to consider other professions. By his senior year, he was still undecided between pursuing a career in "Divinity, Law or Physick." Fortunately, he was able to defer the decision for another year or two after a minister approached him at his graduation ceremony with an offer to teach school at Worcester.[11] The time would give him the opportunity to clarify his religious beliefs and decide on a profession.

Soon after settling into his new town and school, Adams turned to the self-appointed task of reconsidering the theological premises of his inherited religion and to developing what we would today call a philosophy of life. He contemplated the mysteries of his religion, the "Stupendous Plan of operation" of the universe, and the glory and omnipotence of God.[12] During that critical first year in Worcester, he tackled and settled the great questions of religion and philosophy in ways that would later ground his moral and political principles. The themes of the diary reflect his agenda: nature and God, reason and revelation, virtue and vice, free will and determinism.

Worcester introduced Adams to a small, clandestine group of dissenters and freethinkers. Upon arriving in town, he learned that Thomas Morgan's deist treatise, *The Moral Philosopher*, "had circulated, with some freedom" and that "the Principles of Deism had made a considerable progress among several Persons, in that and other Towns in the County."[13] In his autobiography, he recorded vivid memories of the discussions and debates in which he engaged with a lively clique of Arminians, deists, and atheists. His interlocutors provided the intellectual camaraderie, freedom of thought, and exchange of ideas that the young man searching his soul and stretching his mind found exciting and challenging. By contrast, he lost all patience with the "Frigid performances" of the local Congregational minister and his "Frigid" theology drawn from John Calvin.[14]

Adams spent many "Evenings with these Men, as they were readers and thinking Men, though I differed from them all in Religion and Government, because there were no others in Town who were possessed of so much literature." The group's two principal members were the merchant Ephraim Doolittle and the local register of deeds, Nathan Baldwin, whom Adams described as "great Readers of Deistical Books, and very great Talkers." The equally talkative and inquisitive Adams found these armchair philosophers especially attractive because they were "never rude" or "insolent to those who differed from them." Politics and religion were always at the center of their discussions: "They were great Sticklers for Equality as well as Deism." Though not a radical, he found something appealing in the very subversiveness of his new acquaintances. A third member was the "excentric" shopkeeper, Joseph Dyer, a man "very bitter against . . . the Clergy" and an "Arian by profession." Dyer had apparently written "many Manuscripts especially upon the Athanasian Doctrine of the Trinity," which Adams claimed to have read in their entirety. His favorite and most frequent interlocutor was James Putnam, a lawyer, at whose house he boarded. Putnam's religious views were apparently shaped by his friend Peasley Collins, "who had been to Europe and came back, a Disbeliever in Every Thing: fully satisfied that all Religion was a cheat, a cunning invention of Priests and Politicians." The principal area of disagreement between Adams and Putnam concerned the "Evidences of a future State, and the Principles of natural and revealed Religion." Putnam challenged and Adams defended the idea of "a future Existence" and a very limited conception of revealed religion.[15] Though never quite a deist, Adams was nonetheless influenced by his association with Putnam and the Worcester dissenters. At the very least, they drove him to stake out his own position regarding the principles of religion, natural and revealed.

During his first year in Worcester, Adams was challenged by two ministers—Jason Haven of Dedham, Massachusetts, and Thomas Balch of Norwood—on two critical points of doctrine: the divinity of Christ and the veracity of biblical revelation.[16] Haven and Balch associated the rejection of these principles with an extreme form of Arminianism, and Haven told Adams "very civilly" that "he supposed I took my faith on Trust from Dr. Mayhew." The charge is revealing: Mayhew was the great liberal theologian and pastor of Boston's West Church. Late in life, Adams told Thomas Jefferson that Briant and Mayhew exchanged pulpits with some regularity, thereby giving the teenager an opportunity to hear the Boston minister. In his *Seven Sermons* delivered in 1749 and in all likelihood heard or read by Adams, Mayhew preached that there is a "natural" difference between right and wrong, that we are all naturally endowed with a rational faculty to discern the differences, and that we are morally obligated to choose right over wrong. If Adams did not exactly take his "faith on Trust" from Mayhew, his diary makes clear that he was drawing conclusions remarkably similar to those of the Boston preacher. The young man was particularly influenced by Mayhew's *Discourse Concerning Unlimited Submission and Non-Resistance to the Higher Powers* (1750), which he later told Jefferson he read at age fourteen "till the Substance of it was incorporated into my Nature and indelibly engraved on my Memory." Two weeks after his encounter with Haven and Balch, Adams reported to his friend Charles Cushing that there had been "a story about Town that I am an *Orminian*."[17] He let the rumor pass without comment, suggesting that there was some truth to it, but we also see him struggling to defend even the most rudimentary principles of revealed Christianity. He accepted the immortality of souls on faith, for he could not believe that "Death was an endless Sleep." He also accepted the necessity of miracles and the Bible as revealed truth. Much beyond that, he would not go.[18]

On August 21, 1756, John Adams signed a contract to read law with James Putman. His rejection of a clerical calling had not, in the end, been a difficult one. He wrote to Richard Cranch that the "frightful Engines of Ecclesiastical Co[u]ncils, of diabolical Malice and Calvinistical good nature" terrified him whenever he thought of preaching. In the wake of the Briant controversy and in the light of new intellectual influences, Adams warned Cushing that only those with "the highest opinion of what is called Orthodoxy" were accepted as ministers in New England. He claimed to know more than one preacher distinguished for a "sleepy stupid soul." Experience taught him that "people are not disposed to inquire for piety, integrity, good sense or learning in a young preacher." Instead, they looked for "stupidity (for so I must call the pretended sanctity of some absolute dunces), irresistible grace and original sin."[19] The letters to Cranch and Cushing suggest *some* of the reasons why Adams rejected a career as a minister. His reference to "irresistible grace and original sin" indicate others, about which the diary is informative.

On the day he formally announced his decision to pursue a career in the law, Adams wrote in his diary that his reason for "quitting Divinity was my Opinion concerning some disputed Points."[20] As we shall see, the "disputed Points" that he associated with New England orthodoxy were the well-known "five points" refined by Dutch and English theologians at the Synod of Dort and confirmed in the Westminster Confession. These disputed points were the very ones that Adams had seen Lemuel Briant interrogated about in the home of his father.

Almost from the moment that young Adams began to think about theological and moral issues, he rejected the doctrine that the original sin of Adam "was enough to damn the whole human Race, without any actual Crimes committed by any of them." He shuddered at the Calvinists' claim that mankind had been arbitrarily judged and found guilty of a crime, not because of "their rashness and Indiscretion, not by their own Wickedness and Vice, but by the Supream Being." Adams thought the charge unjust and therefore "a real Injury and Misfortune because it renders us worse than not to be."[21] He also thought the doctrine of unconditional election "detestable," "invidious," and "hurtful." Its purpose was to represent "eternal life, as an unattainable Thing without the special favor of the Father." When combined with the doctrine of limited atonement, the effect was "to discourage the practice of virtue." For Adams, unconditional election was the linchpin of Calvinist theology and practice, but he could not accept a doctrine that denied free will, moral obligation, and the possibility of performing the virtue and piety necessary for everlasting happiness. Writing to a friend, he vowed never to be "persuaded or frightened either by Popes or Councils . . . to believe that the world of nature, learning and grace is governed by such arbitrary Will or inflexible fatality." No, indeed not! "We have much higher Notions of the efficacy of human endeavours in all Cases," declared the twenty-five-year-old John Adams.[22] Likewise, he found the connected teaching of limited atonement—the belief that salvation was not possible to all men and women but only to a few—a "strange religious Dogma." He thought preposterous the teaching that "God elected a precious few (of which few however every Man who believes the doctrine is always One) to Life eternal without regard to any foreseen Virtue, and reprobated all the Rest, without regard to any foreseen Vice." Adams appreciated the "serious gravity" of such a doctrine but could not countenance a religious teaching that "represents the world, as under the government of Humour and Caprice." He found such a precept to be morally destructive and intellectually absurd: even the "Hottentots and Mohawks would reject with horror" the notion that some men and women are predestined to eternal grace and others to eternal damnation regardless of their virtue and vice.[23] As we shall see, the doctrine of free will was central to Adams's rejection of Calvinism.

Thus, Adams dismissed several of the foundational premises of Calvinism: he denied original sin and the total depravity of mankind; he denounced unconditional election; he rejected limited atonement. Moreover, although he did not directly address the related doctrines of the irresistibility of grace and perseverance of the elect, he surely repudiated them as well, for they were meaningful only to the degree that original sin, limited atonement, and unconditional election were accepted. During these early years, Adams seems to have been utterly uninterested in the depth, intellectual rigor, and rich complexities of New England's historic faith. There is no evidence, for instance, that he read or even cared to read the greatest of the American Calvinists, Jonathan Edwards. In rejecting Calvinism, Adams could often sound like an Arminian, but it would be incorrect to describe him so simply. To call Adams an Arminian is to suggest that he still carried in his mental constitution traces of Calvinism's original principles, which, as we shall see, he certainly did not. Although it is difficult to pin down and label Adams's true religious views during this period in his life ("natural religion" may be the closest we can come), we can with some certainty reconstruct and describe the principal philosophic sources that influenced his developing world view.

The Great Mr. Locke

A revealing indication of the direction of Adams's thought as he worked out his relationship with God, nature, and mankind is his reading. We cannot know all the books he perused, but from his diary, literary commonplace book, and autobiography, we can discover the works he thought important.[24] The list is heavy in natural philosophy, ethics, and theology. Adams paid special attention to the English theologians known as Latitudinarians. In February 1756, he copied extracts from Archbishop John Tillotson's sermons. Several months later, he took extensive notes on Joseph Butler's *Analogy of Religion, Natural and Revealed, to the Constitution and Course of Nature* (1736). The commonplace book shows that he read Samuel Clarke "on the attributes of God" and Richard Bentley's *Sermons at Boyle's Lecture* (1692).[25] In the wake of Newtonian science and Lockean epistemology, these liberal churchmen sought to give Christianity a new, stronger foundation grounded in reason, natural law, and free will. They taught that "right reason" was capable of determining God's laws and that all men could attain saving grace volitionally, by leading moral, virtuous, and pious lives. They emphasized man's natural capacity and duty to pursue moral rectitude.[26]

Also conspicuous on Adams's list are such early modern English and Continental philosophers as Bacon, Newton, René Descartes, Thomas Hobbes, Gottfried Wilhem Leibniz, and, above all, Locke.[27] In at least four places in the early diary and in one important letter, Adams copied or paraphrased long passages from the *Essay*.[28] These passages and others of the period show him embracing a Newtonian conception of nature as understood by Lockean epistemology. "In Metaphysics," he wrote, "Mr. Locke, directed by my Lord Bacon, has steered his Course into the unenlightened Regions of the human Mind." Dramatically, Adams compared Locke to Columbus: he had discovered a "new World." The newfound epistemological continent was full of dangers and possibilities: it had "unwholesome Weeds," "unprofitable Brambles," and "motly Savages," but it also had "wholesome fruits and flowers," "useful Trees," and "civilized Inhabitants." Locke, Adams said, taught mankind how to exterminate the weeds and to cultivate the fruits of the human mind. Just as Locke had cleared man's field of vision, so too had discoveries by natural philosophers like Bacon and Newton "done Honour to the human Understanding." Thus in philosophy, mathematics, and astronomy the modern world had advanced far beyond the high culture of the classical world. In that advance, Adams excitedly found the "true sphere of Modern Genius."[29]

In Adams's estimation, Locke's exemplary genius displayed itself above all in his effective demolition of the ancient theory of innate ideas. All knowledge, according to Locke, rests on two fundamental premises: physical reality exists independent of the human mind, and men acquire knowledge only through an inductive process of reasoning that filters and orders the experience of the five senses. The implications of this teaching—what Locke called the "historical plain method" —for all revealed religions were clear: the doctrine of the tabula rasa excluded all innate ideas, among them, most fundamentally, the idea of God.[30] For Locke, the only intuitive knowledge that man has is of his own existence; all other knowledge, even of God, is derived by rational deduction from our experience of the world. Nothing is to be taken on trust or faith.[31] In a single stroke, Locke thus denied that God had imprinted in the minds of men certain indisputable truths.

Locke held that God's existence can and must be proved by reason; it may be confirmed by revelation, which must also stand the test of reason. By stripping away the layers of Scholastic system and dogma, Locke laid bare a simple and direct means of coming to know God. One victim was the Antinomian doctrine—what we might call the "pure" doctrine of Calvinist election—that knowledge of God and his saving grace is stamped on the minds or in the breasts of certain men and women. The God of Locke and Adams is not the mysterious yet intensely personal God of the Puritans. Unlike the Puritans, for whom God's existence and majesty were known through his word and works, the God of Locke and

Adams could be known only through rules of evidence that approximated mathematical demonstration. The God that emerges from the pages of the *Essay Concerning Human Understanding* is an intellectual construct whose existence could be proved by rational demonstration and whose purpose could be established by sober argument. The effect of raising reason above faith and revelation to determine the veracity of Christian doctrine fundamentally reshaped Christian thought and experience. The idea of a natural religion did not originate with Locke but was certainly hurried along by his epistemology. The very title of his treatise on theological questions, *On the Reasonableness of Christianity* (1695), set a tone and an agenda for English and American theological investigation for the next century.[32] In this post-Lockean world, some in England and America undertook to replace the enthusiasm of the seventeenth century with a rational theology, a simple and direct moral teaching, and a moderate and reasonable faith.

No part of the Protestant synthesis escaped Locke's influence. As faith became subject to rational reappraisal, so, too, did morality. "Reason," Locke declared, "must be our last judge and guide in everything," including our relations with fellow human beings and our duties to God.[33] Reason, and only reason, could supply standards for determining rules of good behavior and provide guidance for right living. This teaching not only undercut the doctrine of original sin but thrust powerfully toward Latitudinarianism and Arminianism by linking God's grace to man's free will and good works. Redemption, according to Locke, is the reasonable reward for right conduct.

Adams's first step in constructing a new moral vision was to examine human nature. He was particularly concerned with delineating the origins, nature, and limits of human knowledge. Three years after he had decided on a career, he restated the intellectual issue that he had been grappling with since 1756. The connection to Locke is obvious.

> Tis impossible to employ with full Advantage the Forces of our own minds, in study, in Council or in Argument, without examining with great Attention and Exactness, all our mental Faculties, in all their Operations, as explained by Writers on the human Understanding, and as exerted by Geometricians.
>
> Tis impossible to judge with much Præcision of the true Motives and Qualities of human Actions, or of the Propriety of Rules contrived to govern them, without considering with like Attention, all the Passions, Appetites, Affections in Nature from which they flow. *An intimate Knowledge therefore of the intellectual and moral World is the sole foundation on which a stable structure of Knowledge can be erected.*[34]

Ultimately, according to Adams, it is by examining the "Constitution of our Minds and Bodies" rather than through "supernatural Revelation" that we come to know our rights and moral obligations.[35] Such a premise or strategy—starting with man rather than with God—demonstrates how far Adams had ventured into the rational humanism of his age.

Following Locke, Adams held that knowledge begins with two basic axioms: something exists that one perceives, and one exists, possessing consciousness or the means of perceiving that which exists. These irreducible primaries, existence and consciousness, grounded his intellectual project. For Adams, as for Locke, reality exists independent of man's awareness of it: nature is an autonomous realm, self-sufficient and real in its own right. Awareness of external reality is the beginning of knowledge; everything we know "is acquired by Experience, i.e. by sensation or Reflection." Adams is clear and direct on this point: "[T]hese ideas can enter our minds no other way but thro the senses." From these "slender and contracted Faculties," he notes, "we find our Selves capable of comprehending many Things." Reason, building on sensory accumulation of information and liberated from tradition, authority, and theological system, enables man to know himself, nature, and God:

> all the Provision[s] that he [God] has [made?] for the Gratification of our senses, tho very engaging and unmerited Instances of goodness, are much inferior to the Provision, the wonderful Provision that he has made for the gratification of our nobler Powers of Intelligence and Reason. *He has given us Reason, to find out the Truth, and the real Design and true End of our Existence, and has made all Endeavours to promote them agreable to our minds, and attended with a conscious pleasure and Complacency.*

Sometime between February and August 1756, when he was exploring the unenlightened regions of his own mind and reexamining his philosophical and religious convictions, Adams came to the conclusion that reason was a sufficient guide to questions of religion, science, and morals. "Nature and truth or rather Truth and right," he wrote in May 1756, "are invariably the same in all Times and in all Places," and "Reason, pure unbiassed Reason perceives them alike in all Times and in all Places."[36]

Untutored reason, however, was not enough. Something more was needed, and that something was a method for acquiring knowledge. It was principally "the method," mused Adams, that allowed Newton to discover and demonstrate "the true system of the World." Newton rose above other English scientists of the time because he had "employed Experiment and

[Geometry?]"—that is, induction and deduction—in scientific inquiry. "It [is] the Method then," concluded Adams, "and not the Drudgery of science" that discovers nature's secrets.37 Advocating the "historical plain method" of Locke's *Essay*, he defined "Natural Phylosophy" as "the Art of deducing the generall laws and properties of material substances, from a series of *analogous* observations."

> The manner of reasoning in this art is not strictly demonstrative, and by Consequence the knowledge hence acquired, not absolutely Scientifical, because the facts that we reason upon, are perceived by Sence and not by the internal Action of the mind Contemplating its Ideas. But these Facts being presumed true in the form of Axioms, subsequent reasonings about them may be in the strictest sence, scientifical. This Art informs us, in what manner bodies will influence us and each other in given Circumstances, and so teaches us, to avoid the noxious and imbrace the beneficial qualities of matter.38

Lockean method applied as much to society as to nature. Moral and political philosophers must devote themselves to experiencing the world around them, and they must study the history of mankind. "By curiously enquiring into the Scituation, Fruits, Produce, Manufactures, &c. of our own, and by travailing into or reading about other Countries," Adams asserted, "we can gain distinct Ideas of almost every Thing upon this Earth, at present." Similarly, knowledge of the here and now should be supplemented by an examination of the past. By "looking into Hystory," by observing the "Wealth and Commerce, Warrs and Politicks" of different nations over long periods of time, and by examining "the Characters of their principal Leading Men, of their Grandeur and Power, of their Virtues and Vices," Adams thought moral philosophers could determine how and why nations rise and fall.39

Knowledge of the past and experience of the present give access to a far wider and higher field of vision. "Our minds," Adams noted, "are capable of receiving an infinite Variety of Ideas, from those numerous material objects with which we are surrounded." But rather than being "satiated with Knowledge, our Curiosity is only improved, and increased." Remarkably, "our thoughts are more free and active and clear than before." They "rove beyond the visible diurnal sphere, they range thro the Heavens and loose themselves amidst a Labyrinth of Worlds, and not contented with what is, they run forward into futurity and search for new Employment there. Here they can never stop. The wide, the boundless

Prospect lies before them. Here alone they find Objects adequate to their desires." Given the efficacy of reason and armed with a proper method or art, Adams was astonished at the range and openendedness of human knowledge. At the same time, he recognized that some things are simply inaccessible to the human mind. He agreed with Locke that "The Nature and Essence of the material World" are "conceal'd from our knowledge." Likewise, while he would concede that the existence of God can be inductively demonstrated from the data and lawlike regularity of nature, he denied that God's essence or true nature could be known. The most that man can know about physical reality or ultimate spiritual reality are the "Effects and Properties," the mechanical laws of nature that can be observed or demonstrated through experimentation. Ultimate or final causes are "hid from us in impenetrable Obscurity."[40] Adams lost no sleep lamenting the necessary limits of human knowledge. For either scientific or social purposes, he held, it was the visible effects and tangible properties, not the outlying mystery, that mattered.

Thus did Adams follow Locke's counsel to direct the pursuit of knowledge toward things that are useful here and now. The quest should be practical, utilitarian, and aimed at the immediate improvement of the human condition. The "Primary Endevour," Adams thought, should "be to distinguish between Useful and unuseful, to pursue the former with unwearied Industry, and to neglect with much Contempt all the Rest." There was no need to fear, he warned, that the "subjects of Inquiry will be so few, that the Treasures of useful knowledge will be exhausted." Adams never tired of promoting knowledge that would be useful "in the course of life."[41] He thought the elevation of practice over theory had wrought a revolution in the arts and sciences during the two centuries before the American Revolution. He later found a direct connection between "the advancement of civilization and humanity" and "the inventions in mechanic arts, the discoveries in natural philosophy, navigation, and commerce."[42] To that end, natural philosophy should seek to discover the secrets of nature and master its processes for the purpose of bettering man's lot. Through "the Exercise of his Reason," Adams argued, man "can invent Engines and Instruments"; he can "take advantage of the Powers in Nature, and accomplish the most astonishing Designs." He can also "cultivate and assist Nature in her own Productions."

By pruning the Tree, and manuring the Land, he makes the former produce larger and fairer Fruit, and the latter bring forth better and greater Plenty of Grain. He can form a Communication between remotest Regions, for the benefit of Trade and Commerce, over the yielding and fluctuating Element of water. The Telescope has settled the Regions of Heaven, and the Microscope has brought up to View innumerable millions of Animals that Escape the observation of our naked sight.[43]

The art of reasoning for Adams is the means by which man acquires knowledge of the natural world for the betterment of the intellectual and material lives of the great mass of humanity.

By the same art, man's moral condition could be bettered as well. Ascending the ladder of philosophical inquiry, Adams moved from discerning man's primary and immediate sense experience to recognizing nature's physical laws to examining the rules of the moral universe. Once again, analogous observation unlocks the door to an understanding of man's moral constitution. In much the same way that man can acquire knowledge of nature, he can learn of his moral obligations in this world and assess the likelihood of being accepted into the next by performing them. Thus, when Adams thought about virtue and moral action, he had little if any need for theology, for we have been given "Reason, to find out the Truth, and the real Design and true End of our Existence."[44] Like Locke, Adams was primarily concerned with establishing a demonstrative science of ethics based on an examination of nature and human nature.

Reason and the Moral Law

By clearing reason's field of vision, Adams could tackle the great moral question: "What is the proper Business of Mankind in this Life?" The young man devoted much of his early thinking to answering this query; he broached it directly at teatime with Putnam on a late May Saturday in 1756. Having calculated that, for practical purposes, the amount of time that we might devote to contemplating and pursuing piety and virtue amounted to fewer than four hours a day, the rest being given to sleep, to procuring a mere animal sustenance," or to pursuing such "Phantoms" as honor, wealth, or learning, Adams spelled out his answer in three parts. We should use the little time available to worship God, to love our fellow men, and to practice self-discipline by cultivating the "Habits" appropriate to each. Adams's prescription concludes where a man habitually devoted to this threefold "proper Business" might expect his own life to conclude: "We may then exult in a Con[s]iousness of the Favour of God, and the "Prospect of everlasting Felicity."[45] Moving swiftly from religion to ethics, Adams's answer skates over such issues as the relative weights and interdependencies of piety and virtue. But one main thing is very clear: man's proper business, properly pursued, leads to what Christians called redemption and Adams translated as God's favor and man's felicity.

There is no trace here of the traditional Christian or, more precisely, Calvinist scheme of salvation. Adams's God did not save men by a kind of force majeure that Calvinists termed irresistible grace. Instead, Adams made God's good will and reward depend on man's good deeds as quid pro quo. Divine favor could be secured by the initiative of autonomous and freely acting men who took time and trouble to honor God with praise and thanks, to be good neighbors, and to practice "Habits of Temperance, Recollection, and self Government." Such actions had, as we shall see, the far-from-trivial fringe benefit of affording "real and substantial Pleasure" here and now.[46]

After several years of philosophical reflection, Adams was clearly moving toward two conclusions: first, that scriptural revelation may fortify but is not a source of moral truth, and; second, that man, despite his weaknesses, is a rational being who can derive standards of moral obligation and virtuous behavior from observation of the external world and of the operations of his own mind. For Adams, as for Locke, the moral law of nature was synonymous with reason: "Law is human Reason," he asserted; it governs "all the Inhabitants of the Earth; the political and civil Laws of each Nation should be only the particular Cases, in which human Reason is applied." In order to discern piety and virtue, Adams therefore turned to three objects of investigation: the "general constitution of the World," the "nature of all terrestrial Enjoyments," and the "Constitution of our own Bodies." Thus would be discovered "the Laws which the Wisdom of fifty Centuries, has established for the Government of human kind."[47]

At twenty-one, Adams set down a series of reflections regarding the "general constitution of the world" and the laws that order it. From the observation of nature, he deduced six basic laws. First, nature is governed by universal rules that are accessible to the human mind.[48] Second, the internal organization and structure of all animate and inanimate creation is self-sustaining, harmonious, and purposeful.[49] Third, physical nature is interconnected and co-dependent.[50] Fourth, the various species are self-selecting and self-preserving, that is, "each Species regularly and uniformly preserve all their essential and peculiar properties, without partaking of the peculiar Properties of others."[51] Fifth, the structure of the universe is hierarchical: man is just one link in a chain of being that begins with inanimate objects and culminates with the Creator.[52] Sixth, God must, of necessity, be the Creator of such a universe.[53] For Adams, the very concept of God implied a universal system that was rational, orderly, purposeful, knowable, and governed by these same "general Laws."[54]

From the laws of nature as they apply to animate and inanimate matter, Adams thought he could deduce the laws appropriate to humankind. Among the latter, he hoped to determine and distinguish between laws required for man's survival and those necessary for the attainment of happiness in this life and in the next. One way to do so was to reason backward from effects to causes. By observing empirically the nature of "terrestrial enjoyments" and sufferings—rewards and punishments consonant with divine or natural law—Adams thought it possible to determine the content of virtue and piety. By annexing "Pain to Vice, and Pleasure to Virtue," the Creator had provided man with the means of discovering his laws. Adams came close to suggesting that God had implanted in man a moral sense that made a "Course of Impiety and Injustice, of Malevolence and Intemperance, appear Shocking and deformed to our first Reflections."[55]

By "terrestrial enjoyments," Adams meant the long-term pleasures and rational happiness connected with a good conscience and good works, although he did not entirely exclude the pleasures of the senses. The "real and substantial Pleasure" associated with living a pious and virtuous life was a sign of God's favor, pointing toward "the Prospect of everlasting Felicity." A good life was a certain indication "that the same or a like Disposition of Things may take place hereafter." God's hierarchy of pleasure, according to Adams, rewards, as its "greatest pleasure," the "Discovery of Truth." It is from "a sense of the Government of God, and a Regard to the Laws established by his Providence" that "all our Actions for ourselves or for other men, primarily originate."[56] Hence the discovery of nature's laws and the effort to conform to them provide the greatest opportunity for receiving God's present blessing and future reward.

The most important and fruitful field for Adams was the examination of human nature, or what he often referred to as the "Constitution of our Minds and Bodies."[57] From a very early age, he drove himself to understand and give an account of his own mental operations and those of others. "Let me search for the Clue, which Led great Shakespeare into the Labyrinth of mental Nature! Let me examine how men think," he demanded of himself. Adams always began with himself, turning inward and observing his passions and the operation of his own mental processes: "Here I should moderate my Passions, regulate my Desires, increase my Veneration of Virtue, and Resolution to pursue it, here I should range the whole material and Intellectual World, as far as human Powers can comprehend it, in silent

Contemplation." Not even his parents escaped his inquest. He recorded in the diary a "conjugal Spat" between his mother and father. Rather than joining or refereeing the squabble, he excused himself and retired to his room, where he "took up Tully to compose" himself. He later regretted having done so, for he "might have made some critical observations on the Course and Progress of human Passions" by steadily observing "the faces, Eyes, Actions and Expressions of both Husband and Wife."[58] By closely scrutinizing the behavior and relations of people, Adams thought he could discover the underlying passions and powers that animate human action. Once those passions were brought to light, the job of the will was to tame, regulate, order, and channel them in the light of a rationally discernible moral law.

For Adams, initially at least, the idea of natural law assumed a priori the immortality of souls. His reasoning unfolded in the following manner. The afterlife of the soul could be inferred by observing some of the "general Laws" by which God governs "his great Kingdom." Though difficult to identify, these laws, when they illuminate the "particular disposition of Things" in the physical universe, are strong indicators that "there are other dispositions of Things in other Systems of Nature, analogous and of a Piece with them." Thus, one may conclude from "the flux of the Tide to Day" that "the same Phenomenon may be observed tomorrow." Likewise, "our Experience that the Author of Nature has annexed Pain to Vice, and Pleasure to Virtue . . . renders it credible that the same or a like Disposition of Things may take place hereafter." The same reasoning that presumes a necessary relationship between cause and effect in nature applies no less to man's spiritual state. Similarly,

> Our observing that the State of minority was designed to be an Education for mature Life, and that our good or ill Success in a mature Life, depends upon our good or ill improvement of our Advantages in Minority, renders it credible that this Life was designed to be an Education, for a future one, and that our Happiness or Misery in a future life will be alloted us, according as our Characters shall be virtuous or vicious.

His analogous reasoning on this point makes a leap of faith that clearly falls short of any kind of verifiable demonstration, but the important point is that salvation and damnation are directly related to the degree that persons are "virtuous or vicious." Adams saw the here and now as an

"Education," a "State of moral discipline," in which individuals work out the conditions of happiness. This process of trial and effort produces a "Temper of mind" that, Adams insisted, "is in our Power to acquire."[59] In sum, reason is man's primary tool in determining what is right; his obligation to do what is right is defined by his relationship with God; and his spur to right action is the anticipation of pleasant consequences in this life or in the next.

To a friend distraught over the destruction of his home by fire, Adams advised against mourning the loss of petty and impermanent things. Property and social standing, he admonished Josiah Quincy, distract us from higher duties and lower our sights to mere worldly goods. Viewing the fire as a hidden blessing, he offered consolation: "But if you consider it as a punishment of your Vices and follies, as a frown that is designed to arrouse your attention, to Things of a more permanent Nature, you should not grieve, but rejoice, that the great Parent of the World has thus corrected you for your good." Adams told his friend that it was "irrational" and "unmanly" to worry about losing social status by losing property. Instead, he should seek those things that "wise Men" think important and "which cant be torn" from those who lead "rational" and virtuous lives. "Wisdom and virtue," he implored, "are not dependent on the Elements of fire or Water, Air or Earth." In other words, seek higher things that are "rational and noble" and beyond the vicissitudes of folly and fate.[60]

As we have seen, "Our proper Business in this Life," according to Adams, is not to accumulate wealth, honors, or positions but to pursue those "real and everlasting Excellences"; that is, "to improve our selves in Habits of Piety and Virtue." Adams wrote very little about piety, far less than he did about virtue. He considered it to consist of three basic requirements: It is a habit "of Contemplating the Deity and his transcendent Excellences"; it includes the corresponding habit "of complacency in and Dependence upon him"; it should foster a habit "of Reverence and Gratitude, to God." The emphasis on piety as a "habit" suggests that Adams thought of worship as something other than an intimate relationship, an immediate and felt experience. It seems to partake of a social convention, probably a useful reinforcement for virtue, but very far from the fear and trembling associated with the God of the Puritans. Piety, in Adams's revealing words, was "rational and manly."[61]

Adams was much more concerned with the nature and content of virtue. The true design of Christianity was not to make men "good Riddle Solvers or good mystery mongers," as he thought Calvinists had become, but to make "good men, good majestrates and good Subjects, good

Husbands and good Wives, good Parents and good Children, good masters and good servants." When Adams spoke of goodness, he had in mind the ordinary virtues associated with governance of self and obligations to others. Holding that virtue, like piety, should be experienced and practiced as a "habit," he divided the moral duties that provide a real and substantial pleasure into "Habits of Love and Compassion to our fellow men" and "Habits of Temperance, Recollection and self Government."[62] In this regard, he followed a common eighteenth-century distinction between self-regarding and other-regarding virtues.[63]

The other-regarding virtues play a negligible role in the diary: they sum up in the Golden Rule. Self-governance, on the other hand, dominates the diary as its most visible and characteristic theme. It was for Adams the indispensable foundation of a worthy life and the end to which virtues like moderation, frugality, and industry are directed. Declaring war on all unruly and destructive appetites, he deemed unfit for public office any man who "has left one Passion in his Soul unsubdued." Raging passions "should be bound fast and brought under the Yoke." This could be accomplished by rational commitment to the constructive virtues of prudence, fortitude, justice, gratitude, and benevolence that "are found and proved to be human Duties, and beneficial to society, by Reason and Experience." Such virtues "are Duties of the Law of human nature"; they "are institutions of Reason." Invoking a common nautical metaphor, Adams described the passions as "the Gales of Life," while "Reason is the Pilot."[64] The moral education that young Adams sought for himself and recommended to others aimed to promote certain virtues embodied in the idea of self-mastery.

In a letter to his soon-to-be wife, Abigail Smith, he dramatically explained the importance and rewards of self-rule: "Learn to conquer your Appetites and Passions! Know thyself[.] . . . [T]he Government of ones own soul requires greater Parts and Virtues than the Management of Kingdoms, and the Conquest of the disorderly rebellious Principles in our Nature, is more glorious than the Acquisition of Universal Dominion."[65] The goal of self-knowledge, self-mastery, and self-reliance was rational independence in the fullest sense. The critical self-examination that fills the diary and that so many scholars have attributed to Adams's Puritan upbringing represents his attempt to order his soul according to the new moral dispensation advocated by Locke.[66] Exploring the content of moral virtue by examining human nature and physical reality, he thought he could establish the basis for a wholesome moral life.

A New Civil Theology

We are left with an important question: What role did religion play in Adams's public philosophy? He certainly thought moral self-regulation was possible for all, but he also recognized that individuals require additional supports in the form of customs, laws, institutions, and religion. Accordingly, he thought Christianity should be used as an educative tool in shaping and reinforcing moral virtue. In a diary entry of 1796, a much older Adams provided a clear description of the utilitarian role that religion and America's churches ought to play in cultivating private and public morality.

> One great Advantage of the Christian Religion is that it brings the great principle of the Law of Nature and Nations, Love your Neighbour as yourself, and do to others as you would that others should do to you, to the Knowledge, Belief and Veneration of the whole People. . . . The Duties and Rights of The Man and the Citizen are thus taught, from early Infancy to every Creature. The Sanctions of a future Life are thus added to the Observance of civil and political as well as domestic and private Duties.[67]

Adams did respect Christianity: not for its creeds, councils, priests, prophets, enthusiasts, miracles, or dogmas, but for its moral and political value. It should support the moral principles and civic responsibilities associated with a Lockean regime founded on the law of nature and nations. Belief in the immortality of souls and the sanctions of a future life, Adams thought, provided the incentive and moral backbone necessary to sustain a liberal society built upon the rights of individuals. Late in life, he told Thomas Jefferson that his moral and religious creed could be encapsulated in four short words: "*Be just and good.*"[68] In the end, the religion of John Adams was little more, but certainly not less, than a religion of civic morality.

John Adams's earliest reflections on God and scripture, man and nature, piety and virtue help to illuminate his response to the Revolutionary crisis and the sources of his mature political thought. When he first rose in 1765 to defend the colonial cause, Adams espoused principles that he had been formulating since his graduation from Harvard. As he journeyed from New England piety to Enlightenment rationalism, young John Adams both symbolized and played an important role in defining the nature and parameters of a larger moral revolution that was taking place in the minds and hearts of the American people.

Chapter 2

Lawyer, Statesman, and Lawgiver

On August 22, 1756, after a year of teaching school and much soul searching, twenty-one-year-old John Adams announced that he would begin studying the law. The decision had not been easy. For over a year he had struggled with the most important theological doctrines of Calvinist New England. The change in his religious views and his basic orientation to the world came slowly, hesitantly, and with much trepidation at first. But once the decision was made, he jumped with both feet. Diary entries concerned with religious questions drop off to almost nothing in the months and years that followed. From this moment forward, a very different young man emerges from the pages of the diary. Unburdened by family expectations and liberated from personal guilt, he was now able to pursue whatever career he desired, and his desires seemed limitless.

When he surveyed his situation in 1756, John Adams was simultaneously pessimistic and optimistic about his future prospects. Living in Worcester, Massachusetts in the 1750s must have seemed like living on the western rim of civilization. To his friends, he lamented his miserable condition: "At Colledge gay, gorgeous, prospects, danc'd before my Eyes, and Hope, sanguine Hope, invigorated my Body, and exhilerated my soul. But now hope has left me, my organ's rust and my Faculty's decay."[1] For an ambitious young man of great abilities, the future looked bleak. Unmarried, separated from family and friends, cut off from the library and intellectual world of Harvard, Adams would at times despair over his prospects. Into his diary he poured his frustrations: "I have no Books, no Time, no Friends. I must therefore be contented to live and die an ignorant, obscure fellow." To Jonathan Sewell he complained that he expected "To be totally forgotten within 70 Years from the present Hour unless the Insertion of my Name in the Colledge Catalogue, should luckily preserve it longer."[2]

There can be no doubt that a young John Adams sought to cut a large figure in the world. An untapped natural ability and a seemingly unlimited imagination fueled his ambition. But what in reality could the provincial son of a New England cordwainer, seemingly marooned at a western outpost, do to fulfill his life goals? For the most part, he could only hope to become a great and wealthy lawyer. Perhaps over time he could rise to a judgeship or be appointed to the governor's council. Beyond that, there were few outlets for young men with great talents. In a royal province the highest offices of state were appointed from the center of the empire. In a monarchical society where birth, wealth, and English connections almost always determined one's social and professional standing, the opportunity to pursue and achieve great things was distinctly limited.

Readers of the diary and early correspondence are thus startled when confronted with a young man daydreaming about the wildest schemes and life goals. Corresponding with Sewell on the question of whether modern times afforded greater opportunities for young men of genius relative to those of Tully's Rome, Adams answered enthusiastically in the affirmative. The explosion of knowledge in mathematics, in the natural sciences, and in philosophy had sparked a revolution in navigation, commerce, and printing that Adams thought gave his generation a distinct advantage over Cicero's.[3] As he writes to friends about the deeds of history's greatest generals and statesmen, we begin to see a more confident and hopeful young man. These were the years of preparation.

Fortunately, Adams has provided scholars with a doorway into his thinking, his motives, and his rationalizations as they relate to the objects of his escalating ambitions and deepest longings. He was fascinated during this period with a series of intellectual problems that mark the transition from his concerns over other-wordly grace to his emerging desire for immortality in this world. There were, in particular, three issues that he had to address and resolve before he could choose and launch his career. We may refer to these as the problem of ambition, the problem of genius, and the problem of fame.

The Preparation (1755–1760)

In coming to grips with his own elevated ambitions, Adams thought it would be an "agreeable and useful speculation to inquire into the Faculty which we call Imagination."[4] His purpose was to define it and to examine the positive and negative role that it played in human affairs. He first defined the imagination in epistemological terms: it is the "Repository of Knowledge"; it is the faculty that first retains "all the Ideas of visible objects, all the observations we have made in the Course of Life on Men and Things, our selves," and it then allows us to "recall" and "review" the

"Ideas and Assemblages of Ideas that have been before my Mind" for "our Use, as Occasion requires." Adams was also conscious that the imagination is a "very active and stirring" faculty. "It is constantly in Action," he said, and it "runs backward to past scenes . . . or forward to the future." The imagination, he surmised, allows us to recall past pleasures and pains. Boyhood romps through "swamps, and fields, and Meadows," for instance, will lead one to imagine living with the "wildest Tribe of Indians," sharing in "their Hunting, their Warrs, their tedious Marches, thro swamps and Mountains."[5] In short, it allows us to become more than we really are.

Adams saw in the realm of the imagination two distinct but related functions: it included both "Actuality and Possibility, not only what is but what may be." Our memory, by "reviving past scenes" or creating "new" ones, will suggest "Thoughts and inquiries." These thoughts and inquiries will start "Hints and doubts," and they will furnish "Reason with Materials in our retired Hours." It is with the possibilities, with what might be, that Adams was most interested. In our quiet hours of solitude, he wrote, the "Imagination recalls the Ideas of Things, Men, Actions, Characters, and Reason reduces them to order, and forms Inferences and Deductions from them." After reviewing and processing what is and has been, the imagination leaps forward and imagines what might be: "We take pleasure in fancying our Selves in Places, among Objects, Persons, Pleasures, when we are not; and a still greater Pleasure in the Prospect which Imagination constantly gives us of future Pleasure, Business, Wealth, fame &c."[6] There was for Adams an intimate connection between the faculty of imagination and the impulse of ambition.

Ultimately, this "Prospect of futurity, which Imagination gilds and brightens, is the greatest Spur to Industry and Application." The imagination, he wrote, clearly with himself in mind, "is the scholars spur to study"; it is the "Commanders spur [to] Activity and Courage"; and, most importantly, it is the "Statesmans Spur to the Invention and Execution of Plans of Politicks." But to what particular object did Adams direct his youthful imagination? In the spring of 1759, a daydreaming twenty-four-year-old crossed "the Atlantic," where he fancied himself in "Westminster Hall, hearing Causes in the Courts of Justice, or the Debates in the Houses of Commons or Lords." But in his very next diary entry, the young man returned to earth and confronted the reality of his situation: "I had an acking Void within my Breast, this night," he wrote. "I feel anxious, eager, after something." But "what is it?" he demanded of himself. In what he would years later describe in the *Discourses on Davila* as the "*spectemur agendo*" (the desire to be seen), Adams told himself he felt a "concern for

Knowledge, and fame." "I have," he wrote, "a dread of Contempt, a quick sense of Neglect, a strong Desire of Distinction."[7] And of course these wilderness years in Worcester, removed from the opportunities and avenues of power afforded by Boston and London, served only to ignite his imagination and to inflame his ambition.

The related question or problem of genius also fascinated Adams. What, he demanded to know, is the nature of genius, what are its characteristics, and what are its most important and recognized forms? It was demonstrable, he answered, through the "Invention of . . . new Systems or Combinations of old Ideas." Generally speaking, the characteristics common to all acts of genius are "Order, Method, System, Connection, [and] Plan."[8] The true genius will pull these characteristics together in order to achieve some great and lofty end. Adams then offered a five-tier classification or ranking of genius. The first and presumably lowest rung on his ladder of genius was that associated with mechanical genius. Ascending to the second level was the genius demonstrated by the great poets. Above the mechanic and the poet was the man of scientific genius. Standing on the penultimate level was the man of moral genius, defined by Adams as any man "who has a Faculty of considering all the faculties and Properties of human Nature, as the Senses, Passions, Reason, Imagination, and faith, and of [combining] classing all these into order, into Rules, for the Conduct of private Life." Lastly, the highest and most important form of genius was employed by the great statesman, Lawgiver, or constitution maker. The man of political genius combines and applies the moral rules to "the Government of Society, to procure Peace, Plenty, [and] Liberty."[9]

Finally, and most importantly, Adams addressed the problem of fame. Generally speaking, the passion for fame was both an intellectual and a personal problem for him because it cut two ways. On the one hand, there was a kind of fame that was benevolent and noble in purpose and result. On the other hand, there was a passion for fame that could also serve malevolent and base ends. In other words, there was a fundamental distinction between the Pericleses, Catos, Marlboroughs and Washingtons of history and the Alcibiadeses, Caesars, Cromwells, and Burrs. From the vantage of history, drawing moral distinctions between these men of soaring ambition was relatively easy, but choosing the honorable path in search of fame and glory was by no means so simple or obvious to a young man consumed by such a powerful passion.

Benevolent fame is motivated by a desire to promote the public good and is achieved either by performing some great deed or through an act of unusual genius that benefits the common weal. It should not be confused, however, with altruism or the desire for reputation. Adams, following in the Aristotelian tradition, did not take the well-being or the opinion of others as his polestar or guiding standard. Ultimately, benevolent fame is connected to higher principles that the honorable man seeks for selfish reasons. Such men act because they love that which is noble, good, and just for its own sake. That there are or may be superior or more just ways of living is what prompts the magnanimous man to perfect his own soul, and that motivates him to promote or defend the well-being of his community. In other words, self-interest and disinterestedness are united and directed toward achieving some great and patriotic end. Furthermore, because fame is only possible through the approbation of other men, those concerned with pursuing benevolent fame almost always direct their thoughts and actions toward a particular audience. True and lasting fame relies on "a strong affection for the honest Approbation of the wise and the good both in the present, and in all future Generations."[10] In the end, however, though often torn and obsessed by the opinions of others, the final arbiter for Adams was his own conscience, his own understanding of what was honorable, good, and just. There was for Adams, as there was for Aristotle, a crucial distinction between acting honorably and being simply honored. Fame pursued from base motives or achieved by ignoble means was venal and unworthy of the great and honorable man. He therefore demanded of himself that he "assume a Fortitude, a Greatness of Mind" on his "gradual ascent to fame and fortune." In no place do we better see Adams's having come to terms with the problem of fame than in a 1758 diary entry, where he records and translates a few lines from Tacitus: "Contemptu famae, contenmi Virtutem. A Contempt of Fame generally begets or accompanies a Contempt of Virtue." Fame in this context becomes synonymous with the pursuit of noble ends by magnanimous means.[11]

Malevolent fame was something quite different. Here the actor is motivated by entirely low and base motives. The love of reputation becomes an end in itself, regardless of how it might affect the public interest. If one were to examine the history of all ages and nations, Adams wrote in his diary, "we shall find, that all the Tumults, Insurrections, and Revolutions, that have disturbed the Peace of society, and spilled oceans of Blood, have arisen from the giddy Rashness and Extravagance of the sublimest Minds." Many of the greatest men, he argued, "have been the most envious, malicious, and revengeful." Democracies in particular were easily beguiled by "the Tendency of great Parts and Genius," and to fall prey to their "imprudent sallies." From the demagogues of ancient Greece and

Rome "down to the rude speeches of our American Town Orators," oratorical skill and eloquence "may be employed wisely to persuade," but it is more often "employed wickedly to seduce." These men of great ambition and genius are driven by an "unquenchable Thirst of superiority, and Power." They have the ability to carry the masses of a democratic government "into the wildest Projects and Adventures, to set the World aware of their Parts and Persons, without attending to the Calamities that must ensue."[12] Adams always distinguished between those who sought fame at any price from those who, like himself, would sacrifice success in order to do the right thing.

Ultimately, the problem of fame was more complicated than the simple distinction between benevolent and malevolent fame. Even for the man who sought benevolent fame, Adams had to conclude "that the most refined Patriotism to which human Nature can be wrought, has in it an alloy of Ambition, of Pride and avarice that debases the Composition, and produces mischievous Effects." In fact, "the greater a mans Parts and the nobler his Virtues" the stronger will be his passion for fame, and this passion "is apt to betray men into impertinent Exertions of their Talents." Not only does the man of great ability and genius share with lesser men the spectrum of human passions, but he actually feels them to a greater degree: in such a man, the passions of avarice, love, envy, and the love of glory "are lawless Bulls, they roar and bluster" and they "defy all controul." Adams knew this all too well from personal experience. Though always standing guard against them, he often fell victim to the dangers associated with the passion for fame. He understood that even the most just and virtuous man can be seduced and betrayed by his love of fame "into several weaknesses and Fopperies that tend very much to diminish his Reputation, and so defeats itself." In his own case, he recognized that vanity was his greatest vice.[13] That Adams largely failed to conquer this particular passion should not diminish his life-long struggle to recognize and conquer his own vices.

For Adams, the pursuit and achievement of a true and lasting fame, one that takes the public good as its end, must employ certain means or virtues. Not only must the ends be honorable, but the means employed to achieve the public good must be honorable as well. "If I could but conform my Life and Conversation to my Speculations," he told himself, "I should be happy."[14] In bringing together good ends with good means, the diary itself becomes the principal vehicle by which Adams identified, attacked, and purged himself of all unworthy and destructive passions and vices. We see, for instance, a twenty-three-year-old Adams vilifying himself after a socializing weekend spent in the company of young women: he had "been seduced into the Course of unmanly Pleasures, that Vice describes to hercules, forgetful of the glorious Promises of Fame, Immortality, and a good Conscience, which Virtue, makes to the same Hero, as rewards of a hardy, toilsome, watchful Life, in the service of Man kind."[15] This is hardly the concern of a Puritan. It was his own rather than God's glory that he sought. He used the diary to recognize, confront, and exculpate those vices and passions generally associated with a love of fame for its own sake. Self-examination, self-command, and self-improvement are the principal themes of Adams's diary.

John Adams was always looking inward—surveying, evaluating, and judging the state of his soul—raising his sights and stoking his ambition with dreams of great and heroic accomplishments. After affecting great learning, virtue, and wisdom in the company of friends and adult companions, he chastised himself for showing off and appearing to know more than he really did. He recognized his many affectations as "faults, Defects, Fopperies and follies, and Disadvantages." He then wondered if he might "mend these faults and supply these Defects."[16] To that end, Adams imposed on himself a strict daily regimen of hard work, ascetic denial, and Spartan-like austerity. He constantly cajoled and implored himself to rise early, to apply himself to a rigid system of work and study, to conquer his passions, and to ferret out any weaknesses in his character. In 1756, the twenty-one-year-old Adams "resolved not to neglect my Time as I did last Year":

> I am resolved to rise with the Sun and to study the Scriptures, on Thursday, Fryday, Saturday, and Sunday mornings, and to study some Latin author the other 3 mornings. Noons and Nights I intend to read English Authors. This is my fixt Determination, and I will set down every neglect and every compliance with this Resolution. May I blush whenever I suffer one hour to pass unimproved. I will rouse up my mind, and fix my Attention. I will stand collected within my self and think upon what I read and what I see. I will strive with all my soul to be something more than Persons who have had less Advantages than myself."[17]

But he did not always succeed. Almost three years later, Adams was still fighting inertia. "What am I doing?" he demanded of himself. "Shall I sleep away my whole 70 years." In order to bolster and inflame his flagging spirit after an extended period of lethargy and weakness, Adams sketched a fable of Hercules, adapting the story to his own situation.

Let Virtue Address me—

Which, dear Youth, will you prefer? a Life of Effeminacy, Indolence and obscurity, or a Life of Industry, Temperance, and Honour? Take my Advice, rise and mount your Horse, by the Mornings dawn, and shake away amidst the great and beautiful scenes of Nature . . . all the Crudities that are left in your stomach, and all the obstructions that are left in your Brains. . . . Let no trifling Diversion or amuzement or Company decoy you from your Books, i.e., let no Girl, no Gun, no cards, no flutes, no Violins, no Dress, no Tobacco, no Laziness, decoy from your Books.[18]

And again, just over a year later, feeling as though life was passing him by, we see Adams trying to rouse his imagination and inflame his ambition: "Arose late, again. When shall I shake off the shackells of morning slumbers . . . and get my Thoughts into a steady Train, my Imagination raised, my Ambition inflamed, in short every Thing within me and without, into a Preparation for Improvement."[19]

During these lonely years of preparation, John Adams came to terms with his ambition and his passion for fame. Eventually, he came to see that in the pursuit of fame there must be a necessary connection between ends and means, achievement and effort, justice and virtue. Success, reputation, and fame were not ends in themselves for Adams; they had to be attached to a noble end and to some virtuous action. He would not violate his strict code of character to achieve the favorable opinion of posterity. Above all else, John Adams was a man of strict principle, a man of unyielding integrity, a man of firm justice. He was motivated by a love of fame, but he was also driven by something higher, namely, *principle*.

Never the hypocrite, Adams lived by his own words and avowed principles. He always chose to act in ways that he thought right and just, regardless of reward or punishment. Our point is illuminated by two examples drawn from the pre-Revolutionary period. In 1768, Adams refused a request from Governor Bernard to accept the post of advocate general of the court of admiralty. Despite the lucrative financial rewards and the "Royal Favour and promotion" that almost certainly would have come with the position, he declined to accept on the grounds that he could not lay himself "under any restraints, or Obligations of Gratitude to the Government for any of their favours." Furthermore, he could not support a government that persisted "in a System, wholly inconsistent with all my Ideas of Right, Justice and Policy."[20] The linchpin that united theory and practice in John Adams's moral universe was the virtue of integrity. It was

Adams's greatest virtue, one that even his critics and enemies could not and would not deny him.

Likewise, in 1770, Adams risked falling out of favor with the patriot movement by accepting the legal defense of Captain Preston in the Boston Massacre trial. He accepted the case, he said, in order to defend the rule of law and because "Council ought to be the very last thing that an accused Person should want in a *free* Country." He took the case, he said, because "every Lawyer must hold himself responsible not only to his Country, but to the highest and most infallible of all Trybunals."[21] In word and deed, Adams sought to stand above party; his code of honor would not allow him to sacrifice the principled long-term interests of his country for personal gain. Justice, and a kind of philosophical honor, were for Adams the ultimate ends of his actions.

The Great Lawyer-Jurist (1759–1765)

In October, 1758, John Adams returned home after three years of self-imposed exile. The twenty-three-year-old young man was now ready to launch his career and to slowly begin ascending the ladder of fame. To this point, we have caught just a glimpse of the ends to which a young John Adams would attach his quest for fame. As we shall soon see, there was a direct connection between his passion for fame, the objects of his imagination, and the hierarchy of genius. At the top of his pyramid of imagination was the great statesman and at the pinnacle of his hierarchy of genius was the lawgiver or constitution maker. But for a young man in his twenties, there was still a wide chasm between "Actuality" and "Possibility," between "what is" and "what may be."[22] Braintree was not Boston and Boston was not London.

Immediately after his return, the young man sat down at his desk and took stock of his situation. It is from exactly this moment that we see Adams mounting the ladder of fame. The first question that a young man about to launch a career should ask himself, he wrote in a draft letter, "is what Employment am I by the Constitution of my mind and Body, and by the Circumstances of Education, Rank and Fortune, directed to pursue?"[23] His chosen profession was the law, but his ambitions were clearly much greater than those of a provincial lawyer. From early on, Adams knew that the study of law was "an Avenue to the more important offices of the state." Rather than seeking power and fame for their own sake, he identified the study of law with the "happiness of human Society," an object he thought worthy of the great-souled man. But with the pursuit of the law and a career in politics came many dangers. For Adams, though, "the more danger the more glory."[24] The object of his ambition during this second phase was to become a great and virtuous lawyer. He sought nothing less than "to defend Innocence, to punish Guilt, and to promote Truth and Justice among Mankind."[25]

Having decided on a career, the second question that a young man ought to ask of himself was this: "What is the best Method, the safest, easiest, nearest Road to the proper End of that Employment I have chose?"[26] His answer, in short, was hard work. Between 1756 when he first announced his decision to pursue a career in the law and 1765 when he was drawn into the crisis over the Stamp Act, Adams imposed on himself a strenuous regimen of legal study. The young man went well beyond the requirements of the Massachusetts bar, setting high goals and then methodically achieving them. His Spartan-like plan of study during these years was truly extraordinary. Day after day, month after month, year after year, he plowed through the ancient and great works of the common and civil law. In the common law he read works like Edward Coke's *Institutes of the Lawes of England*, Henry de Bracton's *De Legibus et consuetudinibus Angliae Libri quing*, John Cowell's *Institutes of Lawes of England*, John Fortescue's *De Laudibus Legum Angliae*, Matthew Hale's *The History and Analysis of the Common Law of England*, William Hawkins' *A Treatise of the Pleas of the Crown*, Edmund Plowden's *The Commentaries, or Reports of Edmund Plowden*, and dozens of others. In the civil law he read the Dutch legal scholar Arnaldus Vinnius's notes on Justinian's *Institutes*, Thomas Wood's *A New Institute of the Imperial or Civil Law*, Jean Domat's *Civil Law in Its Natural Order*, John Ayliff's *New Pandect of the Roman Civil Law*, and John Taylor's *The Elements of the Civil Law*. He read a good deal of political philosophy as well, including Johann Gottlieb Heineccius's *Methodical System of Universal Law*, Jean Jacques Burlamaqui's *Principles of Natural Law*, Montesquieu's *The Spirit of the Laws*, and Rousseau's *Social Contract*.

When he was distracted by social events, romance, family quarrels, or boredom, Adams would despair over his commitment and prospects for future glory. "Where is my Attention?" he demanded of himself. "Is it fixed from sunrise to midnight, on grecian, roman, gallic, british Law, History, Virtue, Eloquence? I dont see clearly The objects, that I am after. They are often out of my Sight." On such occasions, however, he would quickly recover his resolve and stoically demand of himself that he return to his study and bend his "soul" to the great treatises and casebooks of the law. "Keep your Law Book or some Point of Law in your mind at least 6 Hours in a day," he demanded of himself.

Labour to get Ideas of Law, Right, Wrong, Justice, Equity. Search for them in your own mind, in Roman, grecian, french, English Treatises of natural, civil, common, Statute Law. Aim at an exact Knowledge of the Nature, End, and Means of Government. Compare the different forms of it with each other and each of them with their Effects on Public and private Happiness. Study Seneca, Cicero, and all other good moral Writers. Study Montesque, Bolingbroke [Vinnius?], &c. and all other good, civil Writers, &c.[27]

Adams soon realized, however, that he could not just keep his nose in the law books of the great Continental jurists and philosophers. Soon after his return to Braintree, the young lawyer accepted and lost his first case. He was humiliated. The case, *Field* v. *Lambert,* involved two neighboring farmers squabbling over the trespass of two horses. Adams scolded himself for his ignorance and henceforth set out to master the details of local and provincial law. Thereafter, he determined that he would seek practical information to complement his book learning. He told himself, for instance, that the next time he ran into a shipmaster, he would ask, "what is a Bill of Lading, what the Pursers Book. What Invoices they keep. What Account they keep of Goods received on Board, and of Goods delivered out, at another Port, &c."[28]

It is also at this time that we see Adams begin to consciously and systematically study the constitution of human nature. By inclination and temperament Adams would have preferred to spend all his time with his books, but he soon realized that to acquire a just estimate of human nature his education would also have to take him into the local tavern, marketplace, and town meeting. Part of his daily study routine now included leaving his study for a few hours every day to observe the ideas, motives, and actions of people in the scenes of day-to-day life. After attending a town meeting, for instance, after observing "the Intrigues, Acts, Passions, Speeches, that pass there," he retired home to reflect on what he had seen and heard. Back in his study, he recorded the evening's events, analyzed the speeches and behavior of certain individuals, and then attempted to dig beneath surface effects for their causes: "What Passions or affections in human Nature are affected by Satyr, by Humour, and Drollery?" he typically asked of himself.[29] By 1758, the reader of the diary witnesses an important change in its function. The primary purpose of the diary is no longer to serve as a mirror for Adams to examine his own soul, but to record the passions, opinions, and interests of those around him.

As John Adams climbed the ladder of fame in the late 1750s and early 1760s, the object of his ambition came into focus and remained remarkably consistent. In 1759, he asked himself in the diary "to what higher object, to what greater Character, can any Mortal aspire, than to be possessed of all this Knowledge, well digested, and ready at Command, to assist the feeble and Friendless, to discountenance the haughty and lawless, to procure redress of Wrongs, the Advancement of Right, to assert and maintain Liberty and Virtue, to discourage and abolish Tyranny and Vice."[30] Several months later, he designed a "Project" to collect "the Anecdotes of the Lives of all the great Lawyers, ancient and modern."[31] In 1761, a month before one of the great turning points in his life, he thought "the object and Designs of the Law" to be "Nothing less than the Preservation of the Health and Properties, Lives and Tranquility, Moralls and Liberties of Millions of the human species." And thus "a Comparison of several Constitutions of Government, invented for those Purposes, an Examination of the great Causes of their Danger, as well as those of their safety, must be as Agreable an Employment as can exercise the Mind."[32]

Despite these flights of imagination, Adams was still plagued by the reality of life in eighteenth-century America. The French and Indian War had surely ignited the ambition of men like John Adams and George Washington, but there were still few avenues to the kind of fame associated with the great statesmen and generals of classical antiquity. The young man lamented that he would never "shine, till some animating Occasion calls forth all my Powers."[33] He did not have to wait long for that "animating Occasion." There were, during this period of legal preparation, two events that inflamed his ambition and gave him reason to believe that he would one day find the means by which to achieve great and lasting fame. The first was the death in 1760 of Chief Justice Stephen Sewell of the Massachusetts Superior Court. The new vacancy on the Court, Adams told himself in the diary, "naturally stirs the Minds of all, who know the importance of a wise, steady and loyal Administration of Justice, to enquire for a fit Person to fill that Place." He then listed in some detail the qualifications for such a post: it matched exactly his course of study in the common, civil, canon and feudal laws for the last several years.[34] The second event was James Otis's argument in the Superior Court of Judicature against the writs of assistance. Adams witnessed the event and recorded for posterity the arguments that he would later say were the opening salvos of the American Revolution. Some sixty years later, he described the impact of Otis's speech on those in attendance: "Every man of a crowded audience appeared to me to go away, as I did, ready to take arms against writs of assistance. . . . Then and there the child of Independence was born."[35] From this moment forward, Adams's life was swept along by events that would one day elevate him onto the world stage.

The Orator-Statesman (1765–1776)

During these formative years, Adams was constantly looking for a cause and a platform from which to launch his career and to satisfy his plan for worldly glory. He found that cause in the Stamp Act. He described the year 1765 as "the most remarkable Year of my Life." The attempt by Parliament to impose what seemed to the Americans an unconstitutional tax provided Adams with the necessary launching pad from which to vault himself from relative obscurity to the forefront of public life in Massachusetts: "That enormous Engine, fabricated by the british Parliament, for battering down all the Rights and Liberties of America, I mean the Stamp Act, has raised and spread, thro the whole Continent, a Spirit that will be recorded to our Honour, with all future Generations."[36] Finally, after years of study, Adams was able to bring his extraordinary legal education directly to bear on a constitutional crisis that was about to engulf his provincial world.

The year 1765 and the passage of the Stamp Act brought forth from Adams his first sallies into the public affairs of colony and empire. Between August and October 1765, he published in four installments his first major political essay, "A Dissertation on the Canon and the Feudal Law." At the conclusion of the "Dissertation," Adams revealed what the Stamp Act meant for America and men like himself. Just as the tyranny of Charles I had turned "the general attention of learned men to government," producing "the greatest number of consummate statesmen, which has ever been seen in any age, or nation," so the Stamp Act "ought in the same manner to engage the attention of every man of learning to matters of power and of right." In the same way that men like Algernon Sidney, John Locke, and James Harrington "owed their eminence in political knowledge" to the tyranny of the Stuart monarchy, Adams hoped that Parliamentary tyranny would produce men of like genius in America.[37] That same year, he also composed "Braintree's Instructions to its Representatives in the General Court," an attack on the Stamp Act for depriving the American colonists of two basic rights guaranteed to all Englishmen by the Magna Carta: the right to be taxed only by consent and to be tried only by a jury of one's peers.[38] Later in the year, he served as counsel for Boston to argue before the Governor and Council that the courts should be reopened without the stamps required by Parliament.

From 1765 to 1776, Adams's involvement in radical politics ran apace with the escalation of events. In 1770 he was elected to the Massachusetts House of Representatives, and in 1773 and again in 1774 he was elected by the House to sit on the Council. Both times, though, his election to the upper house was vetoed by the Governor. During his tenure in the Massachusetts House of Representatives, he served as chief legal counsel to the patriot faction and wrote several important resolutions for the lower house in its running battle with Lieutenant Governor and then Governor Thomas Hutchinson; he wrote an important essay on the need for an independent judiciary; and his "Novanglus" essays are generally regarded as one of the two or three best expressions of the American case against parliamentary sovereignty. By the 1770s Adams had distinguished himself as one of America's foremost constitutional scholars. Throughout the entire struggle with Parliament, he maintained that the dispute with England was constitutional. At issue was the constitutional structure of the British empire. The "whole dispute" turned, he wrote, on "the *fundamentals* of the government."[39]

As events in America rushed toward Revolution, Adams would have cause to revise and elevate the objects of his ambition. In 1774, he was appointed to the First Continental Congress. This event marked a turning point in his life and a dramatic upward ratcheting of his ambitions. Upon learning of his election to the Continental legislature, he wrote in his diary that there "is a new, and a grand Scene open before me—a Congress." The prospect of participating in such an august body with "an assembly of the wisest Men upon the Continent" was inspiring and unleashed in Adams new ambitions and his long repressed imagination.[40] He thought the "Dignity" of the American cause to be "the best and greatest that ever engaged the human Mind." He compared the Congress to the ancient Greek "court of Aeropagus," to the Jewish "Sanhedrim," and to the Asian "Divan"; he thought it "equal to a british Parliament, in wiser as well as better ages." It was to be "a School of Political Prophets," he wrote to his friend James Warren, "I suppose—A nursery of American Statesmen."[41]

Over the course of the next several months he would recall the ideas and actions of the great defenders of liberty and the great statesmen-orators of history. He asked James Warren to forgive his vanity for comparing his situation to that of Demosthenes. He tried to imagine what plans the Congress might adopt were "a Sully, a Cecil, a Pitt, or a Ximenes, a Demosthenes or a Cicero" in attendance. Such characters, Adams thought, should always remain "before our eyes." He was also aware of the great dangers associated with his calling, but he reveled in them never-

theless. Ominously, he recalled the fate and martyrdom of some of histories greatest heroes: "Brutus and Cassius were conquered and slain. Hampden died in the Field. Sydney on the Scaffold, Harrington in Goal."
Politics was "an ordeal Path, among red hot Ploughshares," yet he recognized that certain men of the greatest abilities and ambition must heed
the call of duty and honor.[42] Adams did not hesitate to dedicate his life,
his property, and his sacred honor in defense of justice and American liberties. Only modesty and a sense that he felt himself "unequal" to the task
ahead caused him to begin with a stutter. He worried that his knowledge
of "the Realm, the Colonies, and of Commerce, as well as of Law and Policy" would be inadequate for the trials to come. Indeed, so great was the
task ahead that Adams thought as much knowledge was "necessary for an
American Statesmen at this Time as was ever necessary for a British, or a
Roman Senator." Nevertheless, he was thankful to friends for thinking
him an "apt scholar, or capable of learning."[43]

When he first arrived in Philadelphia, Adams was impressed with a
Congress that contained a "collection of the greatest men upon this continent in point of abilities, virtues, and fortunes."[44] He spoke little during
the first few months, silently taking measure of the great men from the
other colonies. Over the course of the next two years, no man worked as
hard or played as important a role in the movement for independence as
did John Adams. His first great contribution to the American cause was
to draft in October 1774 the principal clause of the Declaration of Rights
and Grievances.[45] He chaired the committee that drafted the Declaration
of Independence, he drafted America's first Model Treaty, and, working
eighteen-hour days, he served as a one-man department of War and Ord-
nance. In the end, he tirelessly worked on some thirty committees. "Every
member of Congress," Benjamin Rush would later write, "acknowledged
him to be the first man in the House."[46] Later, as an American diplomat
in Europe, he labored as though possessed in promoting and protecting
American interests.

Adams's greatest moment in Congress and the culmination of his
Revolutionary career came in the summer of 1776, when he rose in Congress to defend a declaration of independence. On June 10, Congress appointed a committee to prepare a declaration that would implement the
following resolution: "That these United Colonies are, and of right
ought to be, free and independent states; that they are absolved, from all
Allegiance to the British Crown; and that all political connection between them and the State of Great Britain, is and ought to be totally dissolved." On July 1, Congress considered final arguments on the question

of independence. After a year of intense polemics and political wrangling, the fate of an empire and its colonies came down to one day. The outcome was by no means certain; there were still votes to be won. Each side put forward its best man. John Dickinson argued forcefully against independence. When no one responded to Dickinson's prepared speech, Adams rose and spoke extemporaneously in its favor. Like his ancient heroes Demosthenes and Cicero, Adams's passionate but reasoned speech moved the assembly directly to vote in favor of independence. Years later, Thomas Jefferson recalled that so powerful in "thought & expression" was Adams's speech, that it "moved us from our seats." He was, Jefferson said, "our Colossus on the floor."[47] Another delegate, Richard Stockton, is reported to have said that "'The man to whom the country is most indebted for the great measure of independence is Mr. John Adams . . . I call him the Atlas of American independence. He it was who sustained the debate, and by the force of his reasoning demonstrated not only the justice, but the expediency, of the measure.'"[48]

The Lawgiver (1776–1780)

At the same time that Adams was ascending the ladder of fame to the penultimate level of statesmen-orator, he was also preparing to take his final step to the highest level of secular fame and immortality. Shortly after the battles at Lexington and Concord, he began to recognize that reconciliation with England was hopeless and that the time had come for the colonies to declare independence and to constitutionalize the powers, rights, and responsibilities of self-government.[49]

In June 1775, Massachusetts presented to the Congress a letter requesting the authority to begin constructing a new government. Adams immediately spoke in defense of the request. By September 1775, he began to argue almost daily for advising the colonies to draft constitutions and to institute their own governments.[50] "The course of Events," Adams wrote to Richard Henry Lee, "naturally turns the Thoughts of Gentlemen to the Subjects of Legislation and Jurisprudence, and it is a curious problem what Form of Government, is most readily and easily adopted by a Colony, upon a Sudden Emergency." Adams understood better than anyone and was therefore the chief advocate, in and out of the Continental Congress, of the need to create new constitutions and new governments in a timely manner. In his public speeches and in his private correspondence, Adams carried the burden of persuading his countrymen that they had reached a unique period, "when a coincidence of circumstances without example, has afforded to thirteen Colonies, at once, an opportunity of beginning anew from the foundation, and building as they choose."[51] But the moment would not last indefinitely; they had to move quickly and boldly. Finally, in May 1776, in large measure due to the labors of Adams, Congress passed a resolution that recommended to the various colonial assemblies that they construct new governments that would "best conduce to the happiness and Safety of their Constituents in particular and America in General." Adams always thought this resolution "an Epocha, a decisive Event" in the American Revolution.[52] And, with some justification, he thought it America's first declaration of independence.

For several months leading up to the May resolution, members of congress had been questioning Adams for advice on how to frame constitutions. Their ignorance was understandable. There were simply no examples in modern history of nations or states framing constitutions de novo. But Adams had reflected on the subject for some time. Indeed, he had been preparing for this moment his entire adult life. He began immediately to look "into the Ancient and modern Confederacies for Examples." The first and most important question asked of Adams was: "How can the People Institute Governments?" He told his colleagues that they must first "invite the People, to erect the whole Building with their own hands upon the broadest foundation. That this could be done only Conventions of Representatives chosen by the People in the several Colonies, in the most exact proportions." That done, his colleagues wanted to know how and why the people would submit to the new constitution. He answered that if there be any doubt, "the Convention may send out their project of a Constitution, to the People in their several Towns, Counties or districts, and the People may make the Acceptance of it their own Act."[53] As far as we know, John Adams was the first American to advocate having constitutions drafted and ratified by special conventions representing the consent of the people, which one distinguished historian has called America's greatest contribution to Western constitutionalism.[54]

In the spring of 1776, a number of Adams's colleagues in the Continental Congress went home to frame constitutions for their respective states. Novices in the art of political architecture, they appealed to the one man whom they knew had thought longer and harder about constitutional construction than any other American. William Hooper and John Penn of North Carolina, George Wythe and Richard Henry Lee of Virginia, and Jonathan Dickinson Sergeant of New Jersey all went to Adams to ask "what Plan of Government" he would advise. He answered by drafting "a variety of short Sketches of Plans, which might be adopted by the Conventions." So inundated was Adams with such requests, he later joked that he had in his head "as many Projects of Government as Mr. Burke says the Abby Seieyes had in his Pidgeon holes, not however constructed at such Length nor laboured with his metaphysical Refinements."[55] Adams eventually published *Thoughts on Government* (1776) to meet popular demand. The pamphlet circulated widely and constitution-makers in almost all the states employed its design as a model from which to work.[56] Ironically, ten years earlier, the thirty-one-year-old lawyer had desisted from entering "into any Inquiry" concerning "which form of Government, whether Either of the Forms of the schools or any Mixture of them is the best calculated to this End the Salus Populi," because he thought this exclusively "the Inquiry of the Founder of Empires." But now, in 1776, he knew "of no Researches in any of the sciences more ingenious than those which have been made after the best Forms of Government nor can there be a more agreable Employment to a benevolent Heart."[57]

Three years later in the fall of 1779, barely off the ship from his first European tour of duty, his home state of Massachusetts called upon Adams to be the "principal engineer" of a new constitution. He joked with his friend Benjamin Rush that he had taken up a "new trade" as a "Constitution monger," but he assumed the task with grave seriousness. As his early diary and letters show, this was a role that he had dreamed about, coveted, and labored for, since his days as a young law student. The many years of preparation—nearly two decades of study, contemplation and travel—were about to pay off. He was to be the lawgiver—the Solon, the Lycurgus, the Moses—of Massachusetts. Just two years earlier, he had written his wife Abigail asking who would "be the Moses, the Lycurgus, the Solon" for Massachusetts? Throughout his life, this would be his greatest honor. He saw no higher glory than that "which attends the great actions of lawgivers."[58] The Massachusetts Constitution of 1780 was the most systematic and detailed constitution produced during the Revolutionary era. It was copied by other states in later years as they revised their Revolutionary constitutions, and it was an important and influential model for the framers of the Federal Constitution of 1787.

The very *idea* of a founding conjured in the minds of America's Revolutionary generation romantic images of classical antiquities' fabled Lawgivers. The names Lycurgus and Solon, wrapped as they were in ancient legend, were held in high esteem and considered by most eighteenth-century philosophers and statesmen as the greatest figures of antiquity. "The character of the lawgiver," Adams once wrote, "was always preferred by the antients, to that of conqueror." "Who," he asked, "does not esteem the glory of Solon, greater than that of Pericles or Themistocles?" Adams learned this lesson from reading William Temple's long-forgotten seventeenth-century "Essay on Heroic Virtue," which taught that the merits of ancient Lawgivers were greater than those of all other heroes of the ancient world, and that their "Glory" was "higher than that of Conquerors."[59]

The American Revolution made possible for an ambitious few the rare opportunity of recreating and, in a sense, of reliving the actions and deeds of these mythical heroes. The event called forth and unleashed a powerful set of passions deep within the soul of America's Revolutionary leadership: the love of fame and the desire for the immortality associated with the great founders and legislators of classical antiquity.[60] "Fame," Adams later wrote in the fourth of his *Discourses on Davila*, "has been divided into three species." The lowest rung on Adams's ladder of fame was "*Credit*, which is supported by merchants and tradesmen." The penultimate level fame, according to Adams, was "*Reputation*, which is cherished by every gentleman." But the highest and most distinguished species of fame was "*Glory*, which attends the great actions of lawgivers and heroes, and the management of the great commands and first offices of state."[61] Adams was here following a long tradition in the history of political philosophy that ranked the lawgiver or legislator at the top of the ladder of fame. According to Francis Bacon's famous classification, the "conditores imperiorum, FOUNDERS OF STATES AND COMMONWEALTHS" ranked highest on the scale of honor.[62] Adams learned the very same lesson from his principal teacher in political affairs, Machiavelli.[63] In the second volume of his *Defence of the Constitutions of Government of the United States of America*, Adams indicated his own fascination with the ancient lawgivers by quoting the following passage from Machiavelli's *Discourse upon the Proper Ways and Means of reforming the Government of Florence*:

> The highest honor that can be attained by any man, is that which is voluntarily conferred on him by his countrymen; and the greatest good he can do, as well as the most acceptable to God, is that which he does to his country. None are to be compared to those who have reformed kingdoms and commonwealths by wholesome laws and constitutions; but as there have been but few that have had an opportunity to do this, the number is very small that have done it. This kind of glory has always been so much coveted by such as made glory the sole end of their labours, that when they have not had power either

to found or reform a state, they have left models and plans in writing, to be executed by others, who should have, in future times; as Plato, Aristotle, and many others, who have shown that, if they did not found free states themselves, like Solon and Lycurgus, it was not owing either to ignorance or want of good-will to mankind, but to want of power. Heaven, then, cannot bestow a nobler gift upon any man, nor point out a fairer road to true glory.[64]

We simply cannot understand John Adams without recognizing the psychic importance that the role of the lawgiver played in his life. Even as a young lawyer, long before the battle at Lexington, Adams was propelled by this desire for immortal fame. In 1761, he told his diary with a dash of youthful enthusiasm that he was "setting up" to be the "Monitor of all future Legislators, a Character for which by my great Age, Experience, Sense and Learning I am well qualified." And certainly by 1776, few among the Revolutionary generation were as aware and self-conscious about the role they would play as lawgivers than was John Adams. "You and I," Adams memorably wrote to his friend George Wythe,

> have been sent into life, at a time when the greatest lawgivers of antiquity would have wished to have lived. How few of the human race have ever enjoyed an opportunity of making an election of government, more than of air, soil, or climate, for themselves or their children! When, before the present epocha, had three millions of people full of power and a fair opportunity to form and establish the wisest and happiest government that human wisdom can contrive?[65]

It is almost impossible for us in the twentieth century to recapture or to appreciate the meaning and symbolism of this passage. This was a defining moment in world history and John Adams knew it. Time has made stale for us the excitement and burden carried by our Revolutionary forefathers. We no longer have the kind of historical consciousness that would make the allusion to the ancient lawgivers meaningful. Thus we can never really know the inner drives and motives of the Revolutionary generation, nor can we understand the ultimate meaning of their Revolutionary act if we do not come to grips with the attempt by a few great and honorable men to recreate the mythic role of the ancient lawgivers.

Chapter 3

The Spirit of Liberty

A great many books have been published in this century on the causes of the American Revolution. The great question that most attempt to address is why the colonists acted as they did. What motives drove this remarkably free and prosperous people to react so passionately and violently to the seemingly benign if not well-intended actions of English imperial officials? How should we understand the relationship between their words and deeds, ideas and actions, principles and behavior? One obvious place to look for answers to these questions is in the major speeches and pamphlets of the Revolutionary era. But such documents are no longer considered as determinative in explaining the "why" of the American Revolution. Abstruse arguments derived from natural and constitutonal law are no longer thought to have determined the outcome of the Revolution one way or the other. They were not ideas that could have viscerally inspired most Americans to respond to perceived threats of encroaching English power; they could not have been transformed into the psychological imperatives that drive men to revolution.

To an early twentieth-century generation of scholars, the speeches and pamphlets spawned by the Revolutionary crisis represented a form of propaganda that masked underlying socioeconomic interests; to a later generation, such arguments were the result of an ideological syndrome and a paranoid mentality. To the first, the Revolutionaries were self-interested, manipulative, and pragmatic; to the second, they were irrational, delusional, and pathological.[1] When viewed from either perspective, the Revolutionaries' most considered public writings and speeches have been downgraded from deliberate statements of individual principle and action to a second-class status where reasoned discourse appears only as a veil for the truly determinative forces of history.[2] Uncovering hidden and largely unconscious motives—whether they be economic or psychological—and breaking the link between cognition and volition has been the modus operandi of modern historical scholarship. Whether studied from the bottom up or from the top down, twentieth-century historians have almost uniformly assumed a deterministic approach to the study of the Revolution and its causes, an approach that assumes an a priori disjunction between rhetoric and reality.[3]

Thus, it is uncommon today for historians to engage in extended and scholarly analyses of the major Revolutionary pamphlets and speeches.[4] John Adams is a case in point. Remarkably, there have been no systematic studies of his pre-Revolutionary writings, even though Adams was a prolific writer, and his pre-Revolutionary essays are considered among the very best and most influential of all the American patriot writings.[5] Indeed, most general studies of the Revolution rely on Adams more than any other patriot to explain the causes and meaning of the Revolution.[6] Adams helps us to understand the coming of the American Revolution because he wrote both reasoned political discourses and passionate rhetorical broadsides. He appealed to the high and to the low, to the head and to the heart.

To assist us in recovering this forgotten world of John Adams, we begin by considering several questions: Why did John Adams think there was a conspiracy by British officials to enslave America? What evidence did he produce to demonstrate a British design against American liberties? Did his revolutionary political thought represent a reasoned and principled response to a real threat, or was it an expression of a mind overheated by "inflamed sensibilities" and an "exaggerated distrust and fear?"[7] In other words, was John Adams an irrational ideologue, or did he think and act as a rational and prudent statesman?

Conspiracy and the Paranoid Style

Like many modern historians, John Adams saw and understood the role played by conspiratorial theories in eighteenth-century politics. In a series of his earliest published writings, Adams examined the causes of political discord and what we might call the paranoid style.[8] The young Braintree lawyer knew as much as any historian that in the realm of politics there is not always a confluence between public rhetoric and private action, and he also recognized that fears of conspiracy are most often rooted in nonrational sources. Adams's purpose in these early essays was to assist in the reformation and elevation of American public discourse. To that end, he sought to expose the public to the principle in human nature that most warps good conscience and corrupts civil discourse: the principle of "self-deceit," that most "spurious offspring of self-love." From the most wicked and "abandoned minds" to the most "modest, sensible and virtuous of the common people," the human soul, he observed, has an amazing capacity for self-flattery and deception. Even men of wisdom and virtue—those of "clearer understanding, and more happy tempers than other men"—are susceptible to "this unhappy disposition."[9] In these early essays, Adams sought to give a sober and rational account of the rise of political faction, political conspiracies, and political paranoia.

This elemental condition of human nature was for Adams the source of almost all public discord and conspiratorial theories. He thought self-deceit like an intellectual switchboard that transforms, rationalizes, and justifies the lower "prejudices, appetites, and passions." Public discourse is thereby corrupted by charge and counter-charge, each side in a controversy rationalizing its own hidden motives while at the same time reproaching others for "impure designs." Adams saw the problems created by self-deceit and conspiratorial politics as particularly acute in Anglo-American politics. The eighteenth-century mixed constitution in both its English and American variants walked a delicate balance between the aspirations of popular and aristocratic parties. Thus, it was not uncommon for the aristocratic party to charge the democratic with "desire of popularity, restless turbulence of spirit, ambitious views, envy, revenge, malice, and jealousy," while the democratic party maligned the aristocratic with charges of "servility, adulation, tyranny, principles of arbitrary power, lust of dominion, avarice, desires of civil or military commissions." Adams rejected both sides. In such disputes he would rather "quarrel with both parties" than "subjugate my understanding, or prostitute my tongue or pen to either."[10] By standing above the turbulent scenes of eighteenth-century Anglo-American politics, Adams hoped not only to expose the underlying causes of civic discord, but also to encourage a form of public discourse that was more self-consciously reflective, more somber, and, in the end, more staunchly republican.

This is not to say, however, that Adams was advising his readers to remain neutral observers in political contests. The more important political lesson drawn by Adams was that political power should never be given to either the "*Bramble* or the *Cedar;* no, nor to *any mortal*, however great or good." To that end, he sought to educate Americans. He called for an enlightened citizenry that could distinguish between a necessary "reverence and obedience to Government, on one hand," and its "right to think and act" for itself on the other.[11] But Adams was mostly concerned with the latter disposition. Given the universal venality and lust of human nature, he knew that the natural tendency of all governments was to grow in power and for liberty to decline. Drawing on the old maxim that, "All Men would be Tyrants if they could," Adams hoped to foster a republican citizenry that would be naturally suspicious of all civil magistrates.[12] This kind of suspicion was neither paranoid nor delusional; rather, it was independent, reasonable, and public-spirited. Adams's enlightened republican citizen must stand above all party faction and he must keep his rulers "under a strict *inspection*, and a just *controul*." Most importantly, he must "examine and judge for *himself* of the *tendency* of political *principles* and *measures*." For Adams, then, every citizen must "be in some degree a *statesman*."[13]

Adams's independent republican citizen was not to be, however, without principle. There was for Adams a higher principle about which there could be no compromise and for which it was entirely reasonable that good men defend at all costs. The higher standard that Adams's new citizen statesmen must use to judge disputed political principles and party policies was the English constitution and common law. These, above all else, Adams sought to protect from the irrational and overwrought world of day-to-day party politics. After studying for several years the "systems of all the legislators, ancient and modern, fantastical and real, and to trace their effects in history upon the *felicity* of mankind," he concluded that "the liberty, the unalienable, indefeasible rights of men, the honor and dignity of human nature, the grandeur and glory of the public, and the universal happiness of individuals, were never so skillfully and successfully consulted as in that most excellent monument of human art, the *common law* of England."[14] The English constitution and the common law were the means by which human nature was tamed and civilized. No citizen by the common law may "justify a furious beating, bruising and wounding" of another "upon the provocation of a fillip of the finger." Inherent in the English constitution and common law was also the right to resist "sudden violence, for the preservation not only of my person, my limbs and life, but of my property." This right to resist arbitrary uses of power—whether by private individuals or public officials—Adams described as "an indisputable right of *nature*."[15] Most day-to-day political disputes fell into the former category; that is, the partisan politics engendered by popular governments were paranoid in that they were most often the result of intrigue, jealousy, and revenge. But Adams understood and taught that there were rare occasions when citizens ought to be hyper-suspicious of their rulers, and that they might legitimately resist the encroachments of political power on their rights and liberties.

The Adams that emerges from these essays is hardly the victim of an ideological paranoia or of a revolutionary syndrome. Instead, what we see is a sober account of human nature, and a deliberate attempt to elucidate the terms and conditions by which ordinary citizens might transcend the faction, deceit, and paranoia inherent in popular politics. Adams hoped to teach his readers a method by which to analyze objectively and to render judgment on the virtues and vices of their political rulers and the tendencies of their "*principles* and *measures.*" When viewed in the context of these early essays on political faction, human nature, and the law, Adams's later writings take on a wholly new appearance.

The Spirit of Liberty

The Stamp Act for John Adams was more than a "fillip of the finger"; he did not think it grew willy-nilly out of the good-intentioned but short-sighted policies of imperial bureaucrats. The Stamp Act was an early-warning signal indicating that a larger threat was looming on the horizon. Indeed, there was, Adams wrote in his "Dissertation on the Canon and the Feudal Law (1765)," nothing less than "a direct and formal design on foot, to enslave America." Several months later in his "Instructions to Braintree's Representatives concerning the Stamp Act," he repeated the charge and promised to produce "evidence" of such a design.[16] This was a theme about which Adams would write time and again in the years after 1765. He therefore wrote his "Dissertation" and several other essays in the following years to assist his citizen statesman in analyzing the "tendencies," the unseen consequences of British colonial policy. This was not an issue of personal jealousy or party feuds for Adams; he was not interested in the character or even in the actions of the Stamp Act's supporters; rather, he was most interested in their "Maxims, Principles and precepts."[17] Adams's method, therefore, was to look at the principles behind the policies as a means of determining their likely long-term consequences.

The Stamp Act was first and foremost unconstitutional, according to Adams. It violated in two ways the most fundamental principle of the English constitution, namely, the principle of consent. Under the English system of government, the people were represented in its two principal political branches, the legislative and the executive. They retained a popular check on the legislative branch through the principle of election, and they partially controlled the executive through the institution of the jury trial. (The execution of laws in the eighteenth century was carried out by the king's courts.) The Stamp Act violated the rights guaranteed by the "great Charter of Liberties" that no citizen shall be deprived of his property or taxed without his consent, "in person or by proxy." Without a just and actual representation, the customary force of the Magna Carta and the common law forbade Parliament from taxing the Americans. It was a "grand and fundamental Principle of the British Constitution," he wrote, "that no Freeman should be subjected to any Tax to which he has not given his own Consent." The principle of virtual representation advocated by the Stamp Act's defenders was nothing more that a "Fiction of Law, as insensible and irrational in Nature, as it will be injurious in fact if so cruel a Taxation should be grounded on it."[18]

Even more "cruel" and "unjust" than the Stamp Act's violation of the principle of no taxation without representation, indeed, the "most grievous innovation of all," was the extension of the courts of admiralty into the American colonies. The recently passed Sugar and Stamp Acts permitted the transfer of revenue enforcement from regular common-law courts to the newly empowered admiralty courts. In the colonists' eyes, this was an ominous constitutional innovation with massive consequences for the system of colonial justice: unconstitutional courts would now enforce unconstitutional taxes. The admiralty courts, Adams noted, were presided over by one judge without the aid of a jury and they operated under the procedures of the civil rather than the common law. Admiralty judges had the authority to determine both the law and the facts of a case, and they held their seats during the pleasure of the king rather than during good behavior. Particularly galling was the new practice established by the admiralty judges of granting themselves "Commissions on all Condemnations," that is, a cut of the bounty gained from those merchants successfully prosecuted for violating the Navigation laws and now the Stamp Act. In other words, judges would have a financial incentive to convict. The Americans would be subject to the whims, greed, revenge, retribution, and violence of malevolent and selfish judges. They would in effect, he warned, be reduced to a state of the "most sordid and forlorn Slaves . . . the slaves of a slave of the servants of a minister of state." The court denied the most basic principles of English common law, that trials should be "per pares [among equals], or per legem terræ [according to the law of the land]."[19] The new use of reinvigorated admiralty courts to enforce direct taxation of Americans deeply offended Adams's sense of Anglo-American justice, and, in the end, it represented the very definition of tyranny.

To all this, Adams responded by writing his "Dissertation on the Canon and the Feudal Law." The "Dissertation" is an essay in political education directed at Adams's enlightened citizen. He took as his broad theme the historical causes of slavery and the conditions necessary to establish political and religious freedom. For Adams, recent attempts by English officials to establish an Anglican episcopacy in America and to impose the Stamp Act on the colonists represented the introduction onto American shores of a new form of the canon and feudal law. Generally speaking, the purpose of the "Dissertation" was twofold: to serve as both an early warning against an impending threat and to provide a clarion call to rouse the people in defense of their rights and liberties. To that end, he wrote a brief history of the Puritan settlement of New England against the backdrop of the Old World canon and feudal law. The "Dissertation" therefore began with an appeal to history; it simultaneously drew upon and hoped to inspire the colonists' collective memory.

According to Adams, there had been throughout history a direct relationship between the general level of education in any given society and its form of government. The less education, the greater the tyranny, while educated societies had been the most free and self-governing. For Adams, knowledge was power—the power to govern oneself and to live an independent life. But the love of knowledge and its power, he cautioned, had been pursued over time for two very different ends: for tyranny on the one hand, and for freedom on the other. Curiously, Adams informed his reader that the love of power had been both the cause of slavery and the cause of freedom. The love of power had led kings to shake off the limitations of their power, but it had also led common people to pursue freedom and to confine political power to the limits of *"equity* and *reason."*[20]

Throughout most of most of human history, however, princes and nobles had monopolized education and they had knowingly and willfully kept knowledge from the people. In particular, they kept from the people a knowledge of their rights, and the power inherent in those rights. Such rights, Adams declared, are not positive grants of the sovereign; they are not his to give or take away; instead, they are "antecedent to all earthly government—*Rights* that cannot be repealed or restrained by human laws—*Rights* derived from the great legislator of the universe."[21] A veil of ignorance had hitherto prevented the people from assuming their rightful independence and freedom.

Since the rise of Christianity, two great systems of tyranny had enslaved the bodies and souls of the European peoples: the canon and feudal laws. The Catholic church and its "Romish clergy" persuaded mankind to "believe, faithfully and undoubtedly, that GOD almighty had intrusted *them* with the keys of heaven; whose gates *they* might open and close at pleasure." On the basis of the canon law, the church assumed all kinds of powers pertaining to this world and the next, including a "power of dispensation over all the rules and obligations of morality—with authority to licence all sorts of sins and crimes"[22] The feudal law was originally based on a military code of law. Under this system, all conquered lands were under the sovereign proprietorship of a victorious general or prince. On the basis of a strictly hierarchical system, land was unequally distributed down the chain of command. With this subordinate distribution of land there came a variety of "*duties* and *services*, all tending to bind the chains the faster, on *every* order of mankind."[23] Only the king owned land allodially, and therefore only the king was free in the fullest sense.

The final blow to liberty, according to Adams, came when these "*two systems* of tyranny" were consolidated into one great engine of oppression.[24] The result was a people held in bondage by their own ignorance. Over time, as the people of England became more sensible of their oppression, they began to break their slavish chains. Between the Reformation and the first settlements in America, Adams wrote, there was a general enlightenment in Europe, and the people of England in particular gained more knowledge of their rights and liberties. The most important event in the enlightenment and liberation of the common man was the Puritan exodus to America.

The Puritan migration was a moment of worldwide revolutionary importance for Adams. But he was quick to remind his reader that it was not religion alone that peopled America; it was, more importantly, a love of "*universal Liberty*" that caused them to risk life and limb. They sought personal and political freedom as well as religious freedom. Liberty, Adams asserted, is a right given to us by God, but he also reminds the reader that these rights would exist were there no God. Our forefathers, he wrote, purchased their natural right to liberty "at the expense of their ease, their estates, their pleasure, and their blood."[25] Liberty is a right of nature. Adams seems to concede here that there are two—not necessarily related—foundations for rights: God and nature. He often described the dual source of rights, but the divine origin is never given the same weight in his thought as is its counterpart in nature. In just one or two places in the "Dissertation" does Adams connect the rights of nature with God. More frequently, however, explicitly and implicitly, he claims that these rights are derived from nature; that is, that they can be deduced from an examination of the constitution of human nature. Human beings have a natural desire to know, and from that desire is derived an unalienable right to pursue knowledge. More particularly, he said, they have a right to a knowledge of their rulers.

Soon after their arrival, the Puritans established a political system more consistent "with liberty and the rights of mankind." Discarding the mystery of the canon law and the force of the feudal law, they constructed their political institutions and policies on the basis of reason and nature. Drawing from their own experience and from an examination of history, Puritan civil institutions were built in accord with the constitution of human nature and in opposition to the "base services, and servile dependencies of the feudal system."[26] They also knew that the perpetuation of their political institutions was based on the ability of an enlightened citizenry to detect, expose, and thwart the designs of those who would deny the people their natural right to liberty, property, and self-government.

But the Puritans knew that their institutions were not and could not be entirely free from the influence of the past. Because it was impossible for the new immigrants to rid themselves completely of the residue of the canon and feudal law, it was necessary to establish additional fortifications to propagate and perpetuate knowledge. One of their first tasks was to establish colleges and a public school system. A second fortification was the establishment of a free press. The right to the acquisition of knowledge was for Adams the first and primary right. In particular, men have a right to a knowledge of the characters and conduct of their rulers. As a corollary to this right, they have another, namely, the right to revoke the authority of their rulers. Liberty, Adams wrote, is a fragile possession that requires diligent protection.

Adams concluded the "Dissertation" by encouraging and supporting the people and the press in the vigilant defense of their rights and liberties. The exoteric purpose of the "Dissertation," then, was to rekindle and fuel the colonists "spirit of liberty."[27] He feared that the Americans had hitherto shown too much caution, diffidence, and reserve in asserting their rights. Following Locke, Adams lamented that human nature is such that men are more likely to suffer abuses gladly than to defend their rights. The Americans had been too reticent in complaining of grievances and violations of their rights. He therefore called on his fellow colonists to rise above their timidity and to think about their threatened condition. We need, he wrote, a renewed spiritedness and a knowledge of our rights and their origins. These Adams pursued in two ways. He must first impress on the "tender mind" the "sensations of freedom," and then certain "ideas of right."[28] This was no easy task, however. Adams's rhetorical project in the "Dissertation" was to inspire, through historical narrative, a reconsideration of the colonists' heroic past as a means of engaging, elevating, and turning their minds toward larger issues of philosophical right.

On one level, then, Adams wrote the "Dissertation" to restore colonial liberties by appealing to history and sentiment; he was attempting to recover something old and valuable. By leading his audience back to the world of their ancestors, he hoped to reawaken long-forgotten memories. By recalling the virtue, spiritedness, and manliness of their Puritan forbears, Adams challenged the lethargic majority to overcome their natural timidity and caution. He called for a remembrance of things past; he demanded that his friends and neighbors remember the great deeds, virtues, sacrifices, and suffering that their forbears endured to guarantee their present freedoms:

> Recollect their amazing fortitude, their bitter sufferings! The hunger, the nakedness, the cold, which they patiently endured! The severe labours of clearing their grounds, building their houses, raising their provisions amidst dangers from wild beasts and savage men, before they had time or money or materials for commerce! . . . Let us recollect it was liberty! The hope of liberty for themselves and us and ours, which conquered all discouragements, dangers and trials![29]

Adams appealed in the "Dissertation" to his fellow citizens' sense of freedom as something experienced and felt. By invoking an old maxim—that sons ought not to forget their fathers—he hoped to shame the American colonists into defending the blood and toil of those who came before them.[30]

On a deeper level, however, Adams was appealing to the reason and judgment of his fellow citizens. The "Dissertation" was less a call to arms than it was a call to the citizens of America to pick up their books. An unstated purpose of the "Dissertation" was to provide Adams's citizen statesman with a certain kind of education. The "spirit of liberty" that he was attemping to rekindle "would be little better than a brutal rage" without such knowledge. But in what exactly were Adams's thoughtful readers to be educated? He implored his fellow citizens to reexamine "the grounds of our privileges, and the extent in which we have an indisputable right to demand them against all the power and authority, on earth." More ambitiously, however, Adams's enlightened statesman should begin more philosophical "reasearches into the grounds and nature and ends of government and the means of preserving the good and demolishing the evil."[31]

At the very least, Americans should study the history of liberty. Adams would first have his enlightened citizen study the history of New England freedom. They should examine both "the nature of that power and the cruelty of that oppression which drove" their ancestors from their homes in England, and the "views and ends, of our own immediate fore-fathers, in exchanging their native country for a dreary, inhospitable wilderness." He would next have them "search into the spirit of the British constitution; read the histories of ancient ages; contemplate the great examples of Greece and Rome; set before us the conduct of our own British ancestors who have defended for us the inherent rights of mankind against foreign and domestic tyrants."[32]

For his more ambitious and philosophical students, however, Adams recommended that they go beyond history to study "the laws of nature" and to "search for the foundations of British laws and government in the frame of human nature, in the constitution of the intellectual and moral world." Equating English rights and liberties with the Lockean laws of nature, Adams reminded his reader that "British liberties are not the grants of princes or parliaments but original rights, conditions of original contracts, coequal with prerogative and coeval with government." Many of these rights, he insisted, "are inherent and essential, agreed on as maxims and established as preliminaries even before a parliament existed." In order to inspire his citizen-statesmen to seize the opportunity and to aspire to great thoughts and deeds, Adams drew a historical parallel between the colonists' present situation and that confronted by the English in the seventeenth century. In the very same way that the tyranny of the Stuarts encouraged the best minds in England to reflect on the nature and role of government, producing a generation of philosophers and statesmen such as Clarendon, Southampton, Selden, Hampden, Faulkland, Sidney, Locke, and Harrington, Adams hoped that the recent actions by Parliament would produce in America a new generation of statesmen and philosophers dedicated to freedom and self-government. By encouraging this kind of research agenda, Adams hoped to enliven the American "spirit of liberty."[33]

This notion of a "spirit of liberty" was one that Adams repeated over and over again in his pre-Revolutionary essays.[34] What exactly was this spirit? What were its characteristics? Spiritedness for Adams was both a *sensation* and an *idea*. It was something felt and thought. The spirit of liberty united in one soul certain "sensations of freedom" and certain "ideas of right" or justice. Liberty, for Adams, meant freedom from foreign domination, freedom from unjust government coercion, freedom from other individuals, and finally, freedom from the tyranny of oneself. In short, it meant self-government in the fullest sense. A free people, he warned, ought to be jealous of their rights and liberties, and they must always stand on guard to protect them. An empirical observation of human nature demonstrated to Adams that freedom is something always tenuous and precarious, and history proved it. The decline and fall of the Greek city states and the Roman republic and the recent history of England proved the point. Indeed, freedom is something extraordinarily rare. Few people have it, and those that do must fight to keep it. For that reason, Adams proclaimed, the American experiment in free government should be cherished and honored.

Ultimately, the "spirit of liberty" for Adams was the virtue necessary to acquire and then keep one's political and civil liberty. The Americans, he wrote, have a "habitual, radical Sense of Liberty, and the highest Reverence for Vertue."[35] The spirit of liberty "is and ought to be a jealous, a watchful spirit." The motto and maxim that he chose to define the spirit of liberty was "Obsta Principiis," that is, to resist the first beginnings. Adams wrote, then, as a kind of early-warning system against the "early advances, these first approaches of arbitrary power." The preliminary advances of power, he wrote, are the most dangerous because, if not prevented, they establish precedents until only a "recourse to nature, violence and war" will remedy the patient.[36] Following Machiavelli, Adams was willing to concede that periodic crises are good for the health of the body politic. "Calamities," he said, "are causticks and catharticks of the body politick. They arouse the soul. They restore original virtues. They reduce a constitution back to its first principles." The colonists have been "terrified" into rediscovering and restoring "the noble foundations of their ancestors."[37] The Americans have a manly sense of their own freedom that is to be cherished and protected at all costs. For these reasons, Adams in later years could describe the American Revolution as being first and foremost a revolution "in the Minds of the People."[38]

"Revolution-Principles"

By 1774, a dénouement had been reached. With the passage of the Coercive Acts, tyranny was no longer threatened, it had arrived. Adams was now convinced like never before that there was a conspiracy afoot to destroy American liberties. The time had finally come, he wrote, to expose "the wicked policy of the tories, trace their plan from its first rude sketches to its present complete draught, show that it has been much longer in contemplation than is generally known—who were the first in it—their views, motives, and secret springs of action, and the means they have employed."[39] In his "Novanglus" essays, Adams named names and produced a smoking gun.

The conspiracy to restrict and even deny colonial rights was, according to Adams, first hatched by a transatlantic "junto" of British ministers and their American minions. The foremost actors in the junto included Lords Bute, Mansfield, and North on the English side, and Governor Francis Bernard, Thomas Hutchinson, and Andrew Oliver on the American side.[40] By 1774 and with the help of hindsight, Adams was able to trace the actions and policies of the junto from as early as the administration of Governor William Shirley (1741–1757), but the real design of the junto only became apparent during the administration of Governor Bernard (1760–1770). The end of the Seven Years' War was the turning point. In just a few short years, the English policy of salutary neglect ended, and, to many Americans, almost one hundred and fifty years of colonial self-government seemed threatened. In addition to the schedule of unconstitutional duties and taxes imposed by the Sugar, Stamp, Townshend, and Tea Acts, British officials over the course of the next decade would dramatically increase their regulatory control over the colonies. Adams provided his readers with a long list of the new rules, powers, and courts of the new imperial bureaucracy.

In 1764, the American Act, in addition to issuing a variety of new duties, prescribed a series of regulations designed to tighten the navigation system. The number of customs officials in America was substantially increased, absentee officials were ordered back to their posts, and the whole customs bureaucracy was given greater authority and protection. A squadron of British warships was sent to America as an arm of the English customs service, and the navy was granted greater powers to inspect American ships. The powers and jurisdiction of the admiralty courts were greatly expanded, and a newly centralized vice admiralty court was established in Halifax.[41] Likewise, the Townshend Acts of 1767–68, dramatically increased the enforcement powers of British officialdom in the colonies. A new five-man American Board of Commissioners of the Customs was established at Boston with the support of four new regiments of British soldiers to exercise direct control over American customs and to enforce rigorously the Navigation Acts. Four new vice admiralty courts were established in North America with both original and appellate jurisdiction. Furthermore, an expanded issuance of general writs of assistance would enhance customs inspections. These general warrants gave its holder almost unlimited authority to enter any house or building, day or night, on the suspicion that it might contain smuggled goods and illegal contraband. To American Whigs, these writs violated the ancient English right against unreasonable searches and seizures.[42]

In addition to unconstitutional taxes, a growing network of regulatory rules administered by a standing army and an ever expanding phalanx of imperial bureaucrats, Adams added to the junto's list of usurpations the destruction of the colonial charters. Top on his list was the unconstitutional practice of plural officeholding. Adams claimed that Hutchinson, for instance, was hoarding for himself and his family the powers of the legislative, executive, and judicial branches of government. Hutchinson had simultaneously been chief justice, judge probate in Boston, lieutenant governor, and a member of the council. This, Adams decried, was "too many offices for the greatest and best man in the world to hold." The Triumvirate of Bernard, Hutchinson, and Oliver had slowly over time and "by degrees, and before the people were aware of it, erected a tyranny in the province." With all their constitutional springs and wheels set in motion, the junto was well placed to "promote submission to the stamp act, and to discountenance resistance to it."[43] No less threatening to Adams was the assumption of the governor's salary by the Crown in 1773 and a threat to do the same with judges.

Finally, in 1774, Parliament passed the Coercive Acts. The Massachusetts Government Act and the Administration of Justice Act were particularly galling and ominous in their portent for colonial self-rule. The Massachusetts Government Act arbitrarily changed the Massachusetts Council to a body appointed by the Crown, each councilor continuing in office at the king's pleasure. The Massachusetts governor was now given complete power to appoint and dismiss all executive and inferior judicial officers, including justices of the peace and sheriffs. Superior court judges would be nominated by the governor for appointment by the king. Juries were to be chosen by the sheriff instead of being democratically elected by the people of the towns. Adams feared this last would potentially mean that Tory appointed sheriffs would only select Tory juries, thereby insuring the ability of the administration to impose and enforce any law or tax on the people that they chose. Such juries, for instance, might also have the authority to muzzle the press with libel convictions.[44] Finally, town meetings were barred without the consent of the governor, except for annual election meetings. The Administration of Justice Act empowered the Massachusetts governor to transfer to Britain or any other colony royal officials accused of committing capital crimes while serving in the line of duty.

The key that allowed Adams to open and enter into the secret intentions of the Triumvirate was the publication of Governor Francis
Bernard's "Principles of Law and Polity, Applied to the American
Colonies." Bernard's essay was the smoking gun that allowed Adams to
expose the concealed intentions and hidden design of certain English
ministers and their American co-conspirators. First written for imperial
bureaucrats in 1764 but not made public until 1774, the "Principles"
served in large measure as the basis for the Coercive Acts.[45] Unveiling
the junto's long-standing design required of Adams that he quote from
Bernard's pamphlet in some detail. That Bernard first sent his "Principles"
to imperial officials in 1764 suggested to Adams "that the project of new
regulating the American colonies were not first suggested to him by the
ministry, but by him to them."[46]

Bernard's chief recommendation called for a massive restructuring of
the American colonial governments. He proposed this be done by first having Parliament claim the absolute right to legislate for the colonies in all
cases whatsoever. Adams found three specific proposals particularly noxious and incriminating: first, a recommendation that Parliament tax the
colonies for a revenue and without their consent; second, that the colonial
charters be declared void and that new colonies be created by redrawing
and consolidating provincial boundaries; and third, that an American nobility be appointed by the king first for life and eventually on a hereditary
basis. Under Bernard's plan, the receipts of colonial taxation would go to
paying the salaries of the governor, lieutenant governor, and the common
law and admiralty judges. "And thus the whole government, executive and
judicial," Adams warned, "was to be rendered wholly independent of the
people . . . and absolutely dependent upon, and under the direction of the
will of the minister of state."[47] Bernard's plan would not only change in
rather dramatic ways the colonial governments, it would in effect destroy
one hundred and fifty years of colonial self-government.

The evidence drawn by Adams to implicate Hutchinson's culpability
was no less damning than Bernard's. Unlike Bernard, Hutchinson was a native son of Massachusetts; he was "bone of our bone, born and educated
among us."[48] His crimes, therefore, were all the more heinous. Adams presented two sorts of evidence against Hutchinson. The first was personal.
Hutchinson, according to Adams, had sold his soul to advance his personal
power and fortune. His accumulation of political offices—legislative, executive, and judicial—was a clear violation of the principle of the separation
of powers. The second kind of evidence enumerated by Adams to expose
Hutchinson's role in the junto concerned his "principles and practices."[49]

In 1773, in two messages to the Massachusetts General Court, Hutchinson came out publicly in support of the Declaratory Act's principle that Parliament was absolutely sovereign in America. More ominously, however, the American public several months later came to learn that Hutchinson's private views—views that he was sharing with English officials—were even more threatening to their rights and liberties. With the assistance of Benjamin Franklin, then living in London, Boston Whigs published Hutchinson's correspondence to Thomas Whately, former secretary to the Treasury under George Grenville. In one of these letters, Hutchinson called for "an abridgment of what are called English liberties." What had long been suspected of Hutchinson was now confirmed.

The public accusation of a conspiracy against American liberties was a serious charge that John Adams did not take lightly. What was really at stake here? Why was the American reaction against British colonial legislation so swift, so passionate, and so violent? Why did they use such inflated rhetoric? Why did Adams and the other Revolutionaries write and speak as if their lives, their fortunes, and the security of their families were threatened directly?

To a penetrating and far-seeing thinker like John Adams, the principles, policies, and actions of British imperial officials and the American junto represented a real threat to colonial liberties. Behind the facade of British denials, he saw in the accumulating and sometimes minor laws directed at America an undeniable reduction in their liberties and the engine for future tyranny, and that is what counted. Not unreasonably, Adams feared that a growing web of commissioners, customs officials, placemen, and judges with direct connections to England, all supported by an army's bayonets, would sap America of its political and moral independence. In the end, whether there was or was not an actual design by power-hungry ministers and their loyalists in America to enslave the Americans is and was a secondary issue. After some ten years of real and direct assaults on American self-government, it was entirely reasonable for Adams to employ the rhetoric of conspiracy in order to awaken and mobilize Americans in defense of their traditional political and moral order.[50] Indeed, it was prudent, if not wise, for Adams to argue that despotism be stopped in its design phase rather than waiting until it appeared on one's doorstep fully developed. But Adams's enlightened citizen, not to mention the unenlightened citizen, would not always be able to see and certainly would not always be moved to act by dry constitutional arguments. Fully in control of his own rhetoric, Adams sought to awaken Americans from their nondogmatic slumbers.

Anticipating the claims of twentieth-century historians, eighteenth-century Tories accused Adams and the other Revolutionaries of appealing to the low, the unjust, and the most ignoble passions of the people. This is a serious charge, then and now, and one that required from Adams a serious reply. The American people, he declared, are too "sensible and virtuous" to be duped over a long period of time into thinking that they are being enslaved when in fact they are not. Unlike his Tory critics, Adams firmly believed the people capable of understanding "the difference between true and false, right and wrong, virtue and vice." On the basis of that judgment, it was only proper, he thought, that the people be given all the information necessary to make these moral and political distinctions. Adams was more than willing to concede, however, that he was in part appealing to a particular passion in the people. The "latent spark" to which he appealed was nothing less than a love of liberty, which, he said, was wrought into the constitution of human nature. Intimately connected to this love of liberty was "a resentment of injury, and indignation against wrong. A love of truth and a veneration for virtue."[51] From Adams's perspective, these are entirely noble and just passions founded on a conscious, deliberate, and rational understanding of political life.

How, then, should the Americans respond to the Coercive Acts? That was the great question for all Americans in 1774. There was for Adams a spectrum of attitudes and responses to which the people might attach themselves. At the two extremes were the spirit of passive obedience and the spirit of anarchy.[52] He regarded both with disdain and considered each anathema to true liberty. In the end, passive obedience and anarchy led to the same result: tyranny.

Throughout the entire Revolutionary period, Adams feared and loathed the people's occasional lapses into timidity and their submissive acquiescence to authority. "In the course of a few months," he wrote in 1767, "they have cooled down, into such a tame, torpid state of indolence and inattention; that the missionaries of slavery, are suffered to preach their abominable doctrines, not only with impunity, but without indignation and without contempt." Conversely and without contradiction, there were times when the people, under the inflammatory leadership of demagogues, had been whipped into an ideological frenzy and deceived into supporting a "total suppression of equity and humanity." Adams would have nothing to do with the peoples' passive obedience, nor would he sanction their occasional anarchic impulses. By contrast, he labored his entire life to live by certain "Rules" with regard to the people. His prime directive was never to "deceive the People, conceal from them any essential truth, nor especially make myself subservient to any of their Crimes, Follies, or Excentricities."[53] Adams saw himself not as a partisan of the patriot cause but rather as one of its most principled statesman.

During the 1760s, Adams had, of course, attempted to foster an enlightened spirit of liberty as the principled mean between the extremes of subservience and anarchy. By 1774, however, resurrecting the spirit of colonial liberty was no longer sufficient to restore colonial rights and liberties. The design against American liberties was now so obvious to him and the threat so imminent that a new and radical course of action was required. The time had come for the Americans to invoke what Adams called "revolution-principles."[54] In that moment, he ceased being a conservative defender of colonial rights and liberties and became a Revolutionary republican.

Adams knew that the call for "revolution-principles" was dangerous, and that it often inclined toward the spirit of anarchy. Despite the charges of Tory writers, he drew a sharp distinction between his "revolution-principles" and the spirit of anarchy. Adams's revolution-principles were guided by the highest concern for reason, justice, and virtue; they were, he said, the principles of "Aristotle and Plato, of Livy and Cicero, and Sydney and Harrington and Locke"; they were "the principles of nature and eternal reason."[55] By contrast, Adams thought the spirit of anarchy was propelled by the lowest passions, injustice, and vice. He worried throughout the pre-Revolutionary period that the spirit of anarchy would overcome and destroy the good sense and justice of the American cause. At home between sessions of the Continental Congress, Adams happened upon a former client whose greeting genuinely alarmed him: "Oh! Mr. Adams. What great things have you and your colleagues done for us! We can never be grateful enough to you. There are no courts of justice now in this province, and I hope there never will be another!" Adams hardly knew what to say. His sense of what the controversy with Britain was all about was deeply offended. "Is this the object for which I have been contending?" he asked himself. The leaders of the Revolutionary movement "must guard against this spirit and these principles or we shall repent of all our conduct," he warned.[56]

Adams's invocation of "revolution-principles" was remarkable for its somber, rational, and levelheaded appeal to facts, precedents, and principles. Revolutions were not to be undertaken for light and transient reasons; they must be pursued with caution, moderation, and prudence.

There must be objectively definable principles and observable conditions that justify such a momentous step. For Adams, the boundary line between resistance and revolution was the constitution. He always sought constitutional solutions to constitutional problems, but when that was no longer possible, a "recourse to higher powers not written" was entirely justified.[57]

At the heart of Adams's "revolution-principles" was the doctrine of equality, the principle "that all men by nature are equal." Equality is the basis for political consent and consent is the necessary precondition for the social contract. Advancing a Lockean interpretation of the English constitution, Adams said that such principles are the foundation "on which the whole government over us, now stands." Thus, when it can be demonstrated that a prince has a "manifest design" to annul the contract, the people have a right to disregard his authority. Indeed, "a settled plan to deprive the people of all the benefits, blessings and ends of the contract, to subvert the fundamentals of the constitution, to deprive them of all share in making and executing laws, will justify a revolution."[58] Even then, Adams warned, the people are slow to rouse. The "most sensible and jealous" among them are willing to suffer a long train of abuses and to overlook a thousand mistakes by their government. They will almost never resist their governing authorities until repeated and multiplying oppressions "have placed it beyond a doubt, that their rulers had formed settled plans to deprive them of their liberties" and "to break down the fences of a free constitution, and deprive the people at large of all share in the government and all the checks by which it is limitted."[59] The call to "revolution-principles" was the option of last resort for Adams.

Generally speaking, Adams was entirely opposed to the resort to "original powers" and the destruction of property, private or public.[60] In 1774, he took on a politically charged civil case, *King v. Stewart,* in which the loyalist Richard King sought to obtain damages after a patriot mob had destroyed his home and property.[61] Adams found the actions of the rioters particularly noxious. After a local mob accused King of being a prospective Stamp Act officer, they broke into his house in the dark of night, terrorized his pregnant wife and children, and then destroyed furniture, windows, and private papers. Adams's address to the jury, echoing James Otis's speech at the writs of assistance case, was a stirring defense of a man's inalienable right to live undisturbed in the privacy of his home:

> An Englishmans dwelling House is his castle. The Law has erected a Fortification round it—and as every man is Party to the Law, i.e., the

> Law is a Covenant of every Member of society with every other Member, therefore every Member of Society has entered into a solemn Covenant with every other that he shall enjoy in his own dwelling House as compleat a security, safety and Peace and Tranquility as if it was surrounded with Walls of Brass, with Ramparts and Palisadoes and defended with a Garrison and Artillery.[62]

Writing to Abigail during the King case, Adams drew a critical distinction between the legitimate and illegitimate, just and unjust actions of popular mobs. "All too often," he wrote, "private Mobs," hiding under the veil of legitimate political deprivations, were secretly motivated by "Resentment for private Wrongs or in pursuance of private Prejudices and Passions." These private mobs, he told Abigail, "I do and will detest." Following Locke, Adams condemned these forms of private justice as the necessary preconditions for a return to the state of nature. The anarchic liberty that results from men being judges in their own cases was entirely inconsistent with true liberty. For Locke, as for Adams, true liberty was possible only through law. "*Where there is no law*," Locke had insisted, "*there is no freedom.*"[63] Adams was one of America's greatest champions of the patriot cause, but he could never sanction the violence of Whig mobs in defense of anything other than fundamental rights and principles.

There were times, however, when "Popular Commotions can be justifyed." Adams defended the resort to original power "in Opposition to Attacks upon the Constitution." Such extreme measures should only be taken "when Fundamentals are invaded, nor then unless for absolute Necessity and with great Caution."[64] It was precisely on these grounds that Adams condoned the actions of the Boston Tea Party. In his diary, he described the Tea Party as "the most magnificent Movement of all" and "an Epocha in History." He was extraordinarily proud of the virtuous "Dignity of the patriots."[65] In his public defense of the tea raiders, Adams provided a principled and reasoned argument for when the resort to revolutionary first principles was justified and when it was not. He understood as well as anyone that civil disobedience was generally ruinous to the health of the body politic, but there were times when "tumults, seditions, popular commotions, insurrections and civil wars" are defensible in the name of just causes.[66] Only when it became absolutely clear that petitions and nonimportation agreements had failed to halt the advance of British assaults against colonial liberties did Adams call for and support direct action.

In defense of the Tea Party's actions, he built his case by quoting from a variety of modern natural-law writers (a list that included Grotius,

Sidney, Puffendorf, Barbeyrac, and Locke) to illustrate the conditions un-der which a people might resist the arbitrary laws or whimsical dictates of their elected or unelected government. According to Hugo Grotius in *The Rights of War and Peace* (1625), private action may be taken against civil authorities when "'the way to legal justice is not open.'" In his *Discourses Concerning Government*, Sidney had written that there are times when "'extrajudicial'" means of "'preventing or punishing injuries'" are necessary. Such conditions exist when magistrates break "'the laws of God and men'" without themselves being subject to a court of justice. Several times throughout "Novanglus," Adams quoted approvingly Locke's dictum that the people are slow to revolt, that they are willing to suffer a long train of abuses before undertaking radical and often violent action. According to Locke, resistance was justified when governments violate the constitution or the terms of the social contract: "'For when men by entering into society, and civil government, have excluded force, and introduced laws for the preservation of property, peace and unity, among themselves; those who set up force again, in opposition to the laws, do *rebellare*, that is, do bring back again the state of war, and are properly rebels.'"[67] Parliament's passage of the Tea Act was just that: it was "an attack upon a fundamental principle of the English constitution." Hence Parliament and not the colonists were the true rebels. According to Locke, when "legislators act contrary to the end for which they were constituted," they are *guilty of rebellion.*[68]

This controversy surrounding the Tea Act was a moral and a consti-tutional issue for Adams, and the American response was legitimately grounded on the "revolution-principles" enunciated by Locke and Sidney. The issue for Adams came down to this: "If parliament has a right to tax us, and legislate for us, in all cases, the destruction of the tea was unjusti-fiable; but if the people of America are right in their principle, that par-liament has no such right, that the act of parliament is null and void, and it is lawful to oppose and resist it, the question then is, whether the de-struction was necessary?"[69] This, Adams said, is a question for reason, jus-tice, and prudence to determine. They could have, he suggested, landed and "stored" the tea until the issue had been resolved. But such action would only have conceded to Parliament the right to tax the colonies—a principle against which they had "struggled for ten years." Unwilling to forever subject themselves and their posterity to the commands of "Egypt-ian taskmasters," the actions of the Boston Tea Party, Adams declared, were "absolutely necessary, and therefore right and just." Driven to the brink of annihilation, the colonists had no other choice: if they did noth-

ing, they would be enslaved; if they acted and failed, they would be enslaved; but if they acted and succeeded, they would regain their liberties.[70] By first calling on the people to revive their ancient spirit of liberty
and then educating his fellow citizens in revolution-principles and the
first principles of government, John Adams played a crucial role in shaping and defining the moral and intellectual revolution that led to the War
of Independence.[71]

Chapter 4

The Principles of Liberty

For John Adams, the controversy with Great Britain was, from beginning to end, constitutional. The Anglo-American contest, he wrote in his diary, was "upon the greatest Question ever yet agitated"; it was a dispute over "the foundations of the constitution."[1] Colonial reaction to parliamentary legislation had less to do with taxes than it did with the political and administrative innovations that were changing the nature of their historic constitution and clashing with their most cherished beliefs concerning the just foundations of government. Of all the British laws directed at the colonies in the years between 1763 and 1774, the one that Adams found most threatening to colonial liberties was the one that least affected their pocketbooks, the Declaratory Act. The taxes associated with the Sugar, Stamp, and Townshend Acts were not the primary issue for Adams, nor were the regulations, bureaucrats, and soldiers. All these were simply consequences of a more dangerous underlying principle. What united the Americans was the claim that Parliament was absolutely sovereign in America. The Declaratory Act was for John Adams the prime mover that gave life to the policies of unconstitutional taxes and courts. At stake was nothing less than the colonists' freedom and right to govern themselves.

In 1775 John Adams wrote a comprehensive study of the constitutional relationship between the center of the British empire and its colonial peripheries.[2] The "Novanglus" essays were a systematic attempt to describe the origins, nature, and jurisdictional boundaries of the imperial British constitution. The central question that sparked Adams to write was clear and simple: Does the authority of Parliament extend to the colonies in all cases whatsoever? Revolving around the central question orbited several other difficult issues: To whom did the colonists owe allegiance, Crown or realm, king or Parliament? Who were the true constitutional innovators, Parliament or colonies? Did the revolutionary settlement of 1688 apply to America?

Generally speaking, Adams's argument in "Novanglus" can be divided into two categories, one negative and the other positive. His first task was to challenge the claim that the colonies were or ever had been subjects of the British state or English realm, and therewith subject to the authority of Parliament. The second and more important task, however, was to present a positive argument defining the true nature of Anglo-American relations. This he ingeniously did by synthesizing two very different kinds of arguments: one from feudal law and another from the laws of nature. Adams's first position was to demonstrate that the Americans were linked to the British empire by a quasi-medieval allegiance to the person of the king. More subtly, however, he advanced a second argument that connected colonists to the king by consent and the laws of nature. Ingeniously, he drew together in one argument Coke's feudal understanding of allegiance with Locke's radical theories on consent and natural law. In the "Novanglus" essays, John Adams walked into and across the frontier of Anglo-American political practice and thought. The result was a highly original and systematic interpretation of the British imperial constitution.[3]

Imperium In Imperio

To understand how apologists for British authority defended the Declaratory Act is to understand in part the growing differences between American and English interpretations of the English constitution. The position of British officialdom was ably summarized by Adams's interlocutor in the "Novanglus" essays, Daniel Leonard, writing under the pseudonym of *Massachusettensis*. Leonard's argument in brief was this: the constitutional authority of Parliament did and must extend to the colonies. This was so because history proves it and theory demands it. Historically, the American colonies, Leonard argued, were and always had been a part of the British state and empire. His fundamental argument was that "when a nation takes possession of a distant country, and settles there, that country though separated from the principal establishment or mother country, naturally becomes a part of the state." All territories acquired (annexed or conquered) by England over the centuries—that is, Wales, Ireland, the Channel Islands—were part of the empire and subject to the authority of Parliament, regardless of whether they were actually represented or not, and regardless of whether they had their own legislatures, as with Ireland. The American colonies were, he claimed, in exactly the same relationship to England and Parliament as were Ireland, Wales, and the Channel Islands. The colonies were part of the British state, "equal" with all its other "ancient possessions."[4]

Theoretically, the colonies must be under the sovereignty of Parliament, Leonard insisted, because "two supreme or independent authorities cannot exist in the same state." Such an *imperium in imperio* would be "the heighth of political absurdity." A sovereign authority existing within a sovereign authority was to Leonard, as it was to all constitutionalists in the Anglo-American world, a contradiction in terms. It was a truism of eighteenth-century politics that there must be some final and absolute authority somewhere in every political state. If the Americans were a part of the British empire, they must then be subject to the supreme authority of the state, "which is vested in the estates of parliament." While it was true that each of the colonies had its own legislature, they were nevertheless subordinate and limited to "regulating their own internal policy." This, according to Leonard, is the traditional understanding of sovereignty. To deny it, he said, would be a constitutional innovation. This is how the mother country and the colonists' ancestors had always understood the relationship; that is, that the colonies were and would always remain subject to Parliament. For Leonard, there could be "no possible medium between absolute independence" on the one hand, and "subjection to the authority of parliament" on the other.[5] The position of British officialdom could admit of no middle ground between these two extremes.

Leonard's rhetorical purpose was to back Adams and the American Whigs into a corner. If the colonies were not subject to the authority of Parliament they were for all purposes independent. If they were independent of Parliament, they were effectively independent of the imperial Crown as well (indeed, he says, they may even be independent of the person of the king), which was created by an act of Parliament with the accession of Queen Anne and the unification of England and Scotland (1707). By the terms of the Glorious Revolution and the Act of Union, the nature of the king's role in the realm had changed; his position had been downgraded to fit into the limited boundaries and harmony of a mixed constitution. Leonard seemed to be suggesting that if one denies allegiance to the king-in-Parliament, one must, by definition, deny the Glorious Revolution and the post-1688 constitutional settlement. This was a powerful argument and entirely within the Whig tradition. If the American colonists owed allegiance solely to the person of the king of Great Britain, they would find themselves in the absurd position of having a king for Rhode Island, a king for Massachusetts, a king for Virginia, and so on. Such a system, Leonard warned, would put the union of the extended British polity in chaos, and it would ultimately give the king new and potentially abusive powers. The end result would be the reestablishment in both colonies and realm of an absolute monarchy. Leonard argued that if the American interpretation of the imperial union were to triumph, it would challenge or change the nature of the monarchy in the realm, thereby upsetting the famed balance in the English constitution. Indeed, were the American interpretation to prevail, Leonard feared that the benefits of the English constitution and the traditional rights and liberties of Englishmen would be forever lost. Leonard's challenge to Adams was grounded on solid Whig principles.[6]

The Post-Nati *or the Case Against Parliament*

Stuck on the horns of a theoretical dilemma, Adams was forced by Massachusettensis to confront and dissolve the distinction between absolute dependence and total independence. This could only be done by first challenging two underlying assumptions of British thought: first, that the colonies were dominions of the British empire, and, second, that the colonists were subjects of the English kingdom, realm, or state. Adams flatly rejected both assumptions as historically untrue and theoretically impossible; thus he had to uncouple the linkage between parliamentary sovereignty and the notion of a unified British state.

Historically, almost all of the American colonies, Adams wrote, were founded and settled *post-nati* (after the accession of James I and the unification of the English and Scottish Crowns in 1603), but before the establishment of parliamentary sovereignty in 1688 and before the creation of Great Britain through the Act of Union in 1707. In other words, most colonies were founded before there was a kingdom of Great Britain, a king-in-Parliament, or a sovereign Parliament. During the Stuart reign, when most of the colonies were founded, there was a united Crown in England and Scotland, but not a united Parliament; each nation had its own legislative body but shared the same king. In the very same way that Englishmen owed no allegiance to the Scottish Parliament and vice versa, so, too, the Americans owed no political attachment to England. To support this argument, Adams invoked Sir Edward Coke's opinion in *Calvin's Case*:

> I beg leave to observe here, that these words in the foregoing adjudication [*Calvin's Case*], that "the natural person of the King is ever accompanied with the politick capacity, and the politick capacity as it were appropriated to the natural capacity"; neither imply nor infer allegiance, or subjection to the politick capacity, because in the case of King James the first, his natural person was "accompanied" with three politick capacities at least, as King of England, Scotland and Ireland:

yet the allegiance of an Englishman to him did not imply or infer subjection, to his politick capacity as King of Scotland.[7]

If it were simply true that the colonists owed allegiance to the En-
glish Parliament, Adams pointedly asked, why not then to the Scottish
Parliament as well or even solely to the Scottish Parliament? After all,
Charles I, grantor of the Massachusetts charter, was the king of both
Scotland and England. Furthermore, most of the colonists who founded
Massachusetts Bay were born *post-nati*, Adams asserted, which meant, as
judged by Coke in *Calvin's Case*, that they were "free natural subjects of
Scotland, as well as England." It was simply not true, he concluded, that
the colonies were or could be a part of the British empire or state. The
very suggestion was a gross abuse of political rhetoric: "The terms 'British
Empire' are not the language of the common law," Adams retorted, "but
the language of news papers and political pamphlets. . . . This language,
'the imperial crown of Great-Britain,' is not the stile of the common law,
but of court sycophants."[8]

Nor was it true, according to Adams, that the colonists were subjects
of the English kingdom or realm. Under the English constitution, such a
connection would have required that "every foot of land should be represented, in the third estate." He was quick to note that "there is not an
acre of American land represented" in the estates of Parliament. Parliament therefore could have no supreme authority over the Americans because the Americans have never been represented in Parliament. To
accept the supremacy of Parliament in the colonies would be to renounce
the British constitution, and it would reduce the colonies to the oligarchic rule of not only a few British grandees but the whole English people, for "king, lords, and commons will constitute one great oligarchy." It
was intolerable to suggest that the common people of Great Britain were
absolutely sovereign over their fellow subjects in America. The Americans understood the English constitution in a different light: "Metaphysi-
cians and politicians may dispute forever," Adams noted, "but they will
never find any other moral principle or foundation of rule or obedience,
than the consent of governors and governed."[9]

To suggest, as Massachusettensis did, that the Americans "'must be'"
subject to "'the supreme power of the state'" was to assert that power,
naked power, was the glue that held the empire together. This seemed to
Adams to be precisely what Massachusettensis and British officialdom
were arguing. By drawing on analogies with Ireland and Wales, theorists of
the British empire sought to establish parliamentary sovereignty over the

American colonies on the grounds that they, too, were conquered nations. It was absurd to suggest, Adams contended, that the American colonies had ever been conquered and annexed to the English realm. First, he said, America "never was conquered by Britain." It was, if anything, a "discovered" country. Furthermore, no territory, he claimed, could be annexed to the realm of England without an act of Parliament, and no such act existed in the case of the American colonies. In this regard, the American situation was entirely different from that of Wales and Ireland. Both Wales and Ireland were conquered dominions of the English Crown until such time as they consented to be incorporated into the realm with parliamentary representation, as with Wales, or until such time as they consented to be subject without representation to parliamentary laws when expressly named, as with Ireland. Where was the Poyning's Law—which required the Crown's prior approval of all laws passed by the Irish Parliament—for America? Adams demanded to know.[10] His logic was irrefutable: if it were true that the colonies had never been annexed to the realm, they could not by definition be a "Part of the Kingdom, and consequently not subject to the Legislative Authority of the Kingdom."[11] Ultimately, each colony was a separate and distinct realm, and the king of Great Britain was the sovereign ruler over each. Hence the king of Great Britain was also the "king of Massachusetts, king of Rhode-Island, and king of Connecticut."[12]

Adams then turned to Leonard's theoretical claim that sovereignty cannot be divided. With this, Adams wholeheartedly agreed. Sovereignty cannot be divided, he said, but there can be parallel sovereignties. By this he meant that the colonial legislatures were the supreme political authorities in America and that Parliament was the supreme political authority regulating the commerce of the empire. The Anglo-American crisis of the eighteenth century was a conflict over the jurisdictional boundary lines between mother country and colonies, and John Adams thought he knew exactly what that boundary line was: it "is a line fairly drawn between the rights of Britain and the rights of the colonies, namely, the banks of the ocean, or low-water mark, the line of division between the common law and civil or maritime law."[13] The colonists, by their charters and through long usage, had consented to Parliament's regulation of the empire's overseas dominions, "but we never thought parliament the supreme legislature over us, but from necessity, and that necessity we thought confined to the regulation of trade, and to such matters as concern'd all the colonies altogether." They were, then, entirely independent of Parliament's authority over their internal concerns, but they had willingly consented to Parliament's control over the empire's external commerce. This tacit agreement between provinces and metropolis was, over time, elevated in the minds of the colonists to the status of an unwritten imperial constitution. Adams thought he had found a formula that could mediate between absolute dependence on the one hand and absolute independence on the other:

> The whigs allow that from the necessity of a case not provided for by common law, and to supply a defect in the British dominions, which there undoubtedly is, if they are to be governed only by that law, America has all along consented, still consents, and ever will consent, that parliament being the most powerful legislature in the dominions, should regulate the trade of the dominions. This is founding the authority of parliament to regulate our trade, upon *compact* and *consent* of the colonies, not upon any principle of common or statute law, not upon any original principle of the English constitution, not upon the principle that parliament is the supreme and sovereign legislature over them in all cases whatsoever.[14]

As Edmund Burke would later suggest in 1777, an imperial constitution had begun to develop during these years out of "mere neglect; possibly from the natural operation of things, which, left to themselves, generally fall into their proper order."[15] The uncodified imperial constitution that had evolved during the seventeenth and eighteenth centuries, at least from the American perspective, sanctioned the separate provincial charters and subsequently limited Parliament's authority over the internal affairs of the colonies.

If the American colonies were not dominions of the British state or the English realm nor under the authority of Parliament, what then were the true grounds of the relationship between the colonies and Great Britain? Where did they fit in the imperial structure? What was the nature of their allegiance to the British throne? Were the colonies conquered, discovered, or colonized lands? Indeed, who owned America? These thorny questions forced Adams to reexamine the origin and foundation of the relationship between provinces and metropolis.[16] The result of his inquiry was a sophisticated, subtle, and unique interpretation of the unwritten Anglo-American constitution.

King and Colonies

The connecting thread that bound the autonomous dominions of the empire together was, according to Adams, the allegiance of the colonists through their charters to the English Crown. But what were the terms or conditions under which the colonists were related to the kings and queens of Britain? Adams's answer to this difficult question was subtle and moved along two planes. In a provisional first response, he conceded a kind of semifeudal relationship between king and colonies. Sounding themes first expressed in the "Dissertation on the Canon and the Feudal Law," Adams attempted to reconstruct the climate of opinion that prevailed in England when the colonies were first founded. When the colonists first settled the Americas, they were confused by "two ideas," one derived from the feudal and the other from the canon law. According to a pure theory of the feudal law, if an English king conquered by armed force the territories in America owned by the natives, he would then have been "sovereign lord of the land" by right of conquest. Such territory would have been held as feudal property, that is, ultimate ownership or sovereignty over that land would redound to the king and not to the realm or to Parliament. Moreover, because the pope claimed sovereignty over all the land in the world, those Christian princes who ruled in his name—or, as in the case of Henry VIII, who had claimed the pope's authority for himself and for the English throne—claimed a right to all land discovered by their subjects. These absurd notions, Adams noted, deluded the English nation at the time the colonies were first settled, but they were nevertheless accepted in a limited way.[17]

The colonists, Adams argued, *chose* to bear allegiance and to hold their land from the Crown. They joined with the king in a medieval social contract, a *pactum subiectionis*, that is, a contract that established the terms of a political relationship between magistrate and subject, ruler and ruled.[18] Allegiance, Adams said, was a traditional feudal concept that simply meant homage and fealty to a superior lord, in this case, the king. By feudal law, fealty implied a reciprocal relationship between lord and vassal; it had no connection to parliaments, lords, or commons. By the terms of this relationship, the duty incurred by the vassal was to be a faithful servant to his lord liege and to help defend him against his enemies. This obligation was his fealty, his *fidelitas*. In return for the homage and fealty of his subjects, the king would provide his community of allegiance with protection.[19]

Adams then distinguished three ways in which a country or an individual might be subject to a king according to feudal law: to his person, regardless of whether the king was in the realm; to his Crown, which meant allegiance to "whatsoever person or family wore that crown" regardless of any revolutions that it might endure; to his Crown and realm or state, in which case the king was inseparable from his kingdom and allegiance was due to king-in-Parliament. The American colonies, Adams argued, were subjects of the British monarchy in the second sense.[20] There were also two ways in which a people or persons could be subject to both a king's Crown and to his person: One may be subject to the holder of the Crown without Parliament by conquest, as were the people of Wales after their conquest by the English but before their consent to annexation by Parliament (which gave them representation in Parliament), or as the Irish were after their conquest but before Poyning's law; or, one may be subject to the person of the king by descent as were the Scots after the accession of James I and before the Act of Union. As we have already seen, Adams rejected any analogy between the American colonies and Wales and Ireland. His first line of argument, then, was to draw a parallel between the colonies and preunion Scotland. In other words, the colonists' relationship to the British throne was to the sitting king in his personal capacity. "We owe allegiance," he said, "to the person of his majesty king George the third."[21]

Ironically, then, Adams's case for the American Whigs seems to be grounded on a feudal or a modified feudal relationship with the British throne. Indeed, he conceded as much. By the terms of the first Massachusetts charter, the colonists owed allegiance to Charles I and his descendants. Intimately connected to this feudal relationship was, of course, a property relationship.

> Holding lands, in feudal language, means no more than the relation between lord and tenant. The reciprocal duties of these are all personal. Homage, fealty, &c. and all other services are personal and to the lord; protection, &c. is personal to the tenant. And therefore no homage, fealty, or other services can ever be rendered to the body politick, the political capacity, which is not corporated but only a frame in the mind, an idea. No lands here or in England are held of the crown, meaning by it, the political capacity—they are all held of the royal person, the natural person of the king.[22]

This definition of the feudal relationship between king and subject raised several difficult problems relative to the ownership of land in America. Clearly, Adams was no more interested in making the king absolutely sovereign over America than he was in having Parliament supremely sovereign. His next move, therefore, was to soften and redefine the colonists' relationship with the king.

According to a pure theory of the feudal law, if an English king had conquered by armed force the territories in America owned by the natives, he would have been "sovereign lord of the land" by right of conquest, in which case the colonies would be in a situation not unlike that of Ireland or Wales before their incorporation in or subjection to Parliament.[23] But a pure theory of feudal law does not apply to America, according to Adams. The Americas were not conquered, they were discovered. It was not at all clear from feudal law that lands discovered were immediately and legally the possession of the king. Besides, even if the king's property claims were legitimate, his majesty had never fulfilled the most basic duty of the feudal relationship, that is, he had never provided protection to the colonists. By implication, Adams seemed to be suggesting that even the most tenuous link between the colonists and the king was absolved by nonperformance, leaving the colonists in something of a state of nature.[24] The question of ownership and control therefore had to be settled on entirely different grounds.

The Charters and the Laws of Nature

On what basis, then, were the colonies owned and governed? "Scarcely a thing is involved in more systematic obscurity," Adams remarked, "than the rights of our ancestors, when they arrived in America." The discovery, exploration, purchase, and settlement of the American colonies was entirely unprecedented in English history. There was nothing in the common law that covered colonization; it was simply "*casus omissus.*"[25] Traditionally, the common law as it had developed between the reigns of Richard I and James I was "confined to the realm, and within the four seas." There was no provision in the common law for the governance of discovered colonies by the authority of Parliament, nor did the common law officially recognize the authority of the Crown to "grant charters to subjects to settle in foreign countries." Furthermore, the colonists' relationship to the king was not based on conquest, marriage, or descent. The colonists were emigrants from the English state; they were not its representatives. And there was nothing in the law of nations that "requires that emigrants from a state should continue, or be made, a part of the state."[26] Indeed many of the emigrants, particularly those in the northern colonies, were fleeing what they considered a tyrannous and corrupt regime. They were asserting their Lockean right of "withdrawing themselves, and their obedience, from the jurisdiction they were born under, and the family or community they were bred up in, and *setting up new governments* in other places."[27] The colonists emigrated to America, Adams wrote in the "Dissertation," to escape "the struggle between the people and the confederacy aforesaid of temporal and spiritual tyranny." Some came to escape religious persecution but almost all came to fulfill a "love of universal *Liberty*."[28]

The king, by his prerogative, did have the authority to prohibit a subject from emigrating by issuing a writ "Ne exeat Regno."[29] By the same token, the king had the authority to "permit his subjects to leave the kingdom," which he did, but that is all. Theoretically, then, the colonists were entirely free not only of Parliament but of the Crown as well. In almost a direct paraphrase of Locke's *Second Treatise*, Adams wrote that the first generation of colonists were bound by their allegiance not to take arms against the king of England, "but their children would not have been born within the king's allegiance, would not have been natural subjects, and consequently not intitled to protection, or bound to the king."[30] Their continued allegiance to the Crown would have at the very least required a tacit consent to his authority. In this way, the American colonies were entirely different from preunion Scotland.

Once the American colonists took their leave of England with the king's permission, they were beyond the common law, the authority of Parliament, and even beyond that of the king. At this point, Adams very subtly challenged the claim that English kings had any right to claim land in the Americas by discovery. Strictly speaking, the Americas were not vacant lands. Indigenous peoples inhabited much of the North American continent. "How," Adams asked, "came the dominions of king Philip, king Massachusetts, and twenty other sovereign, independent princes here, to be within the allegiance of the king of England, James and Charles?" Adams denied that the Americas were any more "within the allegiance of those princes, by the common law of England, or by the law of nature, than France and Spain were." Discovery and settlement by the king's subjects did not give the king of England a right "to the lands, tenements and hereditaments of the native Indians here." In other words, the American colonists could not arbitrarily claim "discovered" land as a right in the name of the British throne. The colonists, Adams noted, "were sensible of this, and therefore honestly purchased their lands of the natives."[31] Implicit in this, is a suggestion that the kings of Europe had no authority in America. This subtle shift in argument not only denied the authority of Parliament in America, but it also suggested that the king's authority in America was dubious as well. The founding history of the Plymouth colony provided Adams with an instructive example:

The first planters of Plymouth . . . had not charter or patent for the land they took possession of, and derived no authority from the English Parliament or Crown, to set up their government. They purchased land of the Indians, and set up a government of their own, on the simple principle of nature, and afterwards purchased a patent for the land of the council at Plymouth, but never purchased any charter for government of the Crown, or the King: and continued to exercise all the powers of government, legislative, executive and judicial, upon the plain ground of an *original contract* among independent individuals for 68 years.[32]

If the colonists were outside the common law, from what source, then, did they derive the authority of their laws? They were most certainly not grounded on statutory or common law; instead, they are derived from two sources: "the law of nature and the compact made with the king in our charters." By resorting to philosophical first principles, Adams was substantially changing the terms of debate. Standing underneath and supporting his view of the traditional English constitution were certain rights common to all men at all times. When a subject left the realm with the king's permission, "he carried with him as a man all the rights of nature." Indeed, English liberties were nothing but "certain rights of nature reserved to the citizen by the English constitution," which cleaved to the colonists when they left England. These same rights would not have been alienated had the colonists gone to "Outaheite, or Patagonia, even altho' they had taken no patent or charter from the king at all." The American colonists were not bound by any English laws, statute or common, excepting those to which they had consented (i.e., Parliament's regulation of trade). The colonists, Adams said, had a "right by nature" to establish English common law in America or any other law system as long as it was not inconsistent with their professed allegiance to the king. Those who discovered and founded the American colonies could begin tabula rasa, he said, with "eternal reason, and the law of nature" as the basis of their constitutional and legal codes. The first colonists could have "erected in this wilderness a British constitution, or a perfect democracy, or any other form of government they saw fit."[33] From the beginning, the colonies were independent of Parliament and were self-governing realms in their own right.

The relationship between king and colonists was therefore defined by the charters. This argument from the charters took on a special importance in Adams's mind. By casting the colonists' expatriation from England and first settlement in America in Lockean terms, he seemed to be saying that the charters represented an original social contract. In other words, these social compacts were more than *pactum subiectionis*; they were *pactum societatis*.[34] The bonds that tied individuals together in these new communities were contractual and volitional; they were not natural and perpetual. The covenants between the individual members of the Plymouth colony, the Connecticut towns, and those of the Massachusetts Bay Company were of more importance to Adams than were the pro forma compacts between king and subject. Drawing from loyalist Thomas Hutchinson's *History of the Colony of Massachusetts-Bay* (which no doubt gave him much pleasure), Adams recounted the founding histories of several colonies. Rather than simply assuming an almost unlimited prerogative over the colonies, the Stuart kings granted the colonists charters that established, limited, and defined the nature of the relationship between lord and subject. The terms of this new relationship stipulated that the colonists "should enjoy all the rights and liberties of Englishmen forever, in consideration of their undertaking to clear the wilderness, propagate christianity, pay a fifth part of oar, &c." Adams reported that "such a contract as this has been made with all the colonies, royal governments as well as charter ones. For the commissions to the governors contain the plan of the government, and the contract between the king and subject, in the former, as much as the charters in the latter."[35] Because Crown and Parliament had, for the most part, neglected the colonies for the first one hundred fifty years of their existence, the charters gained indigenous force and were sanctified through usage, custom, and prescription. Indeed, the charters came to represent proto-constitutions in the minds of the colonists.[36]

In a very subtle move, Adams trimmed the colonists' allegiance to the king from one grounded on Coke's quasi-medieval teaching in *Calvin's Case* to one squarely within the radical social contract tradition of Locke's *Second Treatise*. He summarized his final teaching in this way:

> And from this extensive survey of all the foregoing cases there results a confirmation of what has been so afore said, that there is no provision in the common law, in English precedents, in the English government or constitution, made for the case of the colonies. It is not a conquered but a discovered country. It came not to the king by descent but was explored by the settlers. It came not by marriage to the king but was purchased by the settlers of the savages. It was not granted by the king of his grace, but was dearly, very dearly earned by the planters in the labor, blood, and treasure which they expended to subdue it to cultivation. It stands upon no grounds, then, of law or

policy, but what are found in the law of nature, and their express contracts in their charters, and their implied contracts in the commissions to governors and terms of settlement.[37]

Ingeniously, Adams conflated into a unified whole a historical argument
about the founding of the colonies with a more theoretical argument
about natural rights.

"Novanglus" was not a popular pamphlet like Paine's *Common Sense*.
It appealed more to the head than to the heart, more to the lawyer than
to the cordwainer. It would not have sent many an inflamed Son of Liberty to the barricades. "Novanglus" may not have been read by many
colonists but it certainly would have provided the most thoughtful and
influential American Whigs—the delegates to the Continental Congress
and the second tier of pamphleteers, organizers and preachers—with a
seemingly endless reserve of arguments. For some but not all, support for
or resistance to the American cause was to be determined by sober reflection on the justice or injustice of the colonial case.

Fundamental Law and the Written Constitution

In a very real sense, this was not a debate between English Tories and
American Whigs; it was, rather, an argument between transatlantic
Whigs. It was an intramural debate between two competing Whig interpretations of the British constitution and the meaning of the Glorious
Revolution. For English Whigs, the Glorious Revolution meant the victory of Parliament over the Crown; for American Whigs, 1688 represented the victory of liberty over arbitrary government. Remarkably, each
side in the controversy saw itself as the true guardian of the British constitution and the other as an "innovator" and a corrupter of the constitution's true principles. Ironically, English Whigs could legitimately
denounce the Americans for their Tory-like rejection of Parliamentary
sovereignty while the American Whigs could legitimately denounce the
English for their Tory-like rejection of a British constitution grounded in
fundamental or higher law. At issue, then, were two mutually incompatible Whig interpretations of the British constitution. Increasingly, in the
years between 1764 and 1776, Adams and other American Revolutionaries would come to define a constitution in terms of a written document
grounded on fundamental principles, while the British glorified their
evolving, unwritten constitution.

In the wake of the revolutionary settlement of 1688, English Whigs
increasingly came to view the British constitution as the product of an

evolutionary accretion of common and statutory laws. And certainly by the second half of the eighteenth century, most Britons came to see their constitution as synonymous with the omnipotence of Parliament, unencumbered by the dictates of natural reason and the limitations of natural law. Essentially, the British constitution became whatever Parliament said it was. According to William Blackstone, the leading English constitutional theorist, there could be no distinction between the "constitution or frame of government" and the "system of laws." Parliament's authority, he said, was for all practical purposes unlimited. "If the parliament will positively enact a thing to be done which is unreasonable," Blackstone wrote in the *Commentaries on the Laws of England,* "I know of no power in the ordinary forms of the constitution, that is vested with authority to control it; and the examples usually alleged in support of this sense of the rule do none of them prove, that, where the main object of a statute is unreasonable, the judges are at liberty to reject it; for that were to set the judicial power above that of the legislature, which would be subversive to all government."[38] In other words, Parliament had become identified in the minds of Britons with the constitution itself.

In America, however, the Glorious Revolution represented a step in a continuing correction of the English constitution—a correction that would restore the English constitution to its pristine and original principles, the most important of which was the principle of consent.[39] Although it is true that the Americans supported overwhelmingly the Glorious Revolution and the doctrine of parliamentary sovereignty as applied to the realm, they never consented to a revolutionary settlement that included "the dominions thereunto belonging."[40] Instead, they consented to their own charters and the unwritten, customary, imperial constitution that had been developing over the course of one hundred fifty years.

Ironically, Adams and the other Revolutionaries were caught in a kind of constitutional time warp. They were defending a particular, if not a peculiar, reading of the seventeenth-century English constitution. The first foundings of the American colonies in the early seventeenth century and their isolation from and neglect by the mother country created a situation where time, in a constitutional sense, stood still. The imperial English constitution consented to by the Americans was that which existed before 1688. It was Coke's constitution,[41] the English constitution as interpreted by Sir Edward Coke in his celebrated opinions in *Calvin's Case* and *Dr. Bonham's Case;* it was, in other words, a constitution that defined the colonists' allegiance to the Crown and one that limited the powers of king and Parliament by the common and natural law.[42] Adams firmly believed that the English constitution was grounded on certain permanent and unalterable principles that could not be violated by king or Parliament. From his earliest ruminations on the English constitution, we see an attempt to distinguish between fundamental and statutory law. Adams understood English common-law rights, rights existing from time immemorial, to be a unique reflection or manifestation of the more basic laws of nature. He celebrated the historic English constitution precisely because it was in agreement with the laws of nature.

Between 1761 and 1776, John Adams moved toward a constitutional theory that sought to identify, protect, and enshrine certain basic rights and liberties from the intrusions of government. In the process, he began to develop the notion of a written constitution grounded on an unwritten natural law. To fully appreciate Adams's unique understanding of the British constitution, we must return to 1761. This was the year of James Otis's legendary speech on the writs of assistance, witnessed and recorded for posterity by a young John Adams. In his argument before the provincial Superior Court, Otis declared that Parliament could not violate the traditional rights of Englishmen or the fundamental principles of the English constitution. The issuance of general writs granting royal customs officials broad powers to search and seize smuggled contraband represented "the worst instrument of arbitrary power, the most destructive of English liberty, and the fundamental principles of the constitution." It violated "one of the most essential branches of English liberty," that is, "the freedom of one's house. A man's house is his castle; and while he is quiet, he is as well guarded as a prince in his castle."[43] Paraphrasing Coke's dictum in *Dr. Bonham's Case*,[44] Otis proclaimed parliament's impotence in passing unconstitutional laws: "As to Acts of Parliament. An Act against the Constitution is void: an Act against natural Equity is void: and if an Act of Parliament should be made, in the very Words of this Petition, it would be void. The executive Courts must pass such Acts into disuse. . . . Reason of the Common Law to control an Act of Parliament."[45] If Coke was arguing in *Bonham's Case*, as most scholars seem to agree, that statutes should be narrowly interpreted in the light of the common law, Otis's argument must be seen as magnifying, even transforming, Coke's dictum into a constitutional argument. Otis's position was clear: acts of Parliament "against the Constitution" and "against natural Equity" were void, and the king's courts "must pass such Acts into disuse." This was not a theory of judicial review in the modern sense but, in going beyond Coke, Otis was saying that the powers of Parliament were limited and controlled by the "the reason of the common law" and that the courts have the authority to enforce those limits.[46]

Otis's speech had a massive impact on the young lawyer from Braintree: it woke him from his constitutional slumbers and refocused his understanding of the English constitution.[47] From this moment forward, Adams saw the English constitution as limiting Parliament's authority through an unwritten constitution that incorporated the laws of nature. In the "Dissertation," he stated clearly that English liberties are manifestations of original rights that are natural and superior to the grants and prerogatives of king and Parliament. The source of these rights is the constitution of human nature.[48] Several months later, in his "Instructions to Braintree's Representative," Adams denounced the Stamp Act as "unconstitutional" and "inconsistent with the Spirit of the Common Law, and with the essential Fundamental Principles of the British constitution." Adams was certain that that "old sage Coke" would have found the extension of the vice admiralty courts to America a violation "of that fundamental law, Magna Carta."[49] In the wake of Boston's violent reaction to the Stamp Act, Adams stood before Governor Francis Bernard to urge that the courts be opened despite the absence of stamped paper. Invoking Coke's constitution with a dash of Locke, he urged the governor to open the courts and to disregard a Parliamentary act in violation of fundamental law:

> The Stamp-Act, I take it, is utterly void, and of no Binding force upon Us; for it is against our Rights as Men, and our Priviledges as Englishmen. An Act made in Defiance of the first Principles of Justice: an Act which rips up the foundation of the British Constitution, and makes void Maxims of 1800 years standing. Parliaments may err; they are not infallible; they have been refus'd to be submitted to. An Act making the King's Proclamation to be a Law, the Executive Powers adjudg'd absolutely void. There are certain Principles fix'd unalterably in Nature. . . . This Act has never been received from Authority, therefore in a legal Sense we know nothing of it.[50]

Three years later, Adams again confronted imperial officialdom over the injustice of the Sugar and Stamp Acts. In 1768 customs officials seized John Hancock's sloop *Liberty* for smuggling in violation of the Sugar Act. Brought before a juryless admiralty court (subjects of the realm convicted of the same parliamentary act were tried under the common law and before a jury of their peers), Hancock secured John Adams for his defense. Like James Otis in the writs of assistance case, Adams went beyond the immediate legal issues to consider the fundamental principles of justice and the British constitution. Here, Adams told the court, "is the Contrast that stares us in the Face!"

> The Parliament in one Clause guarding the People of the Realm, and securing to them the Benefit of a Tryal by the Law of the Land, and by the next Clause, depriving all Americans of that Priviledge. What shall we say to this Distinction? Is there not in this Clause, a Brand of Infamy, of Degradation, and Disgrace, fixed upon every American? Is he not degraded below the Rank of an Englishman? Is it not directly, a Repeal of Magna Charta, as far as America is concerned.[51]

In the years between 1761 and 1775, John Adams and many other Americans came to interpret the British constitution as embodying ancient rights and liberties common to all Englishmen which in turn were discoveries of more basic laws of nature. He made an important but neglected distinction between that which was *constitutional* and that which was *legal*.[52] Contrary to British jurists like Blackstone, Adams was quickly coming to the view that there was and must be a fundamental distinction between the "constitution or frame of government" and the "system of laws." For acts of Parliament in violation of the fundamental law to be deemed unconstitutional required that there be some standard, some permanent constitution against which to judge legislation null and void. The king and the king's courts, Adams asserted, were obligated to declare null and void those acts of Parliament in violation of the British constitution's fundamental law. Such authority, however, required that the British constitution be interpreted in such a way that the distinction between legal and constitutional would become meaningful, actionable, and enforceable.

Very early in the conflict with Britain, Adams advanced an interpretation of the English constitution that could only be described as uniquely American. Writing as the "Earl of Clarendon to William Pym," Adams informed his English interlocutor that the American people had a "deeper knowledge" of the English constitution than do most British officials. Indeed, he said, they had "discovered the most accurate judgment about the *real* constitution." Adams was prepared to present "a formal, logical, and technical definition" of the English constitution. Rejecting all traditional definitions, he denied that it was the "practice of Parliament" or the "judgments and precedents of the King's courts," or "custom," or all in one. A constitution grounded on such "fluctuating and variable" principles would be nothing but "wind and weather." It was possible, he thought, to speak in terms of the British constitution's "essentials and fundamentals."

Unlike British officialdom, the colonists knew that the "law of nature" is "one principle foundation" of the "true" British constitution.[53]

Adams began his unique reformulation of the British constitution with two analogies, one anatomical and the other mechanical. The British constitution was best studied, he noted, by comparing it to the constitution of the human body and to the constitution of a clock. All constitutions, whether they be physiological, mechanical, or civil, must have an end, and the first task of a physician, a clock maker, or a states-man was to determine the end of the examined constitution. For the hu-man body, its *telos* is good health; for the clock, the measurement of time; and for the civil constitution, its end is "the good of the whole commu-nity." Civil constitutions, like the human body and clocks, can be kept healthy and running if statesmen or constitutional physicians mind and nurture their day-to-day functions, but there are limits beyond which constitutional physicians may not go. There "are certain other parts of the body, which the *physician* can in no case have any *authority* to *destroy* or *deprave*; which may properly be called *stamina vitae*, or *essentials* and *fun-damentals of the constitution*."[54]

Generically speaking, Adams defined government as "a frame, a scheme, a system, a combination of powers, for a certain end, viz the good of the whole community."[55] Several years later in his debate with William Brattle over the independence of the judges, he wrote that the "British constitution is a fine, a nice, a delicate machine, and the perfection of it depends upon such complicated movements, that it is as easily disordered as the human body."[56] These rather static definitions allowed Adams to study the British constitution through a uniquely American lens. He in-terpreted the British constitution as though it were written or fixed, even though it obviously was not. "Were I to define the British constitution," he wrote, "I should say it is a limited monarchy, or a mixture of the three forms of government commonly known in the schools, reserving as much of the monarchical splendor, the aristocratical independency, and the democratical freedom, as are necessary, that each of these powers may have a controul both in legislation and execution, over the other two, for the preservation of the subjects liberty.[57]

Adams surely knew that the English constitution had evolved over time, but he chose to emphasize in his definition the fundamental princi-ples, the *stamina vitae*, that had endured from an "immense antiquity." For Adams, the British constitution was something fixed; its "*essentials* and *fundamentals*" were defined, limited, and enduring through the common law; it was something that could be dissected and studied; its *stamina vitae* could be precisely identified, nurtured, and protected. The two *stamina vitae* that Adams thought fundamental to the British constitution were representation and jury trials. He eloquently summarized his view of the British constitution in the following terms:

> Thus it seems to appear that two branches of popular power, voting for members of the house of commons, and tryals by juries, the one in the legislative and the other in the executive part of the constitution are as essential and fundamental, to the great end of it, the preservation of the subject's liberty, to preserve the balance and mixture of the government, and to prevent its running into an oligarchy or aristocracy; as the lords and commons are to prevent its becoming an absolute monarchy. These two popular powers therefore are the heart and lungs, the main spring, and the center wheel, and without them, the body must die; the watch must run down; the government must become arbitrary, and this our law books have settled to be the death of the laws and the constitution. In these two powers consist wholly, the liberty and security of the people: They have no fortification against wanton, cruel power: no other indemnification against being ridden like horses, fleeced like sheep, worked like cattle, and fed and cloathed like swine and hounds. . . . This is the constitution which has prevailed in Britain from an immense antiquity: It prevailed, and the House of Commons and tryals by juries made a part of it, in Saxon times, as may be abundantly proved by many monuments still remaining in the Saxon language.[58]

Several years later in the "Novanglus" essays, Adams capped his definition of the British regime. Strictly speaking, the British constitution, he said, was a limited monarchy. In reality, however, and based on the authority of Aristotle, Livy, and Harrington, Adams thought the British constitution much more like a republic than anything else. According to his authorities, a republic is *"a government of laws, and not of men,"* and that was precisely the traditional British constitution as Adams saw it. Despite being hereditary and with an extensive prerogative, the English monarchy was "bound by fixed laws," as was Parliament.[59] For Adams, then, there was in the British constitution a controlling rule of law standing above and beyond, guiding, limiting, and controlling the competing powers of Crown and Parliament.

Taxation without representation and the extension of the vice admiralty courts represented to Adams an ominous loss of the colonists' most basic rights and liberties guaranteed by the English constitution. By 1776, as Parliament exercised and pushed the boundaries of its authority in

America, Adams and his fellow Revolutionaries began to reconceptualize and radicalize their notions of what a constitution was or should be. The revered English constitution, the model for so many colonial charters and governments, not only had failed to resolve the imperial question, but to Americans like John Adams it came to be seen as fundamentally flawed in its own right. In his effort to understand and come to terms with the inadequacies of the British constitution, Adams confronted and began to think through new ways of understanding the very nature of constitutional government. It became clear that the immediate issue of the jurisdictional boundaries of the imperial British constitution was a secondary issue. In the end, the conflict between the center and the peripheries of the British empire could not be resolved precisely because there was no standard, no written constitution by which to sort out the conflicting claims of Parliament and colonies. Mother country and colonies had each developed and sanctified through long usage constitutional customs that were unreconcilable.

The idea of a written constitution was the device by which Adams and the other American Revolutionaries finally broke from the medieval common-law tradition of Coke and fully embraced the modern natural-rights philosophy of Locke. A written constitution was the product not of history, custom, usage, or the "artificial reasoning" of common-law lawyers; it was, rather, the product of philosophy and free will, reason and choice, deliberation and consent. Implicit in the "Novanglus" essays is a feigning nod to Coke's medieval understanding of the English constitution, but far more important to Adams's final teaching is his very subtle smuggling of Locke's radical natural-rights/natural-law teaching into a uniquely American form of constitutional government. Although Adams on several occasions associated the rights of nature with God or Nature's God, his strongest statements on the subject always find the origins of man's rights in "the frame of human nature, in the constitution of the intellectual and moral world."[60] Following in the footsteps of Locke, the laws of nature for Adams are not the dictates of God impressed into the hearts of men, nor are they a body of "higher" moral laws that exist outside or independent of man's natural constitution; they are, rather, the rational deductions of human reason, they are laws the purpose of which is to enable all men in a society to protect their natural rights to life, liberty, and property. In order to avoid the violence, insecurity, and arbitrariness of the state of nature, the laws of nature encourage men to covenant with one another and to transfer their right of self defense to a neutral arbiter in order to create a political community whose purpose is the preservation of peace and justice. This is precisely how Adams interpreted the covenants that created most of the American colonies in the seventeenth century, and it was basis on which he would advocate the creation of new Revolutionary constitutions.[61]

By 1775, Adams was advocating that new constitutions be drafted and governments established on the basis of the consent of the governed. In order to found new governments, it was necessary to "reallize the Theories of the Wisest Writers and invite the People, to erect the whole Building with their own hands upon the broadest foundation," since "the people were the Source of all Authority and Original of all Power." These ideas, he said, were "new, strange and terrible Doctrines to the greatest part" of those who heard them. Sovereignty was now identified with the people themselves rather than with Parliament, Crown, or with government generally. It was not so much that these ideas themselves were "new, strange and terrible"—they had, after all, been known at least since Locke's *Second Treatise*—but rather that they would actually be employed to throw off a government long established in order to create new governments de novo. What was new, radically new, was that the people's will was to be captured by special conventions to create and then ratify written constitutions as fundamental law. As early as June 1775, Adams was calling on the Continental Congress to immediately "recommend to the People of every colony to call such Conventions immediately and set up Governments of their own, under their own Authority."[62] As the leading advocate in the Continental Congress for the construction of new constitutions, Adams was one of John Locke's greatest underlaborers. Through drafting and ratifying conventions, Adams found a mechanism by which to convert theory into practice; he found a means by which to translate the English philosopher's radical natural-rights theory into practical and functioning governments. By lifting the constitutional convention above ordinary acts of legislation, Adams and his fellow Revolutionaries created a process by which written constitutions could be sanctified as permanent and fundamental laws.[63]

Part II

Principles of Political Architecture

Chapter 5

A Guidebook for Lawgivers

Some thirty years after publishing his great work of political theory, *A Defence of the Constitutions of Government of the United States of America* (3 vols., 1787–1788), John Adams lamented to John Taylor of Caroline that his treatise had been "misunderstood, misrepresented, and abused, more than any other, except the bible."[1] To many thoughtful eighteenth- and twentieth-century readers, the *Defence* has always been something of an enigma. James Madison wrote that "men of learning will find nothing new in it. Men of taste, many things to criticize." But he also predicted that "it will, nevertheless, be read and praised" and "become a powerful engine in forming public opinion." "The book," Madison conceded, "has merit." Equally ambivalent is the appraisal of the historian Gordon S. Wood, who calls the *Defence* "the finest fruit of the American Enlightenment," while at the same time describing it as "anomalous" and "irrelevant" to the ideological politics of the new republic.[2] In recent years, the *Defence* has become a neglected classic of American history and political thought.

From the moment of its publication, the *Defence* was denounced by some as antirepublican.[3] Contemporaries charged Adams with advocating aristocracy and monarchy. In our time, historians have rarely differed from his partisan opponents. One scholar has gone so far as to suggest that Adams was attempting "to bring back the 'old regime'" and that he should therefore "be viewed as the political theorist of an American 'restoration.'"[4] In the face of these charges, what are we to make of Adams's claim to having been misunderstood and misrepresented? This chapter reopens the case of John Adams and his books on government. By taking a fresh look at why and for whom he wrote this "strange" and difficult treatise, we may better judge its meaning and significance and, therewith, the justice of his claim.[5] Our first task, then, is to reconstruct the events and climate of opinion that moved Adams to write.

The *Defence* is not an easy book to locate in context. Adams composed it while living in England as America's first minister plenipotentiary to the Court of St. James. When he began to write, both sides of the

Atlantic were stirring with great events. Holland was in the middle of successive revolutions, France's ancien régime was tottering on the brink of revolution, and in America popular upheaval seemed to threaten the new governments. Historians have thus studied and situated the *Defence* in the light of two very different social and political contexts. Some have argued that Adams's treatise is best understood in the context of his Massachusetts experience. According to these historians, he was inspired to write by Shays's Rebellion and by reports from friends back home describing a decline in virtue and social stability in New England.[6] Others have situated the *Defence* in a European context. They argue that Adams was first provoked by a debate largely indigenous to French reformers, and that he embraced the views of conservative anglophiles like Jean de Lolme.[7] Both positions have merit, and each contains an element of truth. On numerous occasions Adams explained to correspondents that events in America and Europe prompted him to begin writing the *Defence*. At the very least, the composition of the *Defence* owes a great deal to the sense of crisis that he felt as he viewed these transatlantic convulsions.

Adams was also influenced by another kind of experience. In the preface to the *Defence*, he noted that his treatise had been written "to lay before the public *a specimen of that kind of reading and reasoning which produced the American constitutions.*"[8] Adams's reading and reasoning provided the central lens through which he filtered and interpreted the great political and social events of the day. He considered the lessons learned in his library to be the decisive experience from which to construct a theory of political architecture. Ultimately, to reconstruct Adams's political thought we must examine his confrontation with the Western political and philosophical tradition.[9] This larger task is the explicit theme of the chapters that follow.

Transatlantic Context

In early October 1786, John Adams barricaded himself behind piles of books at his office in Grosvenor Square, London, and began to write his *Defence of the Constitutions of Government of the United States of America*. Adams later recalled that he did not begin organizing and collecting the materials that went into the first volume until he returned from a diplomatic mission to Holland the month before and that he did not put pen to paper until shortly after October 4. He would live for the next few months in a self-imposed state of "Phylosophic Solitude."[10] Drawing on his many years of reading and research, the first volume took just three months to write: It was completed in January 1787 and published the following month. The second volume appeared that summer, and the third was completed by December 1787. Pressed by Revolutionary events unfolding on both sides of the Atlantic, Adams was forced to rush the volumes to press in the hope that they might be of some immediate use.[11] The fourth volume, the *Discourses on Davila,* was originally published as a series of essays in John Fenno's *Gazette of the United States* between April 1790 and April 1791.[12] It was the only volume he wrote while living in the United States.

Adams first developed a proto-image of the *Defence* sometime in 1784 or 1785. He initially conceived the idea of writing a treatise on government after spending an evening of political debate in Paris with his son John Quincy, Thomas Jefferson, and the marquis de Lafayette. The conversation left an indelible impression on Adams. Years later, he reminded Jefferson of how Lafayette had "harangued" the Americans about "the plans then in Operation to reform France." Adams recalled having been "astonished at the Grossness of his Ignorance of Gover[n]ment and History." It was the "gross Ideology" of Lafayette and the reformers associated with Turgot that "first suggested" to him the "thought and inclination" to write "Something upon Aristocracy."[13] By early 1786, he was telling Jefferson and European correspondents that he had "half a mind to devote the next ten years to the making of a book upon the subject of nobility."

> I wish to inquire into the practice of all nations, ancient and modern, civilized and savage, under all religions,—Mahometan, Christian, and Pagan,—to see how far the division of mankind into patricians and plebians, nobles and simples, is necessary and inevitable, and how far it is not. Nature has not made this discrimination. Art has done it. Art may prevent it. Would it do good or evil to prevent it? I believe good, think what you will of it. How can it be prevented? In short, it is a splendid subject; and, if I were not too lazy, I would undertake it.[14]

Within ten months, Adams found the incentive and the will power to begin research on this "splendid subject." During the next few years, his speculations on "aristocracy" became more focused and responsive to events unfolding around him.

In August 1786, Adams went to The Hague to ratify the recently signed commercial treaty between the United States and Prussia. The highlight of his trip was a visit to Utrecht, where, in a great constitutional victory for the Dutch Patriots, new magistrates were being sworn into office. In an undated letter fragment to his son-in-law William Smith,

Adams described this event as an unprecedented instance in European history of an "old established Government, laid in the Dust . . . and a new one erected from the Foundation, by the Sovereign Will of a free People." He seems to have been profoundly affected by this incident. The constitutional reforms at Utrecht, combined with the "reports of Similar Revolutions" in the other Dutch republics and general conversations with the Patriots, "threw" him "into a train of thinking" about the course of world events during the last thirty years.[15]

During the long trip back to England, Adams reported to Smith that he had fallen into a deep sleep and a "long Dream." Whether real or contrived, this fascinating letter is noteworthy because it suggests that Adams wrote his treatise with a reformist or revolutionary intent; that is, to assist revolutionary republicans on both sides of the Atlantic as they began to reform their political institutions.

> I thought that the natural Principles of Government had taken so deep root, as to have produced Revolutions in America, Ireland, and Holland, and seemed to be pushing forward, with great vigour. But it was a question whether there might not be more heat than light, and whether there was not danger that Innovations might not be judiciously made which would require other Changes before mankind would be satisfied. Where shall we go for Advice? I dreamed that I made a Visit to the other World to my friend De Mably in the Celestial Regions, whom I found in company with Aristotle [and] Plato consulting upon the best *advice* to be given to the United States, Holland Ireland and all People and Countries in Similar Circumstances.

Nowhere else does Adams disclose in such an intimate way the philosophical character of his book. The central problem addressed by his celestial advisors was how the "Legislator" should, on the one hand, avail himself of the natural aristocracy "for the equal benefit of the People, and how on the other shall he prevent" the ambitious and talented few "from doing Mischief."[16] It was to this great question that Adams principally addressed himself in the first volume of the *Defence*.

Adams's ultimate purpose in writing the *Defence* is highlighted in an 1809 letter to Samuel Perley in which he offered "a few hints" (it was in fact his most explicit statement on the subject) as to the origin, context, and purpose of his *Defence*. He there traced the composition of the *Defence* to the arrival in France of Benjamin Franklin in 1776. The Pennsylvanian had come with a copy of his state's newly drafted unicameral constitution, which was "immediately" but incorrectly "propagated throughout France" as "the plan of government of Mr. Franklin." Adams recalled that Louis XVI's comptroller-general, Baron Anne-Robert Turgot and his circle of young reformers—the marquis de Condorcet, the duc de la Rochefoucauld d'Enville, Pierre Samuel Dupont de Nemours, and the marquis de Lafayette—"became enamored with the Constitution of Mr. Franklin."[17] When Adams arrived in Paris four years later with a copy of his own Massachusetts constitution, the French intelligentsia initiated a fierce debate over the question of constitutional forms. The first round began in 1784 when Richard Price, the English dissenting minister, published as an appendix to his *Observations on the Importance of the American Revolution* a letter that he had received from Turgot criticizing the American constitutions for imitating the English form of government. The passage that later provoked Adams to write, said of the American constitutions:

> Instead of collecting all authority into one center, that of the nation, they have established different bodies; a body of representatives, a council, and a governor, because there is in England a house of commons, a house of lords, and a king. They endeavor to balance these different powers, as if this equilibrium, which in England may be a necessary check to the enormous influence of royalty, could be of any use in republics founded upon the equality of all the citizens; and as if establishing different orders of men were not a source of divisions and disputes.[18]

Adams understood Turgot's letter to be a celebration of Pennsylvania's unicameral constitution and a condemnation of the Massachusetts constitution. As long as the ideas and "visionary language" of European philosophers remained confined to elite circles, Adams saw little need to respond to their utopian plans. But "circumstances" had lately occurred that threatened to connect and give life to these disembodied ideas.[19] In September 1786, just after Adams's return from Holland, Louis XVI called for a meeting of the Assembly of Notables, and at the same time news of social and political unrest in Massachusetts was reaching Adams in England.

> I never thought of writing till the Assembly of Notables in France had commenced a revolution, with the Duke de la Rochefoucauld and Mr. Condorcet at their head, who I knew would establish a government in one assembly, and that I knew would involve France and all Europe in all the horrors we have seen; carnage and desolation, for fifty, perhaps for a hundred years.

At the same time, every western wind brought us news of town and county meetings in Massachusetts, adopting Mr. Turgot's ideas, condemning my Constitution, reprobating the office of governor and the assembly of the Senate as expensive, useless, and pernicious, and not only proposing to toss them off, but rising in rebellion against them.

"In this situation," Adams recalled, "I was determined to wash my hands of the blood that was about to be shed in France, Europe and America, and show to the world that neither my sentiments nor actions should have any share in countenancing or encouraging any such pernicious, destructive, and fatal schemes." With this context in mind, "I wrote my defence of the American Constitutions," he declared.[20]

Let us now try to piece together the general context in which Adams wrote his *Defence*. By his own account, he wrote the *Defence* in three distinct phases, each provoked by events European and American. The first volume was inspired by a request from Dutch Patriots for advice on how to construct republican constitutions and by news from New England of "seditious meetings" and "riotous assemblies" threatening to dismantle the state governments.[21] The second and third volumes were prompted by the meeting of the French Assembly of Notables and Shays's Rebellion in the winter of 1786–87. The fourth volume, the *Discourses on Davila*, was inspired by the meeting of the French Constituent Assembly in 1789 and by the rise in America of a new form of ideologically partisan politics. As France and America moved from one crisis to another, Adams worried that these seemingly isolated eruptions of social and political discontent were connected by a common thread. He saw behind these political events a single force that defined, propelled, and directed their basic impulse. The prime mover in each case was a political philosophy that he associated with Turgot and Condorcet. Thus, his primary purpose in writing was to challenge their constitutional ideas and to thwart any influence they might have with American and French reformers. This was the formal cause and principal context in which he wrote.

An American Audience

Why did John Adams feel compelled to respond to Turgot's letter criticizing the American constitutions with a three-volume treatise? The *Defence*, which runs to over a thousand pages, would seem to be an entirely inappropriate response. What would have driven him to such fantastic lengths? More to the point: Who did he think would read such a tome, and what did he think his audience would do with the information once read? As we shall see, the *Defence* was written on two levels and for two very different audiences.[22]

Uppermost in Adams's mind when he began to write was a concern that Turgot's criticism of the American constitutions and his known preference for a unicameral legislature might be adopted by agitators in America who were threatening to tear down existing constitutional structures. In his "Preliminary Observations" to the *Defence*, he noted that there had been "from the beginning of the revolution in America, a party in every state, who have entertained sentiments similar to those of M. Turgot." Radical parties in Pennsylvania and Georgia had framed constitutions "upon his principle" of organizing all legislative power into one central body. And, now, in the fall of 1786, Adams was receiving reports from Boston that "certain committees of counties . . . and other conventions" were meeting, threatening to depose "the governor and senate as useless and expensive branches of the constitution." He described his fellow countrymen as "running wild, and into danger, from a too ardent and inconsiderate pursuit of erroneous opinions of government, which had been propagated among them by some of their ill informed favorites, and by various writings which were popular among them." He listed Paine's *Common Sense*, Catherine Macaulay's *History of England*, and Mr. Burgh's *Political Disquisitions* as some of the offending books. Adams thought these writings "excellent" and "useful" in some respects, but he also thought them "extremely mistaken in the true construction of a free government."[23]

But without question, it was Turgot's letter that Adams most feared. He considered Turgot an eloquent and influential advocate of simple unicameral democracy. This bureaucrat-cum-philosophe had been the darling of the reform movement in France, but his influence—or so Adams thought—extended to America through his close association with Franklin. It was precisely because of the great international respect commanded by Turgot's character and achievements that Adams thought him the most dangerous opponent of good government.

Adams was not particularly disturbed by the turmoil in Massachusetts until he learned that "sympathies in America had caught the French flame." In 1787 he was warning Americans to be on their "guard" against the influence of French ideas. He blamed events in Massachusetts on an "ardent and inconsiderate pursuit of erroneous opinions of government" by his fellow countrymen. He was convinced by the time he came to write the *Defence* that Turgot's letter had "contributed to excite . . . discontents among the people," and he therefore felt it "necessary to examine it" and to show Turgot's theory to be in error so that the American people "will not be misled by his authority." So important was the task at hand that Adams compared his critique of Turgot to no less than Locke's "labored reasonings" to "show the absurdity of Filmer's superstitious notions." In a society governed by popular opinion, it was imperative that he challenge and correct the "mistakes of great men," so that their errors could no longer "countenance the prejudices of numbers of people, especially in a young country and under new governments."[24]

Adams therefore took up his pen to defend the American body politic from a deadly virus, a virus that he thought threatened the American experiment in popular government. The immediate purpose of the *Defence* was to repel the subversive influence that Turgot's ideas might have in America. Adams feared that Turgot's condemnation of some American constitutions as antirepublican would be used as a justification for abandoning the existing constitutions, and that his principle of "government in one centre" would serve as a blueprint for the building of new ones. At the very least, then, Adams was attempting to shape and reinforce public opinion against the erroneous and subversive ideas of European philosophers. By attaching Americans to their revolutionary constitutions and by defending the status quo where he thought it defensible—that is, where it incorporated the "triple equipoise" of government—Adams hoped to shield the existing constitutions until they could be realigned and reinforced with a more exact understanding of how to perfect the separation and balance of powers.

On a very different level, however, Adams was *not* defending the American constitutions at all.[25] Despite the work's title, he was defending only those constitutions with "three orders, and an effectual balance between them." Massachusetts, New York, and Maryland were the only states with constitutions he thought worthy of unqualified defense.[26] In the special case of these three, he was defending them on one "point only," and that being the "side on which they are attacked." Turgot, Adams wrote, had assailed these constitutions "for aiming at three orders and a balance." But, had Turgot or any other constitutional "Warrior" attacked them "for not making their orders distinct and complete" or "where they are not defencible," Adams would have been "the last man in the world" to defend them. Several years later, he told an American publisher who wanted to reprint a new edition of the *Defence* that his treatise was "not and never was intended for a general Defence of the American Constitutions." He was defending only those constitutions that separated and balanced in the legislature three orders. Adams thought all other constitutions hopelessly deficient. He privately conceded to Jefferson that two-thirds of the state constitutions were indefensible. They were no "better than those of the Italian Republicks" of the late middle ages and were bound to produce the same "disorders and Confusion."[27]

In both the preface and conclusion to the *Defence,* Adams suggests that the American state constitutions—including his own—were flawed, some dangerously so, and all needed to be repaired in one way or another. The very nature of the revolutionary situation in the years immediately after 1776—the impending foreign danger and threatening social chaos— forced the leaders of the various colonies to hurry their deliberations, to expedite the constitution-making process, and to ratify and adopt governments that were less than perfect. "Called without expectation" and "compelled" by the exigencies of the times to "suddenly erect new systems of laws for their future government," the framers of the first state constitutions had performed their task admirably under truly difficult circumstances. Instead of following the "whimsical and fantastical projects" of foreign philosophers, the revolutionary generation had "adopted a promising essay towards a well-ordered government." Given such extraordinary circumstances, it is "astonishing," Adams remarked, that "they have been able to do so much." Their accomplishments were unparalleled in human history. But the original founders and constitution makers of the various states, had "been too little prepared by their early views, and too much occupied with turbulent scenes, to do more than they have done."[28] In no way could these first attempts at constructing constitutions be considered as final. At the deepest level, Adams thought America's experiment in constitution making was deficient and incomplete.

Luckily for the Americans, however, during this period of peace, relative social harmony, and virtue, they have the "best opportunity" to correct their first mistakes. In fact, not since Adam and Eve, Adams speculated, had providence offered to "so small a number" his trust to begin anew. If they are to succeed and fulfill this sacred trust, they must reform their constitutions immediately. Adams was extremely sensitive to the fact that the "institutions now made in America will not wholly wear out for thousands of years." It was necessary, then, that "they should *begin* right." If they erred in designing wise institutions at the beginning, they would "never be able to return, unless it be by accident, to the right path." Adams feared that "misarrangements now made" would "have great, extensive, and distant consequences." Thus, it was absolutely critical, he repeated time and again, that American constitution makers should "begin well." The Revolutionary generation must start by "preserving" the principles on which they had originally united, but ultimately it was bequeathed to the post-Revolutionary generation to correct and improve and then finally "complete" the American project in constitutional government.[29]

To that end, Adams addressed the *Defence* to an American audience. To complete and perfect their constitutions, the post-Revolutionary generation must "make themselves masters of what their predecessors have been able to comprehend and accomplish but imperfectly." Thus, Adams wrote with a specific and a very special audience in mind: He directed the *Defence* at those young "men of genius and science," who might "pursue the subject to more advantage" for the purpose of initiating a "complete reformation of every thing yet wrong" with the state constitutions. He hoped that his books on government would be read by "young Americans who wish to be masters of the subject," so that they "may be at no loss for information" when framing new constitutions or rewriting old ones. By writing a treatise on the science of government with the aim of turning "the younger gentlemen of letters in America to this kind of inquiry," Adams hoped that he could have "an effect of some importance" on his country. With time and the necessary corrections, he thought the Americans capable of achieving "the most perfect form of government."[30]

As an instructor of potential constitutional reformers, the most useful and important lesson that Adams could share with his students concerned the method and the modes of reasoning used by the revolutionary statesmen to frame the best of the state constitutions. He predicted that because information about "the formation of the American governments" had hitherto been "little known or regarded either in Europe or in America," the subject may "hereafter become an object of curiosity" to reformers of the post-Revolutionary generation.[31] Adams wrote to share with his readers the results of many years of reading, study, and reflection on the science of politics. For those who would reform or refound the American constitutions, the *Defence* provided a method for acquiring the proper knowledge of constitution-building.

Adams offered the *Defence* to his American audience as a diagnosis of the causes that threatened the health and well-being of the American constitutions, but he also intended that his books prescribe a remedy for the constitutional ills which afflicted the new state governments. Having written a model constitution copied by at least two states and having been the principal architect of another, he intended the *Defence* to be a blueprint, a set of instructions on how to perfect and finish the revolutionary experiment in constitution making. By mapping the historical terrain and by leaving to posterity the reasoning and principles that informed his most mature reflections on the science of politics, Adams hoped to complete his final act of lawgiving, for "it is the master artist alone who finishes his building."[32]

A European Audience

The second audience to whom Adams addressed his book was European. During his many diplomatic missions to Holland, Adams had consorted with the leaders of the Dutch Patriot movement, and, while in France, he was in close contact with a number of philosophes and encyclopedists who would later play important roles in the French Revolution. As early as 1781, he was supplying Dutch, French, English, and Spanish reformers with copies of his revolutionary writings and with many of the state constitutions. In his role as a propagandist for the American cause and as a consultant to many of the Dutch and French reformers, Adams was close to the pulse of the European revolutionary underground. He would later claim to having been "an *eye* witness of two revolutions in Holland," and he claimed to have been an "*ear*-witness of some of the first whispers of a revolution in France in 1783, 1784, and 1785." In the years that followed he gave "all possible attention to its rise and progress."[33] By the time he left Europe in 1788, Adams knew that he stood on the brink of a new world order, that the course of human events had been fundamentally altered by the American Revolution.

Adams was first pulled into the swirl of revolutionary events in Europe during his diplomatic missions to Holland.[34] Far from being the stodgy conservative described by modern historians, Adams actually "dabbled" in and encouraged revolutionary changes in both Holland and France throughout the 1780s.[35] As much as any American, he sought to export the principles of the American Revolution to Europe. "America," he wrote Francis Dana from Leyden, "has been too long silent in Europe. Her cause is that of all nations and men."[36] It was principally in Holland that Adams imported and most exploited his talents as an agitator and revolutionary. To that end, he established close relations with leading Dutch radicals in the hope of turning their attention to the American cause. He quickly published his "Novanglus" essays in Dutch, and, of even greater importance, he republished in Holland a complete edition of all the constitutions of the thirteen American states. In 1780, at the behest of Hendrik Calkoen, "the giant of the law in Amsterdam," Adams publicly answered a series of questions about America and its revolution. The result was

"Twenty-Six letters upon Interesting Subjects Respecting the Revolution in America."[37]

Dutch radicals and reformers first enticed Adams to write a treatise on the science of politics. In correspondence at the time, he described how his "friends in Holland," leaders of the Dutch Patriot movement like the Mennonite minister F. A. Vanderkemp, Jean Luzac, editor of the *Gazette de Leyde;* and the philosopher-nobleman Baron Van der Cappellen tot den Pol, were then "much employed in revolutions." Being "little read in history" and even "less in government," the Dutch Patriots sought advice from Adams on questions of government and constitutional construction.[38]

It was natural for the Dutch to turn to Adams. In much the same way that the French regarded Franklin as an American Lycurgus, the Dutch treated Adams as though he were an American Solon. In the eyes of many, he was "one of the principal founders of American freedom—the legislator of Massachusetts Bay (for he drew up its admirable constitution)."[39] In the midst of their own constitution making, the Dutch turned to the one man who, more than any other, had guided and shaped the revolutionary constitutions of America. "In several conversations there," Adams recalled, "I had occasion to mention some things respecting governments which some of these gentlemen wished to see on paper." Upon his return to London in September 1786, he "began to collect the materials" for the Dutch revolutionaries, but the context for writing soon took on a new urgency and the project quickly expanded into something much larger.[40]

Even more than his desire to help the cause of the Dutch Patriots, indeed, more than any other cause, Adams wrote to influence events as they began to unfold in pre-Revolutionary France. His was inspired by a rumor emanating from Paris that "the Assembly of Notables"[41] would soon be called, and the attendant fear that "the Duke de la Rochefoucauld and Mr. Condorcet" would provide the political and intellectual leadership for the reform movement. The "express purpose" of the *Defence* Adams was to say over and over again was to serve "as a warning voice to the People of France."[42] When he began writing the *Defence* in October 1786, the first meeting of the Assembly of Notables was less than four months away. He began the second volume just as the Notables were sitting down to begin their work.[43]

From his vantage in London, Adams thought the summoning of the Notables "one of the most important events of the age." He saw and described the present epoch to John Jay as "the most critical and important in Europe, of any that has ever happened in our times," and he reported to Jefferson that "all Europe resounds with Projects for reviving States and Assemblies." But from at least 1786 and possibly as early as 1783, Adams was convinced that any kind of revolution in France guided by the "utopian speculations" of democratic philosophers would have dire consequences for Europe and America. He was desperate for information, imploring his friends in Paris to keep him abreast of the proceedings. Jefferson sent Adams a number of pamphlets "giving a summary account of all the meetings of a general nature which have taken place heretofore." Many of the early reports seemed promising. Lafayette told Adams that the affairs of France, "considered in a constitutional light, are mending fast." Despite the rise of a certain "party spirit" in the assembly, Lafayette predicted that France would have in twelve or fifteen years the best constitution in the world, with the exception of the American constitution. Adams immediately wrote back to Lafayette, peppering him for more information: "Pray do the 3 estates sitt altogether in the same room & debate together? & is the vote determined by the majority of members, or by the Majority of the Estates!"[44] Constitutional rather than social reforms were thought by Adams to be the most important.

Initially, Adams was not unsympathetic to the call for the reform of French institutions and policies. After many years on the Continent, he supported those who were becoming "impatient under the yoke of servitude" and who were now "disposed to compel their governors to make the burden lighter." Their demands for reform were more than justified in Adams's opinion. He told Lafayette that he supported "a little more liberality in Religion, in Commerce, in letters, & in Politicks." These gentle reforms, he thought, "would not only augment the felicity of France, but be a good Example to the rest of Europe." He was particularly delighted to hear that the freehold qualification for representation in the provincial legislatures had been reformed on a "liberal scale," requiring that legislators possess only "ten livres" in personal wealth—thirty less than required in democratic Massachusetts! Adams was convinced that the "fermentation" in France would "terminate in Improvements of various kinds." By introducing a few liberal social reforms, he hoped that the burdens of "Superstition, Bigotry, Ignorance, Imposture, Tyranny and Misery" would be lessened.[45]

By the fall of 1787, however, Adams was openly skeptical about the direction of the reform movement. He now doubted whether French legislators had enough "confidence in one another, and in the common people" to endure a "revolution." The whole state of European affairs seemed

so confused to Adams that it was becoming increasingly difficult to predict "what turn of affairs may take." News from France in September 1787
was "discouraging" and by November, all attempts by the French to "obtain provincial and national assemblies, threatens much confusion."
French legislators seemed more concerned, according to Adams, with
"enchanting Eloquence" and "brilliant Phrases" than with the introduction of sober constitutional principles. Remarkably, by December, almost
two years before the French Revolution would begin to take shape and almost four years before Burke would publish his *Reflections*, Adams was beginning to make out the logic and to see the unintended consequences of
this embryonic revolution. On December 10, he told Jefferson with extraordinary prescience that "to think of Reinstituting Republicks, as ab-
surdly constituted as were the most which the world has seen, would be
to revive Confusion and Carnage, which must end in despotism."[46]

Just as he was finishing the first volume of the *Defence*, Adams took
one more swipe at Turgot's idea of government in "one centre." The historic meeting of the Assembly of Notables was just a few weeks away and
he felt increasingly obliged to speak to the people of France. Adams advised the French nation of the danger it would face if it did not adopt his
constitutional prescriptions. Fearing it would instead adopt the constitutional principles of Turgot and Condorcet, he concluded with a warning:
A single-house assembly in France would be moderate for a few years, but
only so long as there was fear that "an exiled royal family, or exiled patricians or nobles, are living, and may return; or while the people's passions
are alive, and their attention awake, from the fresh remembrance of danger and distress." Adams described how a unicameral assembly would almost certainly turn itself over time into an aristocratic body. These new
and old aristocrats will slowly lull the people into giving them more and
more power until they had become a hereditary aristocracy for life. Such
a body would become "a simple aristocracy or oligarchy in effect, though
a simple democracy in name." Then would begin the fight over control of
the first office of the assembly. In the quotation that follows, Adams provided readers of the *Defence* with an extraordinarily prophetic description
of what actually happened in the French Constituent Assembly of 1789
and what necessarily followed over the course of the next ten years as a
consequence of having adopted Turgot's plan:

> But, as every one of these is emulous of others, and more than one of
> them is constantly tormented with a desire to be the first, they will
> soon disagree; and then the house and the nation gradually divides

itself into four parties, one of which, at least, will wish for monarchy, another for aristocracy, a third for democracy, and a fourth for various mixtures of them; and these parties can never come to a decision but by a struggle, or by the sword.[47]

Possibly more than any person of his generation, Adams saw from a very early date the potential danger of a political and social revolution in Europe guided by the ideas of Turgot, Condorcet, and their circle of liberal reformers.[48] He had little confidence in the leadership qualities of France's liberal reformers, and he worried that they would be "unskilfull and unsuccessful asserters of a free government." To Jefferson he wondered if the "Duke of orleans" had the wherewithal to "make a Sterling Patriot and a determined son of Liberty." He compared the French Patriots to "young Schollars from a Colledge or Sailors flushed with recent pay or prize money, mounted on wild Horses, lashing and speering, till they would kill the Horses and break their own Necks."[49]

In the end, Adams was deeply suspicious of a revolution led by political reformers addicted to the theories of the philosophes and encyclopedists. After his return to Boston in 1788, he predicted to friends that a revolution in France would produce "forty years of War and blood in consequence of it without offering a Shadow of Liberty or any other Advantage."[50] He was truly frightened by the course of events he saw developing in Europe, particularly as they might influence political unrest in America. In the years that followed the French Revolution, Adams became increasingly convinced that what he had suspected and feared when he began writing the *Defence* had been substantially confirmed by the Reign of Terror and the rise of Napoleon.[51]

Although provoked at each stage of the writing by events then unfolding in America and Europe, the first three volumes of the *Defence* were held together by one overarching purpose that gave meaning to the whole. It was Turgot's letter, and later Condorcet's *Quatre Lettres d'un Bourgeois de New Haven, sur l'Unité de la Legislation* (1787), and the influence their ideas were having on constitutional reformers in Europe and America that defined for Adams the nature and purpose of the *Defence* and *Davila* essays.[52] Believing in the power of ideas, he was convinced that the theories and constitutional principles associated with the Turgot-Condorcet-Rochefoucauld circle would derail the oncoming French Revolution and would have a profound effect on the future of republican government in

America. Rather than concern himself with the manifestation of those ideas as he saw them being actualized in political events, Adams went to their source, confronting and challenging the forces that gave birth to them. In this way, he hoped to mitigate the continued influence of these ideas in France and America.

John Adams wrote his *Defence of the Constitutions of Government of the United States* in competition with French constitutional reformers as a guidebook for Lawgivers. The work is a manual of political architecture that identifies, collects, and organizes the basic materials or fundamental principles necessary for constitutional construction. To that end, the book implicitly describes the spirit, method, and modes of reasoning necessary for present and future legislators. The four volumes that compose Adams's *Defence* provide the kind of research, the kind of "reading and reasoning," necessary for the successful design and construction of constitutions. In this regard, the *Defence* is not unlike Aristotle's *Politics* or Montesquieu's *Spirit of the Laws,* while the *Discourses on Davila* bear a striking resemblance to Machiavelli's *Discourses on the First Decade of Livy.* The principal purpose of both books is the education of the lawgiver. When viewed in this light, the *Defence* becomes something more than just the anomalous, antirepublican tract of a disordered mind described by modern historians; it may be seen now as a new and positive contribution to a transatlantic debate over the science of politics in revolutionary societies.

Chapter 6

The Science of Politics

John Adams's *A Defence of the Constitutions* stands at a turning point in eighteenth-century political thought and practice. This glorious but traumatic interlude in Western history—a period bracketed by the Stamp Act of 1765 on the one side, and Napoleon's 1799 coup d'etat on the other—was one of those unique and epochal moments in history when theory meets practice, a time that fundamentally alters and realigns the course of human events. In the years between the signing of the American Declaration of Independence and the ratification of the French Constitution of 1790, fifteen or sixteen constitutions were framed in America and Europe. The world had never seen anything like it. In 1815, John Adams described "the last twenty-five years of the last century, and the first fifteen of this" as "the age of revolutions and constitutions."[1]

Standing behind and giving shape and guidance to this period of revolutionary constitution making was a generation of political thinkers who were following and working out the implications of Locke's investigations into "the True Original, Extent and End of Civil Government." The middle decades of the eighteenth century were awash with philosophical treatises on government and a variety of blueprints for constitutional reformers. The age delighted in theories of government, constitutions, and codes. In the wake of Hobbes and Locke, Spinoza and Grotius, Sidney and Harrington, political philosophers were debating and asking questions about the origins and best form of government: Was government the creation of a social contract, was it a Divine creation, or did it evolve spontaneously over time? What was the best form of government: a monarchy, a democracy, an aristocracy, or a mixed republic?[2]

This intellectual debate accelerated in the years following the American Revolution and came to a head with the French Revolution. Prior to these two momentous events, political philosophy had been restricted largely to the world of ideas, to the utopian models of "idle speculators." Surely no thinker prior to the war for American independence thought that his plans for social, political, and constitutional reform would actually be used to reconstruct an entirely new social order that would begin ominously with the "Year One." The American Revolution changed all that. Suddenly political philosophy was of immediate practical value and its consequences real. At the same time that philosophers were debating questions of first principles and constitutional forms, they were also reintroducing into the political discourse of the period a long-revered tradition associated with the "lawgiver" or "legislator" of classical antiquity.[3]

The hope that flowed from the American Revolution followed by the horror of the French Revolution brought home to European philosophers not only the importance and immediate relevance of their ideas, but also the enormous burden of responsibility that went along their new roles as potential legislators. Not since the mythical days of Plutarch's famous lawgivers had philosophers and the intellectual class such an opportunity to bring down from the heavens their plans for worldly reconstruction. "Since we began the career of constitutions," Adams wrote, "the wisest, most learned, and scientific heads in France, Holland, Geneva, Switzerland, Spain, and Sicily, have been busily employed in devising constitutions for their several nations."[4] The success or failure of the European movement away from a thousand years of Popery and Monarchy hinged on the development and successful institutionalization of a new science of politics. With the dawn of a new European order there came a free-market competition among intellectuals to be crowned the new Lycurgus or Solon of the modern world. The French, in particular, seemed enamoured with the resurrected idea of the lawgiver. The abbé Mably and Jean-Jacques Rousseau competed to draw up a new constitution for Poland, and Rousseau composed a second for the island of Corsica. Many years later Adams noted sarcastically how French philosophers had dreamed about and competed for the honor of being designated the "Legislator of the new world."

> If you recollect the ambition of the French philosophers, and their ardent desire to be distinguished by foreign states and princes; the examples of J. J. Rousseau, Abby Condilac, D'Alembert—Diderot—La Harp &C. you will not be surprised that the report of such glory to de Mably, as to be the Legislator of the new world & of hundreds of millions of future people became a 'scandal to philosophy' and spread jealousy and envy throughout the whole coterie of which Grimm was a principal member.[5]

As philosophers and potential lawgivers, the great question that consumed this generation—the great generation of Hume, Montesquieu,

Rousseau, Smith, and many others—concerned the method, the modes of reasoning, the science of politics that the philosopher-statesman and law-giver ought to employ in the theoretical and practical business of consti-tutional construction. Hence the most important task assumed by eighteenth-century political thinkers was to reduce morals and politics to a science. Indeed, the science of politics became in these years *the* science par excellence.[6]

Within the context of this larger European debate over the method and science of politics, John Adams wrote his *Defence of the Constitutions of Government of the United States of America.* In the last chapter, we ex-amined the immediate intellectual and political contexts that inspired Adams to write the *Defence* and the *Davila* essays. But the vigorous debate that Adams took up with the *philosophes* during the 1780s was actually part of a much older controversy in the history of political thought, a de-bate concerned with defining the boundaries and methodologies of polit-ical science and constitution making, and the role that the lawgiver ought to play in constructing new political forms. The two eighteenth-century giants in this debate were, of course, Montesquieu and Rousseau. Ulti-mately, however, this debate had much deeper roots that can be traced back to the seventeenth century, to Bacon and Descartes and their com-peting views over scientific method. We must now turn our attention to that debate and the long tradition of political philosophy that Adams consciously identified his writings with and against.

Adams and the Tradition

Though many of America's Revolutionary generation wrote and spoke of a science of politics, none developed the idea in a systematic way. "I know not how it is that mankind has an aversion to the study of the science of government," Adams wrote. He wondered if the subject was too dry. "To me," he told Alexander Jardine, "no romance is more entertaining."[7] Adams took more seriously than any other American of his time the bur-den of establishing a methodological foundation for the political sciences. But what exactly did Adams mean by a *science* of government? How did he define science, and how did he relate it to the study of politics? Indeed, how did he understand the scientific tradition? The starting point for any study of Adams's political thought must begin with his methodology.

Adams began the *Defence* with a question: Why, if there has been so much advancement in the arts and sciences and in the general practice of government over the course of the preceding three or four centuries, has there been so little improvement in the science of politics during the same period? He thought it unfortunate that the refinement and reformation of manners and the general development of natural philosophy, technology, and commerce in Europe had not resulted in a corresponding development in the political and moral sciences. Adams was genuinely perplexed that a "knowledge of the principles and construction of free governments" should have "remained at a full stand for two or three thousand years."[8] Two years before he published the first volume of his *Defence*, Adams lamented that the "academies in Europe" had neglected the study of government and "the science of society." He noted that a "general spirit of inquiry" into the science of government, that "noblest" form "of all knowledge," had fallen "much behind other arts and sciences."[9] Adams offered his books on government to the public as a remedy to this defect in public knowledge.

The philosophical burden of the *Defence* was to show the ways in which America's Revolutionary constitutions were constructed "merely by the use of reason and the senses." Unlike the constitution makers of classical antiquity, Adams and his fellow American lawgivers had not been granted "interviews with the gods, or were in any degree under the inspiration of heaven." The American constitutions, Adams remarked, "exhibited, perhaps the first example of governments erected on the simple principles of nature."[10] What were the "simple principles of nature" on which those constitutions were grounded? To what objects in nature should "reason and the senses" be directed? More to the point, how were those principles discovered or determined, and what were the modes of reasoning that the American constitution makers employed in their revolutionary experiment? The *Defence* is an attempt to answer these questions: it is an attempt to demonstrate *how* the Revolutionary governments were constructed theoretically. Ultimately, its purpose was to teach future lawgivers and reformers how to think when designing and constructing new constitutions.

Buried among his unpublished papers is a set of rough notes from which Adams pieced together much of the *Defence*. Included in this material is an extraordinary fragment that makes possible a new way of viewing this enigmatic book.[11] Never published as part of the *Defence*, the fragment reveals in dramatic fashion the scientific tradition from which Adams developed his theory of political architecture, and it helps the reader to unlock a new entrance into the organization, purpose, and meaning of this difficult treatise.

The stated purpose of the fragment was to first illuminate "the true method of pursuing the Study of the Arts and Sciences," and second, to enumerate "the great Men to whom We are indebted for the ancient discovery and modern revival of it." Adams's negative purpose was to counter "some celebrated Academicians," who had lately advanced the thesis that "experience and examples" have nothing to do with one of the most important of the sciences, "that of Government." In all likelihood, Adams was here referring to Turgot, Condorcet, and other French philosophes. Adams clearly identified two opposed traditions of scientific reasoning in the fragment: one advocating an empirical a posteriori inductive mode of reasoning, and another advancing a rationalist a priori deductive method. By challenging what he considered bad science and by developing a "right method of philosophizing," Adams hoped to lay the methodological groundwork for a science of politics that could distinguish between "attainable and unattainable knowledge." In other words, he was challenging the deductive method of hypothesis and system building with the inductive method of fact and experience.

Interestingly, Adams argued that the revolution in modern science usually associated with Francis Bacon and Isaac Newton had actually originated in the ancient world. "It is not true," he suggested, "to say that the right use of Reason and the right conduct of the Understanding in the Investigation of Truth, and the Acquisition of knowledge is a late discovery." He identified Hippocrates and Democritus and "some of the Writings of Aristotle" as having first comprehended "that Observation and Experience were the only means of acquiring a knowledge of Nature." Adams preferred the "experimental Philosophy" of Aristotle's *History of Animals* to the "Conjecture," the "fictions of Imagination, and the Spirit of System" found in his *Physics*.[12] And when a new generation of men in the modern era had "little by little, introduced a new science" and seemingly smashed all that had gone before it, Adams found they had really "only revived a Method which had been practised in Antiquity."[13]

Adams credited "Chancellor Bacon" with initiating the revolution in modern science, a revolution grounded on resurrected modes of reasoning dormant for over a millennium. He thought Bacon the "first among the moderns" to have abandoned the "vague and obscure Philosophy" of the scholastics. It was Bacon who had left "words for things" and who "sought in the observation of Nature, a real knowledge, founded in fact." It was Bacon who first "opened a wider field" and who perceived the "general Principles which ought to be fundamental in the study of Nature." And it was Bacon who "dared to form the design of rebuilding Science from the foundations which he had laid on the rock of Nature." Adams considered this last achievement to have been Bacon's greatest. Though his Lord Verulam "hinted at a great number of discoveries which have since been made," it was his reconstruction of science on the basis of a new method that marked his true greatness.

Descartes followed Bacon and was credited by Adams for opening "some courses in experimental Philosophy." But Adams was suspicious of Descartes for having admitted of "certain inward Sentiments of Evidence which it is not easy to comprehend and which may misguide Us in the conduct of the Understanding." He saw in Descartes the beginning of the hypothetico-deductive method. Adams did credit Descartes, though, with discovering certain principles in "Geometry and Algebra," if only because they "pointed out the path to Newton."

For Adams, as for almost every educated person of the eighteenth century, the development of modern science reached its zenith in the work of Sir Isaac Newton. Adams, however, was much less impressed with Newton's actual scientific discoveries than he was with Newton's formulation of a new concept of science, of its methods and modes of analysis. The Newtonian revolution was based, according to Adams, on "the Art of introducing Geometry and Algebra into natural Philosophy and by combining Experiment with Calculation." Adams maintained that Bacon rediscovered the method of induction but that Newton had subsequently applied the theory in brilliant fashion to astronomy and optics, thereby validating and extending its methodological premises. What Bacon had only suggested, Newton brought to fruition.

The last philosopher considered by Adams to have contributed to the development of this empirical science of nature was "Mr. Locke, whose Writings demonstrated that all materials, the elements and Principles of human knowledge, are derived only from Experience and Analogy." Those who attempt to read this "enlightened Phylosopher," Adams noted,

> are Conducted through a Course of experimental Phylosophy, and are Shown that every Sensation and every Reflection is an Experiment. There is a continual appeal to his own Apprehensions Judgements, Reasonings and Arrangements, and to his own Reflections on his own Intellectual operations. He is perpetually [   ] to analyze his own Ideas and Notions, to compare them with the nature of Things, to be accurate in his definitions and steady and sincere in the use of words.

Adams concluded the fragment with a passing reference to the one philosopher who, more than any other thinker of the eighteenth century, had actually applied the empirical method to political questions, namely, Montesquieu. Curiously, though, it is not to *The Spirit of the Laws* that Adams turns. Rather, he quotes from the preface to Montesquieu's little-known and little-read "Temple of Gnidus," where the author satirizes the hubris of the "hypothetical" philosopher: "'I have laboured these thirty years in the composition of a work of twelve pages, which is to contain all that We know concerning Metaphysicks, Politicks and Morals, and which the great Authors have wholly forgotten in the volumes which they have written concerning those sciences.'" Adams agreed with Montesquieu that it was the "hypothetical" mode of reasoning—what Adams called a "hydropical distemper"—that had retarded the development of the political sciences in the eighteenth century. Not until "Experience and Fact shall be more consulted," Adams concluded, could the science of politics expect to make any progress in the modern era.[14]

How could the methods and the modes of reasoning peculiar to the natural sciences be applied to things political? What sort of political epistemology should lawgivers use and employ when designing constitutions? These were the central questions for Adams.

A Machiavellian Moment

In the very same way that Adams saw two methods of reasoning in the natural sciences, he also thought there were two modes of reasoning in the political sciences. On the one hand, there was a tradition of political epistemology—a tradition he often identified with Plato, Rousseau, Paine, and Condorcet—that built political systems on the basis of "Imagination, Hypothesis [and] Conjecture."[15] The tradition of political science that Adams felt the greatest kinship with, however, is best seen in an 1814 letter to John Taylor, where he explicitly stated that he had fortified himself in the *Defence* behind the writings of "Aristotle, Livy, Sidney, Harrington, Dr. Price, Machiavel, Montesquieu, Swift, &c."[16] To that list he might well have added Cicero, Polybius and Hume, all of whom he mentioned on separate occasions as having influenced his theory of political architecture.[17]

The pivotal figure here is Machiavelli. In the same way that Adams credited Bacon with having recovered a methodological tradition in the natural sciences reaching back to classical antiquity, he also claimed that the "world" was "much indebted" to Machiavelli "for the revival of *reason* in matters of government." Machiavelli was for Adams a kind of missing link, an important bridge between the political science of the ancient world and the empirical political tradition of the modern age.[18] Adams thought Machiavelli the central figure in the resurrection of an empirico-inductive tradition of political science. It is no small coincidence, and should be kept in mind, that Bacon—the man Adams described as having "introduced a new science" based on a "revived Method which had been practised in Antiquity"—thought the best method for the political sciences was "that which Machiavel chose wisely and aptly for government; namely, *discourse upon histories or examples.*"[19]

Machiavelli—certainly the Machiavelli of the *Prince*—would seem to be an odd candidate, at least from the perspective of a Revolutionary republican, for the honor of being crowned the "restorer of true politics." What could Adams have meant by this? At the very least, he probably meant to say that Machiavelli had resurrected in his *Discourses on Livy* the constitutional tradition of mixed government associated with Sparta, Carthage, and Rome. That he would describe Machiavelli as having restored *"reason"* in the matters of government suggests that he meant something more. In all likelihood, it was the Florentine statesman's methodological approach to the political sciences that so impressed Adams.

Machiavelli began his *Discourses* by identifying his audience and by describing his purpose in writing. The book was intended to guide a certain kind of man (i.e., young men of merit worthy of governing) toward the knowledge necessary to found, perpetuate, or reform civic institutions. He planned to share with this audience his "long experience and assiduous research" into the course of human affairs. In particular, he would provide his readers with a "real knowledge of history."[20] A certain kind of reasoning about political things would seem then to be an important element in Machiavelli's political philosophy and reform project.

The *Discourses* were written in the form of a commentary on Livy's history of ancient Rome: it empirically observed and analyzed the policies and actions of Rome's rulers and citizens between 753 and 293 B.C. Machiavelli recounted the events, persons, and processes by which Rome was formed and brought to greatness, and he charted the causes for its decline. To that end, he examined the evolution of Rome's constitution, its political institutions and military organization, its internal dissensions and external growth, and the virtues and vices of its greatest statesmen and soldiers. In this way, Machiavelli's modes of reasoning were very different, for instance, from those found in Plato's *Republic*, Hobbes's *Leviathan*, or Rousseau's *Social Contract*. The *Discourses*, the *Florentine Histories*, and even *The Prince* employed a method that seems much closer to that of

Aristotle, the classical historians, and to Polybius in particular.[21] Adams credited Machiavelli's political science, like Bacon's natural science, with initiating a revolution by resurrecting a certain kind of classical political reasoning.

At the heart of Machiavelli's political science was a methodological approach that encouraged the political scientist to study man as he really *is* rather than as he *ought* to be, and the best way to examine man as he is, was through history.[22] Metaphysical and religious considerations were to be disregarded. Armed with this rule of procedure, Machiavelli claimed to have discovered and introduced "new principles and systems as dangerous almost as the exploration of unknown seas and continents." He claimed to have opened "a new route, which has not yet been followed by any one."[23]

How does the explorer find his way in uncharted seas? In the very same way that developments in the navigational sciences permitted Columbus to explore unknown seas and continents and advances in the optical sciences magnified Galileo's sight, so it was Machiavelli's development and application of a new political science, a new constitutional compass, that permitted the constitutional pilot to chart new seas and to discover lost and forgotten worlds. Machiavelli's political science examined the histories of states, ancient and modern. These political bodies or social organisms he called "mixed bodies" which, like "all the things of this world have a limit to their existence." Feigning a kind of decayed Aristotelianism, Machiavelli said of these "mixed bodies" that they have a natural course, a telos, "ordained for them by Heaven," but the history of most regimes demonstrated that their lives had been unusually short. Very few republics had run their entire course and fulfilled their natural end. This was because most republics throughout history had allowed their constitutional forms and structures to become "disorganized." Indeed, "all human institutions," Machiavelli wrote, "contain some inherent evil that gives rise to unforeseen accidents."[24]

Much in the same way that Newton had established certain "Regulae Philosophandi," Machiavelli had prescribed certain "regola generale" for rulers, legislators, and students of political science. After studying how men really do live, the fundamental axiom on which Machiavelli built his science of politics was the premise that human nature has always been and is everywhere the same. Man was the same in pagan Greece as he is in Christian Florence. In the thirty-ninth chapter of the first book of the *Discourses*, Machiavelli established the primary "regola generale" that guided his approach to politics:

> Whoever considers the past and the present will readily observe that
> all cities and all peoples are and ever have been animated by the same
> desires and the same passions; so that it is easy, by diligent study of the
> past, to foresee what is likely to happen in the future in any republic,
> and to apply those remedies that were used by the ancients, or, not
> finding any that were employed by them, to devise new ones from the
> similarity of the events. But as such considerations are neglected or
> not understood by most of those who read, or, if understood by these,
> are unknown by those who govern, it follows that the same troubles
> generally recur in all republics.

The historical observation of all states, Machiavelli argued, demonstrated
that governments, not unlike "heaven, the sun, the elements, and men"
do not change "their motions and power."[25] Thus, the natural state of human affairs, according to Machiavelli, was one of instability and "perpetual movement," and that movement was in one of two directions: states
are either healthy and ascending, or they are cancerous and declining.
Countries may differ entirely one from another in their manners and
mores, but they are all rising or falling according to the same laws of nature.[26] What was most obvious to Machiavelli, even from a superficial examination of world history and the events of his own day, was that states
seem to follow a pattern of relative health and growth, followed by internal decay and eventual decline.

By collecting and collating a wide variety of observable political phenomena and by analyzing the way consequences proceed from certain
causes in political life and human nature, Machiavelli thought he had
found the key to establishing a universally valid political science. History
for Machiavelli was not progressing toward some ideal state of perfection.
Despite all of the changes and upheaval known in human history, the rise
and fall of states follow a familiar and recurring order. Machiavelli
thought the lessons of the past were therefore applicable to the present
and the future. On this view of human nature and history, he was able to
claim for political science the ability to draw valid generalizations or rules
for governing and constitution making and the power to predict the future of most governments.[27] By taking human nature as always and everywhere the same and by studying history as the social phenomena of the
political scientists' empirical observations, Machiavelli laid the basic
groundwork for a style of historical writing and a mode of political science
that would develop over the course of the next three centuries.[28]

Among the modern students of the Machiavellian political science
was Bolingbroke.[29] In his *Letters on the Study and Use of History* (1738),

Bolingbroke developed and extended the insights of Machiavelli's empirical political science. Bolingbroke self-consciously attempted to develop a science or philosophy of history that would uncover the underlying rules and principles that exemplified "the invariable nature of things." Such principles are discoverable by induction from historical example. "He who studies history as he would philosophy," Bolingbroke wrote, "will soon distinguish and collect them, and by doing so will soon form to himself a general system of ethics and politics on the surest foundations, on the trial of these principles and rules in all ages, and on the confirmation of them by universal experience."[30]

The science of history called for by Bolingbroke extended and deepened the empirical approach to politics. The statesman's study of history, Bolingbroke argued, must encompass the experience of as wide a variety of actors and events as is possible: "History, therefore, of all kinds, of civilised and uncivilised, of ancient and modern nations, in short, all history that descends to a sufficient detail of human actions and characters, is useful to bring us acquainted with our species, nay, with ourselves." Historical study provided man with a "map of the country," by which "to guide ourselves." According to Bolingbroke, history provided men with an empirical basis for moral and political action. By history, though, Bolingbroke did not mean the antiquarian collection of facts, nor did he mean the recitation of events and heroic deeds for imitation. The ultimate goal of history was to dig beneath the surface for the "immediate and remote causes" of events. Here, at the level of cause and effect, history becomes "philosophy teaching by examples." The ultimate goal of history, then, was to "reduce all the abstract speculations of ethics, and all the general rules of human policy, to their first principles."[31] This was a philosophy of history that John Adams could take hold of and apply to his own science of politics.[32]

On the title page of his personal set of Enrico Caterino Davila's *Historia delle guerre civili di Francia*, Adams copied from Bolingbroke's fifth letter *On the Study and Use of History* a passage describing one of the principal purposes to which history could be used by philosophers and statesmen:

> Man is the subject of every history; and to know him well, we must see him and consider him, as history alone can present him to us, in every age, in every country, in every state, in life and in death. History, therefore, of all kinds, of civilised and uncivilised, of ancient and modern nations, in short, all history that descends to a sufficient detail of human actions and characters, is useful to bring us acquainted with our species, nay, with ourselves.[33]

This entry provides an important clue as to the nature and purpose of Adams's own *Discourses on Davila*. At the end of the first discourse, Adams interrupted Davila's historical narrative to turn his readers thoughts "for a few moments to the constitution of the human mind."[34] He then follows with a lengthy discussion of human nature over the next eleven chapters.

Historians have often wondered why Adams chose the writings of an obscure Italian historian as the basis of a political treatise published for an American audience in the 1790s. What was his point in using Davila's *History?* Were Adams's *Discourses* on Davila's *Historia delle guerre civili di Francia* written in self-conscious imitation of Machiavelli's *Discourses* on Livy's *History of Rome?* The answers to these questions are found in Bolingbroke.

Adams, like Bolingbroke, did not study history randomly; he did not think all histories or chronicles equally good, nor did he simply study the events of history for their imitative value. History for Adams and Bolingbroke meant something much more. We can only surmise what Adams learned from his reading of Bolingbroke, but it does seem likely that he was shaken from his historical slumbers when he read the famous fifth letter from *The Study and Use of History*. For it was here that Bolingbroke would have taught Adams that "Naked facts, without the causes that produced them, and the circumstances that accompanied them, are not sufficient to characterise actions and councils." It was important for statesmen to examine and compare the works of different historians. Some obviously would be preferable to others in that they illuminated a deeper level of the human experience. The one historian recommended by Bolingbroke, the one who had achieved this higher purpose, was the "noble historian" Enrico Caterino Davila. Our plot thickens when we learn that Bolingbroke thought Davila's work "equal in many respects to Livy."[35]

There can be little doubt that Bolingbroke's recommendation of the Italian historian influenced Adams. According to Bolingbroke, Davila had been suspected "of too much refinement and subtlety." He had been accused of penetrating "the secret motives of actions," and "in laying the causes of events too deep."[36] It was precisely this quality that recommended Davila to Bolingbroke and to Adams, and it was this quality that linked Davila with his near-contemporary Machiavelli in the mind of John Adams. In his commentary on Machiavelli's *Florentine Histories* in the second volume of the *Defence,* Adams quoted Machiavelli to the effect that, "'The most useful erudition for republicans is that which exposes the causes of discord; by which they may learn wisdom and unanimity from the examples of others."[37] Adams was most interested in historians like Machiavelli and Davila: those who sought to find the remote causes of events, causes that were "too deep" for most historians to see. Adams chose historical narratives like Machiavelli's *Florentine Histories* and Davila's *Historia delle guerre civili di Francia* precisely because they sought to "'unravel the secret springs'" that govern the political life of all nations. In fact, all the historians and philosophers that Adams uses in the *Defence*—Polybius, Dionysius Halicarnassus, and even Plato—could be said to have fulfilled to a greater or lesser degree this necessary historical criterion.[38] Indeed, their selection for inclusion in the *Defence* was intimately linked with their ability to get beneath the surface of social phenomena.[39] In contrast to the a priori theories of *philosophes* like Condorcet, Adams described the *Defence* as "an attempt to place Government upon the only Philosophy which can ever support it, the real constitution of human nature, not upon any wild Visions of its perfectibility." Thus, paraphrasing Bolingbroke, Adams wrote that "History is philosophy and policy teaching by example—every history must be founded in philosophy and some policy."[40]

The Science of Politics

At the core of John Adams's political science was the attempt to apply the scientific method of Bacon and Newton to the "moral and intellectual world."[41] He took seriously the possibility that politics could be reduced to a science, not unlike physics or biology. In an unpublished fragment written at about the same time that the *Defence* was being composed, Adams set forth his methodology in direct opposition to that of the marquis de Condorcet, whom he mentions by name as his antagonist.[42] Adams wrote his *Defence* and the *Davila* essays, in large measure, to counter the a priori hyperrationalist tradition of political science that he associated with Descartes and Condorcet. He was suspicious, if not overtly contemptuous, of all theories, hypotheses, or conjectures that could not be demonstrated empirically or inferred from observation and the experimental laboratory of history. The scientific method associated with "Imagination," "Hypotheses," and "Conjecture" had consequences for political life that Adams found both dangerous and destructive. The tendency of such theorists was to denigrate common sense for the "fancy" and reasonings of their own genius.[43] Against the rationalist philosophers, Adams thought that a genuine science of politics must rest on two general principles. First, the "Science of Government," he wrote, "can be learned only from experience." Indeed, he thought experience "the only Source of human knowledge." Second, the political sciences, no less than physics, ought to be "founded in or derived from Experiment."[44] Experience and experiment, then, understood and controlled by observation, analogy, and induction—these were the tools used by Adams in establishing methodological guidelines for an empirical approach to the political sciences.

Adams defined the limits and boundaries of the political sciences by the fence of human experience, beyond which lay the ethereal realm of speculation and imagination. He therefore began his political studies by following the method outlined in the first aphorism of Bacon's *Novum Organum:* "Homo naturae minister et interpres, tantum facit et intelligit, quantum de naturæ ordine re vel mente observaverit, nec amplius scit, aut potest." That is, "Man, being the servant and interpreter of Nature, can do and understand so much and so much only as he has observed in fact or in thought of the course of nature. Beyond this he neither knows anything nor can do anything."[45] The idea of political science as "mimetic"—that is, the notion that the student of political science must first learn to imitate nature and her processes—was central to Adams's empirical approach to politics.

What does it mean to follow or imitate nature? In his marginalia to Condorcet's *Outlines of an Historical View of the Progress of the Human Mind* (1794), Adams indicated the procedure that he had followed in his own study of things political. In discussing the fourth great epoch of human progress, Condorcet had criticized the political philosophy of Greek antiquity (presumably Aristotle) for having studied empirically all "existing governments," a method that he thought "was not enough to convert politics into an extensive science." Condorcet concluded that "even in the writings of the philosophers" the science of Greek political life appeared more as "*a science of facts* than a true theory founded upon general principles." Adams's response to Condorcet throws into sharp relief their competing approaches to the political sciences. "Is there any science, not of facts?" he scoffed. "Newton's science is empirical. Principles drawn from nature are drawn from facts. What is nature but facts? How can reason acknowledge anything but facts and inferences from facts."[46]

What were those "simple principles of nature?" What were the hard "facts" that the political scientist ought to study? Adams later would say that his "plain writings" had "nothing to recommend them but stubborn facts, simple principles, and irresistible inferences from both." Indeed, he would tell John Taylor of Caroline that it had been his lifelong "maxim" to "study government as you do astronomy, by facts, observations, and experiments."[47] The difficult problem for Adams, of course, was how to apply a Newtonian scientific method to the study of human experience and things political.

Universal history provided Adams's student of the political sciences with the necessary laboratory, and the "facts," the "elements" of nature that he observed, were the constitutional and political histories of all republican governments. In particular, he ought to examine the "systems of legislators," the constitutions designed by such great lawgivers as Lycurgus, Solon, Charondas, Zaleucus, Romulus, and many others. Because the experiments of ancient lawgivers were not "finished in many thousands of years," Adams noted, the modern student of politics could observe the long-term consequences, the ultimate effects of certain constitutional arrangements. Understanding this methodological assumption helps to explain, then, the peculiar organization and substance of his *Defence*. It should become more obvious to us why Adams attempted to collect massive amounts of information "from the history of all ages." Like the natural scientist, Adams was collecting, classifying, and collating as much political phenomena as was possible in order to test and verify the theories of Turgot and Condorcet against a tradition of political theory that had argued for mixed government. "The principles of nature which relate to government cannot all be known," he advised the student of politics, "without a knowledge of the history of mankind."[48] History, then, has a particularly didactic value for the political scientist. A broad historical survey of the ancient, medieval, and modern republics, inductively analyzed, would help the political scientist discover the natural and immutable "facts" and "principles" of politics.

Central to Adams's scientific method was the critical role played by experiment. What does it mean to experiment in the political sciences, and how does one test and verify those experiments? Unlike the natural scientist who can test and verify his experiments in a laboratory, the political or moral scientist cannot, or at least should not, perform experiments on human beings. How, then, can the empirical political scientist determine with any degree of certainty which is the best form of government, and how is that proven?

Adams was acutely aware of the difficulty confronted by the political philosopher or lawgiver: "The systems of legislators are," he wrote, "experiments made on human life and manners, society and government." He compared the ancient lawgivers "to philosophers making experiments on the elements. Unhappily, political experiments cannot be made in a laboratory, nor determined in a few hours. The operation once begun, runs over the whole quarters of the globe, and is not finished in many thousands of years."[49] The French Revolution, Adams would later argue, was a classic example of why the method of the natural scientist should not be applied directly or literally to human affairs. The unicameral legislature adopted by the Constituent Assembly in 1789 was, he lamented to Richard Price, "but an experiment, and *must* and will be *altered*." "The form of government they have adopted," he wrote Francis Adrian Vanderkemp in 1790, "can in my humble opinion be nothing more than a transient experiment. An obstinate adherence to it must involve France in great and lasting calamities." Prophetically, he warned that "a demagogue" might "overawe a majority in a single elective assembly."[50] Adams would repeat over and over again how Condorcet's failure to distinguish between the experimental method of the natural scientist and that of the political scientist had resulted in the Reign of Terror. If Adams's political scientist should not try untested theories on society, in what way, then, can it be said that his science was "experimental"?

One of the principal tasks of the first volume of Adams's *Defence*, for instance, was to "find a number of examples" of simple democratic governments, to examine their history, and to trace the process of corruption and degeneration common to them all. Likewise, the second volume "contained three remarkable Courses of experiments in the Science of Legislation."[51] The *Discourses on Davila*, with their history of the French civil wars of the sixteenth century, served the same pedagogical function. From this immense data base, Adams traced how the theories of philosophers and legislators had actually worked in practice. That is, he observed and followed the consequences of certain constitutional ideas as they were confronted by reality. Just as the student of the medical sciences would not practice surgery on live specimens, so the political scientist must not perform untested political experiments on society. Adams tested and measured theory against the lessons of history and experience, and both against the reality check of human nature.

A legislator or political scientist following Adams's methodology would also want to ask of history if certain kinds of constitutional forms have effects common only to that particular constitutional genus, regardless of time or place. Furthermore, he would probe the past to determine whether the theory of simple democratic government had demonstrated over time the desired republican effects prescribed by its advocates, or, whether the philosopher's theory had unintended consequences of an undemocratic nature? In tackling these difficult questions, Adams studied the histories of various ancient, medieval, and modern republics as though he were a natural scientist conducting experiments: "every tryal was intended and contrived to determine the Question whether Mr. Turgots System would do." Adams's political scientist must first define and catalogue the variety of constitutional orders that exist or have existed by the nature of their institutional arrangements, then observe the historical process of change or degeneration common to all regimes, but ultimately the task was to dig deeper, to "unravel the secret springs" of human action.[52]

The phenomenon of nature that Adams studied was neither static nor uniform. He could account for no regime that had not changed over time. In this regard, the *Defence* is rather different from Montesquieu's *Spirit of the Laws.* Montesquieu's primary concern, like that of the natural historian or botanist, was to collect and classify certain phenomena: the various forms of government. Adams, by way of contrast, was concerned primarily with cause and effect, with explaining why constitutions change over time. Despite his great admiration for Montesquieu, Adams found *The Spirit of the Laws* to be an "unfinished work." He thought that Montesquieu had not sufficiently analyzed his "very useful collection of materials" and had therefore failed to expose the underlying causes that generate constitutional change.[53] A *Defence*, in this regard, is more like Aristotle's *Politics* than *The Spirit of the Laws.*

From the perspective of Adams's science of politics, how should the political scientist explain this process of change? Why do some constitutions change and degenerate more quickly than others? Indeed, why do they change at all? Adams's inductive analysis led him to find design flaws in the construction and arrangement of certain constitutional structures. Solon's constitution for Athens, for instance, the worst of the ancient constitutions in Adams's view and the shortest in duration, failed because it gave full executive, legislative, and judicial power to the demos. The Carthaginian constitution, admirable for both its long duration and its resemblance to several American constitutions, proved unworkable over time because it lacked a sufficiently powerful executive to mediate between the senate and the people's body. And Lycurgus's Spartan constitution, the best and longest lasting of the ancient constitutions, was doomed in the end because it was grounded on a moral code of self-denial that cut against the grain of human nature. These design flaws pointed to a more fundamental cause of change. By examining inductively the effects of a vast array of constitutional structures and institutional arrangements, Adams hoped to trace back to their origins, the efficient cause, the engine that propelled, shaped, transformed, and finally led to the eventual degeneration of all governments throughout history. In other words, Adams's political scientist must begin with the observed phenomena of constitutional history, the known effects, and then proceed to resolve or break down these phenomena in order to discover their operative causes.

Ultimately, historical particulars were intelligible only in the light of general causes, approximate and ultimate. By observing historically "the generation and corruption of all kinds of governments," Adams learned that the process of change common to all constitutions proceeded "from the same qualities in human nature." Here, at the level of human nature, Adams found the constant, the uniform, the universal cause of constitutional degeneration. "All nations, from the beginning," Adams claimed in the *Defence*, "have been agitated by the same passions." The "general principles of nature," he later told John Taylor, "have never been known to change." Thus it was "the duty of philosophers, legislators, and artists to study these principles; and the nearer they approach to them, the greater perfection will they attain in their arts." In the end, Adams found in human nature the efficient cause of all constitutional change. It was here, at the level of the human passions, that Adams claimed to have discovered certain "uniform" and constant "laws" which "regulate the moral and political world," no less than those which govern "the vegetable and animal kingdoms."[54] The political scientist would find in human nature the universal cause, the spring that propelled and changed all systems of government through history.

According to Adams, the political sciences had been in a condition of stasis since classical antiquity because lawgivers and philosophers had not adequately taken into account or attempted to understand the true wellsprings of human action. "The generation and corruption of governments," Adams wrote, "which may, in other words, be called the progress and course of human passions in society, are subjects which have engaged the attention of the greatest writers." Adams did not think that most lawgivers (he mentions Lycurgus and Solon by name) had studied adequately or understood fully the passions peculiar to political life. He chastised ancient and modern political philosophers for not having "studied nature, the whole of nature, and nothing but nature." Adams also recommended that his student lawgivers observe and study the various manifestations of human nature in "society and universal history," and "from these we may draw all the real principles which ought to be regarded.[55]

Human nature, then, was the bedrock from which Adams analyzed all social phenomena and from which he would reconstruct a sound political edifice. It was important for the political scientist to study man's natural constitution because it alone provided the key for interpreting the course of regimes past, present, and future. Ultimately, by coming to a thorough understanding of human nature, the lawgiver would be able to ground his regime on uniform and necessary principles. "How is the nature of man, and of society, and of government, to be studied or known," Adams asked, "but in the history and by the experience of human nature in its terrestrial existence."[56] Without an adequate understanding of human nature, particularly of the passions peculiar to political life, Adams did not think it possible for a lawgiver to avoid or overcome the tendency to build political systems according to pure principles derived solely from a priori deductive reasoning.

In the context of seventeenth- and eighteenth-century political thought, Adams's contribution to the development of what Tocqueville would later call a "new science of politics" was unique and significant. He certainly thought that he had developed a method for the political sciences that was an important advance over all other theories. Years later, he claimed to Thomas Jefferson that he had established a method for the political sciences that was "new to Lock[e], to Harrington, to Milton, to Hume to Montesquieu to Rousseau, to Turgot, Condorcet, to Rochefoucault, to Price . . . and at that time to almost all Europe and America."[57] Whether true or not, John Adams stood with an elite few in the eighteenth century who were consciously attempting to establish political investigation on a scientific foundation. Indeed, we see in Adams as serious an attempt to apply a systematic methodology to political questions as we do in Hume, Montesquieu, Rousseau, or Smith. He took these methodological questions so seriously because he thought that a true science of politics must follow sound methodological criteria and be grounded on established guidelines of investigation.

Chapter 7

The Science of History

Any serious study of A *Defence of the Constitutions of Government of the United States of America* must, sooner or later, confront the almost universal scholarly opinion that the work lacks order, coherence, and a unifying plan.[1] The first and most influential volume of the *Defence* is divided into three large sections. The first studies twenty-five democratic, aristocratic, and monarchical republics of the modern world. The second examines the theories of several well-known philosophers, writers on government, and historians. Here Adams considers the opinions and philosophies of Jonathan Swift, Benjamin Franklin, Dr. Richard Price, Machiavelli, Montesquieu, Harrington, Polybius, Dionysius Halicarnassensis, and Plato. He also discusses in passing the ideas of Aristotle, Livy, Thomas Hobbes, Bernard Mandeville, François La Rochefoucauld, Jean de Lolme, and Jean-Jacques Rousseau. The last third studies seventeen democratic, aristocratic, and monarachical republics of the ancient world. The second volume and part of the third "contain three long Courses of Experiments in Political Philosophy," a trilogy of case studies that examine the Italian republics of the Middle Ages.[2] The last half of the third volume is an analysis and critique of Marchamont Nedham's essay on *The Excellency of a Free State, or the Right Constitution of a Commonwealth*, published in 1656.[3] The appended fourth volume of the *Defence*, the *Discourses on Davila*, consists of thirty-two essays, eighteen of which are straight translations from the Italian historian Enrico Caterino Davila's *Historia delle guerre civili di Francia* (1630). The *Discourses* recount the battles, intrigues, factions, and assassinations during forty years of French civil war in the late sixteenth century. Adams interrupts Davila's historical narrative after the first discourse, however, with fourteen essays of "useful reflections" discussing the "constitution of human nature," drawn in part from Adams Smith's *The Theory of Moral Sentiments* (1759). As it stands, the *Defence* is unwieldy and uninviting; indeed, it is seemingly without method or a comprehensive design.

Adams began the first volume of the *Defence* with a preface in which he discussed the nature and intention of his work. Curiously, the preface contains a manifest claim that the work as a whole *does* have a design and that it follows a methodological formula. In a crucial but neglected passage, Adams unfolded a blueprint of the method and system that he had applied to design his own model constitutions. He compared his mode of reasoning to "the method of a wise architect." Adams's method followed a five-step process: first, a study of the theories of government by the best authorities in the art of constitution building; second, a historical examination of the most celebrated "buildings" and forms of constitutional government; third, a comparison of the best forms of government in history and "the principles" of political philosophers; fourth, an inquiry into "how far" theory and practice "were founded on nature, or created by fancy"; and fifth, a comparative analysis of the "advantages" and the "inconveniences" of the best models and theories.[4] This procedure in effect, like an ancient inscription, provides the key to unlocking the mystery of a book that seems at first sight to be merely a "disordered conglomeration" of uncontrollable material. For those who would construct or reform constitutions, the *Defence* provided a method for acquiring the proper knowledge of constitution building.

The first step, the examination of the various theories of government, was simply the point of departure for Adams's scientific investigations. The wise architect should first collect competing theories of constitutional design and consult the writings of political philosophers for the purpose of determining which is best. The evaluation process, however, can only be done by experiment, by measuring, testing, and verifying the various theories against historical practice and the principles of nature. Competing theories can be legitimate only to the degree that they can be demonstrated as actually having worked in "practice." The second and fourth steps—the study of history and human nature—represented for Adams the two crucial requirements for the development of a sound political science. To that end, the four volumes of the *Defence* were devoted to uncovering the true springs of human nature as they were revealed in the constitutional histories of over fifty ancient, medieval, and modern republics. These were the "facts" of nature, the raw data, the material reality that the political scientist must take as the object of his study. History had a particularly didactic value for Adams. Having identified the "facts" of nature that form the subject matter of the political sciences and having established a method by which this information should be organized and processed, Adams thought he had defined and formalized the boundaries and procedures for a true science of politics.

Adams's study of history in the important first volume was divided into two broad parts, modern and ancient. The first examined Turgot's theory of simple government in the light of modern history. The principal question for Adams was whether modern history provided any examples of simple unicameral democracies. Applying the empirical method to a survey of over twenty-six modern republics, Adams could find no such examples. The second part of the *Defence* considers the Platonic, the Aristotelian, and the Polybian theories of constitutional revolution against the backdrop of ancient history. The principal question addressed by Adams was to determine why every ancient regime was incapable of maintaining constitutional stability for an extended period of time. He could find no ancient republic that did not eventually undergo a process of change, a downward cycle of decay and degeneration.

Modern Republican Theory

Following his introduction, Adams began the *Defence* with some "Preliminary Observations" in which he established the context for the entire work. In the years between 1778 and 1786, he wrote, three of Europe's most respected statesmen and philosophers—the Baron Anne-Robert Turgot, the abbé de Mably and Dr. Richard Price—had "turned their attention to the constitutions of the United States," writing and publishing "their criticisms and advice." Adams knew these three men personally, he greatly respected their characters, and he considered their motives for writing as being grounded on "the purest intentions."[5] He credited each with having elucidated a number of "excellent things" about American society and government. Many of their theories and sentiments, however, particularly those concerned with questions of constitutional construction, could not in Adams's opinion be properly reconciled "to reason, experience, the constitution of human nature, or to the uniform testimony of the greatest statesmen, legislators, and philosophers of all enlightened nations, ancient and modern." In particular, Adams was troubled by Turgot's criticism of the American Revolutionary constitutions and, more importantly, by this *philosophe*'s presumption in favor of unicameral government. He feared the potential influence Turgot's opinions might have on constitution makers in America and France.[6] Adams also associated this theory of simple democratic government with the ideas of Milton, Nedham, Franklin, Paine, Condorcet, La Rochefoucauld d'Enville, and later with the Jacobins of the French Revolution.

The first task of the *Defence*, therefore, was to test and verify Turgot's theory of government against history and human nature. In a nation of equal men, Turgot thought there was no need to promote or to create artificially "orders" and "bodies" for the sake of "equilibrium." He believed that each American state should have a unicameral legislature and a severely restricted executive. He preferred, in other words, the Pennsylvania constitution to that of Massachusetts. Before Adams could scientifically dissect and analyze Turgot's theory of government, however, he thought it important to first reconstruct the meaning of Turgot's rather mysterious prescription for "collecting all authority into one centre, that of the nation." In the preliminary observations, Adams offered the following as a partial description of Turgot's meaning: "that an assembly of representatives should be chosen by the nation, and vested with all the powers of government; and that this assembly should be the centre in which all the authority was to be collected, and should be virtually deemed the nation." But how could this single assembly be truly said to represent the nation? Adams demanded to know.

With the eye of a cold realist, Adams cast a Rousseauan shadow over Turgot's plan for simple democratic government. He thought Turgot's language amounted to nothing more than a slick Rousseauan tautology: "The nation will be the authority, and the authority the nation." To Adams this was nothing more than the mumbo jumbo of Rousseau's theory of the General Will. Though it might be true according to the "philosopher of Geneva" that a "society of Gods would govern themselves democratically," the only relevant fact for Adams was that "a simple and perfect democracy never yet existed among men." The only time that there could ever be anything like a General Will is at that one peculiar moment when an infant society wills its political existence, that is, when a people unanimously consents to a social contract creating a body politic. After that, however, the General Will can mean nothing more than majority rule, which is to say, rule of the numerically stronger. The "one centre" that represents the "nation" is in fact no such thing; it is rather only a representation of a party interest. It was only because Turgot's ideas pandered to the innocent "prejudices" of America's new and still revolutionary society that Adams thought it necessary to respond to the "absurdity" of such "superstitious notions."[7]

The same could not be said of Marchamont Nedham's constitutional ideas. Adams took this seventeenth-century English propagandist and defender of Cromwell's commonwealth as the most eloquent and forceful advocate of simple democratic government. Adams thought Nedham's *The Excellency of a Free State, or The Right Constitution of a Commonwealth* "a valuable morsel of antiquity well known in America," and he thought it had many "partisans" there. Adams was so respectful of Nedham that he devoted well over two hundred pages of the third volume to a point-by-point refutation of the Englishman's ideas.

Nedham's defining principle of a free and simple government was the idea of responsibility. For Nedham, the superiority of simple government rested on the premise that it was more directly responsible to the desires and rights of the people than was mixed government. According to Adams, Nedham's "fundamental principle and undeniable rule" was "'that the people, (that is, such as shall be successively chosen to represent the people,) are the best keepers of their own liberties.'" And behind this basic premise lie four fundamental assumptions about the superiority of simple democratic government in promoting a free society: only simple democratic government was "suitable to the nature and reason of mankind"; only in a simple democratic government could the people identify and eradicate sources of abuse and tyranny; only in a simple democratic government with frequent elections could corruption be prevented and faction dissolved; and only in a simple democratic government could rulers be selected according to merit and virtue. Thus, only a simple democratic government was thought responsible to the rights and liberties of the people.[8]

Modern History

Employing the Baconian experimental method, Adams examined Turgot's theory of simple democratic government against the backdrop of history and the test of experience. The principal historical questions that he asked of the Frenchman's theory came in two sets: First, had such a regime ever existed in fact? Could the theory even be tested according to the experimental standards of political science? Second, if an historical example could be found, what was the long-term historical record of such a regime? Had it been a success or a failure and was it a just or an unjust regime? These questions and their answers occupy the first part of the *Defence*.

Adams considered the first question illegitimate, but it was nevertheless the question that gave shape and organization to the *Defence*. The burden of proof, Adams argued, rested with those who assert the positive. He did not think it necessary "to prove that no such government has existed; it is incumbent on him who shall embrace the opinion of M. Turgot, to name the age, the country, and the people in which such an experiment has been tried."[9] Nevertheless, Adams was willing for the sake of argument to disregard the rules of logic. A cursory survey of ancient and modern history suggested to him that no simple democratic government had ever existed. Turgot's theory was a "speculative phantom, that all enlightened men know never did, and never can exist." Yet, he continued, throughout history, several governments have resembled Turgot's favorite model. Rising to the bait, Adams was willing to examine republics that have been considered democratic or that have given the people some share of the government. Thus, he invited his readers in the first chapter of the first volume to travel with him "to some of those countries and to examine their laws."[10]

In what followed, Adams visited and examined over fifty modern and ancient regimes that could be denominated republican. In each case he systematically examined and described the form of government, the institutional arrangements, and the history of each regime as it changed over time. His purpose in conducting this survey was twofold: first, to determine if these republics were democratic in fact or name only, and, second, to determine whether their democratic elements were owing to particular circumstances, "which do not belong to any other people, and prove it to be improper for any other, especially the United States of America, to attempt to imitate it."[11] At the very least, Adams hoped this kind of information would provide useful instruction to future constitution makers about the multiplicity of forms that governments can take, their individual histories, their structure and institutional arrangements, the mechanisms by which they evolved into new forms, and the effects of those forms and changes on the character of the people.

After surveying the so-called modern democratic republics of San Marino, Biscay, seven Swiss cantons, and the United Provinces of the Low Countries, Adams was forced to conclude that none were in fact simple democratic republics. At the end of his survey of the modern republics, he recapitulated his argument and summarized his conclusions. The experience and history of the modern republics demonstrated conclusively one undeniable point: most governments that have been called republics have in fact consisted of democratic, aristocratic, and monarchical elements. Every government that Adams examined, whether it be democratic, aristocratic or monarchic, had decisive elements borrowed from the other forms. Based on contemporary and historical evidence, Adams concluded that no simple democratic governments had ever existed in modern times. Therefore, "if M. Turgot had made any discovery which had escaped the penetration of all the legislators and philosophers who have lived before him, he ought at least to have communicated it to the world for their improvement; but as he never hinted at any such invention, we may safely conclude that he had none."[12]

Ever the scientist, Adams would not leave any stone unturned. He thought it necessary to consider every possible variable and anomaly, every exception to his established rule. The scientific method demanded that he give special consideration and attention to regimes that resembled or seemed to resemble simple democracies. Adams discovered three democratic anomalies that depended either on unusual circumstances for their existence or on elements that were inappropriate considerations for lawgivers: first, regimes that exist because of ancillary geographic conditions; second, regimes that exist because of unusual times or unique circumstances; and third, regimes that exist because of some extraordinary antidemocratic principle or institution (this third anomaly will be discussed in the context of Sparta in the last section of this chapter).

Among those republics often held up as an example of a simple or pure democracy was the tiny, inaccessible, sparsely populated mountain republic of San Marino. Adams's investigation, however, indicated that this isolated enclave was no democratic republic in fact and that its duration was due entirely to ancillary conditions. Adams found that far from being a pure democracy, San Marino's republican institutions were highly aristocratic. The government of this small city-state included a primitive separation of powers and a moderately aristocratic senate.[13] That the people of San Marino were able to remain free and independent for such a long period was not at all surprising to Adams. The principal factors that ensured San Marino's freedom and longevity were its size and location. Isolated and inaccessible, it was secure from the threat of foreign invasion. In a community of only "five thousand souls," a community where every man is personally known to every other, the form of government can be more democratic as "it is scarcely possible that any thing like tyranny or cruelty can take place."[14] It should not be forgotten, Adams warned, that the harsh and primitive conditions of this ethnically, religiously, and culturally homogeneous people are not appropriate or applicable to America: They are not conditions or qualities that would inspire such a heterogenous and commercially minded people.

> A handful of poor people, living in the simplest manner, by hard labor, upon the produce of a few cows, sheep, goats, swine, poultry, and pigeons, on a piece of rocky, snowy ground, protected from every enemy by their situation, their superstition, and even by their poverty, having no commerce nor luxury, can be no example for the commonwealth of

Pennsylvania, Georgia, or Vermont, in one of which there are possibly half a million of people, and in each of the others at least thirty thousand, scattered over a large territory.[15]

San Marino was thus a totally inappropriate model for American or French reformers. It was the product of accident, good fortune, and unique geographical circumstances. Situated as it was at the top of "a very high and craggy mountain, generally hid among the clouds," conditions alone had suppressed the natural human desires for avarice and ambition.[16] Following in the tradition of the Solonian or Montesquieuan lawgiver, Adams deemed the form of government of this fascinating little republic to be appropriate only to its unique if not remarkable circumstances.

The second anomaly discussed by Adams throughout the three volumes of the *Defence* was of regimes that had been able to sustain unicameral legislatures during highly unusual times or periods of national crisis. The obvious case here was during wartime, foreign or civil. It was during these special moments in a nation's history that the people and their leaders are willing to sacrifice their private interests for those of the public good. Adams did not have to travel very far to find this sort of anomaly. During the Revolutionary War, for instance, Americans had been governed by a unicameral Continental Congress and, at times, they had even carried on the war "without any government at all." During such periods of extraordinary national danger, the passions that are the source of interest, faction, and majority tyranny are momentarily deflated and sacrificed in the name of the larger common interest, but such abnormal times and unusual sacrifices cannot be expected to last for very long. Adams was therefore not at all surprised to learn that in the years after the peace the nation had broken out in seditions and public uprisings. The rare moments, when "it is the duty of a good citizen to hazard and sacrifice all for his country" cannot and should not be taken as the standard on which to construct constitutions that are meant to last in perpetuity. In "ordinary times," one should not expect the people and their leaders to sacrifice their personal interests for those of the public. Indeed, it was the "duty and interest of the community not to suffer it." The kind of public virtue that was required to sustain the necessary harmony, justice, and peace in a unicameral legislature over long periods of time runs counter to human nature. "When we know human nature to be utterly incapable of this content, why should we suppose it? Human nature is querulous and discontented wherever it appears, and almost all the happiness it is capable of arises from this dis-contented humor. It is action, not rest, that constitutes our pleasure. All we have to do is to guard and provide against this quality; we cannot eradicate it."[17]

Ordinary people simply cannot long endure such sacrifice. Even in America, where a brief experiment was conducted in building and run-ning unicameral governments and where the people had demonstrated a remarkable degree of self-denial and service to the common weal, it should not have been a surprise that the dominant forces of human na-ture would not lay dormant for very long. In America where the people were more equal, more independent, and more virtuous than in any other place, they had also proven themselves to be more "addicted to luxury" than any other people in history. During the War for Independence, the expansion of the paper money supply had enticed this nation of virtuous agrarian warriors into "a greater degree of luxury than ought to have crept in for a hundred years." The very equality that Turgot thought was the ba-sis of unicameral governments was indeed the active agent that tended to dissolve the people's virtue into warring interests and factions. In a free republic,

> a citizen perceives his fellow-citizen, whom he holds his equal, have a better coat or hat, a better house or horse, than himself, and sees his neighbors are struck with it, talk of it, and respect him for it. He can-not bear it; he must and will be upon a level with him. Such an emu-lation as this takes place in every neighborhood, in every family; among artisans, husbandmen, laborers, as much as between dukes and marquises, and more—these are all nearly equal in dress, and are now distinguished by other marks. Declamations, oratory, poetry, sermons, against luxury, riches, and commerce will never have much effect. The most rigorous sumptuary laws will have little more.[18]

To expect the people and their representatives to sustain this elevated degree of virtue in a unicameral legislature, Adams exhorted his audience, "would be as reasonable to say that all government is altogether unneces-sary, because it is the duty of all men to deny themselves, and obey the laws of nature and the laws of God."[19] As noted above, the only time that anything like a general will can emerge from an association of people is when they are emerging from a state of nature and joining together for the purpose of establishing a body politic. The very necessity of this social contract and the establishment of a neutral arbiter in the form of a coer-cive state power demonstrated that the laws of nature are not naturally binding on mankind. If men would only "consult their reason, and obey their consciences," Adams wrote, "the law of nature would be sufficient for the government of men." But such is not the case for most men and women most of the time. For Adams, a unicameral legislature would simply be a recreation of the state of nature:

> We certainly know, from the known constitution of the human mind and heart and from uniform experience, that the law of nature, the decalogue, and all the civil laws, will be violated, if men's passions are not restrained; and, therefore, to presume that an unmixed democratical government will preserve the laws, is as mad as to presume that a king or senate will do it. . . . Why then is the world any longer amused with a speculative phantom, that all enlightened men know never did, and never can exist?[20]

If the common people cannot be expected to practice and sustain a high degree of virtue for very long, the same is particularly true of those who would govern them. The kind of magnanimous and disinterested pursuit of the public good that defined the great statesman was limited by two factors. The first is that the people generally turn to the great-souled man only in times of great need. Only in times of "distress and danger, when they think no others can save them" will the people elect leaders and statesmen of extraordinary virtue and merit. Once the crisis has ended and "the danger is over," they will "neglect" their national saviors, those rare and magnanimous statesmen, for "others more plausible and indulgent." And once peace and social order have returned, "the people will have the men whom they love best for the moment, and the men whom they love best will make any law to gratify their present humor." A second factor that limited the role of disinterested statesmen during normal times is that such men are genuinely rare and are not to be found in every generation. Even if the people were wise enough to always look to the virtuous legislator for guidance, such men are few and far between. They are a "race" of men not "quite extinct; but the examples are so rare, that he who shall build his frame of government upon a presumption that characters of this stamp will arise in succession, in sufficient numbers to preserve the honor and liberty, and promote the prosperity of his people, will find himself mistaken." It would therefore be "madness in a legislator to frame his policy upon a supposition that such magnanimity would often appear."[21]

When framing laws or constitutions, reformers and constitution makers must take man as he really is and as he is wont to act under normal conditions. The exceptional virtues that the common people and their leaders will often demonstrate during wartime and periodic national crises cannot be duplicated or sustained for any extended period of time, and should therefore not provide the standard by which to construct constitutions intended to endure beyond the occasional and necessitous burst of patriotism. It would be foolish and dangerous to take as one's standard how man might be or ought to be:

> There have been examples of self-denial, and will be again; but such exalted virtue never yet existed in any large body of men, and lasted long; and our author's argument requires it to be proved, not only that individuals, but that nations and majorities of nations, are capable, not only of a single act, or a few acts, of disinterested justice and exalted self-denial, but of a course of such heroic virtue for ages and generations; and not only that they are capable of this, but that it is probable they will practise it.

When framing a constitution, the lawgiver must study the common people as they really are, with their passions and interests and, furthermore, he must not expect virtuous statesmen to be a regular feature of political life. For "to talk of founding a government upon a supposition that nations and great bodies of men, left to themselves, will practice a course of self-denial," Adams warned in his typically provocative way, "is either to babble like a new-born infant, or to deceive like an unprincipled imposter."[22]

Ancient Theory

When Adams turned to the ancient republics, his scientific purpose was different: he asked of history a new set of questions. The ancient republics provided Adams's historical science with a new kind of laboratory and with a new kind of historical experiment. True to his method, Adams began his survey of the ancient republics by first assembling "together the opinions and reasonings of philosophers, politicians, and historians, who have taken the most extensive views of men and societies." The political thinkers he considered most important in this regard were Plato and Polybius.

> Let me proceed then to make a few observations upon the Discourses of Plato and Polybius, and show how forcibly they prove the necessity of permanent laws, to restrain the passions and vices of men, and to

secure to the citizens the blessings of society, in the peaceable enjoyment of their lives, liberties, and properties; and the necessity of different orders of men, with various and opposite powers, prerogatives,
and privileges, to watch over one another, to balance each other, and
to *compel* each other at all times to be real guardians of the laws.

Adams was particularly keen to have his audience study these philosophers because, as he said, their "writings were in the contemplation of
those who framed the American constitutions."[23] Guided by Polybius and
Plato, Adams's principal concern in this section of the *Defence* was to analyze the ancient republics in order to determine how and why these once
great republics had degenerated over time. His task was to identify the
constitutional defects of each regime, the inherent design flaw that would
eventually weaken, corrupt, and finally destroy the constitution's structural integrity. This important subject, Adams pondered, has "engaged
the attention of the greatest writers."[24] His goal was to deepen and extend
the level of his empirical study beyond the rather static examination of
the modern republics.

Following Aristotle, Polybius, and Cicero, Adams accepted the traditional categorization of regimes into three natural or generic forms of government—the one (monarchy), the few (aristocracy), the many (democracy)—with three corresponding deviations or corruptions from the
pure form.[25] He included in the *Defence* a long section from Book Six of
Polybius's *Histories* (paraphrased by Machiavelli in his *Discourses on Livy*),
and he repeated the Polybian taxonomy of the various forms of government and the theoretical diagnosis of their degeneration.[26] Polybius
taught Adams that "reason" and "experience" demonstrated "the tendency of each of the simple forms of government to degenerate" into their
opposites: monarchy inevitably degenerates into tyranny, aristocracy into
oligarchy, and democracy into ochlocracy or anarchy. The real force of
the Polybian argument, though, was that all six forms were part of a larger
cycle of decay and degeneration. This happened because in each pure or
improperly mixed form of government, "there is a certain vice implanted
by the hand of nature." In the "process of time," it was "ordained" that the
pure form would eventually be perverted and would degenerate into its
opposite, or corrupt form.[27]

Monarchy, the first and original form of government, initially serves
the interests of the community. Eventually, however, the monarchy is corrupted when the natural virtues of the first king are eroded by the principle of hereditary succession. Descendants of this first king govern their

citizens by arbitrary power rather than by natural authority, a power that eventually becomes corrupted, vicious, and tyrannical. Unwilling to bear this oppression, the best and most courageous citizens conspire to over-throw the tyrant. The people, grateful to their saviors, choose from this natural aristocracy those who most deserve to assume the reins of gov-ernment. Like the original monarchy, the first generation or two of aris-tocratic rulers govern in the name of virtue and the public welfare. But the aristocracy cannot sustain the substance and the integrity of its form of rule for very long before it too becomes overbearing and abusive. After some time, the aristocracy is replaced by a thoroughly oppressive oli-garchy. The dramatically widening gulf between rich and poor that ensues gives the people just cause to revolt and replace the oligarchy with demo-cratic rule. The people, jealous of their liberties and proud of their claim to rule, initially govern with moderation and justice. Gradually, however, the people turn their liberty into wanton license and their equality into the redistribution of all wealth. The democratic regime soon becomes an indiscriminate mob of warring factions lasting only until the most power-ful demagogue is given martial powers to restore law and order. Thus the cycle has completed its turn and begins anew.

As much as he admired and used the Polybian cyclical model, Adams thought it inadequate or flawed in two fundamental respects. First, the Polybian theory of regime change discussed the cycle of constitutions as a matter of fact and in a rather mechanical fashion: it did not sufficiently go to the underlying causes of that change. Adams found Polybius much too resigned in arguing that the process of decline and degeneration was "ordained" by nature. Second, Adams found Polybius's portrait of human nature far too "charitable," particularly in the light of modern thinkers like "Hobbes, Mandeville, Rochefoucauld, Machiavell, Beccaria, Rousseau, [and] De Lolme." Adams rejected Polybius's claims that the first king would rule wisely and honestly, that the first aristocracy would govern with caution and moderation, and that the first democracy would administer its affairs with decorum. He thought it more likely that as soon as any one of these pure forms felt itself "secure in the possession of their power," they "would begin to abuse it."[28]

The inadequacies of the Polybian system help to explain why Adams turned to the often neglected eighth and ninth books of Plato's *Republic* for the ultimate explanation of why constitutions universally undergo a process of decline and degeneration. Given his generally negative view of Plato's philosophy, it is curious that Adams would so enthusiastically endorse the Platonic theory of constitutional revolution.[29] Plato, he explained, "has given us the most accurate detail of the natural vicissitudes of manners and principles, the usual progress of the passions in society, and revolutions of governments into one another."[30] The Platonic account, like no other, attempted to uncover the underlying causes that propelled all constitutions to change from one form to another.

The Platonic theory of constitutional revolution differed from the Polybian in significant ways. First, Plato asserted the existence of five and not six forms of government. Second, the transition from one form to another in the Platonic account is not cyclical as it is in Polybian theory. Instead, the Platonic theory is linear and dialectical, that is, the seeds of dissolution are inherent in each regime. In the process of change from one regime to another there is an intermediate stage when the thesis and antithesis struggle for control. Rather than evolving into its opposite—monarchy into tyranny, for instance—Plato's simple regimes come into being from the preceding one, descending downward from better to worse. Third, the forces that begin the process of change are less a consequence of some structural flaw in the constitution than they are a product of certain deeper elements inherent in human nature.

In the same way that there are five kinds of political regimes for Plato, so there are five kinds of human characters or soul types. Just as there is a certain kind of human soul that primarily desires wealth, for instance, so there is a corresponding regime, the oligarchic, that esteems riches. Adams was sympathetic to the Platonic account because he saw in it something that was missing from most other theories: it found the ultimate cause of constitutional decay in human nature and, more particularly, in the progress of the passions. He thought Plato's theory important because it showed "the mutability of simple governments in a fuller light," and that "fuller light" of which Adams spoke was Plato's discussion of "the usual progress of the passions in society."[31] Adams agreed with Plato that there is a direct parallel between the process of constitutional transformation and the human soul. He also agreed with Plato that simple governments were most susceptible to degeneration because they are the least capable of controlling the human passions.

Ultimately, however, the Platonic theory failed, according to Adams, because it did not adequately draw the correct conclusions from its otherwise sound premises, namely, the necessity of mixed and balanced government. "What shall be done to prevent" the process of constitutional corruption? Adams asked of Plato. Although Plato did not recommend a mixed and balanced constitution, he did nevertheless establish the premises "from whence the absolute necessity of such orders and equipoises may be inferred; he has shown us how naturally every simple species of government degenerates."[32] Plato's theory, as such, was not Adams's, but Adams did appreciate the attempt to connect human nature to constitutional forms, and he appreciated Plato's understanding of the relationship between the progress of the passions in society and the consequent process of constitutional decay. For these reasons alone, Adams could recommend Plato to all future lawgivers. But Plato's theory, in and of itself, was not enough to satisfy the demands of Adams's political science. The experimental nature of his science required that he illuminate theory with empirical evidence. Thus, "in order to show the theory of Socrates, as reported by Plato, in a clearer light, and to be convinced that he has not exaggerated in his description of the mutability in the characters of men and the forms of government, we should look into the history of those ancient republics from whence he drew his observations and reasonings."[33] Fully one-third of the first volume of the *Defence* is devoted to a survey of over eighteen ancient republics, which, like his account of the modern republics, Adams divided into democratic, aristocratic, and monarchic. Included among the democratic republics are Carthage, Athens, Corinth, Rome, and a number of smaller Greek republics. The aristocratic republics discussed are those of Rome, Lacedaemon, and Crotona. The monarchical republics surveyed include those of the ancient Germans, Phaeacia, and Ithaca.

Ancient History

What can the histories of the various ancient republics teach American and French legislators in the light of the theories of Plato and Polybius? What particular historical phenomena was Adams attempting to examine? Because he could find no ancient republic—as he could find no modern republic—that had been governed for any significant amount of time by one of the pure constitutional forms, Adams focused in the last third of the *Defence* on the very best ancient regimes: governments that mixed and balanced the three pure forms. Inevitably, however, the competition for power and the uneven distribution of power eventually transformed even these hybrid forms into one of the simple forms. The history of classical Greece was of particular value to Adams in providing constitution makers with negative models of government:

> The history of Greece should be to our countrymen what is called in
> many families on the continent a boudoir, an octagonal apartment in
> a house, with a full-length mirror on every side, and another in the

ceiling. The use of it is, when any of the young ladies, or young gentlemen if you will, are at any time a little out of humor, they may retire to a place where, in whatever direction they turn their eyes, they see their own faces and figures multiplied without end. By thus beholding their own beautiful person, and seeing, at the same time, the deformity brought upon them by their anger, they may recover their tempers and their charms together.[34]

Adams's primary task in studying the ancient republics was to demonstrate how the "vice" inherent in the "generation and corruption of governments" was inextricably linked with "the progress and course of human passions in society."[35] He used the histories of the ancient republics to illuminate how and why the corruption of a monarchy most often led to despotism, how and why power-seeking aristocracies transformed themselves into oligarchies, and how and why pure democracies invariably degenerated into chaos and the reign of anarchy. Any lawgiver who attempted to "'set up any one of the former three sorts of government,'" could be assured, Adams warned, that "'it will not be of any long duration; for no precaution will be sufficient to prevent its falling into the other that is analogous to it, on account of the affinity which there seems to be in this case betwixt perfection and imperfection.'"[36]

The formula that Adams applied to his examination of the ancient republics began by describing the original constitution of each regime as it was framed by a founding lawgiver. He began his examination of Sparta, for instance, by describing the form of government designed by its famed legislator, Lycurgus. The constitutions of Solon from Athens, Charondas from Sybaris, Zaleucus from Locris, Romulus and then Numa from Rome are all described and evaluated. There were exceptions, of course. Some regimes did not have lawgivers, and the information about the first foundings of other city-states was unavailable to Adams. But he preferred to examine regimes that had an identifiable starting point. All of the ancient constitutions examined by Adams were mixed to one degree or another, but "an equal mixture" of all three of the natural forms "was never known in Greece."[37] Nevertheless, despite the attempts of the antique lawgivers to mix and balance their constitutions, their handiwork was doomed to failure. Adams could find no ancient republic that did not experience the process of decay and degeneration.

Generally speaking, Adams was able to discern and distinguish among three kinds of ancient regimes: first, those that failed almost immediately; second, those that succeeded temporarily; and, third, those that succeeded for an extended period of time. His ultimate purpose in studying these three kinds of ancient republics was to discover the vice, the inherent flaw of each original constitution, and then to demonstrate how that mechanical flaw was manipulated over time to further the interests and passions of ambitious individuals or certain social orders, thereby setting in motion the familiar cycle of decay and decline.

Among those ancient constitutions examined by Adams that failed almost immediately after its founding moment was the Athenian constitution framed by Solon. The Athenian constitution was important for Adams because in the eighteenth century it was often held up for emulation as an example of a true democratic republic. More to the point, the "fundamental principle of Solon's government," Adams wrote, "was the most like M. Turgot's idea of any we have seen." That fundamental principle, Adams noted, "preserved to every free Athenian his equal vote in the assembly of the people, which he made supreme in all cases, legislative, executive, and judicial." But even the Solonian constitution was far from the kind advocated by Turgot. To stabilize his regime Solon was forced to establish "a greater variety of orders, and more complicated checks" than could be found even in the American constitutions. Solon established four independent orders—an assembly of the people, an assembly of four hundred, an assembly of archons, and the Aeropagus—and "yet all were insufficient," declared Adams, "for want of the three checks, absolute and independent." Almost from the beginning, Solon's attempts to establish constitutional equilibrium were ineffectual; they "produced a never-ending fluctuation in the national councils; continual factions, massacres, proscriptions, banishment, and death of the best citizens." The Solonian constitution lasted for less than one hundred years. In the end, it degenerated into the tyranny of Peisistratus during Solon's lifetime. The fate of the Solonian constitution was, according to Adams, inseparable from its design and construction. The anarchy and tyranny associated with Athens and many other Greek states was directly related to the lack of balance in their constitutions. Quoting Thucydides, the lesson Adams drew from the Greek city-states was that "'Such things ever will be, so long as human nature continues the same.'"38

The second kind of constitution catalogued by Adams was one that had been reasonably successful over time. His illustrating example was Carthage. Adams described Carthage as a large and populous commercial republic that was reasonably well ordered by a mixed constitution. The long duration of its government, lasting some five hundred years, was proof that their constitution was "good." The Carthaginian constitution was particularly worthy of study because it resembled "those of the States of America, more than any other of the ancient republics, perhaps more than any of the modern." It could be compared to the American revolutionary constitutions because it had a mixed constitution that balanced monarchic (two suffetes), aristocratic (senate) and democratic powers, and because the monarchy and senate were annually elected by the people. It also had two additional orders thrown into the mix, further helping to divide power: they were the committee of 104 elected by the senate to watch over the ambition of the great families, and, elected from this body was a subcommittee of five who administered for life the supreme tribunal of criminal jurisdiction.

Why did this admirable constitution not last longer than it did? What were the ultimate sources of its decline? The fundamental flaw of the Carthaginian constitution, according to Adams, was its maldistribution of power among the three principal political orders. The executive authority was limited and had no veto over legislation. Most of the executive power and all of the legislative was lodged in the senate and the people's body. Moreover, if the senate was not unanimous in its legislation, the decision-making process reverted back to the people. Adams's final judgment on Carthage was that its constitution was weighted much too heavily in favor of the senate and the people's body, which, over time, became corrupted and hungry for power. The greatest flaw in the Carthaginian constitution was that it lacked a sufficiently powerful executive to mediate between the aristocracy and the people.

Finally, we come to Sparta, the most successful of the ancient regimes. Adams thought the Spartan constitution worthy of special consideration because of its long duration and because of its historic reputation as the virtuous republic par excellence. Framed by the mythic lawgiver Lycurgus, the Spartan constitution lasted upward of eight hundred years. In an age of revolutionary constitution making, the memory of the Spartan republic captured the imagination of both conservatives and radicals. Hence, Adams thought it important to examine Lycurgus's constitutional design with some care.

Lycurgus was unique among the lawgivers of the ancient world for having consciously identified the central problem of constitution making: "that every form of government that is simple, by soon degenerating into that vice that is allied to it, and naturally attends it, must be unstable." Lycurgus's constitutional innovation was to unite "in one all the advantages of the best governments, to the end that no branch of it, by swelling beyond its bounds, might degenerate into the vice that is congenial to it."

He constructed a government that mixed the three natural sociopolitical orders—that is, monarchy, aristocracy, and democracy—in such a way that "while each was mutually acted upon by *opposite powers*, no one part might outweigh the rest." The result was a constitutional ballast that "equally *poised* and *balanced*" the "contrary powers."[39] From the standpoint of its separation and balancing of powers, Adams thought Lycurgus's constitutional structure the best-modeled in the ancient world. "This system," he wrote, "preserved the Lacedaemonians in liberty longer than any other people we have heard of ever enjoyed it." He could pay the Spartan lawgiver no higher compliment than by saying that his constitutional handiwork resembled the English constitution more than any other in the ancient or modern world.

But it was not Lycurgus's mechanical balancing of Spartan social orders that Adams most admired. He recognized that the Spartan regime was held together by something much stronger than its institutional arrangements. What most impressed Adams was Lycurgus's profound, though flawed, understanding of human nature and his application of that knowledge to his Spartan constitution. Adams followed Polybius in praising Lycurgus for having been the first constitution maker to discover the causal relationship between the process of constitutional decay and the laws of "necessity and the laws of nature." It had been said of Lycurgus that, while in Crete, "he had acquired a deep insight into human nature, at least he had informed himself fully of the length and breadth, the height and depth, of the passion of ambition in the human heart." In particular, he studied those passions that most relate to political life: "the love of esteem, of praise, of fame, of glory." Ambition, in a word, was the passion that Lycurgus "understood better than any other legislator"; he made it the linchpin and "the foundation of his institution." It was for this reason that Adams could agree with Plato's description of Sparta as "The ambitious republic."[40] Ironically, Lycurgus's understanding and application of ambition to the Spartan constitution made it the best and the worst of the ancient republics.

Lycurgus employed ambition as a dynamic force that simultaneously energized and harmonized the regime in two important ways. First, he confirmed and enlarged the "ancient dignities" of the nobles. The authority of the monarchy was significantly deflated by transferring all of the executive power to the senate; likewise, the heart of the legislative power—the authority to originate laws—was given to the aristocracy. The people's assemblies were authorized only to confirm or reject the laws proposed by the senate. "Here is indeed," Adams wrote, "all authority nearly collected into one centre, and that centre the nobility." But Lycurgus did not rest there. Seeing that the "king and people were both too weak" and that aristocratic ambition would never rest until it had effectively destroyed its competitors, Lycurgus sought to "counter-balance" the "restless" ambition of the senate. This he did by employing ambition in a second way, by contriving "a kind of solemn alliance to be perpetually renewed" between king and people, "by which the senate might be awed into moderation." Lycurgus consummated this alliance by ordering the king and ephori (representatives of the people) to take an oath every month. The king "swore to observe the laws," while the people swore "to maintain the hereditary honors of the race of Hercules [the king and his family], to revere them as ministers of religion, to obey them as judges, and follow them as leaders."[41] The purpose of this alliance was to channel the ambition of both the king and the people toward a kind of civil religion.

Still, because the aristocracy controlled the king and dominated the people, it was necessary for Lycurgus to counteract this constitutional imbalance with "other precautions." He did this by directing the whole nation toward one end. Lycurgus reinforced his constitutional order with a strict moral code that would temper factional disputes and foster the good of the community over partial interests. In order to extinguish every "appetite, passion, and affection in human nature," Lycurgus reformulated and rechanneled ambition as "an enthusiastic passion for the glory of the republic, and the race of Hercules." He hoped to foster in his citizens a "pride" in the "glory of the descendants of Hercules and of their republic" and he hoped to perpetuate in them a "superstitious attachment" to both. The Spartan lawgiver created a new-model man through laws that divided property equally; banished gold and silver; prohibited travel and intercourse with strangers; outlawed arts, trades, and agriculture; and discouraged literature. The laws were reinforced by civic institutions that required all citizens to attend public meals and to participate actively in warlike exercises. Moreover, Lycurgus's public philosophy sought to obliterate the individual by teaching all citizens to view themselves as "the property of the state" and by stating that "parents should not educate their own children." Separated from the rest of humanity, the Spartans "lived together, destitute of all business, pleasure, and amusement, but war and politics." Eventually, the Lacedaemonian constitution imploded when the moral glue that held it together became diluted by the introduction of new objects of ambition. After the conquest of Athens, the Spartans acquired "a taste of wealth" and a passion for travel and "foreign manners." Eventually, their leaders divided into factions "and nothing appears afterwards in the history of Sparta but profligacy, tyranny, and cruelty, like that in Rome under the worst of the Caesars."[42]

Lycurgus's political experiment may have been successful if measured simply in terms of its duration, but Adams warned his contemporaries against adopting such a model on two counts. First, he thought the English had demonstrated that the Spartan constitution could be improved upon.[43] Second, Adams condemned the antiliberal nature of the Spartan constitution. He found abhorrent the Spartan ideal of virtue and citizenship.[44] "The institution of Lycurgus was well calculated to preserve the independence of his country," he wrote, but the Spartan lawgiver had little regard for the happiness and liberty of his people. Adams saw in Sparta precisely the kind of political experimentation that his methodology was designed to counteract: "The plan was profound, and means were with great ability fitted to the end; but, as a system of legislation, which should never have any other end than the greatest happiness of the greatest number, saving to all their rights, it was not only the least respectable, but the most detestable in all Greece."[45] Adams's discussion of the Spartan republic plays an important role in the *Defence*. Just as Lycurgus attempted to warp human nature toward a preestablished theoretical end, so too did Condorcet and the French Revolutionaries in the eighteenth century. In the case of Lycurgus, that end was the fulfillment of ambition; in the case of Condorcet, it was equality. For Adams, human nature in all its dimensions provided constitution makers with a yardstick by which to judge between just and unjust regimes. Human nature, studied as it really is and not as it ought to be, was the cornerstone of Adams's political science.

In the end, from these "few short sketches of the ancient republics," Adams was able to draw three generic but important conclusions: first, all of the ancient republics had, to one degree or another, components from all three of the basic orders; second, the prosperity and duration of each was directly related to the degree that each was mixed and balanced; and third, "they all were indebted, for their frequent seditions, the rise and progress of corruption, and their decline and fall, to the imperfection of their orders, and their defects in the balance."[46] A fourth conclusion might be added as well. In a large number of the ancient republics Adams found that the constitutional order was supported by auxiliary controls or by antirepublican elements. Many of the ancient republics were held together by strong religious controls, many were supported by slave economies, and most limited citizenship to property owners.

The ancient republics, Adams concluded, should not be used as models to be copied by eighteenth-century constitution makers. He found much to be admired in these tiny republics, but their usefulness as models for the present was limited primarily by what they taught lawgivers to avoid. The extraordinary geographical circumstances of some republics and the exceptional, antiliberal controls used by others, made them ill-suited as models for America or France.

Chapter 8

The Science of Human Nature

The study of politics for John Adams ultimately meant the study of human nature: it meant an inquiry into "how far" the theory and practice of politics "were founded on nature, or created by fancy." Thus the "first inquiry," the question that Adams thought most important for constitution makers concerned "what kind of beings men are?"[1] He began his examination of man's natural constitution by asking two important questions: First, how should the political scientist study human nature, and second, what aspects of human nature should be taken as most fundamental, most universal, most applicable to political life?

Adams's answer to the first question should not surprise us. Knowledge of human nature ought to be obtained through an application of the scientific method of Bacon and Newton. The method that he applied to the study of human nature took two general forms. The first was subdivided into two elements of personal experience. On the one hand was internal experience, that is, the introspective observation of the working of one's own mind and passions; on the other hand was external experience, that is, what one learned from observing the actions of others. The second method adopted by Adams was what we might call the method of vicarious experience, the primary form of which was the study of history, particularly histories that attempted to "unravel the secret springs" of human actions.[2] The biographies of great statesmen or generals, for instance, provided a unique insight into the basic or pervasive human drives and desires.

Adams's analysis of human nature was not comprehensive: his intention was not to present a full account of the passions, of reason, of the will, or of conscience. Instead, his aim was much more limited and specific. He was mostly if not entirely interested in studying human nature as it reveals itself in a social and political context. The passions that he studied were those that define and shape man as a social being, particularly those that are directly relevant to political life; he was concerned with the passions that come to life and are inflamed by power, authority, and ruling. In other words, he studied the passions most relevant to the work of constitution

148

making. Adams claimed to have identified the passions that have governed mankind from the Roman republic to the American republic, from the Mohawks to the Hottentots. These qualities of human nature were for Adams unlimited, eternal, and universal. Indeed, they govern every member and rank of society from kings to aristocrats to yeoman farmers, and they govern every kind of political organization from the family to the town hall to the national legislature.

Adams's most developed account of human nature is to be found in the *Discourses on Davila*. Although the basic outline, assumptions, and implications of his investigations into the "first inquiry" were implicit in the first three volumes of the *Defence*, Adams felt they were in need of fuller development by the time he came to write the *Davila* essays. At the conclusion of the first discourse, therefore, he determined that he could not proceed with the history and political lessons of the French Civil Wars until he had first turned his readers' attention "for a few moments to the constitution of the human mind."[3] In the twelve discourses that follow, Adams provided his future lawgivers with an extended and occasionally brilliant analysis of human nature and its relevance to constitution making.

Human Nature and the Laws of Nature

As we now know, John Adams was not a Calvinist, nor did he accept a Calvinist view of human nature: he never thought man evil, wicked, sinful, or even bad by nature, nor could he go as far as some ancient and modern writers who had seen "human nature through a more gloomy medium." He refused, for instance, to join with Machiavelli in "condemning our species" by "pronouncing the greatest part wicked; or going the length of the ancients, in supposing them half beasts; or of some moderns, in calling them half devils." Instead, he admired Laurence Sterne's "fable of Tristram Shandy" more than Mandeville's "fable of the Bees," and he agreed with "Butler rather than with Hobbes." Ultimately, it was "weakness rather than wickedness" that defined human nature for Adams.[4] His account of human nature was thoroughly secular and in accord with the most advanced Enlightenment theories of the time.

To fully understand the "constitution of the human mind" and its implications for political life, Adams thought it necessary to "take an extensive view of the subject."[5] It was not enough to say that man was weak by nature and therefore not to be trusted with unlimited power. The political scientist must take into account human reason and the passions, motives, and behavior, the virtues and vices common to most men in most situations, and he must represent man in such a way as to take into account the universal attributes of human nature relevant to the work of political architecture.

Following the modern natural-rights tradition initiated by his English predecessors, Adams began his account of human nature by taking man as he naturally is or as he might have been in a state uncorrupted by social convention. To that end, he invoked the device of the state of nature made famous by Thomas Hobbes and John Locke. Stripped bare of the many layers of social convention, Adams hoped to see true man, with his deepest and strongest drives and desires. An integral part of examining natural man for Adams was to determine whether there are certain laws in the natural state that man is obliged to respect for his own good and for the good of society as a whole. Associated with this task were two related questions: If there are indeed natural laws that man is obliged to follow, how are they known, and are they sanctioned by rewards and punishments?

According to Hobbes and Locke, human behavior is best understood by examining the passions. To that end, they developed the notion of a state of nature from which they were able to ask anew an old question in the history of political philosophy: Is man by nature a social animal? Their answer would revolutionize modern political thought. Hobbes and Locke denied the almost unanimous claim of classical political philosophy that man is social and political by nature. Man, they argued, is dominated, driven, and controlled by powerful antisocial passions. With his sights aimed directly at Aristotle, Hobbes concluded that "The Books of the old Moral Philosophers" are wrong in claiming "that the Felicity of this life, consisteth not in the repose of a satisfied mind," or that men may, "as Bees and Ants, live sociably one with another."[6] To the contrary: human felicity consists in a constant and ceaseless drive to satisfy all desires all the time. As a consequence, Hobbes argued, mankind is naturally inclined toward "a perpetuall and restless desire of Power after power, that ceaseth only in Death."[7] Such a desire constantly pits one man against another, thereby making man's natural condition one of constant struggle and conflict. In the prepolitical state, justice does not and cannot exist. Where there is no power to punish, there is no law, and where there is no law, there is only injustice.

Eventually, though, the fear of violent death and the desire for comfort and repose compel men to seek peace and justice. But Hobbes and Locke found that deductive reasoning is the principal means by which man discovers the necessity and benefits of civil society. The passions make government necessary for Hobbes, but reason shows man how to get there. The application of reason to man's untenable natural condition results in the discovery of certain rules by which men might live peaceably together. The first rule of reason, or law of nature, commands man "to seek Peace" and to defend oneself from those who do not value peace. The second law of nature commands men to give up their right to all things, but only on the condition that all others be willing to do the same. The third law of nature dictates that men should perform their covenants. Fidelity to contracts for Hobbes is the primary social law of nature, and its recognition is the necessary step in forming civil society. The rule of reason is not the rule of the state of nature, because most men are not sufficiently guided by reason. Because there can be little trust of contractual performance in the state of nature, because of the inability of men to punish others equitably and fairly for nonperformance of contracts, and because the laws of nature can hardly be law in the true sense of the word—that is, laws with sanctioning rewards and punishments—some kind of neutral arbiter is needed to adjudicate civil disputes between individuals and to prosecute and punish criminals. Eventually, individuals will come to see the reasonableness of joining together in the ultimate contract, the social contract. When all men are willing to give up certain rights, when they agree to perform all contractual obligations, and when they agree to transfer the right of punishment to a neutral arbiter, they reach the stage when civil government can be established. Justice and society, then, are not natural to man qua man; they are profoundly conventional.[8]

Adams accepted a modified Hobbesian-Lockean teaching that identified two fundamental laws of nature: the law of self-preservation and the law of respecting "the rights of others as much as [one's] own." Although he borrowed heavily from the English state of nature theorists, Adams broke from that tradition in significant ways. He conceded that "nature has sanctioned the law of self-preservation by rewards and punishments." The law of self-preservation, with its sanctioning rewards and punishments, is the fundamental fact of human existence. This axiomatic law of nature rewards selfish activity with "life and health, while negligence and indolence are punished by "want, disease, and death."[9] To this point, Adams was in full agreement with Hobbes and Locke.

But when Adams turns to the second law of nature, he dramatically modified the Hobbesian-Lockean natural-law teaching. Whereas Hobbes and Locke posited rational self-interest as guiding men into recognizing universal and reciprocal natural laws, Adams found a new basis for social peace and harmony. He rejected the Hobbesian-Lockean position that man can rationally deduce and then follow the dictates of reason by respecting the rights of others as he would have them respect his own. "Each individual, it is true," he claimed, "should consider, that nature has enjoined the same law on his neighbor, and therefore a respect for the authority of nature would oblige him to respect the rights of others as much as his own." But such "abstruse reasoning," Adams argued, though simple, "would not occur to all men." Reason, though an important element and guide in human life, was hardly a match for the passions. Although it is true that human beings should aim "at a *balance* of affections and appetites, under the monarchy of reason and conscience, within," it is more likely the case that the vast majority of mankind are incapable of living according to the rules of reason. The general run of mankind are driven by much deeper passions.[10]

Ancient and modern authors had not told the whole story about human nature, according to Adams. If it were true, as argued for by "Socrates and Plato, Cicero and Seneca, Hutcheson and Butler," that "reason is rightfully supreme in man," does it not follow that "it would be most suitable to the reason of mankind to have no civil or political government at all"? The assumption that reason is supreme in all men, Adams argued, logically points away from Nedham's simple democracy or Hobbes's Leviathan toward the anarchist alternative: "The moral government of God, and his viceregent, Conscience, ought to be sufficient to restrain men to obedience, to justice, and benevolence, at all times and in all places; we must therefore descend from the dignity of our nature, when we think of civil government at all."[11] But such a position was hardly tenable and could not be taken with any seriousness, according to Adams.

> The law of nature would be sufficient for the government of men, if they would consult their reason, and obey their consciences. It is not the fault of the law of nature, but of themselves, that it is not obeyed; it is not the fault of the law of nature that men are obliged to have recourse to civil government at all, but of themselves; it is not the fault of the ten commandments, but of themselves, that Jews or Christians are ever known to steal, murder, covet, or blaspheme. But the legislator who should say the law of nature is enough, if you do not obey it, it will be your own fault, therefore no other government is necessary, would be thought to trifle.

Any theory of human nature that elevated and took human rationality as its defining standard was thought by Adams to be wholly inadequate to the task of constitution making. Man's nature was not and should not be taken as synonymous with reason. He was willing to concede that some men live according to the dictates of reason, but it would be foolish for political scientists and lawgivers to take as their standard of human nature the reason and abilities of the wise and good. "There are some few," he conceded, "whose whole lives and conversations show that, in every thought, word and action, they conscientiously respect the rights of others." But those who consistently live by reason and benevolence are outnumbered by "a larger body still, who, in the general tenor of their thoughts and actions, discover similar principles and feelings, yet frequently err." When building constitutional structures, Adams thought it imperative for lawgivers always to remember that, "although reason ought always to govern individuals, it certainly never did since the Fall, and never will, till the Millenium." It was important, therefore, for constitutional architects to take human nature "as it is, as it has been, and will be." Any other approach to these questions would be utopian and illegitimate.[12]

A much more realistic and serviceable account of human nature taught that "the passions and appetites are parts of human nature, as well as reason and the moral sense." One need only study the "known constitution of the human mind and heart" and observe the "uniform experience" of mankind to know that "the law of nature, the decalogue, and all the civil laws" are all insufficient to check the passions. Indeed, a faithful study of human nature would show that "the passions are all unlimited" and that they "increase too, by exercise, like the body." The passions and not reason are the most politically relevant elements of human nature.[13]

This incomplete view of human nature was corrected by Adams when he discussed the second law of nature. Because reason does not teach all men to seek peace, nature has therefore obliged mankind to follow another law, "that of promoting the good, as well as respecting the rights of mankind." But this second law, while similar to Hobbes's second law of nature (mandating that men mutually relinquish some of their rights and respect those retained by all), is sanctioned by rewards and punishments entirely different from those described by Hobbes. Hobbes's rational but isolated man must ultimately resort to a neutral and wholly conventional arbiter, in the form of the state, to resolve conflicts and punish transgressors. Adams does concede that selfish asocial passions are strong in man, but he also says that they are countered by "Benevolence, or an affection for the good of others." Indeed, man is, and has always been, a social being, Adams argued, whether he be in "primitive conditions, however savage," or in any "stage of civilization." In fact, Adams could think of no time or place where man has not been naturally "gregarious." It is through his gregariousness that man is, in part, naturally social. Nature has furnished man with certain "passions, appetites, and propensities, as well as a variety of faculties" that promote both individual self-interest and natural community.[14]

Adams also recognized that benevolence is no match for the socially pernicious passions. It is a weak and distinctly limited affection. Most men, he wrote, "confine their benevolence to their families, relations, personal friends, parish, village city, county, province, and that very few, indeed, extend it impartially to the whole community." As an added support to benevolence, nature has therefore added a second quality: "the desire for reputation, in order to make us good members of society." It was here that Adams broke most decisively with Hobbes and Locke. This desire for reputation, or what Adams called the *spectemur agendo*," was a psychological mechanism peculiar to mankind that "expresses the great principle of activity for the good of others."[15] It is this universal human propensity, the *spectemur agendo*, that Adams took as the primary datum of human nature and social cohesiveness.

Generically, the meaning of the *spectemur agendo* is most easily understood by its literal translation: "Let us be seen in action."[16] To observe, and to be observed, is the strongest natural inclination of humankind. This basic passion, wrote Adams, "is the great spring of social activity." Men will always compare themselves to the actions and deeds of others, particularly with those whom they "most frequently converse." Friends, relatives, and one's closest "circle of acquaintances" provide the social sphere, the audience, and ultimately the gauge to which one looks for praise or censure. Within this tiny circle, all men, even the lowliest, seek "a kind of little grandeur and respect."[17]

The *spectemur agendo* performs its function in two important ways. On the one hand, virtue and social cooperation are rewarded in this life by the most effective of all rewards, "the *esteem* and *admiration* of others." On the other hand, vice and antisocial behavior are punished by the most effective of all punishments, by the fear of "*neglect* and *contempt*." The voice of nature has balanced in man's natural constitution a desire for praise with a fear of censure.

> The language of nature to man in his constitution is this—"I have given you reason, conscience, and benevolence; and thereby made you accountable for your actions, and capable of virtue, in which you

will find your highest felicity. But I have not confided wholly in your laudable improvement of these divine gifts. To them I have super-added in your bosoms a passion for the notice and regard of your fellow mortals, which, if you perversely violate your duty, and wholly neglect the part assigned you in the system of the world and the society of mankind, shall torture you from the cradle to the grave."[18]

In the very same way that man seeks the approbation of others, he proportionately dreads the neglect and disapprobation of those around him. Moreover, not only does man "desire the consideration of others," he will, more often than not, compare his station in life with those around him.[19] When men compare their position and reputation favorably vis-à-vis their friends and enemies, they rejoice, but when they see that others receive greater rewards and respect, they proportionally suffer a greater degree of affliction.

The fear of neglect and contempt, in particular, is a real and deciding passion in mankind; it is almost as powerful as the fear of death: "The desire of the esteem of others is a real want of nature as hunger; and the neglect and contempt of the world as severe a pain as the gout or stone. It sooner and oftener produces despair, and a detestation of existence." Men live and die for the recognition and acceptance of their fellows. Thus, "the *final* cause of this constitution of things," Adams determined, could be discovered with relative ease:

> Nature has ordained it, as a constant incentive to activity and industry, that, to acquire, the attention and complacency, the approbation and admiration of their fellows, men might be urged to constant exertions of beneficence. By this destination of their natures, men of all sorts, even those who have the least reason, virtue or benevolence, are chained down to an incessant servitude to their fellow creatures; laboring without intermissions to produce something which shall contribute to the comfort, convenience, pleasure, profit, or utility of some or other of the species, they are really thus constituted by their own vanity, slaves to mankind.[20]

In this extraordinary statement, Adams has established man as a social being and the relatedness or interconnectedness that he naturally shares with others. This passion "to be observed, considered, esteemed, praised, beloved, and admired by his fellows," observed Adams, "is one of the earliest, as well as keenest dispositions discovered in the heart of man." It is, in short, "the great leading passion of the soul," and "the history of mankind is little more than a simple narration of its operation and effects."[21]

For Adams, the science of government was reducible to understanding the passion for distinction, and the entire art of political architecture ought to be grounded on devising institutional arrangements for the purpose of regulating and channelling its dangerous and beneficial tendencies. Indeed, he thought it the "principal end of government" and the chief object of the lawgiver "to regulate this passion, which in its turn becomes a principal means of government."[22] For Adams, the desire for self-preservation was the principal prepolitical passion, the premise on which his science of politics developed a doctrine of natural rights, consent, and the social contract. But when discussing forms of government and constitutional architecture, the desire for self-preservation drops out of the discussion altogether and is replaced by man's fundamental social passion, the desire for distinction. The *spectemur agendo* is *the* political passion that must be reckoned with by the legislator.

Adams's writings on human nature provide an important and original reformulation of the modern natural-law teaching. He grounded this new theory on two fundamental axes: first, man is social or gregarious by nature; and second, sanctions for the laws of nature are woven deeply into the texture of human nature. This means that Adams found in man a natural, social passion. If man is naturally social and political, justice must therefore be preconventional or nonconventional. "Nature," Adams wrote, "has taken effectual care of her own work," and has "wrought the passions into the texture and essence of the soul." Such an ordering of man's constitution "is a determination of our nature, that lies at the foundation of our whole system in the world."[23] This extraordinarily subtle reformulation of the Hobbesian-Lockean natural-law teaching was central to Adams's political project. He found a sanction for natural law in human nature itself and not in divine judgment or through the retribution of the State. Human behavior and the laws of social interaction could now be understood primarily in terms of a mechanistic psychology of the passions, and this is precisely why Adams argued that the science of politics was inseparable from the science of human nature.

The Spectemur Agendo *and the Individual*

By Adams's own account, humankind has a natural longing for attention, congratulation, and admiration that is woven tightly and deeply into its natural constitution. For Adams, this desire for the recognition of others is real and universal, and it can be seen empirically, either by observing the day-to-day actions of the ordinary and the great, or by examining internally the operations of one's own desires, motives, and actions. For those who might doubt the existence of such a propensity, Adams recommended that they walk out into society, any society for that matter, and simply observe its natural operation. One need only watch, for instance,

> the journeymen and apprentices in the first workshop, or the oarsmen in a cockboat, a family or a neighborhood, the inhabitants of a house or the crew of a ship, or a school or a college, a city or a village, a savage or civilized people, a hospital or a church, the bar or the exchange, a camp or a court. Wherever men, women, or children, are to be found, whether they be old or young, rich or poor, high or low, wise or foolish, ignorant or learned, every individual is seen to be strongly actuated by a desire to be seen, heard, talked of, approved and respected, by the people about him, and within his knowledge.

Likewise, an honest and introspective man, by constant and often painful internal examination, can see how this passion drives his own thoughts and behavior. People are always looking inward, trying to determine, gauge, shape, and react to the "sentiments" and "dispositions" of others as concerns themselves. Every man, Adam wrote, feels this need within himself. Self-examination and "tried experiments" will demonstrate to every man that no "exertion of his reason" and no "effort of his will" can eradicate the human passion for attention and the fear of censure.[24]

In addition to its universality, the *spectemur agendo* is hierarchical and is ranked by many gradations, from the simple desire to be seen to congratulations to reputation to admiration to fame and to seemingly unlimited objects of ambition. At its lowest, the passion for distinction is simply a desire to be seen. Why is the poor man ashamed of his estate, Adams asked, when his conscience is clear and his character irreproachable? The answer is because he is unnoticed by those around him and he knows it. The poor soul stands in as much obscurity in the "midst of a crowd, at church, in the market, at a play, at an execution" as he does if he were locked away in a "garret or a cellar." Even worse: such a man "is not disapproved, censured, or reproached; he is only not seen." The poor man is alienated, not from the means of production, but rather from the attention and consideration of his fellow man. Shame rather than hunger is the source of his greatest suffering. To be "not seen," as Adams put it, is "mortifying, painful, and cruel." The worst fate suffered by man, Adams conjectured, is to "be wholly overlooked, and to know it." He sums up this cruel fate by recounting a pathetic story of human alienation. When the station of a man has become so wretched that he is invisible to "man, woman, or child," he finally looks for recognition in "the eyes of his dog": "'Who will love me then?' was the pathetic reply of one, who starved himself to feed his mastiff, to a charitable passenger, who advised him to kill or sell the animal. In this 'who will love me then?' there is a key to the human heart." Stepping up from "the last and the lowest of the human species," the general run of mankind pursue a common, low-grade kind of distinction; they desire a little "attention, consideration, and congratulation." At this level, Adams observed, the passion for distinction is generally sought after "by means which common sense and every day's experience show, are most sure to obtain it; by riches, by family, records, by play, and other frivolous personal accomplishments." Mere visibility, though, is not enough for most men. It is in this constant need to be seen, to compare oneself to others, that the cause of emulation and rivalries can be discovered between people. "There are no men," Adams wrote, "who are not ambitious of distinguishing themselves and growing considerable among those with whom they converse." Ambition and the passion for distinction are "natural to the human soul."[25]

Central to Adams's discussion of the *spectemur agendo* is the way in which that passion intensifies and increases exponentially as individuals rise in the world. As one's social horizon expands, so does one's passion for distinction. Such a passion becomes all-consuming, it inflames and engulfs the soul: "In proportion as men rise higher in the world, whether by election, descent, or appointment, and are exposed to the observation of greater numbers of people, the effects of their own passions and of the affections of others for them become more serious, interesting, and dangerous." The case of the rejected politician is instructive. Rarely are such individuals resigned to their fate, and only infrequently do they return quietly to private life. Instead, their breasts are full of "resentment and indignation, of grief and sorrow, of malice and revenge." The failed politician is more likely to be "employed in projects upon projects, intrigues after intrigues, and manoevres on manoevres, to recover" lost honors.[26] Even philosophers and mathematicians are driven by the passion for distinction and reputation. To be sure, some scholars are motivated by a genuine love of knowledge and truth, but "the universal object and idol of men of letters is *reputation*." Only "*notoriety*" and "*celebration*" can compensate to the scholar "the loss of appetite and sleep, and sometimes of riches and honors." This great desire for "congratulations" is, according to Adams, "the great incentive to the pursuit of honors." It is most obvious in those who seek a career in politics and, more particularly, in those who seek military glory. Adams then painted a vivid portrait of how all men in the military, from the lowest corporal to the most decorated general, look beyond their present position and aspire to something higher. It is this ceaseless desire to "draw the observation of more eyes" that compels mankind to ascend the ladder of social status and to surpass any and all competitors. As men climb the steps of ambition and success, the universal passion for distinction intensifies, expands, and grows "more furious."[27] And because some men have greater abilities or opportunities to attract the notice of the world and because the passion for distinction intensifies with exercise, some men become consumed with a desire to separate themselves from their peers, to vault past their circle of family, friends, acquaintances, and competitors.

At the highest levels, the desire for distinction tends to promote and nurture genius, "and the desire of superiority to create talents." At this level, one finds the special few "who aim at something more" than the simple attention, consideration, and congratulations of their immediate circle of family, friends, and community. Some, Adams observed, are consumed by an ambition that seeks the highest forms of distinction and praise: they seek the approbation, esteem and admiration from the largest audience possible. "Admiration" in particular is what this rare breed seeks. Indeed, they have an uncommon desire for admiration. Such individuals constantly crave more, even when they have no rival. Drawing on a passage in Adam Smith's *Theory of Moral Sentiments*, Adams dramatically described the man of common means but of extraordinary ambition and ability.

> With what impatience does the man of spirit and ambition, who is depressed by his situation, look round for some great opportunity to distinguish himself? No circumstances, which can afford this appear to him undesirable; he even looks forward with satisfaction to the prospect of foreign war, or civil dissension; and with secret transport and delight, sees, through all the confusion and bloodshed which attend them, the probability of those wished-for occasions presenting themselves, in which he may draw upon himself the attention and admiration of mankind.[28]

"This last description of persons," Adams wrote, "is the tribe out of which proceed your patriots and heroes, and most of the great benefactors to mankind." This powerful and constant need for the admiration of others, particularly among the "tribe of the eagle" as Abraham Lincoln once called them, will often manifest itself into two very different ways. On the one hand, it inclines some to "the most heroic actions in war, the sublimest virtues in peace, and the most useful industry in agriculture, arts, manufactures, and commerce," but on the other hand, it promotes "jealousies, envy, enmity, hatred, revenge, quarrels, factions, seditions, and wars" in others. It should never be forgotten by lawgivers that even among patriots and heroes the passion for distinction, "although refined by the purest sentiments . . . is a passion still; and therefore, like all human desires, unlimited and insatiable." This quality of the human heart, Adams said, provides the key to explaining "the history of human life and manners" and "the rise and fall of empires."[29]

If the *spectemur agendo* is the source of man's happiness and social interaction, it is also the cause of his unhappiness and enmity toward other men because it cuts in two directions. It is "a principal source of the virtues and vices, the happiness and misery of human life." When the passion for distinction "receives a happy turn, it is the source of private felicity and public prosperity," but it will often err, producing "private uneasiness and public calamities." Watching others excel, sometimes at our own expense, and the humilation associated with a loss of status and public reputation, is unbearable to many.

> In an army, or a navy, sometimes the interest of the service requires, and oftener perhaps private interest and partial favor prevail, to promote officers over their superiors or seniors. But the consequence is, that those officers can never serve again together. They must be distributed in different corps, or sent on different commands. Nor is this the worst effect. It almost universally happens, that the superseded officer feels his heart broken by his disgrace. His mind is enfeebled by grief, or disturbed by resentment.

So great is the anguish and disgrace felt by most men with a loss of status and reputation that their resentment is easily transformed into a desire for revenge. Hence the rise of competition and rivalry in society. When a man sees a rival gaining more than himself, he feels "a mortification . . . and a resentment of an injustice, as he thinks it." The injured man will almost always accuse "his rival of a theft or robbery, and the public to taking away what was his property, and giving it to another." Jealousy, envy, and rivalry are natural by-products of an ungratified *spectemur agendo*, and they "produce some of the keenest and most tormenting of all sentiments."[30] So awful is the mortification and feeling of public failure that some will commit crimes and cultivate vices to gain attention, while others will simply commit suicide.

What is true of individuals is also true of larger social and political groups. In the very same way that ambition perverted in individuals can lead to rivalries and competitions, so, too, with groups and various forms of social organization. Indeed, "on it turns the whole system of affairs." Within the same city, Adams explained, families, churches, fraternities, schools, colleges, trades, and districts will compete with one another. On an even larger scale, cities, provinces, and nations will challenge one another for superiority.[31] Adams was trying to teach his fellow republicans that the parties emerging in America after the ratification of the Federal Constitution were rooted in the same passions as those then ripping apart the French nation. In America, he ominously asked, are there not rivalries "between north and south? the middle and the north? the middle and the south? between one state and another? between the government of the states and the national government? and between individual patriots and heroes in all these?" The natural remedy against these dangerous rivalries, Adams urged, was a "well-balanced constitution, such as that our Union purports to be." In this dark and fateful hour, it was imperative that faithful republicans and loyal Americans support their Constitution "as our only hope for peace and our ark of safety," at least until the constitution's "defects, if it has any, can be corrected."[32]

Spectemur Agendo *and the Social Order*

Jealousy, envy, and the desire for revenge were not for Adams the only reactions that men have toward the superiority of others. If resentment were the ruling passion of most men, society would be in a condition of nature requiring something akin to Hobbes's Leviathan state to control the rivalries and competitions resulting from man's mortified emulation. Fortunately, this is not how most men react to the superior condition of an elite few. Indeed, the reaction of mankind in general to those endowed with the blessings of fortune and ability is just the opposite. The natural inclination of most men is to stare and gawk, to esteem, admire, and congratulate those of superior rank or abilities. The deference that the common man feels for the superior and the great is as natural to his constitution as is his desire for distinction; indeed, it is a central component of the *spectemur agendo*.

How are the standards and objects of that deference determined? What qualities do men admire in others? Why do certain human qualities

and actions bring attention and congratulation, whereas some are not no-
ticed and others bring inattention and disgrace? Are the objects of attention natural and universal or are they strictly conventional and parochial?
Most of all, how does this human passion order social behavior?

Ultimately, the things that men most admire and esteem are ranked
along a naturally ordered hierarchy of public ends. That ranking, however, is not necessarily related to the final causes of human happiness. In
fact, it presupposes a reversal of what would be ranked as most virtuous by
the philosopher or the liberal mind. "A wise man," Adams said, "will
lament that any other distinction than that of merit should be made."
The liberal mind admires the man of substance and ability, but he carries
almost no weight with mankind in general. Society is much more disposed to rank beauty, strength, and elegance of person over genius, talents, and virtue, and they are more likely to elevate the "gifts of fortune
and birth, wealth and fame" over both. "The homage of the world,"
Adams noted, "is devoted to these last in a remarkable manner." Why
should this be so? To the wise man and to the liberal mind, for instance,
it is a "curious" fact that the final causes of human happiness do not correspond in any way to the things in society that elicit the most attention
and admiration. Although the intellectual and moral virtues, followed by
health, strength, and agility are the qualities most essential to human
happiness, they are secondary in the eyes of the world to those of birth,
riches, and honors. Indeed, it is not genuine happiness or the summum
bonum that most men seek; it is, rather, the simple desire to be seen and
congratulated that most men aspire to. "Beauty in the face, elegance in
figure, grace of attitude and motion, riches, honors, every thing," Adams
observed, are all "weighed in the scale, and desired, not so much for the
pleasure they afford, as the attention they command." Society therefore
ranks the qualities that produce human happiness in an order opposite to
the one that produces genuine happiness.

> The intellectual and moral qualities are most within our power, and
> undoubtedly the most essential to our happiness. The personal quali-
> ties of health, strength, and agility, are next in importance. Yet the
> qualities of fortune, such as birth, riches, and honors, though a man
> has less reason to esteem himself for these than for those of the mind
> or body, are everywhere acknowledged to glitter with the brightest
> lustre in the eyes of the world.[33]

The difficult task for Adams's political scientist is to explain why
mankind value the qualities of fortune over the intellectual, moral, and

personal qualities. Why should beauty, birth, and riches, glitter with a brighter luster in the eyes of the world than wisdom and virtue? A full answer would have required that Adams examine the "physical" causes of human approbation, emulation, and deference, but such causes were thought by Adams to be "wholly unknown" in the eighteenth century. He recognized and understood the limits of the moral and intellectual sciences of his day. In the end, Adams was only able to offer a provisional answer: beauty, wealth, and birth bring the kind of notice that wisdom and virtue do not because they are seen, they are tangible, and they bring attention, whereas the qualities of wisdom and virtue are unseen, submerged, or simply not understood by most people. More to the point, "the gifts of fortune are more level to the capacities, and more obvious to the notice of mankind in general."[34] Democracies in particular, Adams warned, were prone to establishing standards of social approbation at levels that have far less to do with personal qualities than with qualities of fortune.

Take beauty, for instance. Why, Adams asked, "are the personal accomplishments of beauty, elegance, and grace, held in such high estimation by mankind?" They are rarely admired for their purely aesthetic value; instead, they are esteemed only to the degree that they "command the notice and attention of the public; they draw the eyes of spectators." Adams had no doubt that there was "in natural as well as artificial Society a Privileged Order of Beauty." Would Helvetius or Rousseau say, he once asked of John Taylor, "that all men and women are born equal in beauty?" Indeed, is there any philosopher, Adams asked, who will say "that beauty has no influence in society?" So strong is the public taste for beauty in face and figure that it is generally more admired than virtues generally thought to be of greater importance to individual happiness or to the public good. "You may laugh at the introduction of Beauty, among the Pillars of Aristocracy," Adams wrote to Jefferson some years later, but "Beauty, Grace, Figure, Attitude, Movement, have in innumerable Instances prevailed over Wealth, Birth, Talents Virtues and every thing else, in Men of the highest rank, greatest Power, and sometimes, the most exalted Genius, greatest Fame, and highest Merit."[35]

Odder yet is the admiration bestowed on those of illustrious birth. Adams rejected on moral grounds the notion that noble birth "should make a difference between one man and another?" But the inequality of social rank that flourishes in society is rarely, if ever, founded on reason, merit, or virtue. It relies on much more powerful forces: social prejudice and custom. The poor boy who rises from obscurity to wealth never attracts the same kind of attention bestowed on those of illustrious birth. Why, Adams asked, does it matter whether one's noble heritage is "twenty generations upon record, or only two?" The great "secret," he answered, "lies in this: an illustrious descent attracts the notice of mankind." Why should this be so, he asked? Even though the majority will be indignant and envious of the nobility, the nobility nevertheless "attracts the *attention* of the world." In fact, nobility, Adams declared, whether hereditary or elective, is most esteemed in republics; indeed, admiring them becomes a "national habit." A young man who inherits a noble name long admired by the public "attracts the eyes and ears of all companies long before it is known or inquired whether he be a wise man or a fool. His name is often a greater distinction than a title, a star, or a garter."[36]

What is true of noble birth is also true of wealth. Adams began the third *Davila* essay with the most provocative of questions, Why do men pursue wealth? Like Tocqueville's description of the "adventurous American,"[37] Adams says that the "labor and anxiety, the enterprises and adventures, that are voluntarily undertaken in pursuit of gain, are out of all proportion to the utility, convenience, or pleasure or riches." The necessities of life are gained relatively easily, but there are no limits to what men will risk in pursuit of trinkets and baubles.

> For what reason, then, are any mortals averse to the situation of the farmer, mechanic, or laborer? Why do we tempt the seas and encompass the globe? Why do any men affront heaven and earth to accumulate wealth, which will forever be useless to them? Why do we make an ostentatious display of riches? Why should any man be proud of his purse, houses, land, or gardens? or, in better words, why should the rich man glory in his riches? What connection can there be between wealth and pride?[38]

The last question bears repeating, What connection can there be between wealth and pride? For Adams, the answer was simple. Men seek wealth and riches because "there is more respectability, in the eyes of the greater part of mankind, in the gaudy trappings of wealth, than there is in genius or learning, wisdom or virtue." Wealth is driven by pride and the desire for distinction. It is not so much the ease and comfort, beneficence or utility, associated with great wealth that sends men on this frantic quest; rather, it is the desire for "illustration" that propels men to risk life and limb.[39]

Although the tendency of the many to esteem the qualities of fortune over personal qualities may not be in conformity with reason and

philosophy, Adams, in his capacity as a political scientist, was more concerned with recognizing and understanding the reality, the natural
propensity of the people to "consider the condition of the great in all
those delusive colors, in which imagination can paint and guild it," the
reasons why they do, and the social consequences that follow from this
social deference. He recognized that some men will view their condition
vis-à-vis the great and powerful as unjust or unfair, and that they will respond to the rank of their social superiors with envy and jealousy. But
this is not the reaction of most men to the gifts of fortune borne to the
few. Rather than resenting the privileges of the great, the common man
responds favorably and aspires to the good fortune of the social elite. In
fact, the people feel a "peculiar sympathy" with the presumed "pleasures" of the "powerful, celebrated and rich"; they "favor all their inclinations, and forward all their wishes."[40] The natural sympathy that the
common man feels for those rich in the gifts of fortune is a product of
the imagination's representation of an ideal that most men wish for and
aspire to. The rise of distinctions of rank in society is natural, according
to Adams, but less because the few are naturally superior and more because the many are naturally deferential.

At the foundation of Adams's argument, then, was the assumption
that the principle of deference is natural to human beings and that the
many esteem and almost always follow the few. Aristocracies may take on
a variety of forms, but aristocracies there will always be. It was here, in the
"disposition of mankind, to go along with all the passions of the rich and
powerful," that Adams found a key to the origin of the distinction of rank
or orders in society. The "obsequiousness" of the many to the few had less
to do with a utilitarian "expectation of benefit from their good will" and
more to do with a "desire to serve them for their own sake." The common
man is eager to "assist" the great man "in completing a system of happiness that approaches so near to perfection."[41] Deference, seen as a natural
mechanism of the human psyche, is a principal means by which society
controls and orders itself.

Inequality and Aristocracy

No account of Adams's theory of human nature would be complete without a discussion of his views on aristocracy. No subject interested Adams
more than the nature and origins of human inequality. He told Jefferson
in 1813 that he had been "writing Upon that Subject" for almost thirty
years.[42] Without question, Adams's discussion and analysis of inequality

and aristocracy is and always has been the most controversial and certainly the most misunderstood element of his political thought. From the time he published *A Defence,* he has been accused of harboring aristocratic ambitions and of promoting aristocracy throughout America. Responding to his critics, Adams challenged them to find one instance in his writings that could be interpreted as favoring the introduction of aristocratic orders in America. A fair and just interpretation of Adams's political thought turns on this challenge.

When discussing Adams's views on equality and inequality, it is important that we analyze those ideas in the context of his debate with the French *philosophes.* Turgot, it will be recalled, had written that republics should be "founded on the equality of all the citizens, and, therefore, 'orders' and 'equilibriums' are unnecessary, and occasion disputes." But Adams demanded to know what Turgot and the other democratic intellectuals meant by equality? "Are the citizens to be all of the same age, sex, size, strength, stature, activity, courage, hardiness, industry, patience, ingenuity, wealth, knowledge, fame, wit, temperance, constancy, and wisdom?" he asked incredulously. Adams knew of no nation in history and could imagine none in the future where "individuals were all equal, in natural and acquired qualities, in virtues, talents, and riches."[43]

Adams recognized only one kind of equality. Equality meant equal rights and duties, nothing more and nothing less. This conviction—developed in his earliest pre-Revolutionary writings and never relinquished in his later writings—that all men are equal with regard to certain rights that they derive from nature and God formed the bedrock of his political thought. From this position he never wavered. In his own state of Massachusetts, for instance, he delighted in acknowledging that "there is . . . a moral and political equality of rights and duties among all the individuals," and he applauded the fact that there is "as yet no appearance of artificial inequalities of condition, such as hereditary dignities, titles, magistracies, or legal distinctions." But this unique experiment in human history should not mislead political scientists and those who would build new governments. In every state, even in America, there are and always will be "inequalities which God and nature have planted there, and which no human legislator ever can eradicate." This was the kind of bare-knuckled advice that Adams felt compelled to share with potential lawgivers in France and America. These inequalities should be "of great moment in the consideration of a legislator," he advised, "because they have a natural and an inevitable influence in society." The equality of rights that one may find in Massachusetts should not deceive legislators into thinking that men are, should, or could be equal in all respects for any length of time. An unwillingness to study, acknowledge, and take into account the nature and origins of human inequality had been, from Adams's perspective, the great failing of the French intelligentsia.

> That all men are born to equal rights is true. Every being has a right to his own, as clear, as moral, as sacred, as any other being has. This is as indubitable as a moral government in the universe. But to teach that all men are born with equal powers and faculties, to equal influence in society, to equal property and advantages through life, is as gross a fraud, as glaring an imposition on the credulity of the people, as ever was practised by monks, by Druids, by Brahmins, by priests of the immortal Lama, or by the self-styled philosophers of the French revolution.[44]

If men are equal only in regard to the rights they claim by nature, the question for lawgivers becomes the following: What are the inequalities of human nature that are relevant to constitution making? Adams assumed as an undeniable fact of human nature that men are not only different but inherently unequal with regard to strength, intelligence, beauty, virtue, and all the elements that make up the physical and mental constitution of human nature. Equality, for Adams, did not mean sameness: "By the law of nature, all men are men, and not angels—men, and not lions—men, and not whales—men, and not eagles—that is, they are all of the same species." But he was the first to recognize that "Man differs by nature from man, almost as much as man from beast." Physical and intellectual inequalities are unchangeably established "by the Author of nature."[45] Indeed, invoking a familiar eighteenth-century metaphor, Adams spoke of nature as a hierarchical chain of being:

> Nature, which has established in the universe a chain of being and universal order, descending from archangels to microscopic animalcules, has ordained that no two objects shall be perfectly alike, and no two creatures perfectly equal. Although, among men, all are subject by nature to *equal laws* of morality, and in society have a right to equal laws for their government, yet no two men are perfectly equal in person, property, understanding, activity, and virtue, or ever can be made so by any power less than that which created them.[46]

As he would demand of John Taylor some years later, Adams insisted that terms "be defined before we can reason." This he attempted, in part, by a

kind of relentless Socratic questioning. Whether his interlocutor be Turgot, Condorcet, Jefferson, or Taylor, Adams would assault his opponent
with a barrage of questions that were theoretical in nature but solidly
grounded in reality. "Are there, or are there not," he asked, "physical, cor-
poreal, material inequalities among mankind, from the embryo to the
tomb?" "Are there, or are there not," he continued, "intellectual inequalities from the first opening of the senses, the sight, the hearing, the taste,
the smell, and the touch, to the final loss of all sense? Are there not moral
inequalities, discernable almost, if not quite, from the original innocence
to the last stage of guilt and depravity?" And if the answer to these questions was definitively "yes," and for Adams it clearly was, the conclusion
was necessarily obvious: "From these inequalities, physical, intellectual,
and moral, does there or does there not arise a natural aristocracy among
mankind? or, in other words, some men who have greater capacities and
advantages to acquire the love, esteem, and respect of their fellow men,
more wealth, fame, consideration, honor, influence, and power in society
than other men?"[47]

The politically relevant inequalities of human nature originate, however, only in part from one's natural abilities. Physical, intellectual, and
moral abilities are, in and of themselves, insufficient causes of social, economic, and political inequality. Inequality, as it relates to man as a social
creature, is connected too and emanates from the *spectemur agendo:* "God,
in the constitution of nature, has ordained that every man shall have a
disposition to emulation, as well as imitation, and consequently a passion
for distinction; and that all men shall not have equal means and opportunities of gratifying it."[48] The need, the inherent disposition of men to
distinguish themselves from their circle of family, friends, community, and
nation is the *efficient* cause, the source of all social and political inequality. Inequality is directly linked to natural and conventional standards, to
the objects of social status and to the standards of social emulation. If the
doctrine of equality was indeed an invention, a "gross fraud" perpetrated
by French philosophers, it could hardly be the basis for a theory of republican government.

In the *Defence,* and throughout his life, Adams identified three sources
of social inequality, "inequalities of great moment in the consideration of
a legislator": first, inequalities of wealth; second, inequalities of birth; and
third, inequalities of abilities.[49] These inequalities, it should be noted,
were understood by Adams to be *natural,* that is, they could be found in
all societies and throughout all time. They were not necessarily the product of, or owed their existence to, artificially created legal barriers. Indeed,

he thought these and "many other natural and acquired habitual inequalities" were "visible, and palpable, and audible, every day, in every village, and in every family, in the whole world." It was simply wrong, he told John Taylor, to think that

> aristocracy consists altogether in artificial titles, tinsel, decorations of stars, garters, ribbons, golden eagles and golden fleeces, crosses and roses and lilies, exclusive privileges, hereditary descents, established by kings, or by positive laws of society. No such thing! Aristocracy was, from the beginning, now is, and ever will be, world without end, independent of all these artificial regulations, as really and as efficaciously as with them!

Natural human inequality is the basis for the natural aristocracy. By "*natural aristocracy*," Adams meant "those superiorities of influence in society which grow out of the constitution of human nature." He defined an "*artificial aristocracy*," by way of contrast, as "those inequalities of weight and superiorities of influence which are created and established by civil laws." The key concept in Adams's definition of aristocracy—and he insisted on strict definitions—is the notion of "influence." When Adams spoke of aristocracy, he meant "all those men who can command, influence, or procure more than an average of votes." An aristocrat was any "man who can and will influence one man to vote besides himself." Put another way, an aristocrat was a man "who can command or influence *two votes; one besides his own.*"[50]

The special influence that some men hold over others has much less to do with legal distinctions than it has to do with the nature of human inequality and the role that the *spectemur agendo* plays in human affairs. He thought such inequalities were "a part of the natural history of man."[51] For a meaningful science of politics, even for a science of politics in the service of democracy, it was important for Adams to study the natural ranks and orders on which societies organize and arrange their social and political institutions.

Inequalities of wealth, according to Adams, derive principally from inheritance or, more frequently, "from greater skill, industry, and success in business." Those without or with little property—those "in the various trades, manufactures, and other occupations in life"—are "dependent," he wrote, on the rich for their livelihood, whereas even those with modest wealth are often either in "debt" to or under "obligations" to the wealthy. Others, like men of letters and men of the learned professions, who are neither dependent upon nor inside the web of the wealthy man's economic power and influence, are nevertheless "connected with them and at-tached to them." Indeed, even among the wisest that live, "there is a de-gree of admiration, abstracted from all dependence, obligation, expectation, or even acquaintance, which accompanies splendid wealth, insures some respect, and bestows some influence."[52]

Adams's discussion of the inequalities of birth was in his day the most controversial and certainly the most misunderstood element of his polit-ical thought. Again, it is important to remember that Adams was analyz-ing the role of noble birth or prominent families from the perspective of a political scientist and a lawgiver, and not as a partisan of inherited no-bility. As a student of the political and social sciences, history demon-strated to Adams that no society, ancient or modern, civilized or savage, had ever existed that did not make a distinction between its citizens "on account of their extraction." In fact, it was Adams's established opinion "that more influence is allowed to this advantage in free republics than in despotic governments, or than would be allowed to it in simple monar-chies, if severe laws had not been made from age to age to secure it." But why should this be so, particularly in a republic? Among the lesser reasons why the children of illustrious families assume a natural superiority in so-ciety, Adams mentioned their greater advantages of education and earlier opportunities to become associated with public characters and informed of public affairs. Most importantly, however, Adams suggested that a "ha-bitual national veneration" for the names and the characters of a promi-nent family's "ancestors described in history, or coming down by tradition, removes them farther from vulgar jealousy and popular envy, and secures them in some degree the favor, the affection, and respect of the public." It should not be forgotten that Adams is not speaking here of England or France, but of America: "Go into every village in New England, and you will find that the office of justice of the peace, and even the place of rep-resentative, which has ever depended only on the freest election of the people, have generally descended from generation to generation, in three or four families at most." There are in all societies, Adams argued, certain families that accumulate and possess over time "some degree of family pride," and "who have been invariably encouraged, if not flattered in it, by the people." It is crucial to an understanding of his political science to note that, for Adams, the social and political inequality and privilege ac-corded certain families in democratic regimes were a consequence of the people's natural approbation. Thus, the existence of aristocratic families in democracies has a basis in man's natural constitution. Eventually, these families develop a certain "acquaintance, esteem, and friendship with each other, and mutually aid each other's schemes of interest, convenience, and ambition." It was here, in the rise of an elevated sense of family pride, that Adams found the most honorable and the most dangerous forms of political influence.[53]

Lastly, Adams considered those natural, social inequalities based on "merit, or talents, virtues, [and] services."[54] Merit and virtue, he said, produce a kind of reputation and fame that cannot be acquired by or associated with birth or wealth. But men of superior talents and abilities, particularly if they are from modest means, do not carry the same kind of immediate and visible influence that men of wealth and birth do. How, then, does the young man of ordinary means but of extraordinary ability come to the attention of the public? Traditionally, there had been just two means by which superior men of inferior station could attain public reputation and social rank: war and politics. There were some, for instance, who, "in a long course of service in an army, have devoted their time, health, and fortunes, signalized their courage and address, exposed themselves to hardships and dangers, lost their limbs, and shed their blood, for the people." Others, by demonstrating wisdom, learning, and eloquence in the political arena, may acquire "the confidence and affection of their fellow-citizens to such a degree, that the public have settled into a kind of habit of following their example and taking their advice." In order to acquire the admiration and influence reserved by society to the wealthy and noble, the ordinary man of extraordinary abilities must first "acquire dependents to balance the dependents of the great." This he does by diligently applying "the labor of his body, and the activity of his mind," that is, by consistently cultivating and practicing over a long period of time the "more important virtues":

> He must acquire superior knowledge in his profession, and superior industry in the exercise of it; he must be patient in labor, resolute in danger, and firm in distress. These talents he must bring into public view, by the difficulty, importance, and at the same time, good judgement, of his undertakings, and by the severe and unrelenting application with which he pursues them. Probity and prudence, generosity and frankness, must characterize his behavior upon all ordinary occasions; and he must at the same time, be forward to engage in all those situations, in which it requires the greatest talents and virtues to act with propriety; but in which the greatest applause is to be acquired by those who can acquit themselves with honor.[55]

The man of uncommon ability and virtue must work twice as hard and twice as long to mount the stage of public notice. As a philosopher, there can be no doubt that Adams would have preferred that talent and integrity be the ultimate objects of social attention, but as a social scientist, he had learned from a lifetime of empirical observation of daily experience that "Birth and Wealth together have prevailed over Virtue and Talents in all ages." This was so not because of artificial legal supports, but rather because "the Many, will acknowledge no other 'aristocrats.'"[56]

Years later, when Thomas Jefferson asked, "who are the aristoi?" Adams replied that philosophy would answer "'The Wise and Good.'" But he also knew the answer of mankind was very different. There was no place in the world, Adams thought, where the common man did not elevate in his daily practice "'the rich the beautiful and well born'" above everyone else. Even philosophers, Adams mocked, preferred their children to marry the "rich the handsome and the well descended" over "the wise and the good." And regardless of whether he and Jefferson might think such an ordering unjust and founded on "Prejudice, Folly, Ignorance, Baseness, Slavery, Stupidity, Adulation, Superstition," it was nevertheless a "Fact" demonstrated by "natural, moral, political and domestic History." Is "this great Fact in the natural History of Man to be overlooked, forgotten neglected, or hypocritically waived out of Sight; by a Legislator?" he asked Jefferson.[57] His answer was clear and to the point: the natural basis of distinction was precisely what political scientists and legislators must always keep in mind when designing and constructing republican constitutions.

Unlike the French philosophers of democracy, Adams advised his lawgivers to design and construct constitutions on the basis of how men actually live and not on some philosophical abstraction as to how they might or should live. The study and true understanding of human nature represented for Adams the permanent ground on which a wise political architect must build a strong and durable constititution. But in a revolutionary world where any and all utopian hopes became realities in the minds of men, the sober advice of men like John Adams would fall on deaf ears.

Adams's contemporaries failed to appreciate this fact. Too often Adams's analysis of human nature, particularly his discussion of human inequality and aristocracy, has been misinterpreted as a moral and political prescription rather than as a factual description. Responding to his critics on this very point, Adams adamantly denied that he had ever said anything "about the Right of Aristocracy." To the contrary, he had only "remarked the Fact," he said, as a "Chymist or a natural Historian would note down a Phenomenon, as he observed it, in a natural body. And reasoned from Facts."[58] We simply cannot know Adams's political thought without recognizing this fundamental distinction. He spoke of inequality and of aristocracy not as a political partisan, but from the perspective of an impartial spectator. Adams was not advocating but rather was attempting to understand and explain man's social and political behavior in terms of a theory of human motivation.

In his analysis of the constitution of the human mind, in his discussion of equality and inequality and of the rise of social ranks and orders, John Adams trod on turf that few men in post-Revolutionary America dared to walk. Unlike Madison or Hamilton in *The Federalist*, John Adams was not writing for mass consumption. He addressed the *Defence* and *Davila* essays to a very specific audience: to those in America and Europe who were constructing new constitutions or rebuilding old ones. The very nature of his audience and the importance of the task demanded of Adams, or so he thought, that he speak only the truth, that he share with all future lawgivers the findings of his investigations into history and human nature. But sometimes the truth is a bitter pill, and its messenger suffers the slings and arrows of public censure. This is certainly true in democratic regimes, and it was particularly true for John Adams. It is our responsibility, therefore, to recreate faithfully and accurately Adams's arguments and true intentions, to rise above that Whiggish temptation that relegates to historical irrelevance ideas that have seemingly lost in the battle of partisan politics. We must also consider and judge the merits and demerits, the truth or untruth, of ideas that so uncomfortably challenge our most deeply held national symbols.

Chapter 9

Republican Government

In September 1790, John Adams wrote his cousin Samuel Adams asking rhetorically what was to become of the world at this critical moment in history. John was certain that "Every thing will be pulled down." But what, he demanded to know, "will be built up?" This was the great political question for all thinking revolutionaries at the end of the eighteenth century, and it was the question on which Adams parted company with many of his republican comrades. "Are there any principles of political architecture?" he asked. If there are, "what are they?" He mocked the idea that Voltaire, Rousseau, and their French disciples understood such principles. Despite having learned "the principles of liberty" from Locke, he very much doubted whether French Revolutionaries understood "the principles of Government."[1] Most eighteenth-century republicans could agree that Locke's principles of liberty provided the necessary philosophical foundation for the construction of new governments, but they seemed hopelessly divided over the principles of government. Montesquieu's *The Spirit of the Laws* and Rousseau's *The Social Contract* represent the most obvious points of departure. Having brought philosophy down from the heavens, revolutionary statesmen on both sides of the Atlantic now confronted the very real task of translating theory into practice.

The question of the best regime is, of course, as old as political philosophy itself. Years earlier, Adams had charged Pope with flattering tyrants in his famous couplet, "For forms of government let fools contest, That which is best administered is best." Adams thought nothing more fallacious. To the contrary: he thought that history and human nature demonstrated irrefutably "that some forms of government are better fitted for being well administered than others."[2] This is precisely why Adams took his debate with Turgot and Condorcet so seriously. At stake was nothing less than the future of free government. He wrote A *Defence of the Constitutions* "especially" to counter "the weak, vain projects" of the Turgotists, whom Adams saw "were about setting the universe in a blazing bon-fire, by their presumptuous ignorance and shallow jurisprudence."

He charged France's revolutionary philosophers with being slaves to their own formulaic abstractions. Adams thought the circle of young reform liberals who rallied around Turgot's economic and political ideas to be novices "in all that relates to free government" and superficial in "their reading in the science of government." He accused them of understanding "nothing of Government, or the System of Liberty": they never "closely reasoned upon government, as it appears in history, as it is founded in nature, or as it has been represented by philosophers, priests, and politicians, who have written upon the subject. They have picked up scraps, but digested nothing."[3]

The single theme that unites the *Defence* is that a properly mixed and balanced constitution is superior to that of a simple democratic government in a unicameral assembly. Adams therefore wrote his *Defence* with two general purposes in mind: the first was to criticize the theory of simple democratic government then being advocated by Turgot, Condorcet, Paine and radical republicans in America, and the second was to defend the theory of mixed and balanced governments found in some of the American state constitutions. His attack on the theory of simple democratic government was advanced on three related fronts: first, he had to tear down the theory of simple government then popular in France and America; second, he had to correct the common use and abuse of republican language in eighteenth-century political discourse; and finally, he had to expose certain counterfeit theories of republican virtue.

The Critique of Simple Government

The immediate task of the *Defence* was to answer Turgot's claim that the best constitutional form was a simple democratic government. Adams thought Turgot's proposal "the most interesting subject which can employ the thoughts of men," that is, "to consider in what manner such an assembly will conduct its deliberations and exert its power."[4] To that end, he dissected the theory of simple democratic governments, and he examined the political, social, and psychological pathologies to which that constitutional form was particularly vulnerable.

Drawing on his study of history and his examination of human nature, Adams sought to demonstrate that the promise of unicameral legislatures was thoroughly utopian. It was impossible, he thought, for pure democracy to retain its structural and substantive integrity over an extended period of time. Such a government, he warned, "will upon the first day of its existence, be an aristocracy; in a few days, or at least years, an oligarchy;

and then it will divide into two or three parties, who will soon have as many armies; after which, when the battle is decided, the victorious general will govern without or with the advice of any council or assembly, as he pleases." How was this possible? On what basis could he defend this remarkable claim? All communities, according to Adams, naturally divide into three elements or social orders of the one, the few and the many. The inevitable stratification of society was not unlike "air, oil, and water, shaken together in one bottle and left in repose." Eventually "the first will rise to the top, the last sink to the bottom, and the second swim between." This was particularly true, he said, of a free society based on an equality of rights, for in such communities the possibilities and potential of human nature flower most easily.[5] How or why should this division be natural?

The source of this social division was for Adams found in human nature. The hierarchic order of man's natural constitution (i.e., the natural differences of beauty, strength, intelligence, wisdom, and virtue), when combined with the radically inflationary character of the *spectemur agendo* and mankind's natural deference will eventually lead to the development of distinct and thoroughly natural social orders. These differences, Adams remarked, are found in all societies, from the simplest to the most complex. They are natural rather than conventional divisions, and they are the solvents that eliminate the possibility of true democratic equality. Even the most virtuous society emerging from an uncorrupted state of nature will, upon their first election of a new government, choose predominantly from those with the greatest ambition and from those whose influence carries the greatest weight with ordinary people. Men of ambition will always find their way into government or places of power. "There is not a city nor a village, any more than a kingdom or a commonwealth, in Europe or America; not a horde, clan, or tribe, among the negroes of Africa, or the savages of North or South America," he concluded, "in which inequalities are not more or less visible." With time, as society becomes more settled, prosperous, and conventional, wealth and birth are superadded to the natural inequalities. More often than not, the concentration of wealth will lead to a consolidation of social and political power. In other words, the aggressively ambitious will use whatever means necessary to secure the people's appointment. If they cannot enter through the front door, they will enter through the back; if they are legally prohibited from serving in a unicameral legislature, they will "still govern the state underhand." The power and influence of this new aristocracy, Adams observed, though more than reason and equity could justify, would forever dominate in societies as long as human nature shall have passions and imagination.[6]

Adams scholars most often present his analysis of the naturally occuring social orders as though there were just two, the few and the many. But he frequently argued in the *Defence* that in "all independent bodies of men" there seemed a natural division into "three powers, of the one, the few, and the many." Elsewhere in the *Defence*, quoting Machiavelli for support, Adams advised those who frame constitutions to "'take such provisions as may gratify three *sorts* of men, of which all states are composed.'" He seemed to be suggesting that in all societies, natural and conventional, there was indeed some basis for a natural order of the one. This elevated rank did not, however, represent a fixed or an enduring class. Instead, the natural order of the one represented for Adams a type of character, a naturally occuring phenomenon common to all societies. In the very same way that the natural aristocracy arises out of ambition and deference, so too with the elevation of the one. There is in the "constitution of men's minds," Adams explained, a universal need to "determine who is the first man." If left unsettled, the question of who shall become the first magistrate "will forever disorder the state." Among the natural aristocracy, there will always be some "great genius,—some one masterly spirit, who unites in himself all the qualities which constitute the natural foundations of authority, such as benevolence, wisdom, and power; and all the adventitious attractions of respect, such as riches, ancestry, and personal merit." These men of superior abilities and unlimited ambition seek to stand above all others. They do not represent an existing class or social order but only themselves. Thus, among the natural leaders of any society, there will always arise a handful of men whose "hopes and endeavors" are directed toward "universal monarchy." More importantly, the people themselves desire and are naturally disposed to selecting and elevating one man above all others. "It is strictly true," Adams observed, "that there is a strong and continual effort in every society of man, arising from the constitution of their minds, towards a kingly power." There are always a few outstanding individuals in every society who attract the attention and the affections of the people more than all others. Admired and respected, put on a pedestal, these unique individuals "acquire an influence and ascendency that it is difficult to resist." To support his claim, Adams could find no example in his systematic examination of ancient and modern history of either a free or unfree government that did not have a "principal personage." He thought it entirely reasonable to conclude that "the body politic cannot subsist, any more than the animal body, without a head."[7] Better to recognize such human types, Adams thought, than to allow them to corrupt the legislative power.

Doubtless, Adams would have preferred to see wisdom and virtue as the defining characteristics of America's natural aristocracy, but he knew that such was not and could never be the case. It is important to note, however, that Adams did not necessarily see these inequalities as representing a fixed order of classes, at least not in America. Hierarchy would always exist, but the American hierarchy was based on a shifting scale. Although birth, according to Adams, was one of its foundations, America's natural aristocracy had less to do with hereditary institutions or special privileges and more to do with old and distinguished families that for one reason or another had secured the natural deference of the people. Adams's natural aristocracy was primarily an aristocracy of influence. Its authority was possible only because the people naturally defer to those they think their natural superiors.[8] Hence, it would be a grave error to think that Adams wished to alter or reorder the social divisions within America. As long as these distinctions were not reinforced by laws, formalized class distinctions, or hereditary institutions such as the Society of the Cincinnati, it was a price Adams was willing to pay for the privilege of living in a free society.

Nor should it be forgotten, Adams reminded his readers, that even the most wise and virtuous, those most concerned with the public good, will find in their souls an admixture of self-interest and ambition. He was more than willing to concede that benevolence and the more generous affections are important elements in man's natural constitution, but they are too often ineffectual against the self-regarding passions. To support these claims, Adams insisted that "every moral theorist will admit the selfish passions in the generality of men to be the strongest." There was simply no escaping the fact that "self-interest, private avidity, ambition, and avarice will exist in every state of society, and under every form of government." According to Adams, no form of government was more aptly suited to facilitating "the gratification of self-love, and the pursuit of the private interest of a few individuals" than democratic governments with all "sovereignty in one assembly."[9]

Ultimately, what makes these passions genuinely dangerous is that they are insatiable, without bounds, and they grow exponentially with use. Housed in one assembly—an assembly with the entire authority and power of the state—sit the most talented citizens, those "most inflamed with ambition and avarice, and who are most vain of their descent." Indeed, their elevated sense of self-worth only grows as they compete with one another for the greatest honors and prizes offered by the state. In such a condition, the "love of gold grows faster than the heap of acquisition; the love of praise increases by every gratification, till it stings like an adder, and bites like a serpent; till the man is miserable every moment when he does not snuff the incense. Ambition strengthens at every advance, and at last takes possession of the whole soul so absolutely, that a man sees nothing in the world of importance to others or himself, but in his object." Adams singled out these particular passions because he thought them the "aristocratical passions." He thought it "a curious subject of speculation" for lawgivers to examine how these particular aristocratic passions would subdue reason and conscience, "until they become absolute and imperious masters of the whole mind." Assembled in a unicameral legislature—watching, judging, ranking, emulating, and competing with each other—it would be "as rational to expect" that this natural aristocracy of ambition, like "a glass bubble, with a drop of water inclosed in it, will resist the heat of the fire. The vapor within will blast it into dust and atoms." Adams considered the existence of such passions, particularly as they were found in the hyperambitious, "a species of delerium": once indulged and "continually gratified," they become "mad."[10] Time and again, he decried the inflated passions of the aristocracy. Taming and controlling them became for Adams the raison d'être of republican government.

Central to Adams's negative political task, then, was the need to demonstrate how a unicameral assembly would be naturally transformed from a democratic into an aristocratic body. In the very same way that the people choose for their representatives those they most naturally esteem and admire, those same elected officials would likewise elevate from among their own ranks those of superior ambition, talent, or influence to positions of leadership within the assembly. Unicameral assemblies, like the society at large, would naturally divide into three unequal orders. The position of president or speaker, he predicted, would naturally fall to that one "masterly spirit, who unites in himself all the qualities which constitute the natural foundations of authority." The second order would be occupied by the most ambitious or aggressive from among the natural aristocracy. Finally, stand all the rest, "who are nearly on a level in understanding and in all things."[11] Such a body, though a simple democracy in name, would be an aristocracy or an oligarchy in fact.

Adams knew very well that politics was about getting and keeping power. But what are the particular objects of power that inflame the souls of the aristocratic few? Generally speaking, the natural aristocracy will compete, conspire, and fight behind closed doors over public honors, lucrative offices, and the rewards of public power. More particularly, their personal ambition will inevitably be directed at two objects. First, the most "eminent" and "conspicuous characters" of the assembly's second order will compete with one another for control of the executive and judicial functions of government. In other words, they seek administrative control over "the army, the navy, revenue, excise, customs, police, justice, and all foreign ministers." Second, the most pretentious and self-regarding among the natural aristocracy—"those whose fortunes, families, and merits, in the acknowledged judgement of all, approach near to the first"—covet the highest position and will challenge one another to become leader of the assembly.[12]

With these objects in sight, thus begins the great political maelstrom, the frenzied competition for the emoluments of power, and ultimately the party division that is the very essence of simple unicameral governments for Adams. The important question, of course, was how the grasping aristocracy actually gain and then retain control of the democratic form of government. The perpetual hegemony of the aristocracy had almost always been accomplished through corruption, Adams said, "which is worse than a continuation by birth."[13] According to Adams, simple democracies are corrupted in two mutually reciprocal ways: the first is external to the legislature itself, and the second is internal.

Ironically, the corruption of democratic governments and the ascendancy and dominance of the aristocracy begins with the first act and defining characteristic of the democratic form: elections. Adams thought this particularly true in a large country like the United States with its extended electoral districts. The natural aristocracy, because of its advantage in name, reputation, and wealth, will always stand above all others in the eyes of the public. But elections, by their very nature, encourage competition, and "each scene of election will have two or more candidates, and two or more parties." Despite their public declarations to the contrary, these aristocratic parties are not competing with one another to serve as disinterested patrons of the common good. At best, they represent only partial claims to justice and the public interest. More typically, they will sacrifice "every national Interest and honour, to private and party Objects."[14] Adams thought nepotism, patronage, and the spoils system were almost synonymous with democratic elections. By its very nature, Adams decried, the democratic process punishes "unsullied honor, sterling integrity, [and] real virtue." Instead, every flattery and menace, every passion and prejudice of every voter will be applied to; every trick and bribe that can be bestowed, and will be accepted, will be used; and, what is horrible to think of, that candidate, or that agent, who has fewest scruples; who will propagate lies and slanders with most confidence and secrecy; who will wheedle, flatter, and cajole; who will debauch the people by treats, feasts, and diversions, with the least hesitation; and bribe with the most impudent front, which can consist with hypocritical concealment, will draw in tools and worm out enemies the fastest.[15]

Once elected, the aggressive aristocracy continues its march for place and profit. To fulfill their highest ambitions, those with power and influence must conspire to keep them. The patrician order in the house must recruit support from newer, less experienced, more deferential and invariably less able men from the middle or lower orders of the assembly. Seeking reelection, the aggressive aristocracy trades votes, sells offices, and promises to redistribute wealth from one group to another. It does this by creating an ever expanding network of supporters through flattery and bribery. The assemblyman distributes commissions, contracts, and pensions to his friends and constituents. Likewise, members of the third order in the house will attach themselves to the assertive aristocracy for a variety of self-seeking reasons: because their reelection requires the support of these great men, because they are related by blood or business interests, or because they seek favors for themselves or for their friends and family.[16]

John Adams saw and warned against the rise and baneful effects of the phenomenon later known as Boss Tweedism long before his great-grandson, Henry Adams, chronicled its rise in his novel *Democracy*. He feared that a democratic government with all power centralized in one assembly would establish "a system of hopes and fears throughout the state" that would permit the most corrupt among the exceptional few to retain all power and influence. More ominously, Adams warned, the "judges will be appointed by them and their party, and of consequence, will be obsequious enough to their inclinations." As a consequence, "no justice will be attainable, nor will innocence or virtue be safe, in the judicial courts, but for the friends of the prevailing leaders; legal prosecutions will be instituted and carried on against opposers, to their vexations and ruin." Thus, the execution and enforcement of justice will have been "employed, perverted and prostituted to the purposes of electioneering."[17] Without the rule of law, the legal and moral bond necessary to hold a republic together will have been lost.

The corruption engendered by simple democratic governments does not end in the realm of politics. The "system of hopes and fears," Adams lamented, would extend and spread its praetorian net from the political arena to society in general. No area of public life would remain safe from the corrupting influence of electioneering. Artifice, deception, and dissimulation would be the new virtues needed for success in democratic society. The road to promotion for lawyers, doctors, the clergy, and all those directly or indirectly certified by the state would be intimately connected to courting those who control the reigns of power. Even thespians, Adams explained, "must become politicians, and convert the public pleasures into engines of popularity for the governing members of the house."[18] Finally, the aristocracy and their clinging majority would seek to corrupt the press, "that great barrier and bulwark of the rights of mankind." Those writers, editors, and printers who do not accede to the demands of the political majority would be denounced and their newspapers denied access to the avenues of power. With time, Adams predicted, a once-free press would, "with much secrecy and concealment," become a propaganda organ for the majority and a vehicle "of calumny against the minority." Having come to this point, "the whole system of affairs, and every conceivable motive of hope and fear, will be employed to promote the private interests of a few, and their obsequious majority." In such a state, "it becomes more profitable and reputable to be a party man than a public-spirited one."[19] The final corruption of society would lead to a kind of political cannibalism. To view such a scene, Adams referred his readers to Plato's description of the city of pigs in the *Republic*.[20]

In due time, the great and enduring conflict common to all societies—one that eventually overwhelms the competition between the various constituencies of the natural aristocracy—emerges as the struggle between the many who are poor and the few who are well-to-do. "In every society where property exists," Adams noted, "there will ever be a struggle between rich and poor." History demonstrated and the study of the human passions proved the inevitability and naturalness of this division. It was sown into the very nature of man, and among the causes is the inequality of men's faculties.[21] Although the few and the many share the same passions, they do so in varying degrees. In the case of the oligarchs, for instance, their particular or dominant vice is avarice. The controlling vice in the soul of the democrat is envy. In their battle to control a unicameral legislature, the wealthy, by virtue of their influence, will attempt to fleece the poor, and then with time the many who are poor will attempt to plunder the rich.

At first, the poor—docile, obsequious, and deferential—are restrained by prejudice, habit, shame, fear, principle, or religion from attacking the rich and industrious. Eventually, tired of being abused by the various aristocratic factions, the common people organize themselves (often at the instigation of a disappointed aristocrat or demagogue) to pursue their particular class interest against the domineering few. With time, their envy is turned into resentment, and they begin inventing pretexts to seize and divide the property of the wealthy few. The once cringing poor are easily transformed into an insurrectionary and grasping poor. Adams encouraged his readers to "appeal to every page of history we have hitherto turned over, for proofs irrefragable, that the people, when they have been unchecked, have been as unjust, tyrannical, brutal, barbarous, and cruel, as any king or senate possessed of uncontrollable power." When given the opportunity, the "majority has eternally, and without one exception, usurped over the rights of the minority."[22]

The penultimate scene for simple democratic governments occurs when the poor invade the property of the rich: debts are abolished, unequal taxes are imposed, and ex post facto laws are passed. Never content with their booty, however, the democratic plunderers will not rest satisfied after their initial attempt to confiscate and redistribute property. "The idle, the vicious, the intemperate," Adams warned, "would rush into the utmost extravagance of debauchery, sell and spend all their share, and then demand a new division of those who purchased from them." To accomplish their designs, the leaders of the majority only need to allege "'reasons of state'" to justify to their supporters every act of tyranny and oppression against the minority. It was simply a democratic myth, Adams suggested, that the peoples' avarice and their passion for luxury would be any less than that of the aristocracy. "*Sobriety, abstinence* and *severity*," he reminded his audience, were not virtues associated with democracies; indeed, they were virtues more likely to be found among the aristocracy and oligarchy. In this situation, with property so insecure and precarious, the inevitable result, Adams predicted, would be "universal idleness and famine."[23]

Much of the *Defence*, particularly the third volume, was devoted to demonstrating logically and historically "that the desires of the majority of the people are often for injustice and inhumanity against the minority." Pacified by their own emulation and deference on one day but inflamed by envy and resentment on the next, the defining characteristic of the many is inconstancy. In a passage that sounds remarkably similar to something written by James Madison in *Federalist* No. 63, Adams thought no "more melancholy spectacle can be conceived even in imagination, than that inconstancy which erects statutes to a patriot or a hero one year, banishes him the next, and the third erects fresh statutes to his memory."[24] All too often, aristocratic demagogues and their following among the poor would make laws to gratify some present humor; they desire some "forbidden fruit—for injustice, cruelty, and ruin of the minority." Once on their rampage, the people would entirely confuse and misunderstand their own interests. On one day they cry for "*liberty*" and on the next they demand an "*abolition of debts, and division of goods.*" Having overcome psychologically the shame and guilt associated with their takings, the peoples' desire for more would be liberated, and they would demand "a fresh abolition and division every month and every day." In the end, "the idle, vicious, and abandoned, will live in constant riot on the spoils of the industrious, virtuous, and deserving." There was simply no reason to believe, Adams thought, that the people were any more honest or wise than the aristocracy: "they are all of the same clay; their minds and bodies are alike." The effect of democratic tyranny for Adams was no different than it was under oligarchy or monarchy; it was "as real a tyranny as the sovereignty of a hereditary senate, or thirty tyrants, or a single despot." Invariably, the competition for place and profit, first between aristocratic factions and then between the rich and poor, leads to "dispute, and in time, of division, faction, sedition, and rebellion." Denied freedom and justice, the minority in a government ruled by a single assembly would be discouraged, browbeaten, and insulted and, in the end, would have no option left to them but civil war.[25]

In this state of social and political anarchy, the conditions will have been prepared for the final scene of simple governments. Reduced to a state of chaos, confusion, and exploitation, the people will eventually elevate "some one overgrown genius, fortune, or reputation" to cut down the oligarchy or one particular oligarchic faction. Handed the full reigns of power, this new despot "rules the state at his pleasure, while the deluded nation, or rather a deluded majority thinks itself free; and in every resolve, law, and act of government, you see the interest, fame, and power of that single individual attended to more than the general good."[26]

In the end, Adams could draw but one overarching conclusion about simple governments housed in one assembly: "Whether the assembly consists of a larger or a smaller number, of nobles or commons, of great people or little, of rich or poor, of substantial men or the rabble, the effects are all the same,—*No order, no safety, no liberty, because no government of*

law." Human nature suggested and history proved that simple governments could not curb the growth of factions. Indeed, the whole government, Adams charged, was itself a faction. Following Aristotle, Adams
spoke of democratic majorities as factions, and he defined a faction as
any group that pursued partial interests in its own favor and that refused
or denied "perfect equality to every member of the minority." More fundamentally, however, Adams condemned such governments as anticon-
stitutional. Without a separation of powers and a proper mixing and
balancing of society's natural social elements, there could be no limitations on government power, no counter authority to prevent it from violating the rights of individuals or minorities, and no authority to
prevent it from rewriting the constitution at will. At the very least, a single assembly could never be "a steady guardian of the laws." Thus constituted, a unicameral assembly would make the constitution and all laws
"by its own will, execute those laws at its own pleasure, and adjudge all
controversies that arise concerning the meaning and application of
them, at its own discretion." There would be nothing, he warned, that
would restrain such a government from making and executing tyrannical
laws. In no time, it would have possession "of all the cakes, loaves, and
fishes." In such an environment, the laws "instead of being permanent,
and affording constant protection to the lives, liberties, and properties of
the citizens, will be alternately the sport of contending factions, and the
mere vibrations of a pendulum." From beginning to end, "it will be a government of men, now of one set, and then of another; but never a government of laws." Constitutions would be little more than weak and
ineffective parchment barriers; they would be whatever the ruling majority said it was.[27] Consequently, the rule of law—the fixed and permanent protection of property—was impossible wherever all legislative,
executive, and judicial authority was housed in one centralized governing body.

No other element of Adams's political thought was as penetrating or
prescient as his portrait, analysis, and judgment of simple unicameral
governments. He wrote to challenge the emerging democratic myth that
government by the people would necessarily be government for the people. Given the proclivities of human nature and the lessons of history,
Adams was able to denounce simple governments as the constitutional
form most susceptible to both aristocratic corruption and democratic
tyranny. "In all events," he concluded, we must agree, that human nature
is not fit to be trusted with M. Turgot's system, of all authority in a single assembly."[28]

The Use and Abuse of Words

Nothing drove John Adams to greater distraction than the abuse of language and words in the popular political discourse of his time. In his own mind, one of the primary reasons for the retarded growth of the political sciences in modern thought and practice had been the failure of philosophers and statesmen to develop a uniform lexicon and syntax for the science of legislation. The natural and technical sciences had been revolutionized in the seventeenth and eighteenth centuries because the "elements and definitions" used by their practitioners had been systematized and were commonly understood. But in the political sciences, Adams lamented, "there is a confusion of languages, as if two men were but lately come from Babel":

> Scarcely any two writers, much less nations, agree in using words in the same sense. Such a latitude, it is true, allows a scope for politicians to speculate, like merchants with false weights, artificial credit, or base money, and to deceive the people, by making the same word adored by one party, and execrated by another. The union of the people, in any principle, rule, or system, is thus rendered impossible; because superstition, prejudice, habit, and passions, are so differently attached to words, that you can scarcely make any nation understand itself.[29]

When Adams returned to America from Europe in 1788, he was genuinely alarmed by "those habits of fraud, in the use of Language[s] which appear in conversation and in public writings." The rise of partisan democratic politics had inflated and debased the value of words and, therewith, all political discourse. The abuse of words and the manipulation of political rhetoric was thought by Adams to be "the greatest instrument of sophistry and chicanery, of party, faction, and division in society." Words like aristocracy, monarchy, republic, and virtue were all "employed like paper money," he wrote, "to cheat the Widow and the fatherless and every honest man." The term *republic* was being used to describe things "in their nature as different and contradictory as light and darkness, truth and falsehood, virtue and vice, happiness and misery"; the word *king*, "like magic, excites the adoration of some, and execration of others"; the words *virtue* and *patriotism* were "enumerated among those of various and uncertain signification"; and the word *aristocracy* has "been employed to signify any thing, every thing, and nothing." Such words were thought by Adams to be used in a multiplicity of ways, "by different nations, by different writers in the same nation, and even by the same writers in different pages." It was imperative, then, that his student law-givers develop and employ a political language that was "governed more by reason, and less by sounds."[30]

The development of a science of words might begin, Adams advised, with John Locke's chapter in the *Essay Concerning Human Understanding* "'On the abuse of words.'" He did not think the *Essay* contained anything that most men did not already know from common sense and daily experience, but if Locke had never written another word, Adams wrote, it ought to have secured him "immortal gratitude and renown." Adams believed that a comprehensive science of politics must not only have a developed theory of history and human nature, but it must also conform to a uniform science of language. It was impossible, he thought, that entire nations would ever come to a common understanding of the principles and rules of government without comprehending "one another's meaning by words." Americans, in particular, he told William Tudor in 1789, "will never think alike nor act aright untill they are habitually taught to use the same words in the same sense. Nations are governed by words as well as by actions; by sounds as well as sights." Until words had definite and precise meanings it would be in vain, Adams wrote in the *Defence*, to "expect great improvements" in the science of legislation.[31]

As a rule, Adams was willing to accept "custom" as the "standard meaning of words" for the "purposes of common parlance"; but, when developing a political science of words, he thought "something more technical must be introduced." One of the principal purposes of the *Defence* was to impose some order on the meaning and use of words. The most abused of all words in the political sciences, for instance, was *republic*. In fact, Adams thought that it was not only the most "unintelligible word in the English language" but also the most abused word "in all languages."[32] Common usage and custom were not reliable in this instance as the word republic had been defined in an infinite number of ways. Adams identified three of these definitions as used in common practice.

The first was the most imprecise and was therefore illegitimate: its advocates defined a republic as signifying "nothing but public affairs," which meant that any and every form of government, including despotism and a simple monarchy, was a republic. When used in this way, the term had been "applied to every government under heaven; that of Turkey and that of Spain, as well as that of Athens and of Rome, of Geneva and San Marino." More properly, Adams defined despotism as "a government in which the three divisions of power, the legislative, executive and judicial, are all vested in one man." A monarchy, properly defined, "is a government where the legislative and executive are vested in one man, but the judicial in other men."[33]

Historically, the most common usage of the term (commonly identified with Montesquieu) defined a republic as any government in which the ruling sovereignty is located in more than one person or body.[34] This definition had the advantage of distinguishing a republic from a despotism and a simple monarchy. Using this kind of standard meant of course that a republic could take on a multiplicity of forms. "Of Republics," Adams had written in *Thoughts on Government*, "there is an inexhaustable variety, because the possible combinations of powers of society, are capable of innumerable variations." The genus republic could be divided therefore into democratic, aristocratic, and monarchical species, or any mixture of them. It was around this definition, one that Adams called the "strict definition," and one which "the most accurate writers" supported, that he organized the first volume of the *Defence*. Accordingly, the first volume surveys some forty democratic, aristocratic, and monarchic republics of the ancient and modern worlds. Each of these republics, even those of the same species, was unique and organized in its own way. Adams's strict definition meant that the Spartan, French, and English kingdoms were no less republican than Venice, San Marino, or Holland. He did not think that the citizens of these tiny republics had any more liberty than those of England or France. But even this strict definition was inadequate for Adams.[35]

Adams's argument to this point may be summarized in the following way. The science of politics divides the forms of government into three genera: despotism, monarchy, and republic. Republics are in turn divided into three pure species: monarchic, aristocratic, and democratic. The three species of republic may also be mixed in a multiplicity of ways, but Adams's classification of regimes does not end here. He makes one further distinction that is crucial to his ultimate meaning and that is the distinction between "free republics and republics which are not free." A republic relative to a despotism or a simple monarchy is not an unqualified good according to Adams, for it is possible to have a republic "as tyrannical as an oriental despotism." A higher standard is therefore required before it is possible to arrive at the "only true definition of a republic."[36]

It is on the basis of this crucial distinction—between free and unfree—that Adams was able to establish the third and the best definition of a republic. A free republic—"the best of governments, and the greatest blessing which mortals can aspire to"—adds two crucial criteria to the generic definition of a republic.[37] The first and most important criterion revises the general definition of a republic to include the requirement that it be "an Empire of Laws, and not of Men." Adams borrowed the idea and the language of the rule of law from Aristotle, Livy, Sidney, and Harrington.[38] Harrington's authority, in particular, was central to Adams's teaching. In the *Defence*, he quotes from the *Oceana* as follows:

> Government *de jure*, or according to ancient prudence, is an art, whereby a civil society of men is instituted and preserved upon the foundation of common interest; or, to follow Aristotle and Livy, it is an empire of laws and not of men. And government, to define it according to modern prudence, or *de facto*, is an art, by which some man, or some few men, subject a city or a nation, and rule it according to his or their private interest; which, because the laws in such cases are made according to the interest of a man, or a few families, may be said to be the empire of men and not of laws.

Adams is clear for drawing a rigid distinction between free and unfree republics on the basis of this fundamental requirement. In a chapter on the Polish monarchy in the first volume, he cut a sharp distinction between free republics and all others: "An empire of laws is a characteristic of a free republic only, and should never be applied to republics in general." The penultimate definition of a republic, then, is a government "in which all men, rich and poor, magistrates and subjects, officers and people, masters and servants, the first citizen and the last, are *equally* subject to the laws." Equal, fixed, and known laws defined the rule of law for Adams over against the rule of mere will and pleasure. His "first principle" of politics stated that "neither liberty nor justice can be secured to the individuals of a nation, nor its prosperity promoted, but by a fixed constitution of government, and stated laws, known and obeyed by all."[39] The rule of law, then, establishes the necessary condition on which a republic may be demarcated as free.

But the rule of law simply speaking is not a sufficient definition of a free republic for Adams. A second criterion is required. As Turgot had correctly pointed out in his letter to Richard Price, even a government of laws might not necessarily produce just or good laws. In fact, it was quite possible that equal laws, even those made with common consent, could "deprive the minority of the citizens of their rights." A majority could pass laws requiring a uniformity of religion; it could redistribute property from the wealthy to the poor; and it could restrain trade and confine the personal liberty of all equally. "In short," Adams wrote in agreement with

Turgot, a majority "may restrain physical, moral and religious Liberty of all equally, and against the Judgement of many, without motives, Use, or Benefit." Indeed, the consequences inherent in this logic could be pushed one step further. It was not impossible, Adams noted, that "a nation may be unanimous in consenting to a law restraining its natural liberty, property, and commerce, and its moral and religious liberties too, to a degree that may be prejudicial to the nation and to every individual in it." To overcome the possibility that tyrannical or unjust laws may be legislated with common consent and equally applied to all, Adams added the following proviso: equal laws passed by the consent of the governed must be "for the *general interest* or the *public good*."[40] Adams's definition of liberty and republican government goes beyond Price's by demanding that *legitimate* government be also *good* government. But what are the general interest and the public good? We come now to the nub of Adams's definition of a properly free republic.

When examined "more rationally," Adams found that the etymological origins of the word republic demonstrated that it was inextricably linked with a particular notion of justice: "The word *res*, every one knows, signified in the Roman language wealth, riches, property; the word *publicus* . . . signified public, common, belonging to the people; *res publica*, therefore, was publica res, the wealth, riches, or property of the people." The protection of a nation's wealth and property, individual and collective, provided Adams with the original and best definition of a free republic. Justice and the public good are synonymous with the protection of private property and the liberty to pursue it. For Adams, constitutions and the rule of law exist primarily to protect property.

> *Res populi,* and the original meaning of the word republic could be no other than a government in which the property of the people predominated and governed; and it had more relation to property than liberty. It signified a government, in which the property of the public, or people, and of every one of them, was secured and protected by law. This idea, indeed, implies liberty; because property cannot be secure unless the man be at liberty to acquire, use, or part with it, at his discretion, and unless he have his personal liberty of life and limb, motion and rest, for that purpose. It implies, moreover, that the property and liberty of all men, not merely of a majority, should be safe; for the people, or public, comprehends more than a majority, it comprehends all and every individual; and the property of every citizen is a part of the public property, as each citizen is a part of the public, people, or community. The property, therefore, of every man has a share in government,

and is more powerful than any citizen, or party of citizens; it is governed only by the law.[41]

In this extraordinary passage, Adams presents what is probably the most sophisticated definition of a republic written during the entire founding period. One searches in vain in the writings of Jefferson, or even in *The Federalist*,[42] for a definition that so explicitly describes the necessary and sufficient conditions on which republics must be constructed. By defining a free republic as a "government in which the property of the people predominated and governed," Adams established the guiding spirit by which both legitimate and good government, means and ends, could be reconciled and brought together in a harmonious whole. His definition goes beyond a description of institutional arrangements; it demands of republics that they fulfill certain ends or social goods. He defined a free republic as that form of government in which the rule of law protects the property and therewith the liberty of *all* citizens. For "the moment the idea is admitted into society, that property is not as sacred as the laws of God, and that there is not a force of law and public justice to protect it, anarchy and tyranny commence." No nation, he wrote, could be considered civilized or free until it had institutionalized and made inviolable the "precepts" of "'THOU SHALT NOT COVET,' and 'THOU SHALT NOT STEAL.'"[43] Adams therefore identified the public good as synonymous with the universal acquisition, use, and exchange of private property, thus defining the purpose, boundaries, and even the organization of constitutional structures. He found support for his position in the writings of history's greatest "statesman and philosopher," Cicero, who had also defined a republic as a regime where the "laws, which are the only possible rule, measure, and security of justice, can be sure of protection" and where "property of the people should . . . decide the rule of justice."[44] Justice, then, defined as the protection of the free acquisition and exchange of property, is the sine qua non of good government.

A consistent science of political language was thought by Adams to be the necessary foundation on which to build a demonstrable science of politics. Without an established and stable political lexicon, the meaning of certain words—like democracy or aristocracy—would fluctuate, inflating and deflating, in direct relation to the shifting tides of partisan political debate. Adams was fully aware of what polemics and partisan politics were doing to the Americans' understanding of politics and political discourse, and he did not like it. In the emerging world of ideological politics, language was fast becoming a tool of factions and parties willing to use and abuse the meaning of words in the pursuit of power and social authority. Adams was one of the first political thinkers to see the intimate connection between propaganda and the Age of Ideology.

Republican Virtue

Many leading scholars in recent decades have sought to explain the meaning of the Revolutionary and founding periods in terms of an American rebirth of classical republican thought.[45] Several have identified John Adams as a classical republican, one of them going so far as to describe the *Defence* as "perhaps the last major work of political theory written within the unmodified tradition of classical republicanism."[46] It is true that Adams defended a version of the classical theory of mixed government, but he was also the first major American theorist to reject classical republicanism explicitly. The distance that separates Adams from the classical-republican and civic-humanist traditions is most clearly seen in his devastating critique of their central organizing principle: the concept of virtue.[47]

Historians and political scientists have typically misunderstood Adams's relationship to classical republicanism because they have failed to distinguish the different ways in which he was influenced by ancient thought and practice. On the one hand, Adams adopted the traditional theory of mixed and balanced governments that he associated with Polybius, Cicero, Aristotle, and Plato. He also had a qualified admiration for the actual structure and practice of the Spartan and Roman constitutions. In other words, Adams appreciated the forms or institutional arrangements established by many of the ancient republics. But his admiration stopped there. Adams categorically rejected the "spirit" or *arche* that animated many of these regimes, and he had nothing but contempt for the ancient view of citizenship and virtue.

By classical republicanism, I mean the tradition of Greek and Roman thought generally associated with the writings of Aristotle, Polybius, Plutarch, and Cicero. At the heart of classical republicanism was the notion that public affairs should be the concern of the body politic and that the citizenry should assume direct responsibility for the public good. If self-government was to work, the governed must be capable of governing themselves, that is, they must be capable of restraining their own desires and passions for the sake of the whole. Thus, the success or failure of the classical republic rested on its ability to form the character of its citizens so that they could carry out their moral and political responsibilities. The ancient polity was therefore seen as a schoolmaster or as a molder of republican character. Accordingly, republican government was considered a way of life that could not endure without a citizenry schooled in the principles of virtue. The classical republican definition of virtue meant primarily civic virtue, a love of laws and country, and a disinterested service to the public good. The ancients also believed that what made a man a good citizen was ultimately commensurate with what made him a good man. In other words, because the good man could only perfect himself through participation in public affairs, moral and civic virtue were intimately related. The ends of the classical polis were best summarized in Aristotle's pithy statement in Book III of the *Politics*, where he says that the regime "exists not for the sake of living but rather primarily for the sake of living well."[48] Such virtue demands a rigorous restraint of the private passions for pleasure, wealth, and personal superiority. Not only must there be a relative equality of property, carefully regulated by the laws, but the level of wealth enjoyed by each person must be small. Consequently, a well-ordered republic must be characterized by great austerity and purity of morals. Because ancient political thought took its bearings from how man *ought* to live, it required the political state to marshal all its resources to perfect human nature through participation in public affairs in a small, self-governing community.

Adams undoubtedly felt compelled to examine and debunk the classical republican tradition and its understanding and utilization of virtue because he knew that many American and French defenders of simple government were looking to the ancient republics as models to emulate and copy. Despite the temptations that the classical world might hold for eighteenth-century republicans, he recommended that it be used primarily as a casebook example of what to avoid. One of the most important vehicles for the transmission of classical republican ideals to the New World came through the Americans' reading (or misreading) of the first eight books of Montesquieu's *The Spirit of the Laws*. It is significant, then, that close to the end of the third volume of the *Defence*, Adams should take up Book V, the principal chapter on republican virtue in *The Spirit of the Laws*. In typical fashion, Adams wasted no time in moving directly to the central question, "What is virtue?" He immediately denied that either classical or Christian virtue could be the foundation of a republic. For Montesquieu, according to Adams, virtue "is merely a negative quality; the absence only of ambition and avarice."[49] This absence of ambition and avarice translates for Montesquieu into a patriotic love of the republic, a selfless devotion to the public good. Stated positively, the two qualities that undergird this love of the republic are a love of equality and a love of frugality.

Adams did not think Montesquieu's recapitulation of classical virtue well considered. "Can you find any age or country," he asked, "in which republican virtue has existed?" It was simply not true that there existed anywhere in the world or at anytime a people "who loved the public better than themselves." The history of republics was replete with examples of "the most virtuous characters" demonstrating "unequivocal marks of an ardent and unbridled ambition." Even the great republican hero, Cato, had a "thirst for glory, as strong as that of Caesar." Furthermore, it "is not easy to prove," Adams noted, "that a moment ever existed, in a country, *where property was enjoyed*, when the body of the people were universally or even generally exempted from avarice." Historical example only proved for Adams the evidence found in human nature. Is there, he asked, a natural human passion for equality? Adams knew very well that "every man hates to have a superior." Of greater significance, however, was that "no man is willing to have an equal." In fact, "every man desires to be superior to all others." Envy was not a proper foundation for a republican government. Likewise, frugality was not a passion to be found in man's natural constitution. To the contrary, humankind is naturally acquisitive, if not entirely avaricious. No nation, not even Sparta, Adams noted, practiced frugality "but from necessity."[50] The ascetic monk may choose poverty, but the sublime virtues of religion are not a part of human nature, nor are they to be found in any civilization. No man in America could be expected to choose the harsh conditions of precommercial society.

By the end of his critique of Montesquieu, Adams could barely contain his contempt. He concluded his digression by asking rhetorically if we must "bow with reverence to this great master of laws, or may we venture to suspect that these doctrines of his are spun from his imagination?" Adams attributed Montesquieu's apparent love of classical virtue to a philosophical imagination: It was "derived from the contemplation of the reveries of Xenophon and Plato, concerning equality of goods, and community of wives and children, in their delirious ideas of a perfect commonwealth." Whereas Adams himself attempted to establish a science of legislation based on the constitution of human nature, the lessons of universal history, indigenous social conditions, and reasoned principle, Montesquieu and his republican followers had "feigned for the regulation and animation of government that never had a more solid existence than the flying island of Lagado." These utopian schemes were "all mere figments of the brain, and delusive imaginations."[51]

But Adams was forced to take Montesquieu's ideas seriously because he saw in them the inspiration for what he thought were the fuzzy-minded ideas then popular among political agitators in France and America. Mankind has been most often injured, warned Adams, "by insinuations, that a certain celestial virtue, more than human, has been necessary to preserve liberty."[52] By the time the third volume of A *Defence of the Constitutions* was written in late 1787, many of the most theoretical Anti-Federalist pamphlets and essays were being published against the ratification of the Constitution. Most Anti-Federalist arguments for small and virtuous republics were based explicitly on *The Spirit of the Laws*.[53]

Ultimately, Adams criticized the idea of classical republicanism and its applicability for America on three counts. First, he did not think the kind of laws and education needed to sustain a virtuous republic were possible in a country the size of the United States. Adams cited Socrates and Pythagoras as authorities who supported the idea that public-spiritedness and wise laws are not possible "until mankind, were habituated, by education and discipline, to regard the great duties of life, and to consider a reverence of themselves, and the esteem of their fellow citizens, as the principal source of their enjoyment." As he noted, however, the attainment of such virtue was possible only in "small communities, especially where the slaves were many, and the citizens few." It was utterly fantastic to think that the education of a nation as large as that of the United States could ever accomplish so great a task. The American states, Adams noted, are much larger and more populous than the Greek city-states, and "they are growing every day more disproportionate, and therefore less capable of being held together by simple governments." In fact, America demonstrated just the opposite principle to be true. Whereas small republics require the "utmost frugality, simplicity, and moderation" to preserve their liberty, large nations like the United States achieve the same end despite "great degrees of wealth, luxury, dissipation, and even profligacy of manners."[54]

The commercial spirit that seems to animate the American regime points to Adams's second criticism of the "virtuous republic." According to Adams, acquisitiveness and the desire for material luxury are ineradicable elements of human nature. He did consider excessive luxury to be a vice and a potential source of a republic's undoing, but he categorically rejected the notion "that the form of government is best, and the people's liberty most secure, where the people are poorest." Such a government could never be reconciled to human nature. There was no positive passion in human nature for poverty. Lawgivers therefore should not flatter human nature with compliments that have little or no basis in reality. A wise lawgiver must "form a true idea and judgement of mankind, and adapt his institutions to facts, not compliments." He thought it utterly futile, if not dishonest, for philosophers and legislators "to expect self-denial from men" who have the "power to gratify themselves." It is "to disbelieve all history and universal experience." If given half a chance, all peoples will seek wealth and luxury. In a country like America, where there is unbounded freedom to pursue and exchange property, the common people are inspired "with sentiments which hurry them into luxury." The American War for Independence provided Adams with an excellent example of this condition. At first, during the nonimportation crisis and the early years of the war, the American colonists demonstrated such an extraordinary degree of civic virtue that they governed themselves virtually without any government. Later, though, during the war years and later in peace, "the Americans found an unusual quantity of money flow in upon them, and, without the least degree of prudence, foresight, consideration, or measure, rushed headlong into a greater degree of luxury than ought to have crept in for a hundred years."[55] Liberated from the remnants of a stifling mercantilist economy, the American citizen during the war years was able to break free from status restriction and state regulations to pursue and keep unlimited wealth. "The love of poverty," Adams noted, "is a fictitious virtue that never existed."[56] Necessity and not human nature dictated the extraordinary virtue demonstrated by the Americans in the years preceding the Revolution.

The ultimate cause of Americans' seemingly limitless pursuit of material well-being could be found in the natural-rights philosophy that Adams understood as the basis of the American regime. From this natural-rights position, he leveled his most direct attack against the duties-based philosophy of the ancient republics. In a word, he found these virtuous regimes unjust. His critique of Sparta and the institutions of Lycurgus bear this out. Because the Spartan ideal of virtue and citizenship had become a working model for many French and American reformers, Adams saved his heaviest polemical arsenal for the Lacadaemonian republic.[57] As we have already seen, he did have considerable praise for the mixed government established by Lycurgus, despite its minor structural flaws. In the end, however, he condemned the Spartan constitution as "not only the least respectable, but the most detestable in all Greece." To overcome its constitutional imperfections, Lycurgus had to infuse his

Lacedaemonian citizenry with a rigid and stern system of virtue. It was this defining "spirit" of the Spartan regime that Adams found repugnant and objected to most violently. He categorically rejected the measures used by Lycurgus to form the character of his people. The laws of Lycurgus were an attempt to draw out and upward the public-spirited passions of the people. But, in order to achieve this selfless devotion to the public weal, the Spartan lawgiver attempted to eradicate every passion, appetite, and affection in human nature that could be identified as selfish. Lycurgus attempted to reconstitute human nature by neutralizing, channeling, and siphoning the acquisitive desires through a highly regulated system of social control: property was divided equally, gold and silver banished, foreign travel and commerce prohibited, and literature discouraged; children were educated by the state, citizens were required to take meals together, to be in a state of constant military preparedness, and were ultimately considered the property of the state.[58]

Isolated and inward-looking, the Lacedaemonians lived for nothing but war and politics. Sparta was an armed camp that lived "as if fighting and intriguing, and not *life and happiness*, were the end of man and society." The belligerent militarism that defined the Spartan regime was the principal source of its need to homogenize and control the day-to-day activities of its citizenry. This classical definition of liberty as the duty to participate in public affairs was for Adams "little better than that of a man chained in a dungeon—a liberty to rest as he is." Human nature, Adams wrote, "perished under this frigid system of national and family pride."[59] For Adams, classical republicanism in general and the Spartan regime in particular were inhumane and morally objectionable. Because human nature is what it is, Adams rejected the virtuous classical republic as a suitable model for America. Because they coerced and channeled human passions and ambitions away from their natural course, the classical republics were inherently unstable and fragile and so austere as to create unhappiness, even in regimes that actually managed to sustain order.

Fundamental to Adams's political philosophy was a long-standing advocacy of the natural-rights theory and the right to property in particular. In contrast to the classical tradition, Adams reminded his audience that government "should never have any other end than the greatest happiness of the greatest number, *saving to all their rights.*" Adams was quite willing to concede the necessity of virtue in a republic, but, unlike his French counterparts, he was not willing to support laws violating individual rights for the sake of virtue. In a nation where private property was protected as a fundamental right of citizenship, one can expect a "free people" to be "the most addicted to luxury of any." Their equal rights as independent citizens inspires "them with sentiments which hurry them into luxury."[60] The Spartans, by contrast, were equal in their right to be poor and servants of the state. In a regime established for the protection of individual rights, Adams was willing to accept the costs in any trade-off between liberty and the potentially corrupting effects of luxury.

What, then, is virtue, according to Adams, and how shall it be promulgated? We are given some insight into Adams's answer to these two questions when we examine his discussion of the one ancient republic for which he did seem to have some respect, namely, Carthage. Adams thought Carthage more like America than any "other of the ancient republics," and "perhaps more than any of the modern." Carthage was for Adams the classical antipode to Sparta. Its animating or character-giving "spirit" was commerce, considered by most republican theorists to be antithetical to true virtue. So contrary to the purpose of the classical republican ideal was Carthage that Aristotle did not even consider it a regime, in the strict sense. For Aristotle, Carthage was simply a society founded on contractual obligations concerning property and trade; it was a crass commercial society that partook of none of the higher civic, moral, or intellectual virtues that properly define a regime.[61] Adams saw in Carthage, however, a very different society. He thought it extraordinary that "with all their acknowledged eagerness for money, this people were so many centuries untainted with luxury and venality." The Carthaginians had to a remarkable degree "preserved their primitive frugality of manners and integrity in elections." Indeed, they had been able to combine in their national character two seemingly irreconcilable kinds of virtues, the military and the commerical. They were avaricious, but they were not effeminate. The example of Carthage was sufficient proof for Adams "to doubt the universality of the doctrine, that commerce corrupts manners."[62] The new modern virtues for Adams—that is, rationality, moderation, frugality, industry—would foster in the citizens a decent respect for law and a devotion to strict justice.

One of the great responsibilities of constitution making, according to Adams, was to find and construct a form of government "best calculated to prevent the base effects and corruption of luxury, when, in the ordinary course of things, it must be expected to come in." In rejecting the classical solution to this problem, Adams was not willing to accept the costs to liberty associated with state-coerced civic virtue. Rather than instituting a regime whose stated purpose was the creation of a public-spirited citizenry by means of religion and education, Adams believed that a virtuous citizenry could be generated by channeling the passions through a well-balanced constitution. "It is the form of government that naturally and necessarily produces the effect," Adams repeatedly told his student lawgivers in the *Defence*:

> Mankind have been still more injured by insinuations, that a certain celestial virtue, more than human, has been necessary to preserve liberty. Happiness, whether in despotism or democracy, whether in slavery or liberty, can never be found without virtue. The best republics will be virtuous, and have been so, but we may hazard a conjecture, that the virtues have been the effect of the well ordered constitution, rather than the cause.[63]

Adams stated his position on the virtue question most poignantly in a famous exchange with Samuel Adams in 1790. According to his cousin Samuel, the future of republican government depended on "divines and philosophers, statesmen and patriots" uniting "their endeavors to renovate the age, by impressing the minds of men with the importance of educating their *little boys* and *girls*." John Adams had no doubt that education was a necessary component in the inculcation of public virtue, but he did not think it a sufficient condition. Instead, he was "for seeking institutions which may supply in some degree the defect." David Hume was Adams's principal teacher on this point. He agreed entirely with Hume's suggestion "that all projects of government, founded in the supposition or expectation of extraordinary degrees of virtue, are evidently chimerical." Furthermore, Adams did not think it humanly possible "that men should ever be greatly improved in knowledge or benevolence, without assistance from the principles and system of government." Adams did not think that "religion, superstition, oaths, education, [or] laws" could restrain the passions of men, nor their desire for luxury. Only a well-ordered constitution could temper the emulative passions that follow from luxury. "In a country like America," he cautioned, "where the means and opportunities for luxury are so easy and so plenty . . . it would be madness not to expect it, be prepared for it, and provide against the dangers of it in the constitution."[64]

Although Adams was concerned about the corrosive effects of excessive luxury, he was nonetheless impressed with the ability of a liberal constitutional order to foster a kind of virtuous citizenry peculiar to that kind of regime. One could not always expect "great statesmen and warriors" from such a society, but "a regular well-ordered constitution, will never fail to bring forth men capable of conducting the national councils and arms." More to the point:

> It is of infinitely more importance to the national happiness, to abound in good merchants, farmers, and manufacturers, good lawyers, priests, and physicians, and great philosophers, than it is to multiply what are called great statesmen and great generals. It is a miserable servitude, whether you call it a republic or a despotism, where the law is uncertain and unknown; and it is only under the security of certain and known laws, that arts, sciences, agriculture, commerce, and trades, can ever be made to flourish.[65]

Ultimately, Adams rejected the idea that ancient republics produced a higher degree of patriotism and virtue in their citizenry than did societies based on the protection of property and contract and the encouragement of commerce and industry. He thought the vaunted virtues of the classical republics more of a romantic fiction in the minds of some modern philosophers than a true reflection of historical reality. Instead of these militaristic, slave-holding republics, Adams favored a form of government

> which produces a love of law, liberty, and country, instead of disorder, irregularity, and a faction; which produces as much and more independence of spirit, and as undaunted bravery; as much esteem of merit in preference to wealth, and as great simplicity, sincerity, and generosity to all the community, as others do to a faction; which produces as great a desire of knowledge, and infinitely better faculties to pursue it; which, besides, produces security of property, and the desire and opportunities for commerce, which the others obstruct.[66]

This reordering of the virtues necessary to sustain republican government was for Adams the grounds on which a higher, more just civilization would arise. "The love of science and literature always grows," Adams noted, "where there is much public deliberation and debate." Most important to Adams was his belief that a liberal constitutional order would elevate the dignity of individual moral worth because each individual would be responsible for his own actions and his own improvement. It is a mixed and well-balanced government "that makes all the nation of a noble temper," and it is "freedom" which "produces magnanimity and courage." In a regime "where every faculty as well as passion is always on the stretch, great energy of mind appears."[67] At the heart of Adams's notion of virtue was the premise that humankind are rational beings that must exercise their own reason and free will. Virtue cannot and must not be coerced. A virtuous community is one where self-governing individuals voluntarily support the laws because they are chosen; the laws are not to be followed simply out of fear of punishment or deference to superiors. Ultimately, justice and not virtue was the goal of the regime for Adams. In fact, the best inculcator and guarantor of virtue was the institutionalization and guarantee of strict justice.

Chapter 10

The Principles of Government

John Adams loved the study of government; he found "no romance" more exciting. "The divine science of politicks," as he often called it, "is the science of social happiness, and the blessings of society depend entirely on the constitutions of government, which are generally institutions that last for many generations." He thought there "no employment more agreeable to a benevolent mind, than a research after the best."[1] But what form of government did Adams think would best achieve good, just, and equal laws? What were the basic or necessary principles, structures, institutions, and forms of a well-ordered commonwealth?

On the basis of his underlying political science, Adams derived from the study of nature, philosophy, and history three basic but essential principles of political architecture, principles that one finds in all of his constitutional prescriptions from the beginning of his career to the end: first, representation rather than actual assemblies of the people; second, a separation of the legislative, executive, and judicial powers; and third, a mixture and balance in the legislature among the one, the few, and the many. He considered these three principles the only improvements in the science of politics "since the institution of Lycurgus."[2] These core principles were for Adams the foundation and framework on which all constitutions must be constructed. The first two, representation and separation of powers, were distinctly modern inventions: both were logically derived from Lockean natural-rights theory and its corollary theory of consent. Indeed, they represent the two founding constitutional principles of modern liberalism.[3] The last principle, however, the "triple equipoise," as Adams often called it, was hardly a modern invention. With its roots in the theory and practice of classical antiquity, the mixed regime rested on an entirely different theoretical foundation. How, if at all, did Adams reconcile these very different principles?

Adams's political thought, particularly as it is presented in the *Defence*, is often described by historians as having either confused the principle of separation of powers with that of mixed government, or as having simply rejected the former for the latter in the years between 1776 and

1787.[4] Neither claim is true. Adams's political thought represents a unique and powerful attempt to synthesize the classical notion of mixed government with the modern teaching of separation of powers. This was no small achievement, for it had been generally assumed that the two concepts, at least in their more extreme or pure forms, were incompatible.[5] The theory of mixed government was a peculiarly classical notion necessarily related to the question of who should rule, whereas the separation of powers was a uniquely modern idea necessarily connected to the question of the limits or extent of rule. The classical doctrine of mixed government was said to depend on the naturalness of the political community, whereas the modern doctrine of separation of powers was grounded on an artificial construct deduced from the Lockean teaching on individual rights. The mixed regime was about different social orders and their competing notions of justice, but the separation of powers was about individuals and the coercive power of the state. Adams's theory of political architecture stood between the ancients and the moderns, borrowing the best from each and discarding the rest. To understand fully how he reconciled these seemingly irreconcilable principles, we must briefly reconstruct the theory of the mixed regime and the separation of powers as propounded by their most sophisticated and thoughtful advocates.

Aristotle is justly considered the theoretical patron of the mixed regime. His classic formulation of this teaching can be found in Book IV of his *Politics*, a book that Adams read and incorporated into the *Defence*. According to Aristotle, all regimes consist of several elements or social orders, the two most important being the poor many and the wealthy few.[6] Not only are these distinctions made according to numbers and wealth, but they also denote very different concepts of justice or of the common good that naturally exist within the political community. There are, in other words, conflicting regimes or ways of life within the regime as a whole, each devoted to its own notion of justice: the democrats demand equality for equals, and the oligarchs demand inequality for unequals. Whichever class is dominant—that is, whichever class rules and controls the political offices—is, according to Aristotle, the regime. In other words, whoever rules defines the nature of the regime.[7] This leads, however, to the ruling faction's attempt to absolutize its claim to rule against the other orders. Inevitably, as the few and the many battle one another for dominance, the regime settles into the familiar downward cycle of decay and degeneration. The task for Aristotle's lawgiver was to overcome the natural effects of partisanship and to reconcile the competing notions of justice, particularly those between the many poor and the few wealthy. He does this by separating, combining, and recombining the various elements of the regime.[8]

For Aristotle, the best practical—that is, the fully realizable—regime was the mixed regime or what he called a *polity*. Given the natural diversity of all cities or nations, the Aristotelian polity was a compound or a mixture of the various social constituencies and the partial idea of justice peculiar to each. The purpose of the mixed regime was twofold: to protect each element from the usurpations of the other, and to harmonize and thereby elevate the partisan concepts of justice. To that end, Aristotle had the various and contending social elements share in all the powers of government, of which there were three parts or actions: the deliberative, the magistratical, and the judicial.[9] Therefore, the Aristotelian mixed regime gave greater scope and dignity to the role of statesmanship in reconciling the ongoing deliberations and compromises between the partisans of democracy and the partisans of oligarchy.

Theoretically, separation of powers underwent two critical moments during its development. The first was Locke's correction of Hobbes, and the second was Montesquieu's correction of Locke. Locke began with Hobbes's premise: power is the central problem of politics.[10] Following Hobbes, Locke began with a philosophical construct: isolated individuals in a theoretical state of nature. To escape this condition, the reciprocal powers of judging others and defending oneself (rights originally retained by all individuals) are transferred to a civil government by the consent of a temporarily united people. In this way, for Hobbes and Locke, government is entirely conventional. But as this theory initially grew out of Hobbes, it was confronted with one massive difficulty: the solution was worse than the problem. All power in Hobbes's Leviathan state was funneled into one omnipotent sovereign. In order to overcome the theoretical problem associated with Hobbes and the real problem associated with the Stuart monarchy, Locke established and then separated two central powers or functions of government—the power of legislation (the power of clarifying and universalizing the laws of nature under the rule of law) and the power of execution (the power associated with the rights of nature, i.e., self-preservation)—between two different agencies, the king and Parliament. Locke then divided the executive function into federative and civil power. The first was concerned with war and the law of nations, and the second with the execution of legislative laws.

Following in Locke's footsteps, Montesquieu advanced the theory of separation of powers to its recognizable modern form. In his widely celebrated and highly influential *The Spirit of the Laws*, Montesquieu conceptualized a constitution that arranges the "nature of things" such that "power checks power." Following Locke, Montesquieu separated the legislative and executive powers, but his greatest theoretical innovation was the establishment of an independent third power, the judicial. He therefore separated the powers of government among "that of enacting laws, that of executing the public resolutions, and of trying the causes of individuals," and he then put the control of those distinct powers into different and independent hands. A legislature would make the law, an executive would enact the law, and a judiciary would interpret and declare what the law is by resolving disputes. "This beautiful system," Montesquieu wrote, would regulate and control the "necessary movement of things."[11] The addition of an independent judiciary ultimately led to the development in America of the idea of a written constitution, one of the greatest constitutional innovations of Western history.

From Adams's perspective, representation and separation of powers were well-established principles by the end of the eighteenth century. Theoretically, they had received their greatest elucidation in Locke's *Second Treatise* and Montesqueiu's *The Spirit of the Laws*, books hardly in need of defense. Enlightened philosophers and political reformers on both sides of the Atlantic, people as different as Adams and Condorcet, could agree on the desirability of representation and a separation of powers as logical extensions of the natural-rights theory. This is precisely why Adams saw little need to discuss or defend them at great length in the *Defence*. The mixed regime, however, was an altogether different case. As political thinkers in the sixteenth and seventeenth centuries came to develop a pure theory of separation of powers based on the theoretical construct of the state of nature and the rights of individuals, the older theory of the mixed regime was increasingly seen as obsolete and anachronistic. First in America and then on the Continent, it was a doctrine under assault. This fact begins to explain why Adams devoted most of the *Defence* to defending this controversial principle. For thinkers like Paine, Turgot, and Condorcet, it was strictly incompatible with the natural-rights philosophy. Adams disagreed. He thought the principle of mixed and balanced government not only compatible with but absolutely necessary for a constitution of liberty.

Representation

Political legitimacy for John Adams rested on the principle of representation; representation rested on the principle of consent; consent rested on the principle of sovereignty; and sovereignty rested on the principle of rights. The fundamental, irreducible fact of human existence for Adams was the moral equality of all individuals. Each human being is an autonomous, rights-bearing individual with an equal right to self-government. In other words, no human being is naturally the slave or the ruler of another. In the "Declaration of Rights" in his *Report of a Constitution for Massachusetts,* Adams wrote that "All men are born free and independent, and have certain natural, essential, and unalienable rights: among which may be reckoned the right of enjoying and defending their lives and liberties; that of acquiring, possessing, and protecting their property; in fine, that of seeking and obtaining their safety and happiness." How does this autonomous self-governing individual come to live under the rules and dictates of government? By what means does man move from a state of absolute freedom to a state of ordered freedom?

The concept of natural rights served in Adams's thought, first, as an intermediary between precivil and civil man, and second, as the guiding principle or defining purpose for which legitimate government is established. As with Locke, Adams's understanding of rights was directly related to the question of political legitimacy. Because individuals are equal with regard to their rights—that is, equal in their right to self-government—no one may be legitimately ruled by another without his consent. The equal right of all individuals to self-government established the necessary criteria on which legitimate government rests: consent and justice. Because the natural law teaches that all human beings are the sovereign owners and rulers of their own lives, liberty, and property, it is only by the consent therefore of each and every individual that government may be established, and it must be created primarily if not exclusively for the purpose of securing justice for all. The idea of consent, then, was the central organizing principle around which a "body politic" might be formed "by a voluntary association of individuals."[12]

If the consent of all individuals is the necessary condition on which legitimate government is established, it followed for Adams that "the original and fountain of all just power and government is in the people." The right of sovereignty that resides in the "whole body of the people" is both "unalienable and indivisible." At no time in history, according to Adams, had theory been so well translated into practice than in America during the Revolution, when "thirteen governments were taken down from the foundation, and new ones elected wholly by the people, as an architect would pull down an old building and erect a new one." America was the first nation in history to found a new nation in which sovereignty resided "in the whole body of the people."[13] On the basis of this moral foundation, Adams drew two conclusions for political life: First, the people have a right to establish any form of government they think will best protect their rights; and second, the people have a right to invoke the revolution-principle, that is, the right to throw off any government when it becomes despotic or evinces a design of becoming so.

The doctrine of popular sovereignty was Adams's first principle of political architecture. Despite the opinions of some historians, his views on sovereignty and representation did not change in the years between his writing *Thoughts on Government* and the *Defence*. Time and again Adams wrote in the *Defence* that the "original and fountain of *all* just power and government is in the people."[14] The American constitutions defended by Adams, and particularly the Massachusetts Constitution, were grounded entirely on the full sovereignty of the people. This was not sovereignty *shared*, but complete sovereignty.[15] The people's sovereignty under the old colonial governments was shared with the royal or proprietary sovereignty. It was not inconsistent for Adams to say on the one hand that *constitutional* sovereignty originated and rested wholly with the people, and on the other hand to say that *political* sovereignty could be divided among the legislative, executive, and judicial powers of government, no less than among the one, the few, and the many within the legislature. In other words, political power should derive from the people, but it should also be separated from the people. In this way, the people are ultimately sovereign (they retain the right to construct whatever form of government they think best and to throw off that government when it becomes despotic), but they may transfer or loan some of their power to the government.[16]

In his Massachusetts Constitution, Adams, unlike Thomas Jefferson's much more aristocratic draft constitutions for Virginia, made the House of Representatives, the Senate, and the Governor all elected directly and annually by the people. No other Revolutionary constitution so prominently displayed the sovereignty of the people. Likewise, in the *Defence of the Constitutions*, Adams repeatedly put the sovereignty of all branches of government directly and completely in the hands of the people: "The people are the fountain and original of the power of . . . governors and senates, as well as the . . . assembly of representatives." Elsewhere in the *Defence* he wrote that the "body of the people . . . is the fountain and original of all power and authority, executive and judicial, as well as legislative." By this, though, he meant that the people only temporarily cede their political sovereignty. In other words, the people are always the "fountain and original of all power" and they always retain the right to take it back, but they can and should lend that sovereignty to a duly constituted government on certain terms. Conversely, through free and annual elections, a house, a senate, or an executive may return to and appeal to the people's ultimate sovereignty in order to counter the usurping designs of the other branches or elements. Failing that, the people ultimately have the right to invoke the revolution-principle: "the right of a nation to kill a tyrant, in cases of necessity," he wrote in the *Defence*, "can no more be doubted, than that to hang a robber, or kill a flea." Regardless of what kind of government the people have agreed to live under, they always retain the right "to interpose, and to depose for maladministration—to appoint anew." The life of any form of legitimate government, according to Adams, cannot be, "in the nature of things, for a longer period than *quam diu se bene gesserit*, the whole nation being the judge." The right to call a new constitutional convention, or even the right to revolt, is inherent in Adams's doctrine of consent and sovereignty.[17]

Despite recognizing the right of the people to institute whatever form of government they think best for themselves, Adams did think there was a hierarchy of regimes and that a constitutional republic was the best form. In a country as large and populous as the United States (or even the individual states), it would be absurd to expect that "the whole should assemble, to make laws." Representation was the device that made large republics possible. It was necessary, therefore, to deputize representatives to do for the people what they cannot adequately do for themselves, that is, to transfer "power from the many, to a few of the most wise and good."[18] Adams's government would be wholly popular but entirely representative. This was possible because all the branches of government are directly or indirectly derived from the people, and yet the people do not govern directly. Following in the wake of Sidney and Locke, Adams accepted representation as a distinctly modern invention, as one of his improved principles in the political sciences.

The difficult question for Adams and his student constitution makers, though, was in determining exactly who should be represented and by what means. The first principle of political liberty was "Equality of Representation in the Legislature." A representative assembly, he wrote in *Thoughts on Government*, "should be in miniature, an exact portrait of the people at large. It should think, feel, reason, and act like them." But it was also the business of a democratic legislature to do more than just mirror or represent the passions, opinions, and interests of the people. Ultimately, it must transcend the people and assume as its principal task the job of ensuring "strict justice at all times." And this meant that representation must be equal such that "equal interest among the people should have equal interest in it."[19] Adams well knew that the disease most incident to republican government was the problem of social rivalries and the natural competition among the various elements of society.

How could strict justice be guaranteed, and did the republican principle of representation necessarily mean or imply a representation of all the people? Adams's honesty in confronting these difficult questions was unique. In 1776, James Sullivan wrote Adams suggesting that as the American constitution makers prepared to form new governments, they should consider instituting universal male suffrage. Sullivan thought that as all men must live by the laws, all men should be given the vote to voice their support or disagreement for the laws. Adams's response, written in the month after he wrote *Thoughts on Government*, plumbed the depths of consent, representation, and political legitimacy. He posed the basic problem in the following way:

> It is certain in Theory, that the only moral Foundation of Government, is the Consent of the People. But to what an Extent Shall We carry this Principle? Shall We Say that every Individual of the Community, old and young, male and female, as well as rich and poor, must consent, expressly, to every Act of Legislation? No, you will Say. This is impossible. How, then, does the Right arise in the Majority to govern the Minority, against their Will? Whence arises the Right of Men to govern the Women, without their Consent? Whence the Right of the old to bind the Young, without theirs?

These were some of the thorniest questions that confronted constitution makers and statesmen in the years after the American and French Revolutions. In 1776, John Adams was willing to tackle issues that most democratic statesmen would manage to avoid until the twentieth century. In one sense, Adams had a thoroughly modern view of representation. Unlike most of his contemporaries, he was more than willing to concede that women and young people were the moral if not intellectual equals of their adult male counterparts and that they had some claim to demand the vote. Adams's draft constitution for Massachusetts was certainly one of the most democratic of the Revolutionary era, but he was not willing to grant the franchise to everyone. He thought it entirely appropriate, indeed, even necessary, that there be some minimal qualification to vote; otherwise universal suffrage would inevitably lead to democratic tyranny.

Adams was therefore willing to admit standards that were unfair to some but not necessarily unjust. It was necessary, for instance, to set a minimum age requirement. He recognized that a minimum age of twenty-one was unfair but not necessarily unjust to the man who was twenty plus eleven months and twenty-nine days. For Adams, constitution makers "must fix upon Some Period in Life, when the Understanding and Will of Men in general is fit to be trusted by the Public." Likewise, there must be a minimal property qualification. Adams thought destitute men without property to be insufficiently acquainted with public affairs and all too often lacking in independent judgment.

Consent for Adams meant *enlightened* consent. This meant that his citizen-voters must have certain minimum qualifications: they must be men of independence, judgment, and will. That is, they must be self-governing in the fullest sense. Men who could not govern themselves should not in Adams's opinion have the right to govern others. Universal suffrage, he feared, tended to result in two different but not unrelated ends: either toward the confusion and destruction of "all Distinctions, and prostrate all Ranks, to one common Levell," or, it would drive destitute men toward "some Man of Property, who has attached their Minds to his Interest."[20] Ultimately, by giving the vote to the destitute, one ensured rule by an ambitious, wealthy, and manipulative few. Adams worried that universal male suffrage would encourage electoral corruption and that it would ultimately corrupt the constitution itself.

Adams was well aware that he was open to the charge of inconsistency, but he did not think that fair means justified unjust results. To remedy the problem, to ensure the widest possible suffrage, Adams advocated a public policy that would encourage the broadest possible distribution of property. In this he followed the principle (without the prescription) of Harrington's *Oceana:*

> Harrington has Shewn that Power always follows Property. This I believe to be as infallible a Maxim in Politicks, as that Action and Reaction are equal, is in Mechanicks. Nay, I believe We may advance one Step farther, and affirm that the Ballance of Power in a Society, accompanies the Ballance of Property in Land. The only possible Way then of preserving the Ballance of Power on the side of equal Liberty and public Virtue, is to make the Aquisition of Land easy to every Member of Society: to make a Division of Land into Small Quanties, So that the Multitude may be possessed of landed Estates. If the Multitude is possessed of the Ballance of real Estate, the Multitude will have the Ballance of Power, and in that Case the Multitude will

take Care of the Liberty, Virtue, and Interest of the Multitude in all Acts of Government.

Adams was proud that his own state of Massachusetts had, from the time of its founding, instituted a wise policy of distributing public lands as widely as possible. Despite its minimal property qualification, Massachusetts and the other New England colonies had the broadest, the most liberal franchise in the world. He saw no need to change that, and his own draft for a Massachusetts Constitution carried on that tradition.[21]

Finally, Adams's liberal and thoroughly modern view of representation can be seen in an extraordinary passage from the *Defence* where, in a rare dissenting opinion from Aristotle, he challenged the Peripatetic philosopher's view of citizenship. Taking as his text Book VII, chapters 8 and 9 of the *Politics*, Adams criticized Aristotle for arguing that husbandmen, artificers, and merchants could not be true citizens of the polity but were merely instruments useful to civil life and the virtuous regime. For Aristotle, the city or regime is constituted in order to fulfill its ultimate purpose, namely, virtue (wisdom and prudence). To that end, farmers, tradesmen, and merchants worked to "subserve certain uses and conveniences of the city." In other words, they were something less than citizens. Adams had utter contempt for a position he thought so thoroughly uncharacteristic of Aristotle.[22] This notion, according to Adams, forfeits "to the human species the character of rational creatures" and thus foists over men an unnatural aristocracy or monarchy. He thought this "dogma of Aristotle, and the practice of the world . . . the most unphilosophical, the most inhuman and cruel that can be conceived." Adams wanted his system of government open to almost all citizens; he understood all too well that in the course of human life some of the "most splendid geniuses, the most active and benevolent dispositions, and most undaunted bravery" come from the middle and lower classes. He thought that nature's moral equality had given to the natural aristocracy of merit and virtue "an undoubted right to have every road opened for them for advancement in life and in power that is open to any others." As long as a man had some small amount of property, he "may be supposed to have a judgement and will of his own" and should be allowed therefore to participate in public affairs. Adams was confident that farmers, mechanics, and merchants would discover, elect, and elevate to the public stage men of merit and ability from there own ranks "where they may exert all their faculties, and enjoy all the honors, offices, and commands, both in peace and war, of which they are capable."[23]

Separation of Powers

Separation of powers was for Adams the second great invention of the modern political sciences, and it was a central principle of his constitutional theory from the "Novanglus" essays to the *Defence*. He used it consistently as a means by which to criticize the concentration of power in the hands of a king or a democratic assembly. His condemnation of the royal government of Massachusetts in 1774 was spurred by the concentration of legislative, executive, and judicial power in the hands of Bernard, Hutchinson and Oliver.[24] And in 1776 he condemned his fellow Revolutionaries for attempting to concentrate the three powers of government in a unicameral legislature. Following Locke and Montesquieu, Adams had a clear sense of the separate and distinct powers of government and the need to balance them in order to preserve the separation. The "three branches of power have an unalterable foundation in nature," he later wrote in the *Defence:* "they exist in every society natural and artificial; and that if all of them are not acknowledged in any constitution of government, it will be found to be imperfect, unstable, and soon enslaved."[25]

In 1776, as Adams began to think about and develop constitutional plans for the new Revolurionary governments, the principle of separation of powers played a pivotal—if not *the* pivotal—role in his political architecture. In fact, *Thoughts on Government* was one of the first and most important revolutionary pamphlets written in defense of separation of powers. Several months before he officially began to write *Thoughts,* Adams sketched to Richard Henry Lee a first draft of the principle that was to have such an important affect on America's first constitution makers. The legislative, executive, and judicial powers, he told Lee, "comprehend the whole of what is meant and understood by Government." It is only when each of the three natural powers is balanced against the other two, "that the Effort in humane nature towards Tyranny, can alone be checked and restrained and any degree of freedom preserved in the Constitution." Six months later, he formally constructed a constitutional blueprint premised on the separation of powers principle. In *Thoughts on Government,* Adams made it clear that there could be no "impartial and exact execution of the laws," no constitution of liberty, without a separation of the three natural powers of government. He challenged the conceit recently popularized by Paine's *Common Sense* that the liberties of the people would be best secured in a unicameral assembly. Any form of government that did not include a separation of powers was, by definition, a threat to liberty and justice. Such governments "would make arbitrary laws for their own interest, execute all laws arbitrarily for their own interest, and adjudge all controversies in their own favour." Still later, he declared in the *Defence* that the safety of the state "depends upon placing the power of making laws, of executing them, and administering justice, in different hands."[26] Separation of powers was the means by which Adams constitutionalized the republican form of government.

When it came time for Adams to draft his own state constitution, he made the separation of powers the centerpiece of his institutional arrangements. He actually wrote into the text of his "Frame of Government" for Massachusetts that "the legislative, executive, and judicial power, shall be placed in separate departments, to the end that it might be a government of laws and not men." No state constitution constructed during the Revolutionary period was so explicit and openly self-conscious about the need to constitutionalize the separation of powers. (The Virginia constitution of 1776, inspired by Adams's *Thoughts on Government*, came closest to Adams's formulation of 1780.) The foundation for his institutional separation of powers was, of course, that the three powers of government be grounded directly or indirectly on the people. This new "body politic" was to be "formed by a voluntary association of individuals: It is a social compact, by which the people covenants with each citizen, and each citizen with the whole people, that all shall be governed by certain laws for the common good." On that basis, the people were to endow the government with "an equitable mode of making laws, as well as for an impartial interpretation; and a faithful execution of them, that every man may, at all times, find his security in them." With greater clarity and in greater detail than any other state constitution at that time, Adams organized his draft constitution around three independent and separate powers. To that end, he clearly delineated the legislative, executive, and judicial branches by organizing his constitution according to chapters, sections, and articles. But Adams was not an advocate of the pure version of separation of powers that says each power should be rigidly defined, placed in its own branch, and kept entirely separate from the other powers in their branches. Adams well knew that power is by its nature grasping and inflationary. He thought separation of powers viable only to the extent that the three branches could be balanced and given some means of self-defense. In other words, each of the three branches had to be given some kind of check on the encroaching and grasping powers of the others.

The legislative power in Adams's draft constitution was divided bicamerally between a Senate and a House of Representatives, and the governor was given an absolute veto to serve as a balance between the few and the many in the General Court. Among its most general powers of course was the authority to make laws for the "good and general welfare" of the Commonwealth, among which included civil and criminal laws (with punishments), and assessment of taxes in order to "dispose of matters and things whereby they may be religiously, peaceably, and civilly governed, protected, and defended."

Adams had always been an advocate of an independent, strong, unified, and high-toned executive. He understood that the natural tendency of republican governments was for the legislative branch to usurp all powers executive and judicial. In order to prevent legislative manipulation of the executive branch, he designed his independent executive by first, having him elected directly by the people rather than by the legislature (as it was with most of the other state constitutions), and second, by giving him an absolute veto over the legislature.[27] Just as the legislature represented the people's authority in "making, altering, and repealing" the laws, Adams's executive would independently represent "the majesty, persons, wills, and power of the people in the administration of government and dispensing of laws."[28] His executive veto served two functions: the first was to protect and sustain the separation of powers against the much stronger legislative branch, and the second was to give it a legislative power as an additional security against the enactment of unjust laws. In this way, he created a thoroughly republican executive that would have sufficient powers and authority to ensure good government.

The powers of Adams's democratic but muscular executive were twofold: the first magistrate was to execute and administer the laws of the legislature, and he was to have full authority over the organization and execution of defense matters. To those ends, he gave his governor broad appointive and federative powers. He styled his executive a "commander in chief" of the state's defense forces, and he gave this first magistrate full power "to assemble in martial array, and put in warlike posture, the inhabitants thereof, and to lead and conduct them, and with them to encounter, expulse, repel, resist, and pursue, by force of arms . . . all and every such person and persons as shall, at any time hereafter, in a hostile manner attempt, or enterprize the destruction, invasion, detriment, or annoyance of this Commonwealth. . . ." In order to further promote and strengthen the first magistrate's executive and prerogative power, Adams also gave his governor the authority to appoint all judicial and executive officials and all officers of the militia with the advice and consent of his Council. And, in order to maintain an independent, dignified, and disinterested executive so that "he should, in all cases, act with freedom for the benefit of the public," Adams ensured that the governor should have an honorable stated salary, "of a fixed and permanent value, amply sufficient for those purposes, and established by standing laws."[29] One of Adams's great contributions to constitutional theory was his attempt to republicanize the executive power while at the very same time restoring to it some of its original monarchic powers that could make it an effective promoter of the public interest.

Finally, Adams established an independent judiciary. Adams wrote very little during his lifetime about the role of the judiciary in his constitutional system, but he did see it as playing a pivotal role. Throwing off much of their inherited constitutional traditions, Adams and his fellow constitution makers were about to draft and establish written constitutions de novo. The very idea of a written constitution establishing a limited government required that there be a separate and independent judiciary, the primary purpose of which was to defend the constitution itself. First in *Thoughts on Government* and then in his draft constitution for Massachusetts, Adams established a separate judicial authority. He established its importance in no uncertain terms: "The dignity and stability of government in all its branches, the morals of the people and every blessing of society, depends so much upon an upright and skillful administration of justice, that the judicial power ought to be distinct from both the legislative and executive, and independent upon both, that so it may be a check upon both, as both should be checks upon that." To ensure the independence and dignity of the judiciary, Adams provided in the Massachusetts constitution that all "judicial officers, duely appointed, commissioned and sworn, shall hold their offices during good behavior," and that no "Justice of the Superior Court of Judicature, Court of Assize, and General Goal Delivery, shall have a seat in the Senate, or House of Representatives."[30] By these means, Adams hoped that the judicial branch would stand above ordinary law and protect the constitution as the fundamental law.

John Adams built his constitutional structure on the foundation of Lockean natural rights, consent, and the sovereignty of the people, the scaffolding was supplied by the principle of representation, and the architectonic principle that gave the government its general form was the separation of powers. Still, Adams was not satisfied; he was not convinced that "the formation, impartial execution, and faithful interpretation of good and equal laws" could be achieved by these principles alone.[31] Standing on its own, separation of powers was an insufficient principle of constitutional construction. First of all, though separated, the powers of government could never be equally distributed. By definition, the vortex of political power in republican government naturally rested in the legislative branch, and the natural tendency of the legislative was to usurp over time the powers of the other branches, particularly those of the executive. The problems arising from this unbalanced distribution of powers were particularly compounded if the legislature were unicameral. Single-house assemblies would almost always be controlled by an aggressive aristocracy who would govern in the name of some majority at the expense of the minority.

Adams also thought separation of powers a somehow hollow doctrine. It was a theory built on a philosophical construct (isolated individuals in a state of nature) that was not altogether grounded in the day-to-day realities of political life. It did not adequately take into account the social, religious, political, and economic divisions, hierarchies, and rivalries that exist in most communities. In order to ensure that the legislature would pass just and wise laws for the common good, Adams thought something more was needed in addition to separation of powers. That something of course was the introduction of the third of his great principles of constitutional construction: the triple equipoise of the one, the few, and the many in the legislative branch. The integration of the triple equipoise into the separation of powers more than anything else represented Adams's unique contribution to Western constitutionalism. Adams attempted to reconcile the seemingly irreconcilable theory of mixed government with separation of powers, and he attempted to provide the classical notion of mixed government with an entirely new philosophical foundation.

Mixed and Balanced Government

Adams scholars most often identify his political thought with the mixed regime of classical antiquity or with the traditional eighteenth-century English constitution. Indeed, for many, Adams has become the symbolic defender of mixed government during the Founding period.[32] This claim, however, distorts his overall theory of political architecture. Adams was indeed an advocate of mixed and balanced government, but only in the context of the modern doctrines of natural rights, representation, and, most importantly, separation of powers. In the very same way that he was not an advocate of a pure theory of separation of powers, he was not an advocate of a pure or classical form of mixed government. He was for mixing the one, the few, and the many in only one branch of government, that is, the legislative. This makes his theory of the mixed constitution unique in the history of political thought, and it should not therefore be compared to the classical or English versions.

For Adams, mixed government and separation of powers could be employed as overlapping and mutually reinforcing principles. In fact, the theory of mixed government was actually a subsidiary principle subsumed by Adams under the umbrella of separation of powers. Time and again he made clear that the balancing of the one, the few, and the many was to take place strictly within the legislative branch. The integration of these two principles in one constitutional form represented "the only scientific government; the only plan which takes into consideration *all* the principles in nature, and provides for *all* cases that occur." In other words, separation of powers and mixed government, taken as separate and distinct principles, were incomplete or insufficient guarantors of republican liberty; they were incapable of enacting and executing equal laws "by common consent, for the general interest." It was only by combining the two that "all the principles in nature" and all the potential abuses of power could be taken into account and reconfigured so as to promote just ends and the public good.[33] Adams emphasized mixed government over the other principles in the *Defence* because it was the sole principle under attack.

When he first began to write about constitutions in the early 1770s, Adams accepted the traditional rationale for mixed government that had come down through the ages from the Greeks. His principal teachers had been Aristotle, Polybius, Cicero, and their modern students, Machiavelli and Harrington, from whom he learned about the classical categorization of regimes and the related cyclical theory of constitutional change. This rather simplistic teaching presupposed the existence of three natural or ideal forms of government. Years before Adams had written the *Defence*, he declared in a 1772 oration delivered at Braintree, that "there are only Three simple Forms of Government" synonymous with the natural social orders of society: democracy represented the rule of the many, aristocracy the rule of a "few, great, rich, wise Men," and monarchy represented the "Rule of one." Inherent in each of the pure regimes were the seeds of discontent and dissolution. Human nature, never content with what it has, seeks more and more power, and the natural forms of government are inevitably perverted and transformed into their opposite: monarchy degenerated into tyranny, aristocracy into oligarchy, and democracy into mob rule. It was possible, however, to escape or transcend the cycle. In addition to the three simple forms of government and their corrupt alternatives, lawgivers might create an "indefinite variety of other Forms of Government, occasioned by different Combinations of the Powers of Society, and different Intermixtures of these Forms of Government, one with another." The purpose of the mixed regime, then, was to prevent or allay the perversion of the three natural or pure forms of government into their corrupt counterpart. By mixing the three natural political forms in one government, the see-sawing fluctuations that had destroyed the ancient city-states would cease. "Liberty," Adams told his Braintree audience, "depends upon an exact Ballance, a nice Counterpoise of all the Powers of the State. . . . The best Governments of the World have been mixed."[34] By the time he came to write the *Defence*, his understanding and defense of mixed and balanced government had matured and deepened. No longer content to repeat the shallow and rather timeworn formulas of the classics, Adams sought to go beyond them by providing this old theory of government with a deeper, more philosophical defense.

From Adams's perspective two basic problems must be addressed by all republican constitution makers. The first was to find some kind of constitutional device by which to draw out and up the talents of the exceptional few without compromising republican principles. As he later explained to Thomas Jefferson, history and experience demonstrated that the natural aristocracy were "the most difficult Animals to manage, of anything in the whole Theory and practice of Government." What was to be done with them? Should they be recognized and regulated, or should they be simply "massacred" and "eradicated" as French Revolutionaries were about to do? Was there any place for them in republican government? In other words, "how shall the legislator avail himself of their influence for the equal benefit of the public? and how, on the other hand, shall he prevent them from disturbing the public happiness?"[35]

The second and related task for Adams's lawgiver was to constitutionalize the natural social conflict between the few and the many. "The great art of lawgiving," he announced, "consists in balancing the poor against the rich in the legislature."[36] In sum, the great problem of constitutional construction was in reconciling aristocratic ambition with democratic envy. How could the aristocracy be tamed and the democracy sobered? What form of government was most in keeping with human passions and the hierarchic ordering of man's natural constitution?

These difficult questions led Adams to address the "great question," the great theoretical problem of constitutional theory: "What combination of powers in society, or what form of government, will *compel* the formation, impartial execution, and faithful interpretation of good and equal laws, so that the citizens may constantly enjoy the benefit of them, and may be sure of their continuance?"[37] The key to answering these questions, according to Adams, was to find some kind of "resisting force" to counter the self-regarding passions. Adams's constitution would not require voluntary obedience to natural law, virtue, or religion to make it work, nor would it require the rule of magnanimous statesmen. In the place of these traditional republican props, Adams sought a strictly constitutional solution. He looked to the structures of government, to the institutional checks and balances associated with the separation of powers, and then to the legislative triple equipoise of the one, the few, and the many as the means by which to tame the passions. His constitution would be a self-executing mechanism; it would harness and then channel the power driven by the passions in politically and socially useful ways. Just as he was finishing the *Defence*, Adams told Jefferson that he had been long settled in the opinion "that neither Philosophy, nor Religion, nor Morality, nor Wisdom, nor Interest, will ever govern nations or Parties, against their Vanity, their Pride, their Resentment or Revenge, or their Avarice or Ambition. Nothing but Force and Power and Strength can restrain them."[38] Of course, Adams found a partial "resisting force" in the separation of powers, but that alone was an insufficient check. Separation of powers was indifferent to the kind of laws legislated and executed. It did not take into account and could not overcome the rivalries and faction-based legislation that was natural to all societies. In particular, it did not and could not overcome the problems associated with aggressive aristocracies and overbearing majorities.

Adams's general solution to the problems posed by republican government was to mix and balance in the legislative branch of government the one, the few and the many, so as to "*compel*"—this is a key principle for Adams— "to compel all to respect the common right, the public good, the universal law, in preference to all private and partial considerations." Throughout the *Defence*, he repeated the necessity of placing the three natural orders in the legislature so that they might "*compel* each other at all times to be real guardians of the laws." What exactly did Adams mean by this? What mechanisms or compulsions did he think would force the competing social orders to "prefer the public good before their own"?[39]

Ultimately, for Adams, the sociopolitical orders associated with the one, the few, and the many were simply manifestations of the passions and the *spectemur agendo*. The true novelty of his defense of mixed and

balanced government was in giving to "every passion" an "adequate counterpoise." In other words, passion must be made to counteract passion.
This meant, of course, that the legislature first had to be divided, shared,
and balanced among three equal or near equal orders. It was simply not in
the "nature of things," he wrote, to have a "balance without three powers." Unless the three orders were "independent and absolute" and had a
"veto, or negative, to every law, the constitution can never be long preserved." A wise lawgiver, Adams observed, must therefore "take away the
power, by controlling the selfish avidity of the governor, by the senate and
house; of the senate, by the governor and house; and of the house, by the
governor and senate." Adams thought it a basic axiom, a "universal precept," that constitution makers should "trust not to human nature, without a control, the conduct of my cause." Without the legislative triple
equipoise, he thought it would "be impossible that the laws should at all
times preserve their authority and govern all men." History clearly
demonstrated that the one, the few, and the many were equally guilty of
usurping rights when given unlimited power, and that no "wise man"
would trust any one of them with this power. It was therefore necessary
that "every judicious legislator . . . set all three to watch and control each
other." The triple equipoise, he said, must be established as a "dictate of
nature."[40]

Bicameralism was the central component of Adams's mixed and balanced legislature. A two-house chamber would recognize all the passions,
opinions, and interests of the few and the many; it would, in other words,
represent or recreate society at large. On one side stood a house of representatives or a lower house to represent the people at large. A representative assembly would serve as a bulwark of the people's liberties.[41] On the
other side of this balance stood a senate or an upper house to represent the
natural aristocracy. A separate and distinct senate would act as a safety
valve for the natural aristocracy, thereby allowing the government to benefit from the talents and ambitions of the few while at the same time preventing them from overrunning the government. Adams thought it
absolutely necessary and entirely consistent with republican policy to both
elevate and separate the "most illustrious" from the general populace.
"This is, to all honest and useful intents," he said, "an ostracism." Banished
to a senate, the aristocracy would be surrounded and watched on one side
by an assembly and by a governor on the other. By throwing the rich and
proud into their own assembly, Adams's political architect would thereby
disarm the aristocracy "entirely of the power to do mischief," and he would
also be able to take advantage of their "abilities and virtues."[42]

The pivotal role in Adams's triple equipoise, however, was played by the governor, who stood between the few and the many. Armed with an absolute legislative veto, the governor in Adams's schema was to serve as an "impartial mediator." His separate election by the people ensured that he would not simply be a tool of either house. The "greatest desideratum in a government," according to Adams, was a unified executive power "of sufficient strength and weight to compel both these parties, in turn, to submit to the laws." Annually elected by the people, the governor was "the natural friend of the people"; he was their greatest defense against "the avarice and ambition of the rich and distinguished citizens."[43] Adams hoped that his executive would disinterestedly rise above faction and party rivalry and serve as the guardian of the common good.

In the very same way that he had constitutionalized the natural powers of government, Adams attempted to constitutionalize the competition between the natural social orders. By embodying the one, the few, and the many in the legislature to watch and protect each other, he argued that each order with its incomplete concept of justice and the common good would be forced to moderate and elevate its partial claims; they would be "stationed to watch each other, and compare each other's conduct with the laws." Adams even compared this constitutional pulling and tugging to Newton's laws of motion. If properly designed and constructed, this perfect constitutional system would be held together because "'reaction must always be equal and contrary to action.'" In the very same way that Newton's system of universal law demonstrated how "power must be opposed to power, force to force, strength to strength," so too with the constitution of government: the lawgiver must oppose "interest to interest, as well as reason to reason, eloquence to eloquence, and passion to passion." When combined with a separation of powers, a mixture of the one, the few, and the many in the government would produce and necessitate "constancy in all its parts":

> the king must be constant to preserve his prerogatives; the senate must be constant to preserve their share; and the house theirs. Neither can go beyond its line, without being called back by the other. . . . It is to this universal vigilance and constancy, which such a constitution renders necessary and unavoidable, that the laws owe their perpetual superiority, and are able to make kings, nobles, and commoners, ministers of state and religion, and judges too, bow with reverence to its decisions. To this constancy, therefore, is due that delightful tranquility of mind, arising from a sense of perfect security in

the protection of known laws for the enjoyment of life, liberty, honor, reputation, and property.

A constitution with a mixed legislature was therefore superior to all others because it was "best calculated to prevent, to manage, and to remedy tumults, by doing justice to all men on all occasions, to the minority as well as majority; and by forcing all men, majority as well as minority, to be contented with it." It was the only "means of reconciling law and liberty." The legislative triple equipoise would force the various elements in the law-making process to moderate their passions, to look beyond their immediate self-interest, and to compromise with competing interests. The result would be a government capable of producing laws that were just, equitable, and ultimately for the common benefit. Only in a well-balanced government, Adams wrote in *Davila*, could "reason, conscience, truth, and virtue . . . be respected by all parties, and exerted for the public good." With a separation of powers and the legislative triple equipoise, Adams and his fellow constitution makers had discovered a "method of enacting laws that must of necessity be wise and equal."[44]

The Language of Signs

In addition to regulating and limiting the outrages of democratic envy or oligarchic arrogance, Adams thought it possible to arrange government institutions in such a way that the passions could be conducted through channels that seek higher, even nobler ends. Not only must republican government ensure *just* government, Adams thought, but it should also foster *good* government. A truly wise constitution maker, therefore, must also attempt to gratify, encourage, and arrange emulation and the passion for individual distinction "on the side of virtue." The structure of the government itself, its forms and formalities, its institutional arrangements and procedures, could be used, Adams thought, to elevate and foster a more "noble temper" among the citizenry.[45] This is an extraordinarily ambitious claim. What exactly did Adams mean by it? How could it be achieved?

The *spectemur agendo*, it will be recalled, is a passion that can be directed toward either socially destructive or socially beneficial purposes: it could reveal itself in the form of democratic envy and aristocratic aggression on the one hand, or it could be directed toward democratic aspiration and aristocratic virtue on the other. The whole science of government, according to Adams, could "be reduced to the same principle, and be all comprehended in the knowledge of the means of actively conducting, controlling, and regulating, the emulation and ambition" of the most aggressive citizens. Adams thought it possible to arrange the institutions of government in such a way that they would foster the emulation that produces genius and the desire for superiority that creates talents.[46] The question was how to do so.

Adams's answer was unique. He began with the republican axiom that "men aspire to great actions when rewards depend on merit." His task was to first find a means by which to lure the best men to participate actively in government and, second, to connect merit with political office. In order to attract the true men of abilities, merit, and virtue, constitution makers must somehow stir their emulation and inflame their desire for distinction. Adams found his answer with the ancient Romans. No one, he thought, understood the human heart better than the Romans, and no one "made a better use of the passion for consideration, congratulation, and distinction." The Romans employed what Adams called the "language of signs," that is, they attached to the most prestigious public offices certain honors, titles, and public signs of distinction. "*Distinctions of conditions*, as well as of ages, were made by difference of clothing. . . . The chairs of ivory; the lictors; the rods; the axes; the crowns of gold, of ivory, of flowers; . . . their ovations; and their triumphs; everything in religion, government and common life, was parade, representation and ceremony." The purpose of these rewards was to "excite the emulation and active virtue of the citizens." They served as a magnet, drawing out and up the talents of the best citizens in the service of the republic. Adams was quick to recognize that these signs were mere frivolities, that they brought neither profit nor true pleasure, and "yet experience teaches us, in every country of the world, they attract the attention of mankind more than parts or learning, virtue or religion."[47] These honors, above all other public signs, are what attract the attention of the most ambitious if not the best citizens.

It was also important to Adams's plan that these honors be directed toward or attached to the "right objects." In other words, the honor in question must be in recognition of some virtue or service that promoted the good of the public. By this means, the lawgiver would let the people see that virtue was "the only rational source and eternal foundation of honor." At the very least, the lawgiver must give some kind of "intimation" that the titles and honors he establishes as marks of order and subordination were connected to "some particular virtues" associated with the nature of the position. Adams hoped to connect "honor with offices," that is, to annex by law "the names and ideas at least of certain moral virtues and intellectual qualities" to certain offices. Titles like veneration, grace, excellence, honor, serenity, and majesty, for instance, had meanings and rankings that were intended to symbolize and evoke certain qualities.[48] The honor or office itself, then, would attract the men of ambition and talent, but it would also direct that ambition and talent in socially useful ways. Adams hoped that an American language of signs would inspire the most talented, ambitious, and virtuous citizens toward public-spirited actions.

Adams's call for an American language of signs was shocking to his republican friends like Thomas Jefferson and Benjamin Rush. At the heart of old-fashioned republicanism had been the idea that disinterestedness and self-sacrifice were the only virtues that could uplift and sustain the republican form. To that end, traditional republicans had made public office "irksome" and a "burden," and they had demanded of their rulers that their service "be perfectly disinterested." In the name of patriotism, for instance, they would typically ask their officeholders to serve with little or no pay. Adams thought there were three unintended consequences to this antiquated teaching that would be ultimately destructive of republican government. First, without some kind of incentive, the best citizens would not serve. It was a philosophical fiction to suggest that there were sufficient numbers of disinterested statesmen who, over long periods of time, would serve the public without some kind of compensation or reward. Second, only the rich could serve, thus turning the government over time into an oligarchy. All public offices, he warned, "would be monopolized by the rich; the poor and the middling ranks would be excluded." And third, it would introduce "a universal system of Machiavelian hypocrisy into popular elections."[49]

This last consequence Adams worried about the most. He knew "very well that the word 'disinterested' turns the heads of the people by exciting their enthusiasm." He also knew that "those who are most interested, most corrupted, and most determined to carry the commodity to market, are the most liberal in their offers of a price to purchase it, the most ostentatious in professions of disinterested motives." Though history might present to Americans a handful of these disinterested characters over the course of many centuries, it also demonstrated "two thousand instances every year of the semblance of disinterestedness, counterfeited for the most selfish purposes." In the end, this "hypocritical pretence of disinterestedness" would be set up to deceive the multitude, "much oftener than the virtue will be practiced for their good." Worse yet, having gained office through the people's niggardliness and by their own hypocritical pronouncements of disinterestedness, the ruling oligarchy would ultimately demand "gratitude" from the people, and gratitude, Adams warned, could not be the foundation of a truly republican government. "The cry of gratitude," he said, had "established more despotism in the world, than all other causes put together." John Adams was attempting to turn the classical theory of republican government on its head. His new republicanism would be guided by a new principle: that "every public man should be honestly paid for his services" as a matter of justice rather than gratitude.[50] Furthermore, offices that paid well would provide the necessary incentives to attract the best men to serve without the deception and hypocrisy associated with disinterestedness. Justice required it and the long-term well-being of the republic demanded it.

The greatest difficulty in employing the language of signs for republican purposes was to ensure that the distribution of honors be just. Not only does the public good require justice in the distribution of wealth (a function for Adams determined by market processes), but it does so as well with regard to the distribution of fame and honor. If the language of signs did not recognize true merit—that is, the natural aristocracy of wisdom, virtue and abilities—the distribution of honors could be easily corrupted and turned against the public good. This was delicate business. Adams knew that there was no stronger or more universal an appetite in human nature than that which sought distinction and honor, and he also knew that real merit was confined to a relatively small number. The problem, of course, was that "the numbers who thirst for respect, are out of all proportion to those who seek it only by merit." Every man wants his fifteen minutes of fame, as we say today. In a world where the majority of people are scrambling for honors and distinction, "what chance has humble, modest, obscure, and poor merit in such a scramble?" he asked. Most people recognized, indeed, there is "a voice within us," he wrote, "which seems to intimate that real merit should govern the world; and that men ought to be respected only in proportion to their talents, virtues, and services." The problem confronted by lawgivers, however, had been to determine how constitutions could be organized so as to recognize true merit. "How shall real merit be discovered?" he asked. And "who shall judge?"[51]

Of one thing Adams was certain: true merit would never be discovered in a simple democratic government. The distribution of honors in a simple democracy would always be determined by an arbitrary and partisan majority seeking reelection. "In a simple democracy," he warned, "each leader thinks himself accountable only to his party, and obliged to bestow honors, rewards, and offices, not upon merit and for the good of the whole state, but merely to increase his votes and partisans in future elections." Simple democracies, Adams warned, were accountable to no one in the selection and distribution of honors. By contrast, a mixed government afforded greater opportunity for the recognition of true merit than any other form. In a mixed government properly balanced, Adams claimed that it was "rarely possible that real service, merit, and virtue should go unrewarded." In a mixed government, the appointment to offices and the distribution of honors would come under much stricter scrutiny. In marked contrast to a simple democracy, there are in a mixed government "three resources, one in each branch of the legislature, and a fourth in the courts of justice" to watch and guard the distribution of appointments and honors. He thought history clear on this point: "the best appointments for a course of time have invariably been made in mixed governments."[52]

More particularly, Adams thought that the best hope for the selection of real merit lay with an independent executive.[53] It was impossible, indeed, ridiculous to think that the people of a nation as large as the United States, or any one of the separate states, would have sufficient knowledge to choose individuals of the greatest merit for the highest offices and honors. It was obvious that such a contest would be "a lottery of millions of blanks to one prize." Real merit, Adams stressed, was too "remote from the knowledge of whole nations." There was a much greater likelihood, however, that an independent executive would have the personal knowledge of those individuals most endowed with real virtues and abilities and that he would have the means and the necessary judgment to choose men of abilities for positions of public trust. There was also less danger that the selection of individuals for offices and honors by a single person would be corrupted. This is precisely why Adams gave his Massachusetts governor, for instance, the authority to appoint all judicial officials and, most importantly, all officers of the militia. He thought a republican governor much more responsible than a democratic majority in choosing men of true merit, and he thought them much more accountable because "gross corruption in the distribution of offices" is more visible and easily detected when confined to one person. "When the emulation of all the citizens looks up to one point, like the rays of a circle from all parts of the circumference, meeting and uniting in the centre, you may hope for uniformity, consistency, and subordination; but when they look up to different individuals, or assemblies, or councils, you may expect all the deformities, eccentricities, and confusion, of the Polemic system."[54]

In addition to channeling the desire for distinction toward more elevated and public ends, Adams also thought the language of signs could be used for another important purpose. Historically, one of the great problems of republican governments had been to foster and retain the people's attachment and obedience to the laws over extended periods. In monarchies and aristocracies, the people's obedience to the laws had traditionally been secured through force and a standing army. Republicanism, by contrast, had always required of its citizens that they be self-governing, that is, that they voluntarily obey the laws. But this had always proven a difficult task. The tendency of republican governments over time had always been toward anarchy. Adams assumed, however, that if the distribution of public offices and honors could be truly determined on the basis of merit, the people would be much more likely to demonstrate in deed and action their respect and voluntary attachment to the government and its laws. Again, he turned to the Romans for guidance. In that ancient republic, he wrote, "everything was addressed to the emulation of citizens, and everything was calculated to attract the attention, to allure the consideration and excite the congratulations of the people." In this way, the people could "attach their hearts to individual citizens according to their merit; and to their lawgivers, magistrates, and judges, according to their rank, station, and importance in the state." This subordination of ranks and offices Adams thought not only natural but necessary in all governments, and it was particularly important in a republic where the tendency was always toward leveling and disorder. It was critically important, therefore, that the ordinary citizen "sees honors, offices, rewards, distributed to valiant, virtuous, or learned men." That being the case, "he esteems them his own," and is willing to obey their laws, but only "as long as the door is left open to succeed in the same dignities and enjoyments." Adams thought this method of attaching reverence to ranks the only means of "preserving order, or procuring submission to the laws"; it was the only method consistent, he thought, with "the true spirit of republics."[55] Adams well knew that popular government could become as unjust as any aristocracy or monarchy. He therefore sought to provide the republican model with a strong and durable constitution, one that would withstand the corrupting pressures common to the republican form.

Adams's understanding of mixed and balanced government was unique, and should not be confused with either that of the classical philosophers or with that of eighteenth-century Britain. He certainly appealed to the great tradition of the mixed regime, but Adams was also an innovator within that tradition. In both form and content, he was attempting to provide that constitutional design with an entirely new philosophical foundation. Whereas Aristotle, Polybius, Machiavelli, Harrington, Montesquieu, and De Lolme tended to construct their mixed polities on the basis of en-trenched socioeconomic or legally established hereditary orders, Adams saw the differences between the one, the few, and the many as determined by and inherent in the constitution of human nature. The deeper one penetrates into the meaning and originality of Adams's theory of mixed government, the more one sees that it represents a new trend of thought. A *Defence of the Constitutions of Government of the United States of Amer-ica* may very well be the most important reformulation of the mixed and balanced government since Aristotle's *Politics*.

Chapter 11

The Art of Political Architecture

From very early in his public life, John Adams was fascinated with the role played by the lawgivers or legislators of classical antiquity in framing constitutions and codes of law for their respective city-states. The very idea of a lawgiver, though, raised certain difficulties for Adams and the statesmen of the Revolutionary era. Although he clearly relished the opportunity afforded by the Revolution for recreating and reliving the role of the great Legislator, Adams was nevertheless sharply critical of the ancient foundings. The activities of the ancient constitution makers had been shrouded in mystery and their authority was almost always derived from divine sources. Adams reminded his readers in the preface to *A Defence of the Constitutions* that, according to the ancients, "the Divinity alone was adequate to the important office of giving laws to men." Myth, divine authority, artifice, and fraud—all were used to legitimize the authority and wisdom of the classical lawgivers. The ancient method of establishing government by a divinely inspired lawgiver was simply unacceptable for America, where the people are too "enlightened to disabuse themselves of artifice, imposture, hypocricy, and superstition."[1] A new foundation, therefore, a new mode of establishing government was necessary for a people educated in the modern natural-rights philosophy associated with John Locke. But Locke's theory was not without its difficulties for American constitution makers. The ideas of equality, consent, and sovereignty associated with his social contract theory made no mention of how constitutions should be designed and by whom. In fact, it was not clear that a sole constitution maker was consistent with Lockean theory.

Descending from the realm of pure theory, American statesmen in the 1770s and 1780s were confronted with the very real task of converting Lockean ideas into practice. As a leading advocate for the establishment of Revolutionary state constitutions, Adams wrestled with, and thought as deeply about this problem, as any person of his generation. We know that he was one of the first Americans to invoke the use of special constitutional conventions first to draft and then ratify the constitutional will of the people. He advocated the sovereignty of the people as the only moral and legal basis of legitimate constitutional orders, but he understood that the people themselves, or even their representatives, were unlikely to design good constitutions. The idea of a constitutional convention was the first step in overcoming this Lockean oversight, but even a small convention of several dozen men was liable to massive inconveniences and to corrupting passions and interests. Adams therefore supported the idea that constitutions be drafted by special committees elected by the whole convention. Indeed, he came very close to suggesting that a good constitution could be created by only one man. "It is incredible," he told Richard Price, "how small is the number, in any nation . . . who comprehend any system of constitution or administration." Public opinion should be respected and consulted when framing constitutions, but it should never be the guiding principle when it conflicts with common sense, the dictates of reason, and the "formation of a right Judgement of public affairs." Only infrequently and on "small matters," he warned, should lawgivers follow public opinion. The views of the many in such weighty matters were like "a wave of the sea in a storm in the Gulf Stream." Instead, the design and construction of new states "should be guided and aided as well as informed by those [who] are in Possession of all the secrets of the State." The principles of political architecture must in large measure be discovered. Unlike Solon and Lycurgus, America's Lockean lawgivers would not have "interviews with the gods," nor would they be "in any degree under the inspiration of Heaven." Instead, Adams insisted that his student legislators devote many years to the study of history and human nature. Political architecture "requires universal knowledge and great experience." It was not a task for the common man. The kind of knowledge, experience, and wisdom that was "essential to the formation of a right Judgement" in public affairs was limited to the rarest of individuals:

> How few in any age or Country, have been equal to it. In America we should have been very excusable, if we had found none. Neither our Education, our Prospects or Expectations led us to this Frame of thinking. Ages of anarchy and Distraction preceded the formation of such characters as those of Lycurgus and Solon; and long study and laborious Travel, with a single view to discover the best form of Government, were scarcely sufficient for their purpose.[2]

Adams understood that some constitutions, those with obscure or unknown beginnings, had evolved slowly toward perfection. This was certainly the case with the Roman and English constitutions, two of his favorites. At this unique moment in history, however, when the opportunity and the means of building constitutions from calm reflection and deliberate choice were just right, the Americans' Revolutionary effort would have been in vain had they left the formation of their constitutions to chance or accidents. It was critically important that the Revolutionary generation "begin well." Adams warned that "misarrangements now made, will have great, extensive, and distant consequences; and we are now employed, how little soever we may think of it, in making establishments which will affect the happiness of a hundred millions of inhabitants at a time, in a period not very distant."[3] To begin well, however, meant that America's founding generation must be suitably educated for the peculiar task at hand.

What are the qualities that make a good lawgiver, according to Adams? What personal characteristics, what kind of education and training, what qualities of mind, and what kinds of intellectual processes must come together in one man to establish the proper credentials and authority of a single legislator? Just as he was beginning to write the *Davila* essays, Adams sketched his own portrait of the ideal lawgiver:

> The character of a Legislator has in all ages been held above that of [a] hero. Lycurgus and Solon are ranked higher than Alexander or Caesar. The most profound and sublime genius, the most extensive information and the vastest views have been always considered as indispensable. A consumate master of Science and literature, a long experience in affairs of government, travel through all the known world were among the ancients thought little enough for a founder of laws.[4]

Adams understood that the training of a lawgiver was a long and arduous task. "This kind of architecture," he said, "is an art or mystery very difficult to learn, and still harder to practice." It is not like the other arts or sciences. Penetrating and comprehending "all the intricate and complicated Interests which compose the Machine" of state required a "Mind as vast as the Ocean, or Atmosphere." The lawgiver must spend years studying human nature, political philosophy, and history. As early as 1763, Adams could write that it had been his "amusement for many years past . . . to examine the systems of all the legislators, ancient and modern, fantastical and real, and to trace their effects in history upon the felicity of mankind." From Paris in 1780, he told Abigail that it was his "Duty to study" the "Science of Government . . . more than all other sciences."[5] And study he did. With a kind of resolute determination that almost boggles modern sensibilities, Adams threw himself into the study of history, philosophy, jurisprudence, and the law. With his sights focused on the glory and lasting immortality associated with the ancient lawgivers, Adams set for himself a rigorous daily schedule of study.

Adams's training for the role of a lawgiver included not only the study of history and philosophy, but also foreign travel and the observation of how ordinary people live from day-to-day. He observed common and not so common people in their homes and at work, in public meetings, and in private conversation. When Benjamin Rush suggested to him that law-givers ought to think more and watch less, Adams challenged the idea that watching a family at the dinner table was "beneath the Dignity of a Legislator." He scoffed at Rush's elitism and told him that "nothing in human life is beneath the Dignity of a Legislator to consider." Indeed, he insisted that the principles of government "are to be seen in every scene of human life."[6]

Adams was also fascinated with the ways in which politics and religion shape a nation's character and mores. In 1778, when he landed at Bordeaux on his first diplomatic mission to Europe, he traveled five hundred miles through the French countryside with a determination to see this foreign country "with a philosophic eye." He was determined, he said, to "discard all my old England prejudices, my American prejudices, my New England prejudices, my puritan prejudices, my Yankee prejudices, & every other bias, as perfectly as [though] I was travelling in Venus, Mercury, or Mars." The purpose of the journey was to see as "much of the national character, and manners" as possible. After arriving in Paris and exploring its various districts, he went to the theatre, to the opera, and to all the great and small churches; he then travelled beyond Paris as much as he could, to Versailles, into the countryside, and to the great châteaux. He then asked himself a number of questions: "'What View of religion and Government, have produced these Effects? Could a free republick, or any species of free Government exist with such a religion? such manners? such information, and such understandings?"[7] These are not simply the questions of a diplomat; they are the questions of a lawgiver!

Adams's intense, even obsessive desire to observe the effect of local institutions on the French character may have been a conscious attempt to imitate the same kind of journey reported to have once been undertaken by Lycurgus. In order to gain useful knowledge it was said that the Spartan lawgiver had traveled to Egypt and Crete. Adams learned of this legend from Plutarch's *Lives*. Hence he is able to tells us in the *Defence* that the purpose of Lycurgus's mission was to acquire "a deep insight into human nature." The Lacadaemonian lawgiver "informed himself fully of the length and breadth, the height and depth, of the passion of ambition in the human heart." Lycurgus, Adams reported, understood ambition better than all other legislators. The Spartan constitution maker had used and channeled this aggressive passion in such a way as to gain its advantages while mollifying its antisocial propensities. Adams advised those "Statesmen" who would form "a new World" to study "every gradation of the passions, and every shade of their various and opperations on the good or evil of Society."[8]

Following this "Course of Reflection," Adams thought it possible to establish "a System of Rules that may one day produce an Hero or a Legislator, a great Statesman or Divine or some other great Character that may do Honour to the World." In 1772, he sketched a course of study for himself that would one day produce *Thoughts on Government*, the Massachusetts Constitution, and *A Defence of the Constitutions*: "Human Nature . . . and human Life must be carefully observed and studied. Here we should spread before Us a Map of Man—view him in different Soils and Climates, in different nations and Countries, under different Religions and Customs, in Barbarity and Civility, in a State of Ignorance and enlightened with Knowledge, in Slavery and in freedom, in Infancy and Age."[9] Like the Spartan lawgiver Lycurgus, Adams spent much of his life's journey wandering through and studying what he called the constitution of the human mind.

The Lawgiver's Art

The political controversy between Adams and the Turgotists began and ended on the question of constitutional forms, on whether unicameral or bicameral legislatures would better protect the rights and liberties of all citizens. Behind this question, however, defining and shaping its parameters, was a very different kind of theoretical problem that lawgivers must address before they actually begin to construct constitutions: Should lawgivers attempt in the Rousseauan tradition to design the one best constitution in theory, applicable to all people at all times, or, following the advice of Montesquieu, should they design constitutions relative to the customs, habits, and mores of particular peoples?[10] This question goes to the heart of the differences in constitutional design between Adams and the Turgotists. Condorcet designed constitutions on the basis of "what could or should be done."[11] Adams designed constitutions on the basis of both theory *and* practice. Generally speaking, he thought the mixed constitution best, but he also recognized that its design could and should be adapted and adjusted to the moral character of the people over whom it would govern.

At the beginning of Book IV of the *Politics,* Aristotle compared the art of political architecture to that of the gymnastics trainer. Athletics requires not only a consideration of the best training regimen for the perfect physique, but also a knowledge of the best possible regimen for a range of imperfect bodies. Similarly, the political architect not only must consider the best regime in theory, but he must also consider what regime is best for a range of political communities in the light of the very best.[12] Adams thought constitution making an art, and he often compared it to painting or to conducting a symphony. Imitating the method of a Michelangelo or a Handel, Adams advised his constitutional architects first to study and imitate nature as it really is. In the same way that Michelangelo examined the world around him and Handel took into account the various instruments of an orchestra, Adams's student constitution makers must catalogue and study an extensive number of political forms. That done, his lawgivers are then at liberty to arrange and rearrange these constitutional forms in an infinite number of ways in order to construct a beautiful and harmonius whole.[13] This is not to say that Adams's political architect would begin de novo or without guiding first principles.

Following in the tradition of Solon, Aristotle, and Montesquieu, Adams advised his lawgiver to frame constitutions relative to the national character and way of life peculiar to each and every nation.[14] Because not every form of government was suitable for every people, Adams thought it absolutely necessary that the lawgiver first measure the "spirit" of the people for whom he was to frame a constitution and then adapt the best form of government around the animating spirit of that particular society. Forms of government, he told Richard Henry Lee, may be designed in "an infinite Number of Ways," but they must be accommodated "to the different, Genius, Temper, Principles and even Prejudices of different People." In the years after 1776, the Americans were confronted with the daunting task of simultaneously creating anew while at the same time preserving the best of the old and tried. Their greatest difficulty, Adams warned, lay "in forming Constitutions" to suit the varying needs of thirteen "particular colonies." Because the folkways, mores, and habits of the several colonies were different one from another, he advised America's lawgivers to consult and take into account "the Usages, and Genius, and Manners of the people." Prudence, therefore, must be the lawgiver's architectonic virtue; it must guide him as he attempts to reconcile ideas and interests, the best regime with the best practical regime. To all present and future legislators he left a simple warning: "Beware how you make laws to shock the prejudices or break the habits of the people. Innovations even of the most certain and obvious utility must be introduced with great caution, prudence and skill."[15] Practical wisdom must temper speculative theory and the philosopher's desire to make over the world.

Despite the importance that Adams placed on factoring local customs and historical experiences into constitutional designs, it must be noted that he was not a constitutional relativist. He did not recommend that constitutions be designed solely on the basis of prescription, that is, on the basis of tradition and established custom. John Adams was not an American Burke. He never would have said that the best constitution for any given nation was that which was based solely on the prejudices or circumstances of its inhabitants. When Turgot chastised America's Revolutionary constitution makers for imitating the English constitution and for not having taken the opportunity to alter radically the colonial charters, Adams was quick to point out that the state constitutions were the product of both philosophy and traditional practice. America's Revolutionary lawgivers, he said, framed their constitutions less from a servile obedience to the principles of the English constitution than from an attachment to their own indigenous forms of government. Furthermore, the Revolutionary constitutions were not simple copies of the old colonial charters, although they did retain the essence of the better ones. Though mindful of the old ways, American lawgivers constructed their new constitutions according to the principles found in "nature and reason."[16] Adams always insisted that the *art* of political architecture be informed at every step by a *science* of politics.

As we have already seen, the primary purpose of the *Defence* was to elucidate the principles absolutely necessary for the creation of the best practical regime. Adams thought representation, separation of powers, and the legislative triple equipoise to be the essential framework for all governments. These core principles of political architecture that Adams found in nature and reason were not subject to change. They were not unlike the laws that govern the motion of the heavens and the machines that man was building in the light of a Newtonian cosmos. Adams thought government a piece of clockwork, a machine to be designed and constructed on the basis of "principles and maxims, as fixed as any in Mechanicks." But he also assumed that constitution makers must have before them a further range of alternatives. The dozens of ancient and modern republics that Adams studied taught him that lawgivers may employ "a multitude of curious and ingenious inventions to balance, in their turn, all those powers, to check the passions peculiar to them, and to control them from rushing into those exorbitancies to which they are most addicted."[17] Adams knew that his three core principles could be dressed in an almost endless variety of designs, that they could be adjusted and adapted to suit the needs of different colonies or nations. Fortunately for the Americans, the old ways and the standards of nature and reason were synonymous.

The Solonian Lawgiver

In 1776 Adams first tried his hand at constitutional design. In November and December of 1775, he led the charge in the Continental Congress to encourage the separate colonies to begin designing and constructing new forms of government. As the leader of this movement and considered by many the one person who had thought most deeply about how to design constitutions, Adams was frequently called upon to recommend a plan of government. At the behest of several colleagues in the Continental Congress, he drafted a series of constitutional blueprints for constitution makers in North Carolina, Virginia, and New Jersey, all of whom were in the process of constructing new governments for their respective states. Eventually published as *Thoughts on Government*, Adams drew his basic plan of government from the peculiar traditions and the unique social conditions of the southern and middle colonies. Three years later, he was the "principal Engineer" of a constitution for his own state of Massachusetts, a colony whose social structure and customs were substantially different from those of the south. A comparison of these two documents reveals the underlying assumptions that Adams brought to the task of constitutional design and construction.

Both *Thoughts on Government* and the Massachusetts Constitution share the three essential prerequisites Adams found necessary for the construction of any free government: a full representation of the people, a separation of the legislative, executive, and judicial powers, and balance in the legislature among a House of Representatives, a Senate and a Governor. Within this general framework, however, he adjusted and amended the modes and nature of representation of each blueprint to reflect the peculiar social conditions of these very different regions.

Adams thought it was crucial to the very task of constitution making that lawgivers be mindful of the audience for whom they are designing and building constitutions. They should "proceed in all established modes to which the people have been familiarised by habit." Because he wrote *Thoughts on Government* principally for constitution makers in Virginia and New Jersey, it was important that he take into consideration the "Inclinations of the Barons of the south, and the Proprietary Interests in the Middle Colonies." Indeed, *Thoughts on Government* "were calculated for southern latitudes, not northern." In Virginia, for instance, "the Gentry are very rich, and the common People very poor. This inequality of Property, gives an Aristocratical Turn to all their Proceedings." To accommodate the demands of the southern land Barons and the proprietary interests of large landowners in New Jersey and New York, Adams designed a Senate that would be chosen by the House of Representatives, either from its own members or from the people. Likewise, the Governor would be chosen by a joint election of the House and Senate. Because of the authority and power of an entrenched planter class in these states, Adams thought it necessary to design a constitutional framework that elevated and gave a higher tone to the Senate and Governor. The "ideas of equality" that Adams saw as being "so agreable" to the "natives of New England" were simply "disagreeable to the gentlemen in the other colonies," particularly those in the south. By taking the election of the Senate and the Governor out of the direct hands of the people, he was taking account of and giving greater weight to the aristocratic elements of these societies.[18]

This is not to say, however, that Adams did not attempt to introduce certain "innovations" into the southern constitutions. Following his own advice to legislators that they not shock the prejudices or break the habits of the people, he proposed with "great caution, prudence and skill" that elections for all three branches be annual. He was concerned that this highly democratic proposal might be "too popular," and he wondered if annual elections might not be "too frequent" for a state like Virginia. His lawgiver's art therefore left open the possibility that the people could amend their form of government to better suit any changes in the social structure or character of the people. They might alter the length of office held by senators to "seven years, or three years, *or for life*, or make any other alterations which the society shall find productive of its ease, its safety, its freedom, or in one word, its happiness."[19]

A Senate elected annually, for three years, for seven, or even for life! On first reading, this might seem an extraordinary recommendation. Adams made clear in *Thoughts* his strong preference for annual elections, but, as elsewhere, he would leave that decision to the people. Even if the people of Virginia had constructed Adams's principal bugaboo, the unicameral legislature, he would have nevertheless supported their right to do so. The "right of the people to establish such a government as they please," he told Francis Dana, "will ever be defended by me, whether they choose wisely or foolishly." Adams would later confess that he had over-estimated the hold of the aristocratic authority over the minds of the people in the southern colonies. He was therefore delighted to learn that southern constitution makers had adopted governments "even more popular than the 'Thoughts on Government.' "[20]

While bearing many structural similarities to *Thoughts on Government*, Adams's *Report of a Constitution . . . for the Commonwealth of Massachusetts*, was a different sort of constitution designed for a different kind of society. The ideas of equality that so repulsed the land barons of the South defined the peculiar spirit of the people of New England. The Massachusetts Constitution was therefore much more democratic in tone and substance than the prescriptions found in *Thoughts*. Instead of a Senate elected by a lower house and a Governor elected by both legislative houses, Adams recommended for Massachusetts that all branches of the government be elected directly and annually by the people.

In addition to the annual election of the legislative and executive branches, the eligibility requirements for voters that Adams wrote into the Massachusetts Constitution were as liberal as any in America at the time. Accordingly, he wrote into his draft constitution that the principle of representation be based exclusively "upon the principle of equality." Any man, twenty-one years of age and resident in any town for one year preceding an election, possessing a freehold estate in that town of "the annual income of three pounds, or any estate of the value of sixty pounds" was given the right to vote by Adams. Historians have determined that these requirements were highly democratic, preventing few, save those with virtually no stake in the society, from the right to vote.[21]

Adams also extended the basis of representation in the House by changing the way in which districts were allotted their representatives. Formerly, representation had been proportionately based on numbers. Adams changed representation based on population to the number of ratable polls, which, generally speaking, included all free males sixteen years of age and above. Such a change meant that those who were too young or without enough property to vote, but who were nevertheless assessed for taxation purposes, would be counted among the numbers on which representation was based. Consequently, apprentices and grown sons still living in their master's or father's house were counted as a part of the population that Adams's legislature was intended to mirror.[22] No other state constitution put such faith and power in the hands of the people.

Though Adams designed his *Report of a Constitution* around the "spirit" of the citizens of Massachusetts and the customs of their traditional form of government, his draft constitution did attempt to introduce a few innovations that were eventually considered unacceptable by the people of the Bay colony. The delegates to the constitutional convention added to and subtracted from the Adams draft in two significant ways. Most importantly (at least from his perspective), Adams's draft *Report* had included an absolute executive veto. By giving the governor an unqualified veto, Adams intended to make the executive a third branch of the legislature. This power, he told Elbridge Gerry, would elevate the executive into a "Reservoir of Wisdom," from which it could occasionally guide and check the people's representatives, who comprised a reservoir of liberty. He thought this power essential to a well-balanced constitution; without it, the governor would "be run down like a Hare before the Hunters."[23] The Convention dropped the absolute executive veto from Adams's draft constitution, opting instead for a qualified veto. The most important addition to Adams's draft was the inclusion by the Convention of Article III of the Declaration of Rights, which provided tax support for religion. Philosophically, Adams probably would have preferred a stricter separation between church and state, but he was not about to challenge or eradicate one of the oldest and most established traditions of the Bible Commonwealth.

Despite these changes and revisions to Adams's original text, the author was delighted with the final result. He got as much out of the people as he thought could be expected. He had not disguised his "real Sentiments" and the people had received his constitutional blueprint with a kind of manly "Candor." Adams's draft constitution combined the best ideas from the Massachusetts Charter of 1691; it took account of the egalitarian "spirit" of New England culture; and it reconciled principles and theories that Adams had developed as a consequence of his "reading and reasoning." To Edmé Genet, Adams wrote that he hoped that the Massachusetts Constitution would provide a model for "the gradual [Pro]gress of Society, and the slow March of the human Un[der]standing in the Science of Government."[24] It was the most sophisticated and developed constitution produced during the Revolutionary period. Despite the many amendments that have been added to it over the course of the last 200 years, the Massachusetts Constitution is the oldest working written constitution in the English-speaking world.

The core principles of Adams's thought did not change over time, nor did he become more conservative. As a lawgiver in the Solonian or

Montesquieuan tradition, Adams adapted the theoretically best form of government to the society or stage of society for which it was intended. Interests, customs, habits, established authority and political philosophy, all these competing claims were factored by Adams into his Revolutionary constitutional designs for the new American states. *Thoughts on Government* gave the planter states of the south and the proprietary middle states not the best constitution that could be sketched in theory but gave them instead "the best they could receive."[25] Adams, unlike Tom Paine or Condorcet, understood the need to adjust and adapt constitutions on the basis of a community's local traditions and customs. But what of Adams as a pure theorist or as a teacher of lawgivers? Should he design the best constitution based purely on reason and philosophy, or should he develop a flexible art of political architecture similar to the one he employed during the period of Revolutionary constitution making?

Political Theory and the Problems of Constitution Making

In the fall of 1786, while living in a foreign land and in a state of self-imposed "philosophic solitude," far away from the turmoil of local politics, Adams wrote his great theoretical treatise on the political sciences and the art of political architecture. Unlike *Thoughts on Government* or the Massachusetts Constitution, *A Defence of the Constitutions of Government* was written for more than just the people of a single state: it was written for a much larger, transatlantic audience. No longer constrained by the customs and mores of a particular people, Adams now had the opportunity to design the one best constitution de novo, on the basis of reason and philosophy alone. As we have shown throughout the present study, Adams's principal intention was to show present and future lawgivers, American and European, how to design constitutions. The *Defence* is primarily a book about method; it is a manual that provides lawgivers with the information necessary for constructing constitutions suitable for the peculiarities of separate and distinct nations. The *Defence* does offer a generic defense of mixed and balanced government as the best form of government, but it does not prescribe a monolithic or universal blueprint for all nations.

But this is not how historians have interpreted the *Defence*. They have charged Adams with having dramatically changed his political thought in the years after the Revolution. The supposedly egalitarian Adams of the Revolutionary period is said to have become an enemy of republican government; the new Adams had become a reflexive defender of England's mixed monarchy and a proponent of "the absolute necessity of permanent elites." One historian has gone even further in suggesting that a Europeanized Adams had become "imprisoned within a framework," a framework that rigidly prescribed the English constitution as the one universal model for all other nations. The Adams of the *Defence* and *Davila* essays is now said to have viewed "widely diverse social structures as basically similar." Consequently, he "never found it in the least anomalous to consider the same set of constitutional arrangements applicable to the political problems of each." Apparently blind to the differences between cultures, his general "system of balances presumed to fit the conditions of France in 1789 as much as the revolutionary American states in 1776."[26]

But is this what Adams really said or meant to say? A close reading of the *Defence* and *Davila* essays does not support this interpretation. The evidence suggests something quite different. Adams's contemporary critics and modern historians have either misunderstood or misconstrued the kind and level of audience for whom he was writing. The *Defence* does *not* prescribe one universal model—the English constitution—for all nations. Adams's method throughout the *Defence* was to teach American and European lawgivers how to design and build constitutions according to the warp and woof of a nation's inherited political culture. This means that at different places throughout the *Defence* Adams was writing for different audiences. For instance, when he praises or promotes the English constitution or the benefits derived from hereditary aristocracies, it is important that the reader determine the specific audience that Adams was addressing. It cannot be assumed that he was speaking to an American audience. What historians have generally interpreted as a monolithic prescription for America may, in fact, have been a proposal intended primarily or exclusively for European constitution makers. In the very same way that Adams recommended different forms of government for different American colonial societies during the Revolutionary period, he likewise recommended different constitutional forms for different nation-states. It may be helpful at this point to examine more closely the various constitutional forms that he prescribed in the *Defence* and *Davila* essays and the specific audience for whom they were intended.

When Adams began to write the *Defence* in the fall of 1786, there was a general sense in Europe that great reforms, even revolutions, were about to unhinge and transform the ancien régime. But how could the ancien régime and the absolute monarchies of Europe be reformed? While sympathizing with the French Patriots, for instance, Adams was skeptical that their plans for reform would have anything other than dire consequences for Europe. He therefore counseled moderation and an appreciation for the "course of progressive improvement," which European society had undergone during the last "three or four centuries." On the very first page of the *Defence*, Adams described how France and the monarchical nations of Europe were in the process of becoming freer and wealthier. They had over time evolved a rudimentary system of checks and balances; they had erected tribunals to register and ensure the stability and protection of common rights and liberties; they had attempted to limit the power of crown and ministerial government; and, most importantly, property was generally secure and personal liberty seldom invaded. A parallel development, if not a direct result of these republicanizing effects on monarchical government, had been a liberalization of the press and commerce, leading to a general empowerment of the people's political opinions and to an increase in national and individual wealth.[27] The natural evolutionary forces of enlightenment were slowly melting the frozen status society built around the reciprocal liberties and duties of noblemen and peasants.

Adams had grave doubts about the willingness of French intellectuals and legislators to study and appreciate the nature of social and economic change and their relationship to political and constitutional forms. He thought it a gross and chimerical whim that French intellectuals would hold up for emulation the unicameral constitution of Pennsylvania as a model for a people so long habituated to the rule of one man. It was ludicrous, Adams thought, for the French and the people of the other great European kingdoms to think that they could disregard or abolish overnight a hierarchical and deferential social order that had taken root over the course of a millenium. He insisted that the fabric of France's historic social constitution would have to be respected and given its due weight. This meant that French constitution makers could have no illusions in their evaluation of French society. Any attempt at reform in France could not and must not neglect two important facts about French society.

First, Adams did not think the French people capable of managing more than a limited degree of liberty. France, despite recent reforms, was a corrupt nation, and its corruption cut across the various orders of French society. A haughty and depraved nobility governed an ignorant peasantry conditioned to subservience and obedience after centuries of living under the twin tyrannies of the feudal and canon law. The whole nation had been shaped and corrupted by a depraved social morality. But it would be wrong, Adams suggested, to vilify the nobility as the only corrupt element of French society: "It may gratify vulgar malignity and popular envy, to declaim eternally against the rich and the great, the noble and the high; but, generally and philosophically speaking, the manners and characters of a nation are all alike." The French peasantry was no less "vicious, vain, and luxurious" than their social betters. In fact, Adams found that "intemperance and excess" were "more indulged in the lowest ranks than in the highest."[28] A slavish citizenry long acclimated to the ancient rule of absolute monarchs, habituated to the ordered and regimented life of a deferential society, and conditioned by a "Romish clergy" to believe in the omniscience of the Catholic Church could hardly be expected to understand overnight the requirements of freedom and republican self-government. The institutions and customs of the ancien régime had reduced the French people "to a state of sordid ignorance and staring timidity."[29] The French character was, however, formed by more than the status relationships of the ancien régime. There was something unique about the French soul, something that Adams could not quite explain but that he knew to be entirely ill-suited for republican government. They did not possess the virtues—for example, temperance, prudence, frugality, industry—necessary for self-government. "*Panem et aquam, et vinum et circenses,*" Adams said, "are all that they understand or hope or wish for." The temperament of all Frenchmen, rich or poor, was defined by a "fire, impetuosity and vehemence" that tended to be "violent immoderate and extravagant." The passions of a Frenchman, Adams noted, "are always outrageous." A Frenchman in love "must shoot himself or succeed."[30] Such a people were peculiarly ill-suited for democratic government.

Second, rather than condemning and advocating the abolition of hereditary rank, Adams advised French reformers to acknowledge the nature and historic role that the nobility had played in promoting the rights and liberties of all Frenchmen. Although increasingly limited in their authority, the French aristocracy had always assumed the major role in checking the coercive power of the monarchy. The nobility had constantly challenged the king's ministers and prevented "them from running into abuses of power and wanton despotism." They provided a buffer between the monarchical authority and the "obedience of the subjects."[31] Any attempt to eradicate the nobility would be dangerous and foolish, if not altogether impossible. Adams knew that aristocracy was natural to the human condition and that any attempt to destroy it would only lead to its rebirth under different forms and behind different masks.

The principal constitutional reform that Adams recommended to the European kingdoms was "the introduction of democratical branches into those governments." He predicted that if the people and philosophers of Europe aimed at anything more than gradual reform, they would "defeat themselves." It would be impossible for a people sunk so low in public morality to imitate the American revolutionary example successfully. In fact, their reform projects would be ruined if they proceeded by "any other than gentle means and by gradual advances, by improvements in general education, and by informing the public mind." Adams suggested that, with a few institutional adjustments and the security of a few more rights and liberties, Europe might attain a tolerable if not a high degree of civil and political liberty, at least as much as one could hope for given the circumstances.

> If religious toleration were established, personal liberty a little more protected, by giving an absolute right to demand a public trial in a certain reasonable time, and the states [parlements] were invested with a few more privileges, or rather restored to some that have been taken away, these governments [simple monarchies] would be brought to as great a degree of perfection, they would approach as near to the character of governments of laws and not men, as their nature will probably admit of.[32]

Because of their historic past, the future liberalization of those European nations governed by simple monarchies had to come slowly and by a process of general evolution and enlightenment. Adams therefore admonished them to avoid abrupt breaks with the past and to temper their desire for revolutionary change. He was convinced "that if they aimed at any constitution of civil government more popular than the English, they would ruin themselves, after setting Europe on fire and shedding oceans of blood." Adams did not think the people of France capable of sustaining a revolution in the name of republican government on the American model. "What would have become of American liberty," he wrote to John Jay, "if there had not been more faith, honor, and justice in the minds of their common citizens, than are found in the common people in Europe."[33] In other words, his advice for France was identical to Montesquieu's counsel in *The Spirit of the Laws:* slow reform based on the model of the English constitution and the promotion of commerce. Adams would never have denied to the French their right to revolution, but he certainly would have questioned their good sense in using it.

In addition to the absolute monarchies of the Continent, Adams also offered advice in the *Defence* to the relatively free governments of Europe (Holland, Venice, Bern, etc.), and England in particular. On the whole, these nations had an adequate separation and balancing of powers. Despite the existence of democratic institutions and the promotion of liberal policies, he thought the constitutional forms and institutional arrangements of these nations still in need of some adjustment and improvement. He thought them capable of being brought nearer to relative perfection, if only they could make a few minor adjustments. The most obvious and immediate area identified by Adams as needing reform was in the people's representative bodies. "The end to be aimed at, in the formation of a representative assembly," he declared, is to gather a "sense of the people, the public voice. The perfection of the portrait consists in its likeness." He thought the English Parliament, for instance, inadequately and unfairly constituted. To attain just and fully representative institutions, Adams recommended the following adjustments as necessary conditions for genuine constitutional reform: first, numbers or property or both should be the rule; and second, the duration of holding office should be relatively short. More specifically, representation should be devised so as not to encourage corruption. This, Adams advised, may be achieved in four ways: first, elections ought to be frequent and suffrage broad; second, electoral districts ought to be divided into well-defined units; third, the distance that legislators should have to travel ought to be diminished; and fourth, only legal residents of a community ought to have the right to vote.[34]

One of the great misunderstandings among Adams scholars concerns his views on the English constitution. The standard interpretation of his post-Revolutionary career is that he became an unqualified proponent of the English constitution. Adams was always sensitive to the charge that he had become a devotee of monarchism and aristocracy. The accusation that hurt the most came from the pen of his old friend, Mercy Otis Warren, who, in her *History of the Rise, Progress, and Termination of the American Revolution* (1805), claimed that Adams had become "'so enamoured with the British Constitution and the government, manners, and laws of the nation, that a partiality for monarchy appeared, which was inconsistent with his former professions of republicanism.'" There can be no question that Adams deeply admired British constitutional forms and usages. He thought the English constitution the best known to man, and he thought that it had evolved over the centuries into a nearly perfect building for the people of Britain. But he did not develop this opinion as a consequence of his having lived in England in the years after the Revolution or as a result of his having read Jean De Lolme's *Constitution de l'Angleterre* in the 1780s. "My opinion of the British Constitution," he wrote to Warren, "was formed long before I had any thing to do in public life, more than twenty years before I ever saw the British Island." He said that he formed his judgment on the British Constitution as early as the late 1750s when he began reading "Fortescue, Smith, Montesquieu, Vattel, Acherley, Bacon, Bolingbroke, Sullivan, and Blackstone, and De Lolme, and even from Marchmont Needham, Algernon Sydney, James Harrington, and every other writer on government, and from all the examples I had ever read in history, from all I knew of the human heart and the rise, progress, and tendency of the passions in society."[35] During the Stamp Act crisis, Adams publicly and privately described English constitutional forms and practices as the best in the world. The superiority of the British constitution to other forms of government, he told his fellow colonials in 1766, was that it took "Liberty" as "its end, its use, its designation, drift and scope."[36] With the exception of the American state governments, no other constitutional form in the world promoted freedom as much as the English constitution.

In a number of places in the *Defence*, Adams described the British form of government in highly complimentary terms. In fact, so highly did he regard the English constitution that he referred to it as the "most stupendous fabric of human invention." Elsewhere, he described the English constitution as being "the result of the most mature deliberation on universal history and philosophy." At times his praise seemed almost without limits: "Not the formation of languages, not the whole art of navigation and ship-building does more honor to the human understanding than this system of government." Despite this great admiration for the English constitution, Adams did not think it the best constitution simply or the best in theory. It was certainly the best for England and theoretically it was better than almost all others, but he certainly did not think it perfect or the best simply. Adams criticized the English constitution for its imperfect representation of the people in the House of Commons.

> The improvements to be made in the English constitution lie entirely in the house of commons. If the county members were abolished, and representatives proportionally and frequently chosen in small districts, and if no candidate could be chosen but an established, long-settled inhabitant of that district, it would be impossible to corrupt the people of England, and the house of commons might be an immortal guardian of the national liberty. Instead of projects to abolish kings and lords, if the house of commons had been attended to, wild wars would not have been engaged in, nor countless millions thrown away, nor would there have remained an imperfection, perhaps, in the English constitution.[37]

Experience and history taught Adams that the English form of government was the best and certainly the most successful known to mankind. Its forms and formalities had evolved over the centuries into a stable constitutional order. The British constitution was the most successful because it had weathered the test of time.

But if experience and history deemed the English constitution best, theory could only judge it second best. The British constitution, Adams said, was "the most perfect model that has as yet been discovered or invented by human genius and experience, *for the government of the great nations of Europe*."[38] As a model for America, however, it was entirely inappropriate. Theoretically, America's thirteen state constitutions were the best and most admirable in the world. Their superiority to the English constitution rested on the fact, Adams proudly noted, that the people were able to hold frequent and, in some cases, annual elections for their governors and senators. "This improvement, the Americans, in the present stage of society among them, have ventured on."[39]

What was so unique about the "present state" of American society that made annual elections possible? In America, Adams wrote, "the right of sovereignty resides indisputably in the body of the people," because "they have the whole property of land." There are and can be no nobles or patricians in America; "all are equal by law and by birth." For Adams, it was principally the ownership and control of the land by the common people that differentiated the New World from the Old; it was the foundation on which a highly democratic system of government was constructed. Following the Harringtonian formula that "'empire follows the balance of property,'" Adams thought the Americans capable of self-government because the distribution of land there is divided "in such a manner, that nineteen twentieths" of the property is in the hands of the common people.[40]

Adams's survey of ancient and modern republics, including his examination of England, demonstrated that all nations throughout history had permitted social orders based on distinctions of wealth or birth. In every nation he "found *orders*, with very great distinctions." In America, however, "legal distinctions, titles, powers, and privileges, are not hereditary," and thus "no election is confined to any order or nobility, or to any great wealth; yet the legislature is so divided into three branches, that no law can be passed in a passion, nor any inconsistent with the constitution." The great innovation of the American constitutions is that "there are different orders of *offices*, but none of *men*." This is a crucial distinction for Adams. The Americans, he said, "have not made their first magistrates nor their senators hereditary. Here they differ from the English Constitution, and with great propriety." American senators, for instance, "have influence chiefly by the principles of authority, and very little by those of power." Adams concluded, therefore, that Americans had every reason to "exult" when comparing themselves "with England and the English Constitution."[41]

The great virtue and superiority of the American constitutions to that of the English was their having grounded full sovereignty in the people. Americans in 1776 and still in 1786 did not have any meaningful hereditary social orders that needed special representation; their institutional arrangements were based on the separation and balancing of intragovernmental powers only. "In the present state of society, and with the present manners," it was possible for America to have annual elections for all the great offices of state.[42] The Americans, unlike the English, popularly elected, directly or indirectly, the three branches of government and the three principal components of the legislative branch, the natural orders of the one, the few, and the many. In other words, American social conditions, when combined with the elective principal, obviated the need for representation based on social orders.

Adams would only judge the American constitutions provisionally best, however, because, as he said, they were still experiments; they had not yet withstood the test of time. Adams was not simply a partisan for the American system as an unqualified good; he had reservations about the American constitutions, reservations about "whether a government so popular can preserve itself." He understood that the Revolutionary constitutions were experiments to determine whether men were capable of good government based on reflection and choice. It was still an open question as to whether the trial would succeed. As a statesman and as a political scientist (as opposed to a partisan), Adams understood that the American experiment in constitution making was just that, an experiment, one that the good scientist could not judge until the test had run its course. Adams was not without hope, however; he had good reason to believe that the American constitutions would "prove themselves improvements upon the Roman, the Spartan, and the English commonwealths."[43]

Adams did not expect America always to remain in this state of general social equality. He feared that greater and greater disparities in wealth and power would eventually divide America into the few and the many. If a time came when "great quantities of property shall get into few hands," Adams thought it natural and appropriate for the American people to consider amending their constitutions to a "nearer resemblance of the British constitution."[44] Adams never wrote as a partisan for the English constitution as modern scholars would have it, and this kind of prescription in no way represents a change in his political thinking. The very same idea is explicitly stated in *Thoughts on Government*. Adams there left open the possibility that Virginia and the proprietary states might want to amend their constitutions (the length of tenure for senators in particular) at some future date in order to better reflect any changes that might occur in the composition of the social order. As the inequalities of wealth became more pronounced in these societies, as the balance of property shifted from the many to the few, it *might* become necessary to adjust the constitution in order to separate the few from the many. In 1776 and in 1786, he recommended that states include amendment clauses in their constitutions that would allow the people, if necessary, to extend the length of tenure for senators for periods lasting anywhere from three years to life. Adams feared that hereditary and, particularly, monied elites would corrupt annual elections and turn the government into a de facto aristocracy. He always thought it better to give the aristocracy their own representation in a mixed government than to allow them to dominate and control a more democratic government through corruption and the arts of electoral fraud. Nowhere in the *Defence* or the *Davila* essays does Adams advocate the institutionalization of permanent social orders into the American constitutions as the preferred political arrangement.[45] He thought it a regrettable but a necessary alternative when the best form of government had become corrupted. The charge that Adams "drastically changed" his concept of balanced government between 1776 and 1786, that he substituted for the mechanical checks and balances of intragovernmental institutions and powers a balancing of different social orders—the few and the many—does not hold up under close scrutiny.

Chapter 12

Posterity Must Judge

On July 4, 1826, fifty years to the day after the approval of the Declaration of Independence, John Adams and Thomas Jefferson died. From his deathbed, Adams whispered these famous last words: "Thomas Jefferson lives." Literally speaking, he was mistaken. Jefferson had expired some hours before. In another sense, though, he was right. The Jefferson legacy continued to live and prosper, whereas his own historical reputation, figuratively speaking, died an ignominious death. That John Adams is largely forgotten today would have undoubtedly surprised the nineteenth-century Americans who turned out by the hundreds of thousands to listen to the funeral orations delivered all across the United States in honor of these two remarkable men. Despite the invectives hurled at Adams during the 1790s and his subsequent loss to Jefferson in the presidential election of 1800, both men were eulogized across the country in an outpouring of public grief as the inseparable heroes of the American Revolution. They were remembered as they had once been described by their mutual friend Benjamin Rush "as the North and South Poles of the American Revolution." Their apotheosis in the testimonials of 1826 seemed to indicate that both would be forever enshrined as the twin towers of the Revolution.[1]

In what was probably the greatest of all the funeral orations, Daniel Webster captured a common sentiment: Adams and Jefferson, he wrote, had been "so intimately, and for so long a time, blended with the history of the country, and especially so united, in our thoughts and recollections, with the events of the Revolution, that the death of either would have touched the chords of public sympathy." For Webster, history must treat these two men as inextricably bound together: "No two men . . . have ever lived in one age, who, more than those we now commemorate, have impressed on mankind their own sentiments in regard to politics and government, infused their own opinions more deeply into the opinions of others, or given a more lasting direction to the current of human thought." Webster concluded his peroration by noting that Washington's star would now be joined by those of Adams and Jefferson in the constellation of American liberty.[2]

We now know, of course, that John Adams's star has fallen from this American constellation. Of all the Revolution's central figures, Adams has been the least studied. The modern fate of Adams's reputation has hinged to a very large degree on the common scholarly opinion that his political ideas became irrelevant by the 1790s. We are now told—to use a modern colloquialism—that Adams just didn't get it, that he became increasingly reactionary in the years after 1776, that his political thought was never able to accommodate itself to the theoretical innovations of 1787, that he became an advocate of monarchism and aristocracy, that he stood dazed as the insurgent democratic forces unleashed by the Revolution marginalized his philosophical approach to politics. There is, of course, some truth in all this.[3] After his return to America in 1788, he often seemed to be a man out of step with many of his countrymen. Ever the political scientist, his ideas, policies, and rhetoric seemed strangely counterintuitive to the new world of democratic politics.

Contemporary Reactions to A Defence of the Constitutions

Scholars have generally portrayed Adams's *Defence of the Constitutions* as having received an ambiguous if not downright hostile reaction in the wake of its publication. In recent years, however, a great deal of new archival material has emerged that forces us to revise to a very large extent our views on the relevance and significance of the *Defence*. As this new evidence now makes clear, the initial response to its publication was overwhelmingly positive. Benjamin Rush informed Adams that his "excellent volumes upon government" would serve as "the Alcoran [Koran] of my boys upon the great subject of political happiness. You have laid the world and posterity under great obligations by your remarks." Henry Knox, Secretary at War for the Confederation, thought Adams should have entitled his book, " 'The Soul of a Free Government.' " Tench Coxe told John Brown Cutting that the "zeal, ability and learning" with which Adams had "supported the true principles of republican government both in theory & practice reflect the highest honor upon himself and his country." Joel Barlow predicted that the *Defence* would do great service in the United States "by correcting thousands of erroneous sentiments which have arisen from our inexperience, sentiments, which if uncorrected in the early stage of our political existence, will be the source of calamities without measure and without end, both in this country and throughout the world." The Presidents of Harvard and Yale colleges lent their considerable weight in support of the *Defence*. Joseph Willard of Harvard hoped that Adams's "learned and benevolent labors" would "have due weight" with the American people and that they might "profit by it." Yale's Ezra Stiles wrote with even greater enthusiasm: "I have received great Instruction from your learned Labour, which will do more, I believe, toward leading [   ] the Inquiries of American & European Politicians to a [thoro'] Examination of the ancient and modern Polities in Europe, & [thence] to learn what Government human Nature can & cannot bear, than any publication hitherto made. We have needed at this time . . . the very Lights you have furnished."4

Several correspondents recognized immediately that the purpose of the *Defence* was to serve as guidebook for constitution makers. David Ramsey informed Adams that his work was "universally admired in Carolina & I flatter myself that it will be instrumental in [disseminating] right notions of government." He devoutly wished that "the sentiments of it were engraven on the hearts of every legislator in the United States." Silvanus Bourne praised Adams for having "fully explored" "every avenue to the human heart, the true direction of the political magnet . . . and the great [Arcana] in the science of government which had puzzled Philosophers and Statesmen of old." John Trumbull congratulated Adams for having instructed "mankind in the fundamental principles of Government," although he thought that the best thinkers of "even the most civilized nations" were "some centuries behind" Adams's political science. Thomas Brand Hollis told Adams that he had "proved" his "principle most masterly and satisfactorily from History," and that "nothing now remains but that your country may benefit from your labors by putting your principles in execution."5 And that is precisely what they did.

Over the years scholars have also downplayed the impact of the *Defence* on the forming of the federal constitution. Many of Adams's contemporaries, however, both outside and inside the Philadelphia Convention, thought his treatise a "word spoken in season." In several key states, the *Defence* was read with much acclaim, and it was thought to have had a positive influence on the Constitutional Convention. From Massachusetts, Richard Cranch offered elegant testimony to the importance of the *Defence* to American constitution makers: it had come "to America at a very critical moment just before the meeting of the grand Convention at Philadelphia for revising and amending the Confederation, when the Subject matter of your Book will naturally be much talked of, and attended to by many of the greatest States-men from all parts of the United States." From New York, Richard Henry Lee, a Virginia delegate to Congress, told Adams that his *Defence of the Constitutions* had

"reached America at a great crisis," and that it would have a "proper influence in forming the Federal Government now under consideration.
Your labor may, therefore, have its reward in the thanks of this and future
generations." From South Carolina, Thomas Pinckney told Adams that
"We are looking forward with anxious expectation to the result of the deliberations of the federal convention now sitting at Philadelphia. Your
Excellency's Defence of the Constitutions arrived in time to be of utility."[6] And so it did.

Judging by reports from Philadelphia, the *Defence* was widely read and
discussed in the Convention's host city. Just as the Convention was sitting down to begin its deliberations, Tench Coxe described the *Defence* as
being "much and justly admired here." It had, he noted, come "out very
opportunely for the convention." Writing in a Philadelphia newspaper on
June 6, "Sidney" encouraged every American freeman to "furnish himself
with a copy of this invaluable book." More particularly, he urged the con-
vening Convention delegates "to read and study it"; indeed, he thought
"every man who is elected to serve in our assemblies, councils, senates,
congress or convention, subscribe a declaration . . . that he not only believes in the old and new testaments, and that he will faithfully discharge
the duties of his station, but that he has read 'Adams's Defence of the
American Constitutions.'" Also writing from the Convention's host city,
Benjamin Rush enthusiastically told Richard Price that the *Defence* had
"diffused such excellent principles among us, that there is little doubt of
our adopting a vigorous and compounded federal legislature." William
White, the first Episcopal bishop of Pennsylvania, wrote that Adams's
book on government would have "no small Influence on the Deliberations" of the Convention. Possibly the greatest evidence of the influence
of the *Defence* on the Philadelphia Convention comes from the Constitution's most trenchant critics. The Philadelphia Anti-Federalist Samuel
Bryan, writing under the pseudonym, "Centinel," feared "that the principles of government inculcated in Mr. Adams's treatise" had "misled some
well designing members of the late Convention." Likewise, "John Humble" suggested in a Philadelphia newspaper that Adams's *Defence* guided
the delegates in their construction of a complex government.[7]

It also seems likely that several members of the Constitutional Convention read the *Defence*. Here the evidence is more circumstantial, but
it does help to give us a better picture than previously seen by scholars.
Benjamin Franklin told Adams just as the Convention was beginning its
work that his book "is in such request here," and that it had already been
"put to press." William R. Davie, a North Carolina Convention delegate,

informed James Iredell that "Among the late publications of particular merit, a performance of Mr. J. Adams, the American Minister at the British Court, now signally engages the attention of the public." John Jay, though not a member of the Convention but a confidante of several of its most important members and one of the Constitution's most important supporters through his co-authorship of *The Federalist*, told Adams that his book on government "gives us many useful lessons. . . . I consider the work a valuable one, and one that will tend greatly to recommend and establish those principles of Government on which alone the United States can erect any political structure worth the trouble of erecting." Three weeks later, Jay informed Adams that his book was circulating and "does good." He thought it conveyed "much information on a subject with which we cannot be too intimately acquainted, especially at this period, when the defects of our National Government are under consideration, and when the strongest arguments are necessary to remove prejudices and to correct errors, which, in many instances, design united with ignorance to create, diffuse, and confirm." Jay thought the Constitution corresponded "a good Deal" with Adams's "just Principles of Government."[8] Finally, we have James Madison's ambiguous opinion of the *Defence*. It is true that Madison opined to Jefferson in an oft quoted letter that "men of learning will find nothing new in it. Men of taste, many things to criticize." But he also predicted that "it will, nevertheless, be read and praised" and "become a powerful engine in forming public opinion." "The book," he conceded, "has merit." In 1790, Francis Adrian Vanderkemp summed up the opinion of many when he wrote that Adams had been "the soul of the Philadelphia Convention" and that he had "arranged all the essential materials of this Report."[9] As we shall also see below, a close examination of the debates in the Constitutional Convention reveals that several important members used arguments remarkably similar to those of the *Defence*.

The *Defence* did, of course, have a few critics. Typical was the charge made by the Reverend James Madison of Virginia to the effect that "the secret Design" of the *Defence* was to "overturn" the revolutionary constitutions and to introduce the British system of government into America. Adams's plan, he told his younger cousin, was to turn the executive branch of the new constitution into a king and the senate into a house of lords. The Reverend Madison even went so far as to charge Adams with treason. Adams was under the influence of a "foreign Court," he wrote, and was "plotting" to overturn the American governments.[10] There were undoubtedly Federalists in America who favored superimposing the British constitution on America, but John Adams was not one of them.

Writing as a New Jersey "Farmer," John Stevens accused Adams of being a "state empiric, who prescribes one single remedy for all disorders," a system of "Orders and Balances." Stevens then accused Adams of advocating the recognition or creation of "orders, ranks or nobility" and of desiring to foist the British constitution on America. America had no such orders, he retorted, and he hoped that it never would. Stevens even implied that Adams was attempting to "place a king, cloathed with all the dignities and prerogatives of a British monarch, at the head of it." In the end, Stevens actually came out in support of a form of government that was remarkably similar to that advocated by Adams. Stevens's principal disagreement with Adams was over how that government was to be explained and justified. For Stevens, government was an artificial construction and delegation of the people's power, entirely disconnected from the major constituents of society. Adams saw government in the very same way, but he also thought it necessary to go a step further and take into account the social manifestations of human nature.[11]

The most interesting critique of the *Defence*, however, was not published until 1814. John Taylor admitted to having spent over twenty years in writing his five-hundred-page *Inquiry into the Principles and Policy of the Government of the United States*. That Taylor spent two decades producing this massive critique of Adams and that he thought it still worthy of publication suggest that he thought the *Defence* still relevant, all too relevant. The *Inquiry* was written as a response to "Mr. Adams's defence of the American constitutions" but, as historians have neglected to notice, it was also written as a critique of "the essays signed Publius, but entitled the Federalist." He thought both books "had paid too much respect to political skeletons, constructed with fragments torn from monarchy, aristocracy, and democracy." Apparently Taylor did not think *A Defence* outside the mainstream of Federalist thought. For Taylor, this was the mainstream. He chose to focus his attack on Adams because he thought *A Defence* potentially more dangerous to his own favored political system than *The Federalist*. The principal difference between the two texts for Taylor was that *A Defence* was notable for its "erudition" while *The Federalist* was distinguished by its "elegant style."[12]

If ever a book were anomalous and irrelevant, it was Taylor's "letters from the dead," as he called them. The Virginian had certainly read Adams's volumes, but it is not at all clear that he understood their substance. Taylor, for instance, attempted to associate Adams's ideas with

Robert Filmer's defense of the hereditary and divine right of kings in the *Patriarcha or the Natural Power of Kings* (1680). He also accused Adams of attempting to establish hereditary nobility in America. Adams therefore had to be, he said, an advocate "for a natural inequality of moral rights and duties," and his system must require that the government systematically redistribute property, either by "force or fraud," in order to create de novo a landed aristocracy and a sufficiently regal king. Taylor's logic led to the most fantastic claim of all, that Adams was advocating the forcible redistribution of property:

> If this definition is correct, an invasion of property constitutes the essential quality of Mr. Adams's system. A king, a nobility and a hierarchy, cannot subsist without property, and this property must be taken away in some mode from others. . . . Therefore the supposed two orders cannot preserve a political existence, without constantly receiving the profits of two thirds of the property in a nation. This requires a regular system for invading private property to sustain a government consisting of balanced orders.

Adams did not miss the irony of being accused of promoting aristocracy by a plantation owner and slave master. How was it, he would later demand of Taylor, that his most determined critics were almost always Virginia aristocrats, men whose fortunes were gained from birth, marriage, and the forced labor of enslaved blacks?[13]

Many reform liberals in Europe saw the *Defence* in an entirely different light. Dr. Richard Price, the famous English minister and moral philosopher was, with some chagrin, ecstatic about the *Defence*. He rationalized his embarrassment at having published Turgot's letter and thereby sparking Adams to write the *Defence* on the grounds that Adams had made a genuine contribution to the political sciences. The subject of government, he wrote, "was now better understood than ever it was." Two years later, Price was still praising the *Defence*. He thought that Adams had contributed, "with great ability," to the "establishment of a form of government that will be an example to the world."[14] Given Price's international stature, all this was extraordinarily high praise. Writing from Holland, the Dutch reformer A. M. Cerisier told Adams that he had read the *Defence* and that he considered it "as the Breviary of the genuine republican principles, compatible with the nature of society and with liberty, safety and good order." The Englishman Alexander Jardine bestowed on Adams the ultimate compliment. He praised *A Defence* for having advanced the science of government "more than any other thing that has appeared since Montesquieu." He told Adams that he did not think the governments of Europe capable of improving until "we learn from you." The English radical Joseph Priestley, in his *Familiar Letters Addressed to the Inhabitants of the Town of Birmingham*, declared that "though a unitarian in religion," he was a "trinitarian in politics." On political questions, he said that he "always took the part of Mr. Adams against Dr. Franklin." Several years later, Thomas Cooper, English ex-Patriot and intimate of Price and Priestley, said this of the *Defence:* "Mr. Adams's defence of the constitution of the United States . . . is such a condensed view of the merits and defects of the various forms of government, ancient and modern, as is no where else to be found." So enthusiastic about the *Defence* was Cooper that he thought that "*England can show no such work*" and that the "trifling and popular panegyric of DeLolme is not to be compared with it."[15]

The *Defence* also received enthusiastic support in France. When John Trumbull told Adams in 1790 that he wished "every member" of the French Constituent Assembly, then drafting a new constitution for France, "were obliged under pain of expulsion, to read your Defence, & either adopt your principles or confute them," little did he know that Adams's books on government had already become the object of some discussion among French legislators. On August 19, 1789, the Marquis de Lally-Tollendal, one of the Assembly's reform leaders rose and asked of his fellow constitution makers the following question: "If Mr. Adams has written that there could be no government, no fixed constitution, no sure protection of the laws, liberties and property of peoples without the balance of three powers" is it not our responsibility "that we too should yield?" Eleven days later, he declared on the floor of the Constituent Assembly that he would stand and speak with "Lycurgus and Polybius, with Cicero and Tacitus, with Montesquieu, Gibbon, De Lolme, Blackstone, [and] Adams" in defense of mixed and balanced government. Adams even received reports that his *Defence* was "upon the table of every member of the committee for framing a constitution of government for France." In 1795, after the failure of the unicameral constitution of 1791, the Comte de Boissy d'Anglas emerged from a third Constituent Assembly to report a new constitutional plan to the people of France. He made sure to inform them that the ideas of "one of the greatest modern writers, upon government, John Adams" had inspired his committee. From Adams, he said, they had learned "'that there is no good government, no stable constitution, no sure protectors for the lives, the liberty, the property of the people, without the

BALANCE OF THE THREE POWERS.'" Even Charles Alexander de Calonne, Minister of Finance to Louis XVI, praised the *Defence* in his *De L' Etat de La France* (1790) as well as recommending the book in his public "Letter to the King."[16]

Adams and Federalist Thought

When the *Defence* is viewed in the context of the inflamed party disputes of the 1790s, it does appear to be strangely out of place, even anomalous. But the *Defence* was not written as a party pamphlet and should not therefore be judged solely by the standard of ordinary political discourse common to the 1790s. Adams consciously chose to write in a manner that was very different from the political rhetoric of his time. He chose to rise above party dispute: the book was written as a guidebook for constitution makers and statesmen, and it was intended to make a contribution to a tradition of political science that extended from Plato to Burke. Thus, the *Defence* must also be judged by a different standard. If we try to understand Adams as he understood himself—that is, from the perspective of a statesman, a political scientist and a lawgiver—his books on government become much less irrelevant.

For the most part, Adams's failure was one of rhetoric and an unwillingness to speak in the new language of political and ideological partisanship. It is easy to see, for instance, how some Adams scholars could argue that his use of language was trapped in the traditional categories of the classical theory of mixed government. To many of his contemporaries it seemed as though he were speaking with an Old World political dialect no longer understood by New World republicans. Adams understood all too well what polemics was doing to the Americans' understanding of politics, but he would not distort the meaning of his words to pander to the passions, opinions, and interests of America's newly emerging democratic parties. Though not himself always consistent, Adams occasionally relied on older forms of expression that he borrowed from the great tradition of political thought. It was this failure of rhetoric as much as anything that marginalized his philosophical approach to politics. Adams wrote in the language of Aristotle, Machiavelli, Sydney, Locke, Bolingbroke, Hume, and Montesquieu. It might make more sense, then, to pull Adams's books out of their immediate context and judge them relative to works such as *The Politics* and *The Spirit of the Laws*.

It may also be helpful at this point to contrast the purpose and audience of Adams's *A Defence of the Constitutions* with that of *The Federalist*. The authors of *The Federalist* wrote for a mass audience. Despite the theoretical subtlety and innovations of *The Federalist*, its authors were forced to write in a style that would appeal to the passions, opinions, and interests of a democratic society. Their rhetoric was therefore dictated by the need to gain votes. Madison, Hamilton, and Jay wrote, in other words, as partisans. Adams, on the other hand, wrote consciously for a much more select audience. *A Defence* was not written as a piece of political propaganda. Despite its obvious failings, it was intended to be a scientific study of government, encompassing the whole length and breadth of history, one that also provided an account of the constitution of human nature which must be factored into the task of lawgiving. The principles adduced by Adams were not his prejudices or even his opinions; he claimed to have discovered certain truths about political questions. A formal treatise on the science of politics will, by definition, be written in a voice different from that of a political tract. In other words, Adams and the authors of *The Federalist* wrote with a different purpose in mind, and they wrote for a different kind of audience. Hence, each used a different kind of political language.

It is also important to keep in mind that the *Defence* was written for a transnational audience. Whereas *The Federalist*, for instance, was written for a strictly American audience, the *Defence* was written for American and European constitutional reformers. It was therefore necessary for Adams to use a form of political discourse that would resonate with lawgivers on both sides of the Atlantic. This is one reason why, for instance, that Adams used words such as "king," "aristocrat," and "plebeian." It is simply not true to say that Adams's frequent use of these terms represented a new found appreciation for the forms and formalities of the ancien régime. Adams was constantly misunderstood because he used these old concepts representatively rather than literally, without making clear the difference. When he spoke of aristocracy to his American audience, for instance, he was not advocating the creation of a legal, inherited, landed aristocracy; he spoke instead of the natural aristocracy. When he spoke to his European audience, he might very well have been referring to the traditional landed aristocracy. To some degree, of course, the fault must rest with Adams for not having more clearly demarcated these distinctions.

Adams's rhetorical failure was also due in part to the unique circumstances in which he wrote. He did not have the advantages, for instance, of having attended the Constitutional Convention, where his principles and rhetoric would have been subject to serious and searching criticism. The authors of *The Federalist* had the benefit of writing after the Convention and in the light of Anti-Federalist criticism. Had James Madison or Alexander Hamilton, for example, published a theoretical treatise on government before the meeting of the Constitutional Convention, one that included the views that they would later express on the floor of the Convention, undoubtedly they too would have been charged with having been irrelevant. Madison and Hamilton benefited from the Convention's rule of secrecy, the purpose of which was to promote candor and an expression of genuine opinions. Hamilton's famous speech of June 18 defending monarchy and an inherited aristocracy and Madison's speech of June 26 defending a nine-year tenure for the senate were surely out of the mainstream of American political discourse. In fact, Adams would have found Hamilton's plan repugnant and Madison's unwise. He certainly would have disagreed with major planks in Madison's Virginia Plan. Adams would have found Madison's call for the senate, the president, and the judiciary to be elected by the House of Representatives insufficiently democratic and open to aristocratic intrigue.

In order to fairly determine whether the *Defence* was outside or within the mainstream of Federalist thought, we should also judge Adams's treatise relative to the ideas of the participants at the Constitutional Convention. Although there is not one recorded reference to Adams's name in the Convention debates nor to his work, most historians agree that the principles, institutions, and structure of the new national government—a written constitution; the idea of constituent and ratifying conventions; equality of representation; separation of powers among legislative, executive, and judicial branches; a bicameral legislature with checks and balances; an independent and unified executive with a legislative veto—were almost identical to the forms of the Massachusetts Constitution and the blueprint outlined in the *Defence*.[17] The similarities do not end with the institutions and structures themselves. A close reading of the Convention debates demonstrates that many of the positions argued on the floor of the Convention bear striking similarities to the arguments and modes of reasoning enunciated by Adams in his *Defence of the Constitutions*.

Between June 18 and July 2, Alexander Hamilton, Charles Pinckney, James Madison, and Gouverneur Morris, four of the Convention's leading Federalist thinkers, engaged in one of the most fascinating debates of the entire Convention. Although they were discussing the proposed government's general outlines, the immediate subject was the form and tenure of the senate. Underlying that discussion, however, was an exchange of views on the character and future course of American society, its resemblance to English society, and the form of government best suited to protecting the infant nation's long-term interests and liberties. Interestingly, much of this discussion never made its way into public print. The views expressed by Madison and Hamilton over these several days never found a place in *The Federalist*. The arguments elucidated in this remarkable exchange bear many similarities to those found in the *Defence*. By reexamining this extraordinary exchange, we may better reevaluate the question of John Adams's relevance and irrelevance.

On June 18, Alexander Hamilton delivered his infamous "monarchy" speech, in which he spoke about his concept of the best form of government per se, his concept of the kind of society best suited to that form, and the tenure of the senate. Hamilton shocked many in the convention when he declared the British government the best in the world, although he doubted whether it was attainable by the Americans. He grounded his defense of Britain's mixed regime on the writings of Aristotle, Cicero, and Montesquieu. At the heart of Hamilton's reasoning was the classical explanation: "In every community where industry is encouraged, there will be a division of it into the few & the many. Hence separate interests will arise. . . . Give all power to the many, they will oppress the few. Give all power to the few, they will oppress the many. Both therefore ought to have power, that each may defend against the other." Hamilton understood that the few were driven by avarice, the many by envy, and both by ambition. In order to turn these passions toward the public good, Hamilton's mixed regime for America pitted passion against passion as the means by which harmony could be brought to the whole. The British constitution's particular excellence was its having achieved over time exactly that purpose. Hamilton described the British House of Lords as "a most noble institution," that formed a "permanent barrier against every pernicious innovation" attempted by either crown or commons. Thus, Hamilton recommended to the Convention an American senate loosely modeled after the British. In his own draft constitution, he recommended that senatorial electors be limited to those who could demonstrate that they or their wives had "an estate in land for not less than life, or a term of years" (he did not hold this property requirement for the elected themselves), and he recommended that those chosen as senators should hold their seats for life. To complete his system, Hamilton told the Convention that he supported the establishment in America of a hereditary monarchy.[18]

The following week, on June 25, Charles Pinckney returned to the themes of Hamilton's speech. He, too, told the convention that he thought the British constitution "the best Constitution in existence," but he did not think that it could be introduced into America for several centuries. The British constitution, Pinckney argued, was adapted to a very different kind of society. Great Britain, he declared, "contains three orders of people distinct in their situation, their passions and principles." The existence of a hereditary order of Peers in particular made Britain's government entirely inappropriate for America. He thought American society uniquely egalitarian. Following in the Solonian tradition of lawgiving, Pinckney argued that constitutions must be suited to the manners, customs, and interests of the people who will live under its institutions and laws. Because of the general equality of wealth and rank found in America, the republican form was for the time being the best form of government.[19] Pinckney's lament was, of course, Adams's hope.

The next day, James Madison rose to concur but also to amend Pinckney's sentiments. Behind closed doors, Madison sounded more like John Adams and less like Publius of *The Federalist* essays. A high-toned senate, he argued, was necessary to gain a competent knowledge of the public interest and to moderate if not to counter the people's mercurial passions. The principal purpose of a senate, Madison told his fellow delegates, was to check the democracy. Too often, even in a nation as virtuous as America, the people had succumbed to ignoble passions; they had been diagnosed with "symtoms of a leveling spirit" and a passion for "a more equal distribution" of life's blessings. This was particularly true in a free country, Madison continued, where the people easily divide into different and competing factions. He agreed with Pinckney that American society was presently republican, but he could not agree that there would always be a wide distribution of property and wealth. Over time, American social conditions would undoubtedly change. "In future times," Madison warned, "a great majority of the people will not only be without land, but any other sort of, property." More ominously, because of population growth and because of liberal suffrage laws, he assumed that the poor many would eventually grasp all political power. In fact, he warned that signs of a leveling spirit had already appeared in America. In order to frame, therefore, "a system which we wish to last for ages, we should not lose sight of the changes which ages will produce." But how could this danger be guarded against on republican principles? he asked the Convention. How were the rights of the minority to be protected? In order to secure the people against their own representatives but ultimately against themselves, Madison thought it absolutely necessary that the people's trust be divided between "*different* bodies of men, who might watch and check each other." It is critically important to note that Madison is not simply referring to a mechanical separation and balancing of neutral powers, nor is he referring to a bicameral legislature composed of the self-same elements. It made no sense to Madison and the other Federalists to check a democratic assembly with a democratic senate. He was not dividing the legislature between *two* bodies of men, but rather between *different* bodies of men. The distinction is critical.[20]

One of the principal purposes of a senate for Madison was to protect the "possession of different degrees and kinds of property" which results from "different and unequal faculties of acquiring property."[21] This was done most easily, of course, by those who are actually in possession of wealth and property. Whereas Adams spoke of "ostracizing" the natural aristocracy to a senate in order to defang their ambition and influence, Madison spoke of building a "fence" between the people's branch and a branch taken from "a portion of the enlightened citizens, whose limited number, and firmness" might counter the fickle and ill-considered opinions of the lower house. In other words, he hoped to implant in the American constitution both democratic and aristocratic principles. His solution was a senate "sufficiently respectable for its wisdom and virtue" and sense of justice. In order to support wisdom and virtue, stability, and order, Madison thought a nine-year term necessary for the senate. In a federal structure extended over a large republic and with a senate chosen by a house of representatives, Madison assumed, indeed, he hoped that the senate would be filled by citizens endowed with the privileges of birth and wealth. Given that the Americans were "now digesting a plan which in its operation would decide for ever the fate of Republican government," Madison implored his fellow delegates to not only "provide every guard to liberty that its preservation could require, but be equally careful to supply the defects which our own experience had particularly pointed out."[22]

Several days after the exchange between Hamilton, Pinckney, and Madison, Gouverneur Morris addressed the same issue. Some of his arguments and language seem to have been taken almost verbatim from Adams's *Defence*. Morris began by addressing the following question: What is the purpose of a senate? It was, he answered, to check the "precipitation, changeableness, and excesses of the first branch." The "excesses" of the democratic branches of the state constitutions he described as violations of "personal liberty private property & personal safety." What, then, he asked, are the qualities, characteristics, or virtues that are necessary to provide a check to a democratic assembly. Morris conceded that "*Abilities* and *virtue*" were qualities desired in both houses. Something more, though, was required for the senate. He then listed four qualities that define a properly constituted senate. First, the Senate must have a personal interest in checking the people's house, "one interest must be opposed to another interest." Echoing the *Defence* and predating *The Federalist*, he said that vices or ambition must be made to check one another. Second, the senate must have great personal wealth and the aristocratic spirit. Third, the senate must be independent in order to temper the people's spirit, and true independence, he thought, could only be achieved by banishing the aristocracy to a separate house. In language that could have been quoted directly from the *Defence*, Morris bemoaned the fact that the rich had always tried to dominate and enslave the people. It was necessary, therefore, to give them a separate house in order to prevent their usurpations. That way, both the many and the few would be able to control one other. Otherwise, if combined in one house, the rich will eventually establish an oligarchy. Thus, by "combining & setting apart, the aristocratic interest, the popular interest will be combined against it. There will be a mutual check and mutual security." Fourth, going well beyond Adams, he thought that senators should serve life terms. An "independence for life," he thought, would ensure the "necessary permanency." In order to support this independence and permanency, Morris also thought that senators should not be paid and should be appointed by the executive.[23] With the exception of this last cluster of points, Morris's argument was so close to Adams's as to be indistinguishable.

It should be obvious by now that John Adams's political thought was squarely within the mainstream of Federalist thought. He was not an errant knight tilting at phantom windmills. There is virtually nothing in the *Defence* that was not echoed at the Convention. In fact, Adams might very well have found the Convention views of Hamilton, Pinckney, Madison, and Morris too conservative and not sufficiently appreciative of the American character and its capacity for democratic self-rule. Not only did Adams support much of the Federalist persuasion of 1787, but the rationale and modes of reasoning found in the *Defence* bear many striking similarities to the central arguments and principles contained in *The Federalist*. Adams and Madison began their constitutional reasoning at the same point: they sought to address and overcome the central dilemma of social and political life, namely, the enduring conflict between the many and the few. But within the context of that endless struggle, each saw the problem originating from a different source. For Madison, the source had always been overbearing democratic majorities, whereas, for Adams, the real origin was to be found in the designs of intriguing aristocratic minorities. The general theoretical problem was for both born out of a general disillusionment with the political consequences of the Revolution. For Adams and Madison, there was a need to reinforce the Revolution's central principles and institutions, but there was also a need to redesign and rebuild those structures that had proven weak and vulnerable. They both rejected as unjust and illiberal the traditional republican devices—that is, a reliance on patriotism, virtue, and religion—for restraining and overcoming the natural social conflict common to all societies; nor did they think that constitution makers could rely on the continued availability of enlightened statesmen like themselves. Instead, both sought a constitutional solution to the problems most associated with republican government. They both saw written constitutions as self-executing mechanisms that would counter, channel, and elevate the passions, interests, and opinions of the people toward republican ends. They both grounded their constitutional pyramid on the sovereignty of the people. Both advocated a separation of powers with legislative checks and balances and, most importantly, they did so for largely the same reasons. In the end, the differences between Madison and Adams on the fundamentals of constitutional architecture were minimal.

If this is true, we must revise the common scholarly opinion that Adams had somehow moved outside the boundaries of acceptable republican opinion.[24] Not only did John Adams comprehend what was happening to the fundamentals of post-Revolutionary political thought, he was responsible for much of the change. His thought became irrelevant only to the degree that it had become successful. As a constitutional theorist and as a constitution maker, Adams was by proxy the philosophical architect of several state constitutions through his *Thoughts on Government* and he was the principal framer of the Massachusetts constitution which, along with his *Defence*, had some influence on the framing of the Federal constitution and the revision of state constitutions in Pennsylvania and Georgia. Adams's advocacy of a bicameral legislature and an independent executive bears more than a superficial resemblance to the constitutional structure created by the Philadelphia Convention and to the principles and reasoning contained in *The Federalist*. The people to whom his ideas later became irrelevant were nevertheless operating within the framework of a constitutional system that Adams played an important role in creating. It was only after his principal task was finished and forever instituted that his subsequent political career was pilloried in the arena of partisan politics.

Ideology and the Politics of Rhetoric

John Adams's alienation from American popular politics was not caused by the publication of his *Defence of the Constitutions*. New evidence shows that rather than diminishing Adams's public reputation, the *Defence* greatly enhanced it. But we are still left wondering how, why, and when Adams came to be denounced in the 1790s as a defender of monarchy and aristocracy. Because these charges were leveled by many important thinkers in their own right, they need to be taken seriously and examined closely. In order to comprehend fully what happened to Adams's reputation during the 1790s, we need to reexamine two events that clearly did lead to charges that he had renounced his republican views in favor of aristocracy and monarchy. The first, the dispute over government titles and etiquette, was entirely a self-inflicted wound. The second, the controversy surrounding the publication of his *Discourses on Davila*, was inspired by his friend Thomas Jefferson.

One of the first items of business considered by the new American Congress in 1789 was the question of titles, ceremony, and official government protocol. The issue was immediately pressing as both houses of Congress had to determine how they should officially address the highest officer of the executive branch. No one quite knew what style or titles would "be proper to annex to the office of President and Vice President of the United States." The House of Representatives quickly rejected any suggestion that the President should be afforded a special title. Almost unanimously, the House resolved to address the chief executive as "George Washington, President of the United States." The Senate, however, debated the issue for over a month. Adams, Richard Henry Lee, and a majority in the Senate came out strongly in favor of giving the President a regal sounding title. Adams favored addressing the President as "His Highness" or "His most benign Highness," or "His Majesty, the President."[25] Following Adams's lead, a Senate committee recommended that the chief executive be addressed as "His Highness the President of the United States of America and Protector of their Liberties." Recognizing that such high-sounding titles had no support in the House, the Senate soon dropped their recommendation and accepted that of the House.

Almost immediately, the hue and cry went up against Adams for trying to seduce the American people into accepting a British-style monarchy. The charges were, of course, false. Adams had no desire to foist upon the American people an American monarchy or a permanent aristocracy. Personally, he thought titles rather silly, and he despised them as much "as any Quaker, or Philosopher on Earth." Furthermore, he made it perfectly clear that he only favored titles attached to public offices rather than to individual men and their progeny.[26] Though utterly anachronistic in an American context, his reasons in support of titles were brilliant and theoretically sophisticated. His support had nothing to do with his having been corrupted during his time at European courts. Adams thought titles consistent with republican theory and practice (e.g., the Roman republic), and he thought them consistent with his own theory of political architecture.

As we have seen in chapter ten, Adams employed in the *Defence* what he called a language of signs in order to direct the emulation of the most ambitious and talented citizens to "the side of virtue" and to foster a more "noble temper" among the ruling elite.[27] Elevated titles, he thought, would induce men of true abilities, merit, and virtue into public service. Otherwise, the best men would have little incentive to forego the emoluments of private life. We tend to forget that public service in the eighteenth century, particularly at the national level, represented a massive financial burden, particularly for those of middling means. Adams also hoped that the title itself would reflect a certain quality or kind of virtue that its holder would aspire to achieve and reflect in his public actions. Titles, Adams thought, would bring out the best in a republican citizenry.

In his correspondence in the wake of the titles controversy, Adams offered several other reasons for favoring republican titles. First, he thought titles synonymous with the very idea of government. There was no government in the world, he thought, that did not have titles of some kind. Families, clubs, colleges, professional organizations, indeed, almost every form of human association invoked titles of one kind or another. Another important reason for invoking titles was to "make offices and laws respected." Adams did not think the steady, independent, and virtuous part of the community required titles, but "the Profligate, the criminal and abandoned, who have little reverence for Reason, Right or Law divine or human" certainly do. Whereas other forms of government used force, fraud, and corruption to engender obedience to the laws, Adams thought noble titles would command the voluntary respect of the people. If titles "will save you the expense of Gallows, stocks, whipping posts, or the pain of employing them," Adams asked Rush, "why not use them?" The alternative to titles, he wrote, was the coercive power of armies and navies. Furthermore, he thought that by giving titles to the executive officers of the government, "aristocratical pride" would be humbled. For Adams, then, titles played a dual role by controlling the worst elements of society and also in taming aristocratic pride. Titles would help support republican government by providing a constitutional device designed to protect public liberty and order from the intrigues of faction and partisanship. In the end, by honoring "their own creation," he thought, the people would be honoring themselves. Such was the "true spirit of republics."[28]

Adams also had more pressing political reasons for supporting titles. First, he thought such titles served an important diplomatic function. Adams worried that "provincial" titles would unnecessarily cost American diplomats much-needed respect in the courts of Europe. Furthermore, he thought the national government needed additional supports and sources of respect against the downward pull of the state governments. "The state governments will ever be uppermost in America in the Minds of our own People," Adams warned, "till you give a superiour Title to your first national Magistrate."[29] He worried that men of ability still identified with the state governments, thus channeling the peoples' first loyalty to their local officials and governments. Adams was certain that the fate of the new national government depended on raising it above the state governments.

Not until he was being ridiculed in the press and mocked as the "the Duke of Braintree" and "His Rotundity" did Adams realize the folly of his position. He was initially correct to raise the question of protocol, but he should have realized that he had nothing to gain by keeping alive an issue that had been so decisively rejected in the House. James Madison probably had it right when he told Thomas Jefferson that had Adams's *"project succeeded it would have* subjected the *president to a severe dilemma* and given *a deep wound to our infant government."* Jefferson responded by telling Madison that the whole affair *"was the most superlatively ridiculous thing I ever heard of."*[30] The titles campaign was a massive political error for Adams. At the very least, it demonstrated a lack of prudence and sensitivity to popular opinion. Stubborn in his defense of principles that seemed so contrary to the thrust of the Revolution, he became the scapegoat for partisan attacks that plagued him for the rest of his life.

A year after the titles controversy, Adams provoked more bad press with the serial publication of his *Discourses on Davila* in John Fenno's *Gazette of the United States*. Published anonymously between April 28, 1790, and April 27, 1791, the *Discourses* expressed Adams's wholly negative opinion of the French Revolution. He wrote this unconventional series of essays with a twofold purpose: first, to warn Americans against principles then being propagated by French Revolutionaries, and, second, to provide useful guidance to French constitution makers. Adams hoped that his essays would help Americans "to form a right judgment of the state of affairs in France at the present moment." Although he appreciated French intellectuals for "wisely reforming one feudal system," Adams worried that they might be "unwisely" laying "the foundations of another." He was particularly alarmed by reports that an overwhelming majority of the French National Assembly had rejected as models the bicameral constitutions of England and Massachusetts for a single-chamber legislature. The *Discourses* therefore present a direct and open appeal to the legislators of France. "FRENCHMEN!" Adams shouted, learn from the history of your own nation: "Consider that government is intended to set bounds to passions which nature has not limited; and to assist reason, conscience, justice, and truth, in controlling interests, which, without it, would be unjust as uncontrollable." The failure to do so, he predicted, would produce "nothing but another thousand years of feudal fanaticism, under new and strange names."[31]

Adams was particularly concerned with the egalitarian proposals to abolish all distinctions of ranks and to take all political power from both king and nobles. The French, he wrote, had correctly learned from the principles of the American Revolution that "all men have one common nature," and that "equal rights and equal duties" are inferred from that axiom, but they had radicalized the principles of the American Declaration of Independence by interpreting equality to mean as well "equal ranks and equal property."[32] One of the principal aims of the *Davila* essays, then, was to expose to both French and American audiences the fallacy and danger of democratic dogma. His advice to the French was to reform their political institutions slowly on the model of the English constitution.

Years later Adams would write that the *Discourses* had "powerfully operated to destroy his popularity." They were portrayed, he said, as presenting "full proof that he was an advocate for monarchy, of laboring to introduce a hereditary president in America."[33] To understand properly how Adams's public stock crashed following the publication of the *Discourses*, we must examine the role played by Thomas Jefferson in provoking and perpetuating an ideological and political campaign that destroyed Adams's reputation.

Initially, the anonymous *Davila* essays passed before the public with little notice. The calm before the storm ended abruptly in April 1791 with the American publication of Thomas Paine's *Rights of Man*. Jefferson, who had been loaned a copy of the English edition of Paine's book by James Madison, sent it along to Paine's American publisher with a note endorsing the work. In one of the most embarrassing episodes of his life, the note soon appeared as the preface to the American edition of *Rights of Man*. The unauthorized statement recommended Paine's work as an antidote to "the political heresies" that had lately sprung up among the American people. The "political heresies" of which Jefferson spoke was a veiled but easily seen reference to Adams's *Discourses*. The capital was electrified by Jefferson's charge. Almost immediately, the note was reprinted all over the country.

Jefferson was mortified by the editor's transgression of propriety. Immediately he began a letter-writing campaign denying that he ever intended for the note to be published. In the days immediately after the embarrassing publication of *Rights of Man*, Jefferson told George Washington that, though not intended for publication, he most certainly was referring to Adams and the *Discourses on Davila* when he wrote of "political heresies" that had recently grown up in America. He explained to Washington that in conversations with Adams he had openly told the vice-president that he "is a heretic" (a claim that Adams denied absolutely), and he told Washington that he thought Adams an apostate "to hereditary monarchy and nobility." Paine's popular and republican pamphlet would, Jefferson told Washington, "wipe out all the unconstitutional doctrines which their bellwether Davila has been preaching for a twelvemonth." Nonetheless, despite his enthusiastic support for Paine's principles, he flatly denied that he "meant to step into a public newspaper with that in my mouth." To other correspondents, however, he let it be known that he approved entirely of the subsequent newspaper attacks on Adams as proof that "the spirit of republicanism is sound" in America. Jefferson took unrestrained delight in reporting to Thomas Paine that the controversy had "excited the public attention" and, more importantly, that it had caused the public to reexamine Adams's "'Defence of the American constitutions' and the 'Discourses on Davila,'" which it had kindly passed over without censure in the moment." Furthermore, he took pride in having played a part, if unintentionally, in turning the attention of the people away from the "assertions of a sect"—that is, those who had "apostatized from the true faith"—in favor of "King, lords, and commons." Fortunately for America, "Mr. Paine's answer to Burke will be a refreshing shower to their minds." Remarkably, when Jefferson wrote to explain himself to his old friend John Adams, he told a very different story. By "political heresies," he claimed to not be referring to Adams and the *Davila* essays: "Indeed it was impossible that my note should occasion your name to be brought into question; for so far from naming you, I had not even in view any writing which I might suppose to be yours."[34] The claim, in the light of his letters to Washington and Madison, was simply a lie.

In June, young John Quincy Adams rose to defend his father in a series of articles signed "Publicola." Mistaken initially as the work of the vice president, the younger Adams's rejoinder to Paine and Jefferson was a restrained, closely reasoned argument in defense of the British constitution against that of Revolutionary France. In defending his father against the charge of heresy, he quite appropriately asked the American public to consider the full meaning of Jefferson's words: Does Mr. Jefferson, he asked, "consider this pamphlet of Mr. Paine's as the canonical book of political scripture? As containing the true doctrine of popular infallibility, from which it would be heretical to depart in one single point?" John Quincy was quite right to question whether the American and French Revolutions were to be now seen as inextricably bound together and, unbeknownst to most, worshipped as religious orthodoxy. He wondered if he had been laboring under the mistaken opinion that Americans "were possessed of a full and entire freedom of opinion upon all subjects civil as well as religious." Contrary to what Jefferson seemed to be suggesting, John Quincy thought there was no "infallible criterion of *orthodoxy*, either in church or state" in America. The very idea seemed un-American.[35]

Reaction to "Publicola" was immediate. In the weeks and months that followed, an intense but rather lopsided ideological war broke out across the United States over the nature of the English constitution and the American Revolution. In newspapers all around the country, Jefferson and Paine were exalted, while John Adams was abused as an enemy to freedom and squibbed as an advocate of monarchy and hereditary orders.[36] From this moment forward, John Adams was never able to shake off the charge that he was an intellectual traitor to the cause of republicanism.

Jefferson certainly always denied that he intended for his note to be published, but the circumstances surrounding its publication do raise serious questions. If seen in the light of his likely role in suppressing the French translation and publication of Adams's *Defence* in 1787 and his covert role in founding and sustaining Philip Freneau's *National Gazette* in 1791, Jefferson's claim of nolo contendere in the *Rights of Man* controversy seems disingenuous. Jefferson's character was such that he almost always shunned direct public confrontation. Instead, he preferred to provoke and mobilize his party lieutenants or the republican press to engage in public disputes that he wished to affect but not to be associated with publicly.[37] Jefferson's felicity of expression was matched only by his abilities as a political manager and ideological agent provocateur. Unlike John Adams who always put his cards on the table, Thomas Jefferson was a master at palming his ace. He may very well have been the greatest politician of his generation.

Jefferson's explanation of the Adams-Paine episode falls flat for several reasons. First, his note to Paine's American publisher was simultaneously too provocative, and its veiled allusion to Adams and the *Discourses* too subtle by half; it reads as though devilishly calculated. Second, though greatly embarrassed by the event, he seemed all too pleased with the result. He defended his actions on the grounds that his indiscretion had actually stopped an antirepublican juggernaut from delivering America to "king" and "lords." Third, Jefferson never told the American people that publication of the note had been unauthorized. Given the political shock waves created by the affair and given the damage and hurt that he knew it would cause his friend John Adams, it would have been entirely appropriate for Jefferson to acknowledge publicly that he had not consented to the note's publication. In other words, Jefferson permitted the American people to continue believing that he was publicly supporting Paine's book against an American sect of republican heretics. Fourth, Jefferson was no political innocent, unaware of the world of partisan political publishing. He supported, funded, and used the world of Philip Freneau and Benjamin Franklin Bache to support his political career and ideological agenda. Finally, Jefferson never accepted responsibility for the libelous attacks advanced against Adams. In fact, he blamed the ensuing ideological warfare on John Quincy Adams and the "Publicola" essays. He told Adams that public reaction to his note and to *Rights of Man* was negligible until the publication of "Publicola" had ignited the whole affair. Adams might well have reminded Jefferson that American reaction to the *Discourses on Davila* was equally negligible until the publication of Jefferson's note. He did tell the Virginian that the real source of the bitter public controversy could be traced back to the "Striking . . . recommendation" that prefaced *Rights of Man*. Adams insisted that Jefferson tell him "What Heresies" he intended to impugn by his note, and he reminded him that they had never had a full discussion about their respective political philosophies. "It was high time," Adams declared, "that you and I should come to an explanation with each other." Adams then directly challenged Jefferson to "produce Such a passage and quote the Chapter and Verse" from any of his writings that could be interpreted as advocating monarchy and aristocracy. Then and there the issue could have been resolved honorably. But Adams's invitation was left without a reply. Jefferson refused to come clean with Adams. Instead, he preferred to perpetuate the charge behind Adams's back, repeating his libel many more times over the years.[38]

By raising the banner against heresy, Jefferson, assuming the role of America's ideological Holy Father, excommunicated Adams from the Revolutionary faith of 1776, a faith that was now intimately connected to the French Revolution. To believe in one was to believe in the other, and support for the French Revolution became for Jefferson an ideological litmus test as to whether one was truly a republican or a monocrat. Adams's critique of the French Revolution in the *Davila* essays therefore provided Jefferson with evidence on which to convict his old friend of blasphemy. To those who have praised the Virginian as the American apostle of enlightenment and intellectual freedom, Jefferson's marriage of the American and French Revolution as consummating a new religious orthodoxy must seem strangely paradoxical.

Jefferson's friends and foes thought his indiscretion was, if not unintentionally useful to his political career, born of outright political ambition. That George Washington would not respond to Jefferson's explanatory letter strongly suggests that the President did not accept the Secretary of State's story. Even Julian Boyd, editor of *The Papers of Thomas Jefferson* for the period in question, noted that Washington returned Jefferson's letter of explanation with "only an icy silence." In the immediate aftermath of the Adams-Jefferson controversy, James Monroe wrote his fellow Virginian and told him that public honor initially dictated that he explain his political principles "fully to the publick." Riding a wave of popularity, though, Monroe now thought it more prudent for Jefferson to stay silent given the upcoming presidential election. Jefferson's stature, he said, had risen in the estimation of republicans and would remain there simply on the basis of his "short note prefixt to Paines pamphlet." Besides, he had nothing to gain and probably everything to lose by engaging Adams in debate. Writing as "Catullus," Alexander Hamilton accused Jefferson of using the publication of *Rights of Man* "to answer the double purpose of wounding a competitor and of laying in an additional stock of popularity." He then accused Jefferson of intentionally provoking a controversy by indicting Adams as an antirepublican in order that the newspapers across the country would resound "with invective and scurrility against the patriot."[39] By tearing down the vice president, Hamilton thought Jefferson was setting up himself to succeed Washington when the time came. In 1796 and then again in 1800, the Republican party machine—a machine that Jefferson had created and controlled as much as anyone—did their best to revive the polemics of 1791.

Remembering John Adams

John Adams's reputation was irrevocably damaged by the ideological and rhetorical campaign that was waged against him in the early 1790s. In the wake of the *Rights of Man* imbroglio, the *Defence* and *Davila* essays became books about which everyone seemed to have an opinion but few had actually read. Most hurtful to Adams was the knowledge that his discourses had been "willfully misrepresented" by ideological partisans who had not read them, and the misrepresentations were then used as a pretense "for overwhelming me with floods and Whirlwinds of tempestuous Abuse." Over the years, Adams received several anecdotal reports that confirmed his suspicions. Judge Thomas Cushing informed the vice president that he had recently attended a dinner party with Patrick Henry who "harrangue[d]" the guests with a condemnation of Adams's political writings. When it became clear to Cushing that Henry "knew nothing about them," he asked the Virginian if he had ever read Adams's books. Embarrassed, Henry conceded that he had not. Arthur Lee, also in attendance, spoke up in defense of Adams and told the gathering that the *Defence* was "the Work of the greatest Genius that had ever been written in this Country." At another dinner, the Virginia planter and Jeffersonian operative William Branch Giles charged the *Defence* and *Davila* essays with the increasingly common indictment of monarchism. Also in attendance was John Trumbull, who had actually read the volumes. When it became clear to Trumbull that Giles was totally ignorant of their content, he interrupted the Virginian to ask if he might pose one simple question: "Pray Mr. Giles have you ever read those Volumes of Mr. Adams?" Taken by surprise, Giles blushed, hesitated, and stammered that he had not. He took his account, he said, from the newspapers. Curtly, Trumbull chastised Giles and insisted that he had "no right" to give an opinion of books that he had not read. Nancy Allen, hostess for the gathering, then turned to Giles and told him that she hoped his political opinions were not "taken up with so much Levity and upon so little foundation!"[40]

In the years after the end of the Jefferson administration, republican polemicists who had once lampooned the *Defence* began to reassess its value. Many came to find their former position wanting. In 1820, Adams received a remarkable letter from Charles Holt, the former editor of the *Connecticut Bee*, a Republican party newspaper. Holt reminded the former president that he had once been imprisoned under the Sedition Law, passed by the Adams administration in 1798. In other words, he had good reason to dislike Adams and the principles for which he stood. He informed Adams that he had then written and published much against him "as an aristocrat in principle or royalist at heart, no friend to 'the rights of man,' and hostile to the 'republicanism' of the United States." Remarkably, he then admitted that he had not even read the *Defence* in those days. The charges, he wrote, were entirely fabricated. In the intervening years, however, he confessed to having had a change of mind. Having since read Adams's treatise he now "felt abundant cause for disregarding the impressions I then entertained." Paying Adams the ultimate compliment, he now believed in 1820 that the

> good sense of our fellow citizens, in most if not all of the American constitutions, has secured to the people the benefit of your theory, improved from the British system, and established such guards, and preventatives against both anarchy and despotism, as I trust will long present to the world more perfect models and happy spectacles of a nicely balanced and well regulated state, than are to be found in the warm imagination of the most benevolent theorist, or the real history of the all the republics which Greece and Rome, Europe or Asia, ancient and modern has furnished."

Adams would have liked this letter, not so much because its author now agreed with him, but because it demonstrated the kind of intellectual integrity and honesty that Adams so admired.[41]

If the leaders of the Virginia Dynasty—the Madisons, Thomas Jefferson, William Branch Giles, Patrick Henry, and John Taylor—were right in their accusations against the *Defence* and *Davila* essays, it would be entirely proper for modern scholars to say that Adams was an anachronism who missed the intellectual significance and political meaning of the American Revolution. But if they were untrue, it would be incumbent upon us not only to reexamine the significance and relevance of John Adams, but also to look anew at American intellectual and political culture in the years after 1787. According to the best available evidence, Adams was not without cause when he suggested that his writings had been willfully misrepresented by ideological partisans who had not read his books. From that moment forward, he later told Jefferson, a foundation was laid for that "immense Unpopularity, which fell like the Tower of Siloam upon me."[42] In a sense, the problem with Adams's books on government, at least from the perspective of people like Jefferson and Taylor, was that they were *too* relevant. If the *Defence* was so obviously irrelevant and anomalous, why did it provoke such a powerful response? Why was it slandered by Jeffersonian Republicans throughout the 1790s? In an intense and bitterly partisan ideological battle, the *Defence* had to be made irrelevant before it actually became so. It did not simply fall stillborn from the press. This is precisely why John Taylor felt compelled to spend twenty years writing a five-hundred page response to Adams. In the end, by studying the nature, sources, and influences of post-Revolutionary partisan rhetoric, we may come to learn more about the ideology of the Jeffersonian republicans than about the political ideas of John Adams.

John Adams knew that statues and monuments would never be built in his name, but he did hope that posterity would remember and judge him fairly. This book has above all else attempted to do just that. In closing, I would like to draw the readers' attention to three aspects of his life and thought that deserve to be remembered and that may hold some relevance for our present and future.

Unlike Thomas Jefferson and Alexander Hamilton, John Adams did not bequeath to the future a usable theory of political economy. He played a minor role in the major policy battles of the 1790s. Strict versus broad constitutional construction, limited versus expansive government functions, free trade versus protectionism, states' rights versus union, isolationist versus internationalist foreign policy—these controversies have defined American political discourse for over two hundred years. Indeed, the liberal tradition has rarely moved beyond the political issues first debated by Jefferson and Hamilton. This explains to a large degree why they and not Adams seem more relevant to the present.

In a deeper sense, however, Adams's contribution to the liberal way of life was more important. We tend to forget that American liberalism has rarely ever derailed from its original projectory precisely because it runs on a constitutional track first laid by Adams. From his defense of British soldiers at the Boston Massacre trial to his drafting of a Revolutionary constitution for Massachusetts, from his advocacy in the Continental Congress for the establishment of Revolutionary governments to his gentle call for their reform in his *Defence of the Constitutions*, John Adams was arguably the leading constitutionalist of the founding era. His early advocacy of a deliberate founding and of a written constitution as higher law established a sanction of authority and permanence that transcended the impermanent interests, passions, and opinions of the present and future. Moral and political change in America would therefore be limited to recreating, restoring, or fulfilling the principles of America's founding moment. The Talmudic constitutionalism that Adams placed at the heart of American civic life explains to a large degree why our political discourse has never advanced beyond the original policy debates initiated by Jefferson and Hamilton; it established a barrier to the neofeudal aspirations of John C. Calhoun and to the socialist dreams of Eugene Debs. Adams's parchment barriers have proved to be an iron cage for nonliberal traditions, thus the extraordinary uniformity and timelessness that defines American political life. We have good cause then to remember Adams for what he aspired to be and in the end truly was: a founder and a lawgiver.

Many scholars today, inspired by the staleness of American public discourse in recent decades, have begun to search for and to resurrect neglected intellectual and political traditions. Thus the renewed interest in Puritan communalism, Anti-Federalism, classical republicanism, and even Progressivism. This openness to alternative intellectual traditions invites us to reexamine some of Adams's more controversial views. Adams's political science, and his views on equality and inequality in particular, offer a profound alternative to the democratic dogmas of our day. He well knew that the United States and the nations of Europe were in the midst of a democratic revolution unlike any other. But democracy was not a dogma for him, nor was it a religion as it would be for some. Though a friend, Adams was not simply a partisan for the project. Whereas Thomas Jefferson bore almost millennial hopes for democracy, Adams saw nothing inevitable or providential in it. For Jefferson, certainly in the years after 1789, democracy was a good in itself. Adams, by contrast, saw the fragility and darker side of democracy, and he challenged the idea that its progress is unqualifiedly good. He was able, in a way that Jefferson was not, to step outside of the democratic regime and to look more objectively at its virtues and its vices.

Adams's greatness as a political theorist is best revealed in the extraordinary penetration with which he analyzed how democracies democratize, that is, how they destroy old mannners and mores and transform the soul in rather profound ways. The great danger associated with the doctrine of equality is that it generates a downward psychological and moral momentum that is hard to resist or control. He knew that unchecked democratization would eventually liberate the most wicked democratic passions. Anticipating Alexis de Tocqueville, he worried that democratic envy would lead to democratic conformism and ultimately to democratic tyranny. Adams thus perceived with unequaled acuity the dangers to which popular governments are liable. He wrote the *Defence* and the *Davila* essays so that democratic man might see what he has most to fear in himself and what he is permitted to hope for from a democratic revolution.

Democracy, for Adams, was not an answer but a problem to be solved. He insisted that democracy look to a source or a standard outside itself to establish its bearings. Democratic equality for Adams meant constitutionalizing rights, rights held in common by all people. But equality before the law must also promote the natural differences between human beings—that is, inequalities of wisdom, virtue, merit, beauty, etc.—while tolerating conventional inequalities that arise as a consequence of birth and wealth. Adams respected natural inequalities, and he recognized the inevitability of artificial inequalities. A healthy democratic regime must simultaneously foster and control both democratic and aristocratic aspiration. Adams looked deeply into the soul of the democratic revolution that was sweeping the West, identified its defects and weaknesses, built dikes to protect it from its own excesses, and finally, he sought to elevate and ennoble this experiment in self-government by reminding us that democratic greatness must recognize and appreciate the truly great.

From the beginning of his public career until the very end, John Adams always acted on principle and a profound love of country. He devoted his life and mind to the cause of liberty and to the construction of republican government in America. He wanted liberty, equality, and a virtuous republic as much as any Jeffersonian. Adams was no simpleminded partisan, nor was he a naive or foolish advocate of republican government. His understanding of patriotism, honor, and justice would not permit him to abandon the long-term interests of his country for personal political gain. In Adams's view, the preservation of liberty and republican government required that a disinterested few stand uncorrupted above all party and faction. We may take the following words that he wrote to a friend during some of the darkest days of the Revolution as a kind of motto to describe who he was as a man and as a patriot: "Fiat Justitia ruat Coelum [Let justice be done though the heavens should fall]." To live by such words, though, requires a kind of moral independence that honors doing only what is right and just at all times. "I must think myself independent, as long as I live," he wrote to his son John Quincy in 1815. "The feeling is essential to my existence."[43] Adams created in himself a moral universe that we can barely fathom today. He always refused to compromise on matters of principle, and for that very reason, he was not and could never be a successful politician.

As the fiftieth anniversary of the Declaration of Independence approached, the ninety-one-year-old Adams was asked to provide a toast for the upcoming celebration in Quincy. He offered as his final public utterance this solemn toast: "INDEPENDENCE FOREVER." These last words stand as a signature for his life and principles. At a time in our national history when most Americans cynically assume that their political leaders are dishonest, corrupt, and self-serving, we might do well to recall the example of John Adams and restore to posterity the respect and admiration that he so richly deserves.

NOTES

Introduction

1. Benjamin Rush quoted in Joseph J. Ellis, *The Passionate Sage: The Character and Legacy of John Adams* (New York, 1994), 29.

2. Gilbert Chinard thought Adams "one of the most original and penetrating writers of his generation" (*Honest John Adams* [Boston, 1933], xi); Vernon L. Parrington described Adams as "the most notable political thinker—with the possible exception of John C. Calhoun—among American statesmen" (*Main Currents in American Thought*, I [New York, 1927], 320). Harold Laski called Adams "the greatest political thinker whom America has yet produced" (Quoted in Haraszti, *John Adams and the Prophets of Progress* [Cambridge, Mass., 1952], 46). Charles Warren thought that Adams "rightly may be termed 'The Architect of American Constitutions'" ("John Adams and the American Constitutions," *Massachusetts Law Quarterly* 12 [1917], 73). Clinton Rossiter judged Adams to be "the most constructive political mind of the era" (*Seedtime of the Republic* [New York, 1953], 403). Elsewhere, Rossiter wrote of Adams "that no other man in that glorious age of learned statesmen ranged farther afield for instruction and inspiration." "In the realm of political ideas," Rossiter concluded, Adams "had no master—and I would think no peer—among the founding fathers" ("The Legacy of John Adams," *Yale Review* [June 1957], 533, 548). As a political theorist, Joseph Charles ranked Adams as "perhaps the leading man of his generation" (*The Origins of the American Party System* [New York, 1961], 54). Gordon Wood has written that "no one read more and thought more about politics" during the revolutionary and founding period than did Adams (*Creation of the American Republic* [Chapel Hill, N.C., 1969], 568). Pauline Maier described Adams as "perhaps the country's most learned students of politics" (*From Resistance to Revolution* [New York, 1972], 287). J. M Porter and R. S. Farnell thought that Adams, "with his legal mind and massive erudition, probed deeper and wrote more on the proper constitutional order than the other Founding Fathers" ("John Adams and American Constitutionalism," *American Journal of Jurisprudence* 21 [1976], 32–33).

3. This position was most elaborately worked out in John R. Howe's *The Changing Political Thought of John Adams* (Princeton, N.J., 1966), but the most influential statement of this interpretation is to be found in Wood, *The Creation of the American Republic*, 567–92. Wood's chapter on Adams is entitled, "The Relevance and Irrelevance of John Adams," which includes a section on "The Anomaly of the *Defence of the Constitutions*." This interpretation is also accepted by Joyce Appleby, "The New Republican Synthesis and the Changing Political Thought of John Adams," *American Quarterly* 25 (1973): 578–95; and by Lance Banning, *The Jeffersonian Persuasion* (Ithaca, N.Y., 1978), 278–90. There are those, however, who do see an overall consistency in Adams's political thought. See, for instance, Benjamin Fletcher Wright,

American Interpretations of Natural Law (New York, 1962), 120–23; Zoltan Harazsti, *John Adams and the Prophets of Progress* (Cambridge, Mass., 1952), 27; Joseph Ellis, *The Character and Legacy of John Adams*; Richard Alan Ryerson, "'Like a Hare before the Hunters': John Adams and the Idea of Republican Monarchy," *Proceedings of the Massachusetts Historical Society* (Boston, 1996): 16–29; and, most importantly, Ralph Lerner, *The Thinking Revolutionary: Principle and Practice in the New Republic* (Ithaca, N.Y., 1987), 16–29.

4. John Adams to Benjamin Rush, 23 March 1809, *The Spur of Fame: Dialogues of John Adams and Benjamin Rush, 1805–1813*, ed. John Schutz and Douglass Adair (San Marino, Calif., 1966), 139. Standard biographies of Adams include: Gilbert Chinard, *Honest John Adams*; Page Smith, *John Adams*, 2 vols. (Garden City, N.Y., 1962); Anne Husted Burleigh, *John Adams* (New Rochelle, N.Y., 1969); and, John E. Ferling, *John Adams: A Life* (Knoxville, Tenn., 1992).

5. Bernard Bailyn, "Butterfield's Adams: Notes for a Sketch," *William and Mary Quarterly* 3rd Ser., 19 (1962): 239–56.

6. Ibid., 246, 252–53, 255.

7. Peter Shaw, *The Character of John Adams* (Chapel Hill, N.C., 1976), 223.

8. The methodological premises of this school of interpretation were first enunciated in Bernard Bailyn's *The Ideological Origins of the American Revolution* (Cambridge, Mass., 1967). The definitive methodological statement of this mode of interpretation, however, is found in Gordon S. Wood's essay "Rhetoric and Reality in the American Revolution," *William and Mary Quarterly*, 3rd Ser., 23 (1966), 29–30.

9. Howe, *The Changing Political Thought of John Adams*, xv; Wood, *Creation of the American Republic*, 577. From a slightly different perspective, Joyce Appleby and Edward Handler, following the methodology of the ideological historians, have argued that the essential context of the *Defence* is to be found in Adams's European experiences. See Handler, *America and Europe in the Political Thought of John Adams* (Cambridge, Mass., 1964); and Appleby, "The New Republican Synthesis and the Changing Political Ideas of John Adams," *American Quarterly* 25 (1973): 578–95.

10. Benjamin Franklin to Robert R. Livingston, 22 July 1783, in Albert Henry Smyth, ed., *The Writings of Benjamin Franklin* (New York, 1905–1907), 9: 62.

11. David Hackett Fischer, *Paul Revere's Ride* (New York, 1994), xvii.

12. I have relied for my research on *The Works of John Adams, Second President of the United States*, 10 vols., edited by Charles Francis Adams (Boston, 1850–56), hereafter cited as *Works* and relevant volume; and *Papers of John Adams*, 8 vols. to date, edited by Robert J. Taylor et al., (Cambridge, Mass., 1977–), hereafter cited as *Papers* and relevant volume; and *Diary and Autobiography of John Adams*, 4 vols., edited by L. H. Butterfield (Cambridge, Mass., 1962), hereafter cited as *Diary and Autobiography* and relevant volume.

1. Calvin, Locke, and the American Enlightenment

1. John Adams to H. Niles, 13 February 1818, in *Works*, 10: 282–83. Also see JA to Thomas Jefferson, 24 August 1815 and JA to Thomas McKean, 26 November 1815, *Works*, 172–73, 180–83.

2. John T. Morse thought Adams "an admirable specimen of the New England Puritan." *John Adams* (Boston, 1898). Francis Thorpe called him "a Puritan of the

Puritans." "The Political Ideas of John Adams," *Pennsylvania Magazine of History and Biography*, 44 (1920), 3. Paul K. Conkin writes that Adams's "dominant character traits, his habits of thought, even his political ideals, were thoroughly Puritan." *Puritans and Pragmatists: Eight Eminent American Thinkers* (New York, 1968), 109. John P. Diggins goes farthest in describing Adams as a "good Calvinist." *The Lost Soul of American Politics: Virtue, Self-Interest, and the Foundations of Liberalism* (New York, 1984), 55.

3. Bailyn, "Butterfield's Adams: Notes for a Sketch," 238–56; Morgan, "John Adams and the Puritan Tradition," *New England Quarterly*, 34 (1961): 518–29.

4. Morgan, "John Adams and the Puritan Tradition," 518–29. See also Morgan's *The Puritan Dilemma: The Story of John Winthrop* (Boston, 1958). Morgan later expanded this theme to apply to the whole Revolutionary generation in "The Puritan Ethic and the American Revolution," *William and Mary Quarterly*, 3rd Ser., 24 (1967): 8–18. Those who have followed Morgan's lead include Alfred H. Kelly, "American Political Leadership: The Optimistic Ethical World View and the Jefferson Synthesis," in Library of Congress Symposia on the American Revolution, *Leadership in the American Revolution* (Washington, D.C., 1974), 23; Schutz and Adair, *The Spur of Fame: Dialogues of John Adams and Benjamin Rush, 1805–1813*, 18; Shaw, *The Character of John Adams*, 3–24; Ellis, *Passionate Sage: The Character and Legacy of John Adams*, 48, 52–53; Ralph Ketcham, *From Colony to Country: The Revolution in American Thought, 1750–1820* (New York, 1974), 159–60, 166; Smith, *John Adams*, 4, 234; and Jurgen Gebhardt, *Americanism: Revolutionary Order and Societal Self-Interpretation in the American Republic*, trans. Ruth Hein (Baton Rouge, La., 1993), 57, 72–93.

5. Bailyn, "Butterfield's Adams," 255; Diggins, *Lost Soul of American Politics*, 71; Shaw, *The Character of John Adams*, 211–12. For Richard B. Morris, it was "the Puritan, with his deep pessimism about man and his Puritan stress on moral values, that gave so distinctively conservative a cast to Adams's revolutionary thought." "John Adams: Puritan Revolutionary," in Morris, *Seven Who Shaped Our Destiny: The Founding Fathers as Revolutionaries* (New York, 1973), 110. Earl N. Harbert writes that "as much as Jonathan Edwards, Adams was convinced of the imperfection of man." "John Adams' Private Voice," *Tulane Studies in English*, 15 (1967): 98. See also Parrington, *Main Currents in American Thought*, vol. 1, *The Colonial Mind* (New York, 1927), 324; Yehoshua Arieli, *Individualism and Nationalism in American Ideology* (Baltimore, 1964), 134; Clinton Rossiter, *Conservatism in America* (New York, 1955), 114; and Barry Alan Shain, *The Myth of American Individualism: The Protestant Origins of American Political Thought* (Princeton, N.J., 1994), 227.

6. Bailyn, "Butterfield's Adams," 252, 249, 246, 253. For Bailyn and Morgan to demonstrate convincingly how Adams's thinking and behavior could be adequately explained as theological or cultural secularization, they would have had to provide a standard by which to judge how or why the psychological process of secularization took place. Both understood, in Morgan's words, that Adams was "not quite a Puritan," but neither discussed the agent or cause of Adams's personal and intellectual movement away from the Puritan ideal. Morgan, "John Adams and the Puritan Tradition," 525. Two studies that seek to demonstrate how first Calvin and Calvinism and then Cotton Mather and Puritanism were influenced by modern rationalism are Ralph C. Hancock, *Calvin and the Foundations of Modern Politics* (Ithaca, N.Y., 1989), and Michael P. Winship, *Seers of God: Puritan Providentialism in the Restoration and Early Enlightenment* (Baltimore, 1996).

7. On this movement as a colonial-wide intellectual phenomenon, see Claude M. Newlin, *Philosophy and Religion in Colonial America* (New York, 1962); Henry F. May, *The Enlightenment in America* (New York, 1976); Conrad Wright, *The Beginnings of Unitarianism in America* (Boston 1955); Alice M. Baldwin, *The New England Clergy and the American Revolution* (New York, 1928); and Kerry S. Walters, *The American Deists: Voices of Reason and Dissent in the Early Republic* (Lawrence, Kans., 1992). For a very different interpretation of the moral and religious causes of the Revolution see Alan Heimert, *Religion and the American Mind from the Great Awakening to the Revolution* (Cambridge, Mass., 1966).

8. *Diary and Autobiography*, 3: 263. See also Shaw, *Character of John Adams*, 8–9.

9. L. H. Butterfield et al., ed., *The Earliest Diary of John Adams* (Cambridge, Mass., 1966), 60, 63. Hereafter cited as *Earliest Diary*; *Diary and Autobiography*, 3: 262. For a useful discussion of Adams's scientific training under Winthrop see I. Bernard Cohen, *Science and the Founding Fathers: Science in the Political Thought of Jefferson, Franklin, Adams, and Madison* (New York, 1995), 196–236. In a 1782 letter to Abigail, we can see why Adams rejected science as a career, but we also see the how the influence of the scientist's empirical method informed his study of human nature. He reported having visited a "Mr. Lionet," a man of some renown in the scientific community whose "Hobby Horse has been natural knowledge" and who shared with Adams his book about his collection of caterpillars. "Have you the Inclination," Adams asked rhetorically, "to read and inspect Cutts of the Anatomy of Caterpillars—their Names, Blood, Juices, Bones, Hair, Senses, Intellects &c. &c.—Their moral Sense, their Laws, Government, Manners Customs.

I dont know whether he teaches the manner of destroying them, and Saving the Apple Tree. I doubt not the book is worth studying. All nature is so.—But I have too much to do, to Study Men, and their mischievous Designs upon Apple Trees . . . and other Things, ever to be very intimate with Mr. Lionet, (whom I respect very much however) or his Book." (25 July 1782, *Adams Family Correspondence*, ed. L. H. Butterfield et al. [Boston, 1963], 4: 353–54).

10. *Diary and Autobiography*, 3: 262. Adams's recollection of Briant's apostasy and his subsequent quarrel with Boston-area Congregationalists is reprised in Wright, *Beginnings of Unitarianism*, 67–75.

11. *Diary and Autobiography*, 3: 262–63.

12. Ibid., 1: 24.

13. Ibid., 3: 263. For a discussion of Morgan's treatise and its place in eighteenth-century deist thought see Sir Leslie Stephen, *History of English Thought in the Eighteenth Century*, 2 vols. (New York, 1962), 140–42.

14. JA to Nathan Webb, 1 September 1755, *Papers*, 1: 1.

15. *Diary and Autobiography*, 3: 264–66.

16. For Haven, see Clifford K. Shipton, *Sibley's Harvard Graduates: Biographical Sketches of Those Who Attended Harvard College* (Boston, 1956), 13: 447–55; for Balch see ibid., 9 (Boston, 1956), 273–78.

17. *Diary and Autobiography*, 1: 14–15; JA to Thomas Jefferson, 18 July 1818, *The Adams-Jefferson Letters: The Complete Correspondence Between Thomas Jefferson and Abigail and John Adams*, 2 vols., ed. Lester J. Cappon (Chapel Hill, N.C., 1959), 2: 527; JA to Charles Cushing, 1 April 1756, *Papers*, 1: 13. The editors of the *Papers* believe that the misspelling of "Arminian" by Adams was an intentional play on words and was intended as a joke between the two.

18. *Diary and Autobiography*, 3: 265.

19. JA to Richard Cranch, 29 August 1756, *Papers*, 1: 17; JA to Charles Cushing, 19 October 1756, *Papers*, 1: 21–22. By August 1756, Adams was openly condemning much of the New England clergy and its lay followers. His inflated rhetoric suggests that he was opening an emotional and intellectual safety valve that was ready to burst.

20. *Diary and Autobiography*, 1: 42–43.

21. Ibid., 42.

22. JA to Samuel Quincy, 22 April 1761, *Papers*, 1: 48–50.

23. Ibid., 49. Adams's diary records a conversation of 1756 with one Major Greene about limited atonement. Greene presented the Calvinist view of the "Divinity and Satisfaction of Jesus Christ." He argued "'that a mere creature, or finite Being, could not make Satisfaction to infinite Justice, for any Crimes,'" to which Adams responded in the margin, "Thus mystery is made a convenient Cover for absurdity." *Diary and Autobiography*, 1: 6.

24. The only Adams scholar to have addressed this question is John L. Paynter, "The Ethics of John Adams: Prolegomenon to a Science of Politics" (University of Chicago, 1974), 1–55. Paynter makes a convincing case that the primary intellectual influence on Adams during these years was his reading of theological texts of English "rationalist" theologians.

25. Tillotson's influence in America is shown in Norman Fiering, "The First American Enlightenment: Tillotson, Leverett, and Philosophical Anglicanism," *New England Quarterly* 54 (1981): 307–44. Also see Fiering, *Moral Philosophy at Seventeenth-Century Harvard: A Discipline in Transition* (Chapel Hill, N.C., 1981).

26. I have profited from the following studies in the development of English natural theology: Gerald R. Cragg, *From Puritanism to the Age of Reason: A Study of Changes in Religious Thought within the Church of England, 1660–1700* (Cambridge [Engl.], 1950), and *Reason and Authority in the Eighteenth Century* (Cambridge [Engl.], 1964); Margaret C. Jacob, *The Newtonians and the English Revolution, 1689–1720* (Ithaca, N.Y., 1976); Sir Leslie Stephen, *History of English Thought in the Eighteenth Century*, 2 vols. (New York, 1962); Basil Wiley, *The Eighteenth-Century Background: Studies on the Idea of Nature in the Thought of the Period* (Boston, 1962); and Ernst Cassirer, *The Philosophy of the Enlightenment* (Boston, 1955).

27. On the general role played by Lockean philosophy in America, see Steven M. Dworetz, *The Unvarnished Doctrine: Locke, Liberalism, and the American Revolution* (Durham, N.C., 1990), and Jerome Huyler, *Locke in America: The Moral Philosophy of the Founding Era* (Lawrence, Kans., 1995).

28. See *Diary and Autobiography*, 1: 11, 32–33, 38, 40, 43–44, 98–99.

29. JA to Jonathan Sewell, February 1760, in *Papers*, 1: 42–43.

30. John Locke, *An Essay Concerning Human Understanding*, ed. John W. Yolton, 2 vols. (London, 1961), bk. I, chap. 1, sec. 2.

31. See ibid., chap. 4, secs. 12, 18.

32. John Locke, *On the Reasonableness of Christianity*, ed. George W. Ewing (Chicago, 1964).

33. Locke, *Human Understanding*, bk. IV: chap. 19, sec. 14.

34. Draft of a letter to Jonathan Sewell, *Diary and Autobiography*, 1: 123 (emphasis added). Compare with Locke, *Human Understanding*, bk. I, chap. 1, secs. 1–8.

35. *Diary and Autobiography*, 1: 42.

36. Ibid., 98–9, 18, 43–4 (emphasis added), 26.

37. Draft of a Letter to an Unidentified Correspondent, *Earliest Diary*, 71–72.

38. *Diary and Autobiography*, 1: 11.

39. Ibid., 40–41.

40. Ibid., 40–41, 29–30, 38–39.

41. *Earliest Diary*, 71–72.

42. *A Defence of the Constitutions of Government of the United States of America, Works*, 4: 283.

43. *Diary and Autobiography*, 1: 27.

44. Ibid., 43.

45. Ibid., 31.

46. Ibid.

47. Ibid., 117, 41; *Earliest Diary*, 66.

48. "No doubt There is as great a multitude and variety of Bodies upon each Planet in proportion to its magnitude, as there is upon ours. These Bodies are connected with and influenced by each other. Thus we see the amazing harmony of our Solar System. . . . But to rise still higher this Solar System is but one, very small wheel in the great the astonishing Machine of the World. Those Starrs that twinkle in the Heavens have each of them a Choir of Planets, Comets, and Satellites dancing round them, playing mutually on each other, and all together playing on the other Systems that lie around them. Our System, considered as [one] body hanging on its Center of Gravity, may affect and be affected by all the other Systems, within the Compass of Creation. Thus it is highly probable every Particle of matter, influences, and is influenced by every other Particle in the whole collective Universe." *Diary and Autobiography*, 1: 24.

49. "Now every Animal that we see in this Prospect, Men and Beasts, are endued with most curiously organized Bodies. They consist of Bones, and Blood, and muscles, and nerves, and ligaments and Tendons, and Chile and a million other things, all exactly fitted for the purposes of Life and motion, and Action. Every Plant has almost as complex and curious a structure, as animals, and the minutest Twigg is supported, and supplied with Juices and Life, by organs and Filaments proper to draw this Nutrition of the Earth." Ibid., 30.

50. "If we consider a little of this our Globe we find an endless Variety of Substances, mutually connected with and dependent on Each other. In the Wilderness we see an amazing profusion of vegetables, which afford Sustenance and covering to the wild Beasts. The cultivated Planes and Meadows produce grass for Cattle, and Herbs for the service of man. This milk and the Flesh of other Animals, afford a delicious provision for mankind. A great Part of the human Species are obliged to provide food and nourishment for other helpless and improvident Animals. Vegetables sustain some Animals. These animals are devoured by others, and these others are continually cultivating and improving the vegetable Species. Thus nature, upon our Earth, is in a continual Rotation." Ibid., 23.

51. "We don't see Chickens hatched with fins to swim, nor Fishes spawned with wings to fly. We don't see a Colt folded [foaled] with Claws like a Bird, nor men with the Cloathing or Armor which his Reason renders him capable of procuring for himself. Every Species has its distinguishing Properties, and every Individual that is born has all those Properties without any of the distinguishing Properties of another Species." Ibid., 39.

52. "There is, from the highest Species of animals upon this Globe which is generally thought to be Man, a regular and uniform Subordination of one Tribe to another

down to the apparently insignificant animalcules in peppery Water, and the same Subordination continues quite through the Vegetable Kingdom." Ibid., 39.

53. "God whose almighty Fiat first produced this amazing Universe, had the whole Plan in View from all Eternity, intimately and perfectly knew the Nature and all the Properties of all these his Creatures. He looked forward through all Duration and perfectly knew all the Effects, all the events and Revolutions, that could possibly, and would eventually take place, Throughout Eternity." Ibid., 30.

54. Ibid., 25.

55. Ibid., 41–42, 25–26, 43–44.

56. Ibid., 41–42, 31, 25–26, 43–44, 33–34.

57. Ibid., 42.

58. Ibid., 61; *Earliest Diary*, 77; *Diary and Autobiography*, 1: 65.

59. *Diary and Autobiography*, 1: 25–26, 41–42.

60. Ibid., 113.

61. Ibid., 23, 31, 9.

62. Ibid., 8, 31.

63. See, for instance, Adam Smith, *The Theory of Moral Sentiments*, with an Introduction by E. G. West (Indianapolis, Ind., 1976).

64. *Diary and Autobiography*, 1: 33–44; *Earliest Diary*, 53–54, 64–65. Adams used the same metaphor some thirty years later in *Discourses on Davila*, *Works*, 6: 243. See Paynter, "The Ethics of John Adams: Prolegomenon to a Science of Politics," 48 n. 5, for a record of other eighteenth-century usages of the pilot-gale image.

65. JA to Abigail Smith, 20 April 1763, *Adams Family Correspondence*, 1: 5.

66. For the influence of Locke's revolutionary moral theory on American thinking, see Baldwin, *The New England Clergy and the American Revolution*; Huyler, *Locke in America: The Moral Philosophy of the Founding Era*; Thomas L. Pangle, *The Spirit of Modern Republicanism: The Moral Vision of the American Founders and the Philosophy of Locke* (Chicago, 1988); Michael P. Zuckert, *Natural Rights and the New Republicanism* (Princeton, N.J., 1994).

67. *Diary and Autobiography*, 3: 240–41.

68. JA to Thomas Jefferson, 12 December 1816, *The Adams-Jefferson Letters*, 2: 499.

2. Lawyer, Statesman, Lawgiver

1. JA to Nathan Webb, 1 September 1755, *Papers*, 1: 1.

2. *Diary and Autobiography*, 1: 22; JA to Jonathan Sewell, February 1760, *Papers*, 1: 41.

3. JA to Jonathan Sewell, *Papers*, 1: 41–43.

4. *Diary and Autobiography*, 1: 98–100.

5. Ibid.

6. Ibid.

7. Ibid.

8. *Earliest Diary*, 72–73.

9. Ibid.

10. JA to Jonathan Sewell, February 1760, *Papers*, 1: 41.

11. *Diary and Autobiography*, 1: 80; *Earliest Diary*, 91. For a superb discussion of the role that classical or Aristotelian notions of honor played in the American founding,

see Lorraine and Thomas Pangle, *The Learning of Liberty: The Educational Ideas of the American Founders* (Lawrence, Kans., 1993), 235–38, 240–41, 243–50.

12. *Diary and Autobiography*, 1: 221–22, 8, 221–22.

13. Ibid., 221–22, 37, 33–34, 24–25.

14. Ibid., 41–42.

15. Ibid., 73.

16. Ibid., 67–68.

17. Ibid., 35.

18. Ibid., 72–73.

19. Ibid., 132.

20. Ibid., 3: 287.

21. Ibid., 292.

22. Ibid., 1: 99 (emphasis added).

23. *Earliest Diary*, 70–72.

24. JA to Charles Cushing, 1 April 1756, *Papers*, 1: 13; JA to Richard Cranch, 18 October 1756, *Papers*, 1: 20.

25. *Earliest Diary*, 77.

26. Ibid., 70–72.

27. *Diary and Autobiography*, 1: 74, 73.

28. Ibid., 53.

29. Ibid., 82–84.

30. Ibid., 123–24.

31. *Papers*, 1: 127, n. 4.

32. *Diary and Autobiography*, 1: 196–97.

33. Ibid., 133.

34. Ibid., 167–68.

35. JA to William Tudor, 29 March 1817, *Works*, 10: 247–48. For the impact that Otis's speech at the writs of assistance case had on Adams, see his recollections of the case in his autobiography: *Diary and Autobiography*, 3: 276. It is an interesting coincidence that the event that ignited the patriotic ambition of Thomas Jefferson was his having witnessed Patrick Henry's famous speech in defense of the Stamp Act Resolutions.

36. *Diary and Autobiography*, 1: 263.

37. *Papers*, 1: 127.

38. See *Diary and Autobiography*, 3: 282.

39. "Novanglus," *Papers*, 2: 246; see also JA to Moses Gill, 10 June 1775, *Papers*, 3: 21.

40. *Diary and Autobiography*, 2: 96.

41. JA to Samuel Osgood, Jr., 15 November 1775, *Papers*, 3: 309; JA to James Warren, 25 June 1774, *Papers*, 2: 99–100; JA to Joseph Hawley, 27 June 1774, *Papers*, 2: 101.

42. JA to James Warren, 17 July 1774, *Papers*, 2: 109–10; JA to James Warren, 25 July 1774, *Papers*, 2: 117; JA to William Tudor, 4 August 1774, *Papers*, 2: 127; JA to James Warren, 25 June 1774, *Papers*, 2: 99–100. Several weeks before being elected to the Continental Congress, Adams wrote in his diary that "If I should be called in the Course of Providence to take Part in public Life, I shall Act a fearless, intrepid, undaunted Part, at all Hazards." *Diary and Autobiography*, 2: 82. We are reminded at this point of Adams's youthful spur for studying the law: "the more danger the more glory." JA to Richard Cranch, 18 October 1756, *Papers*, 1: 20.

43. *Diary and Autobiography*, 2: 96; JA to James Warren, 17 June 1774, *Papers*, 2: 109; JA to James Warren, 25 June 1774, *Papers*, 2: 99–100.

44. JA to Abigail Adams, 8 September 1774, *Adams Family Correspondence*, 1: 150–51.

45. Adams's role in drafting the Declaration of Rights and Grievances can be seen in *Diary and Autobiography*, 2: 131, 152–53, and *Papers*, 2: 144–52.

46. George W. Corner, ed. *The Autobiography of Benjamin Rush: His 'Travels Through Life' Together with his Commonplace Book for 1789–1813* (Princeton, N.J., 1948), 140. It was later said of Adams: "'I never shall think we shall finally fail of success while heaven continues to the congress the life and abilities of Mr. John Adams. He is equal to the controversy in all its stages. He stood upon the shoulders of the whole congress when reconciliation was the wish of All America. He was equally conspicuous in cutting the knot which tied the colonies to Great Britain. In a word I deliver to you the opinion of every man in the house when I add, that he possesses the clearest head and firmest heart of any man in the congress.'" William Gordon to JA, 27 March 1777, *Papers*, 5: 133.

47. "Notes on a Conversation with Thomas Jefferson," *The Papers of Daniel Webster: Correspondence*, ed. Charles M. Wiltse (Hanover, N.H., 1974), 1: 375. In an 1813 letter to Mr. W. P. Gardner, Jefferson commented on the political importance of Adams's speech: "No man better merited than Mr. John Adams to hold a most conspicuous place in the design. He was the pillar of its support on the floor of Congress, its ablest advocate and defender against the multifarious assaults it encountered; for many excellent persons opposed it on doubts, whether we provided sufficiently with the means of supporting it, whether the minds of our constituents were yet prepared to receive it, &c., who, after it was decided, united zealously in the measures it called for." Quoted in *Works*, 3: 57 ff.

48. *Works*, 3: 56 ff.

49. See *Diary and Autobiography*, 3: 314–15.

50. See *Diary and Autobiography*, 3: 327–30. He would later say that he "embraced with Joy the opportunity of harranguing on the Subject at large, and of urging Congress to resolve on a general recommendation to all the States to call Conventions and institute regular Governments." Ibid., 355.

51. JA to Richard Henry Lee, 15 November 1775, *Papers*, 3: 307–8; JA to John Penn, 27 March 1776, *Works*, 4: 203. For a list of Adams's arguments presented before the Continental Congress in favor of establishing new governments, see *Diary and Autobiography*, 3: 354.

52. *Diary and Autobiography*, 3: 386, 383.

53. Ibid., 352–56.

54. See Wood, *The Creation of the American Republic*, 342. See also Robert R. Palmer, *The Age of Democratic Revolution* (Princeton, N.J., 1959), 214.

55. *Diary and Autobiography*, 3: 358.

56. For the history behind the writing, publication, and influence of *Thoughts on Government*, see the description given in a footnote by the editors of Adams's *Diary and Autobiography*, 3: 331n–32n and the editors' introduction to *Thoughts* in *Papers*, 4: 65–73. For Adams's account of the composition of *Thoughts*, see his letter to James Warren, 20 April 1776, *Warren-Adams Letters* (*Massachusetts Historical Society Collections*, 72–73 [Boston, 1917–1925]), 1: 230–33. The influence of *Thoughts on Government* on the constitution-makers in Virginia is examined in John E. Selby, "Richard

Henry Lee, John Adams, and the Virginia Constitution of 1776," *Virginia Magazine of History and Biography*, 84 (October 1976): 389–400.

57. *Diary and Autobiography*, 1: 298; JA to Mercy Otis Warren, 16 April 1776, *Papers*, 4: 124–25.

58. JA to Edmund Jennings, 7 June 1780, *Diary and Autobiography*, 2: 401n.; JA to Benjamin Rush, 4 November 1779, *Papers*, 8: 279; JA to Abigail Adams, 2 June 1777, *Adams Family Correspondence*, 2: 253; *Works*, 6: 241.

59. JA to William Griffith, 15 April 1800, *Adams Papers Microfilm*, Reel 120 (Microfilm edition published by the Massachusetts Historical Society, Boston, which owns the originals), hereafter cited as *Adams Papers*, Reel 120, etc.; JA to John Quincy Adams, 2 September 1815, Ibid., Reel 122.

60. The classic work on this subject is, of course, Douglass Adair's, *Fame and the Founding Fathers*, 3–26.

61. *Works*, 6: 241.

62. Quoted in Adair, *Fame and the Founding Fathers*, 14–15.

63. Adams's peculiar intellectual debt to Machiavelli is discussed in C. Bradley Thompson, "John Adams's Machiavellian Moment," *Review of Politics* 57 (Summer 1995): 389–417.

64. *Works*, 5: 189. In *The Social Contract*, Rousseau speaks of the legislator as "one who, preparing for himself a future glory with the passage of time, could work in one century and enjoy reward in another." *On the Social Contract, with the Geneva Manuscript and Political Economy*, trans. Judith R. Masters and ed. Roger D. Masters (New York, 1978), 68.

65. *Diary and Autobiography*, Spring 1759, 1: 221–22; JA to George Wythe ["Thoughts on Government"], April 1776, *Works*, 4: 200.

3. The Spirit of Liberty

1. The classic statement of the Progressive historians is Charles Beard, *An Economic Interpretation of the Constitution of the United States* (New York, 1913), and the standard account of the Ideological historians is Bernard Bailyn, *The Ideological Origins of the American Revolution* (Cambridge, Mass., 1967). Bailyn in particular has singled out Adams as a victim of an ideological syndrome. See Bailyn's *The Ordeal of Thomas Hutchinson* (Cambridge, Mass., 1974), 2. Bailyn there describes the Whig "distrust" and "animosity" toward Thomas Hutchinson as "morbid, pathological, [and] paranoiac." Bailyn uses Adams as his first example to demonstrate this irrational antipathy toward Hutchinson.

2. Although differing over the Revolutionaries' motives, the Progressive and the Ideological historians have drawn remarkably similar conclusions about what *not* to study. For Arthur Meier Schlesinger and the Progressive historians, the American Revolution ought not to be studied as a "great forensic controversy over abstract governmental rights" (Schlesinger, "The American Revolution Reconsidered," *Political Science Quarterly* 34 (March 1919): 61ff. For Gordon S. Wood and the Ideological school, the historian should eschew "the nicely reasoned constitutional arguments of John Adams or Jefferson" in order to study the more revealing "enthusiastic and visionary extravagance" of their thinking" (Wood, *Creation of the American Republic*, 121).

3. On the shared philosophic premises of the Progressive and Ideological historians, see the important methodological essays of Gordon S. Wood: "Rhetoric and

Reality in the American Revolution," 3–32; and "Conspiracy and the Paranoid Style: Causality and Deceit in the Eighteenth Century," *William and Mary Quarterly* 39 (1982): 401–41. Helpful correctives to this view are Diggins, *The Lost Soul of American Politics*, 347–65, and Lerner, *The Thinking Revolutionary*, 1–38.

4. Recent exceptions to this trend include: John Phillip Reid, *Constitutional History of the American Revolution: The Authority of Rights* (Madison, Wis., 1986); *Peripheries and Center: Constitutional Development in the Extended Polities of the British Empire and the United States, 1607–1788* (Athens, Ga., 1986); Theodore Draper, *A Struggle for Power: The American Revolution* (New York, 1996), and Robert Webking, *The American Revolution and the Politics of Liberty* (Baton Rouge, La., 1988).

5. Charles H. McIlwain, in his Pulitzer-prize winning *The American Revolution: A Constitutional Interpretation* (New York, 1924), 39, described Adams's revolutionary political thought as "the most elaborate exposition extant of the American interpretation of the constitutional problem of the empire." Even the most comprehensive study of Adams's political thought of the last half century barely mentions the "Novanglus" essays. See Howe, *The Changing Political Thought of John Adams.*

6. Randolph G. Adams, *Political Ideas of the American Revolution* (New York, 1922); Bailyn, *The Ideological Origins of the American Revolution*; Colbourn, *The Lamp of Experience: Whig History and the Intellectual Origins of the American Revolution* (New York, 1969); Gebhardt, *Americanism: Revolutionary Order and Societal Self-Interpretation in the American Republic*; Wood, *The Creation of the American Republic*, and *The Radicalism of the American Revolution* (New York, 1993).

7. Bernard Bailyn, "The Central Themes of the American Revolution, an Interpretation," in *Essays on the American Revolution*, ed. Stephen G. Kurtz and James H. Hutson (Chapel Hill, N.C., 1973), 13.

8. The editors of *The Adams Papers* have collected these differently titled essays under the general designation of essays "On Political Faction, Man's Nature, and the Law." Included in this collection are Adams's "Humphrey Ploughjogger" essays. I have focused on those essays entitled " 'U' to the *Boston Gazette.*"

9. John Adams, "U" to the *Boston Gazette*, 29 August 1763, *Papers*, 1: 78.

10. Ibid., 79–80, 77.

11. Ibid., 80.

12. Adams, "An Essay on Man's Lust for Power" [post 29 August 1763], *Papers*, 1: 81.

13. Adams, "U" to the *Boston Gazette*, 29 August 1763, *Papers*, 1: 81.

14. Ibid. [5 September 1763], 86.

15. Ibid., 84–85.

16. Adams, "A Dissertation on the Canon and Feudal Law," *Papers*, 1: 127; Instructions to Braintree's Representatives concerning the Stamp Act," *Papers*, 1: 133.

17. John Adams, "Humphrey Ploughjogger to Philanthrop," 5 January 1767, *Papers*, 1: 178.

18. "Instructions to Braintree's Representatives concerning the Stamp Act," *Papers*, 1: 134.

19. Ibid., 134–35; "The Earl of Clarendon to William Pym," 13 January 1766, *Papers*, 1: 159. Four years later, Adams was still haranguing against the courts of admiralty: They had, he said, been "forming by degrees into a system that is to overturn our constitution and to deprive us entirely of our best inheritance, the laws of the land." *Works*, 3: 505–10. For a particularly clear-headed description of how the Americans

interpreted the meaning of the extension of the admiralty courts' powers in America, see David S. Lovejoy, "'Rights Imply Equality': The Case Against Admiralty Jurisdiction in America, 1764–1776," *The William and Mary Quarterly*, 3rd ser., 16 (October, 1959): 459–84.

20. "A Dissertation on the Canon and the Feudal Law," *Papers*, 1: 111.

21. Ibid., 112.

22. Ibid.

23. Ibid., 113.

24. Ibid.

25. Ibid., 114, 120.

26. Ibid., 117.

27. Ibid., 125.

28. Ibid., 127.

29. Ibid., 126.

30. This theme is again repeated in Adams's little-read essays from "Governor Winthrop to Governor Bradford." An imagined correspondence between these two great men—the Founding Fathers of the Massachusetts Bay and Plymouth colonies—was intended to remind the Americans of their past, to remind them of the principles on which the colonies were founded. Adams, "Governor Winthrop to Governor Bradford," [January–February 1767], *Papers*, 1: 191–210.

31. Adams, "Dissertation," *Papers*, 1: 126, 123, 127.

32. Ibid., 126.

33. Ibid., 125, 126–27.

34. Cf. "Instructions to Braintree's Representative concerning the Stamp Act," *Papers*, 1: 134; "The Earl of Clarendon to William Pym," *Papers*, 1: 163–64; "Governor Winthrop to Governor Bradford," [26 January 1767], *Papers*, 1: 192, 200, 203, 204. See also "Novanglus," *Papers*, 2: 255.

35. "The Earl of Clarendon to William Pym," 20 January 1766, *Papers*, 1: 163.

36. "Governor Winthrop to Governor Bradford," 9 February 1767, Ibid., 200. This view of the spirit of liberty is supported by Jefferson who, in his draft of the Kentucky Resolutions, said that "confidence is everywhere the parent of despotism-free government is founded in jealousy." "Draft of the Kentucky Resolutions, [Oct.] 1798," in *The Writings of Thomas Jefferson*, ed. Paul L. Ford (New York, 1892–1899, 10 vols.), 7: 304.

37. "Governor Winthrop to Governor Bradford," 26 January 1767, *Papers*, 1: 192. For Machiavelli's advocacy of "terror" as a means restoring the virtues of first foundings, see *Discourses on the First Ten Books of Titus Livius* in *The Prince and the Discourses*, ed. Max Lerner (New York, 1950), bk. 3: chaps. 1, 22, 30.

38. JA to Thomas Jefferson, 24 August 1815, in *The Adams-Jefferson Letters*, 2: 454–56.

39. "Novanglus," *Papers*, 2: 298–99.

40. In an interesting historical analogy, Adams compared the plans and actions of Bernard's American triumvirate to the infamous designs of Edmund Andros, Edward Randolph, and Joseph Dudley in the last quarter of the seventeenth century. Andros, Randolph, and Dudley were despised symbols in Massachusetts history for having played a central role in the nullification of the original Massachusetts charter in 1684 and in the subsequent incorporation of the province into the Dominion of New England.

41. American colonials charged with violating the Navigation Acts were required to go to Halifax to prove their innocence. If they did not appear (and many could not

afford to go to Halifax), British customs officers could, "without offering any evidence in support of their allegation, have the property condemned and sold (pocketing half the proceeds)." Bernard Knollenberg, *Origin of the American Revolution: 1759–1766* (New York, 1965), 167.

42. During this same period, Parliament also passed a law in 1763 preventing westward colonial expansion beyond the Appalachians, and it aggressively renewed enforcement of the White Pines Act. In 1765, the Quartering Act pulled British soldiers back from the frontier for deployment in coastal cities. The troops were quartered in the facilities of colonial governments, pubs, and inns, and in unoccupied dwellings. The cost of quartering and feeding the troops was passed on to the colonial legislatures.

43. "Novanglus," *Papers*, 2: 273–74.

44. "Novanglus," *Papers*, 2: 282–83.

45. See Bailyn, *Ordeal of Thomas Hutchinson*, 86, 189 n. 64.

46. "Novanglus," *Papers*, 2: 237.

47. Ibid., 238.

48. *Diary and Autobiography*, 2: 81.

49. "Novanglus," *Papers*, 2: 277.

50. See Webking, *The American Revolution and the Politics of Liberty*, 153–57.

51. "Novanglus," *Papers*, 2: 228–29.

52. This distinction is of course central to Locke's political thought in the *Second Treatise*. Even in his *First Tract on Government* published nearly 30 years before the *Second Treatise*, Locke was working through this perennial problem: "'Tis not without reason that tyranny and anarchy are judged the smartest scourges can fall upon mankind, the plea of authority usually backing the one, and of liberty inducing the other: and between the two it is, that human affairs are perpetually kept tumbling." (Philip Adams, ed., *John Locke: Two Tracts on Government* (Cambridge, Mass., 1967), 119.

53. Adams, "Governor Winthrop to Governor Bradford," 26 January 1767, *Papers*, 1: 192; *Diary and Autobiography*, 3: 290.

54. "Novanglus," *Papers*, 2: 230.

55. Ibid.

56. *Diary and Autobiography*, 3: 326.

57. Ibid., 3: 301. In 1773, Adams was asked to revise the response of the House of Representatives to Thomas Hutchinson's ill-fated address to the General Court on the nature of the imperial union. The House's first draft, probably written by Samuel Adams and James Warren, was "prettily drawn" and "full of very popular talk and those democratical principles which have done so much mischief in this country." Adams cautioned his friends that arguments "based on nature and eternal and unchangeable truth" ought to be "well understood and cautiously applied." Prudence dictated that the "resort to club law and the force of arms" be limited to cases of necessity only. The Coercive Act provided Adams with that necessity. JA to William Tudor, *Works*, 2: 313.

58. "Novanglus," *Papers*, 2: 230–31.

59. Ibid., 231–32.

60. *Diary and Autobiography*, 3: 299.

61. L. Kinvin Wroth and Hiller B. Zobel, eds., *Legal Papers of John Adams* (Cambridge, Mass., 1965), 1: 106–40.

62. Ibid., 1: 137.

63. Butterfield, ed., *Adams Family Correspondence*, 1: 131; John Locke, *Second Treatise of Government*, ed. Richard Cox (Arlington Heights, Ill., 1982), 34. Adams would have completely agreed with Locke, when he wrote: *"Freedom of men under government, is, to have a standing rule to live by, common to everyone in that society, and made by the legislative power erected in it; a liberty to follow my own will in all things, where the rule prescribes not; and not to be subject to the unconstant, uncertain, unknown arbitrary will of another man (Cox, ed., Second Treatise of Government, 15)."*

64. "Novanglus," *Papers*, 2: 296, 298.

65. *Diary and Autobiography*, 2: 85–86.

66. "Novanglus," *Papers*, 2: 288–89.

67. Ibid., 288–90, 292–93. Adams is here quoting from chapter 19, "Of the Dissolution of Government," sec. 226, from Locke's *Second Treatise*. See Cox, ed., *Second Treatise of Government*, 138.

68. "Novanglus," *Papers*, 2: 296; Locke, *Second Treatise of Government*, ed. Cox, 138–39.

69. "Novanglus," *Papers*, 2: 298.

70. *Diary and Autobiography*, 2: 86; "Novanglus," *Papers*, 2: 298, 232.

71. JA to Thomas Jefferson, 24 August 1815, *The Adams-Jefferson Letters*, 2: 454–56.

4. The Principles of Liberty

1. *Diary and Autobiography*, 2: 77; "Novanglus," *Papers*, 2: 271.

2. Most historians have not been so kind, however, in their assessment of "Novanglus." Moses C. Tyler once described "Novanglus" as a "vast morass of technical discussion, into which no living reader will ever follow the writer, and from which the writer himself never emerges alive." *Literary History of the American Revolution*, 1: 392. More recently, Novanglus has fared no better. Peter Shaw, for instance, has described the Novanglus essays as having been erected "on an emotional basis" and as a "disorganized response to developing events." *Character of John Adams*, 83–84.

3. Adams first worked out the arguments presented in "Novanglus" at least as early as 1773. In that year he wrote for the Massachusetts House of Representatives their reply to Governor Hutchinson's two messages on the nature and extent of Parliament's authority in America. The central arguments contained in the response of the House anticipate Adams's more developed and systematic presentation in "Novanglus" of a radically new theory of dominion, colonial rights, and the limits of parliamentary rule.

4. "Massachusettensis" [Daniel Leonard] in *The American Crisis: The Daniel Leonard–John Adams Letters to the Press, 1774–1775*, ed. Bernard Mason (New York, 1972), 33. See also pp. 39–43.

5. Ibid., 33–34, 39.

6. Ibid., 32–37.

7. "Novanglus," *Papers*, 2: 347–48.

8. Ibid., 250–51.

9. Ibid., 311, 315, 323.

10. Ibid., 315, 361, 373, 361.

11. "Reply of the House to Hutchinson's First Message, 26 January 1773, *Papers*, 1: 319.

12. "Novanglus," *Papers*, 2: 329, 321.

13. Greene, *Peripheries and Center*, 88; Adams, "Novanglus," *Papers*, 2: 313.

14. "Novanglus," *Papers*, 2: 261, 307.

15. Edmund Burke, "Letter to the Sheriffs of Bristol," in *The Works of Edmund Burke*, 16 vols. (London, 1826) 3: 190, quoted in Greene, *Peripheries and Center*, 65.

16. For an superb general treatment of these questions as they apply to the Revolutionary generation as a whole, see James H. Kettner, *The Development of American Citizenship, 1608–1870* (Chapel Hill, N.C., 1978).

17. "Novanglus," *Papers*, 2: 330–31.

18. See Gerald Stourzh, *Alexander Hamilton and the Idea of Republican Government* (Stanford, Calif., 1970), 25–26.

19. "Novanglus," *Papers*, 2: 349–50.

20. Ibid., 345.

21. Ibid., 350–51, 321.

22. Ibid., 379.

23. Ibid., 330.

24. As early as 1765, Adams began to work out the logic of this argument: "Are not Protection and Allegiance reciprocal? And if We are out of the Kings Protection, are we not discharged from our Allegiance. Are not all the Ligaments of Government dissolved? Is it not <a Declaration of> an Abdication of the Throne? In short where will such an horrid Doctrine terminate? It would run us into Treason!" *Diary and Autobiography*, 1: 270.

25. "A case omitted; a situation not provided for."

26. "Novanglus," *Papers*, 2: 330, 327, 311.

27. Locke, *Second Treatise of Government*, ed. Cox, 70.

28. "Dissertation on the Canon and Feudal Law," *Papers*, 1: 113–14.

29. "Let him not go out of the Kingdom."

30. "Novanglus," *Papers*, 2: 327–28; cf. Locke, *Second Treatise of Government*, ed. Cox, 71: "'Tis true, that whatever engagements or promises anyone has made for himself, he is under the obligation of them, but *cannot* by any *compact* whatsoever, bind *his children* or posterity."

31. "Novanglus," *Papers*, 2: 330.

32. Ibid., 317 (emphasis added).

33. Ibid., 328, 330, 353. Here I must dissent from Charles McIlwain's otherwise superb history of the Revolution. McIlwain argued that the most important colonial constitutional argument against Parliament was contained within an imperial context. His point here is to downplay colonial arguments based on the charters and fundamental law. From Adams's perspective, the imperial, charter, and fundamental law arguments were inextricably intertwined.

34. On this distinction in Alexander Hamilton's thought, see Gerald Stourzh, *Alexander Hamilton and the Idea of Republican Government*, 26.

35. "Novanglus," *Papers*, 2: 331.

36. See Greene, *Peripheries and Center*, 19–54; Andrew C. McLaughlin, *Foundations of American Constitutionalism* (Greenwich, Conn., 1961), 13–65.

37. "Novanglus," *Papers*, 2: 373–74.

38. William Blackstone, *Commentaries on the Laws of England* (Oxford, 1765–69; facsimile reprint ed., Chicago, 1979) 1: 126, 91.

39. On this point, see Colbourn, *The Lamp of Experience*, 3–56, 83–106, 185–93.

40. Charles H. McIlwain dates the beginning of the movement toward the Ameri-

can Revolution to 19 May 1649, when Parliament passed an act establishing the Commonwealth. That act read: "Be it declared and Enacted by this present Parliament and by the Authority of the same, That the People of England, and of all the Dominions and Territories thereunto belonging, are and shall be, and hereby Constituted, Made, Established, and Confirmed to be a Commonwealth and Free-State: And shall henceforth be Governed as a Commonwealth and Free-State, by the Supreme Authority of this Nation, The Representatives of the People in Parliament, and by such as they shall appoint and constitute as Officers and Ministers under them for the good of the People, and that without any King or House of Lords." See McIlwain, *The American Revolution*, 21.

41. In using the term "Coke's constitution," I do not mean to suggest that Coke had a constitutional theory or that he understood the English constitution in anything like the way we view America's written constitution. He did not. For Coke, the fundamental law that was the English constitution was an unwritten amalgam of the common law, Magna Carta, statute law, and the form of Parliament. (See James R. Stoner, *Common Law and Liberal Theory: Coke, Hobbes, and the Origins of American Constitutionalism* [Lawrence, Kans., 1992], 27–47.) More importantly, however, I am using this term, "Coke's constitution," from the perspective of the American Revolutionaries. By the middle of the eighteenth century, Anglo-Americans could speak of a British constitution, but they did so from very different perspectives. For some, the British constitution was synonymous with Parliament; for others, building on Coke, the British constitution represented a controlling rule of law that superseded Crown and Parliament. That rule of law, as James Otis and Adams understood it, incorporated the common law, the laws of nature, some statutory law, and the political forms and formalities that had developed in Britain over the course of several hundred years. See John Philip Reid, "In Accordance with Usage: The Authority of Custom, the Stamp Act Debate, and the Coming of the American Revolution," *Fordham Law Review* 45 (1976): 364–65.

42. For an introduction into this peculiar constitutional tradition, see Edward S. Corwin, *The 'Higher Law Background' of American Constitutional Law* (Ithaca, N.Y., 1955); J. G. A. Pocock, *The Ancient Constitution and the Feudal Law* (Cambridge, Mass., 1957); James H. Kettner, *The Development of American Citizenship, 1608–1870* (Chapel Hill, N.C., 1978); Stoner, *Common Law and Liberal Theory;* Thomas C. Grey, "Origins of the Unwritten Constitution: Fundamental Law in American Revolutionary Thought," *Stanford Law Review* 30 (1978): 843–93; R. A. Humphreys, "The Rule of Law and the American Revolution," *Law Quarterly Review* 52 (1937): 80–98; Charles F. Mullett, "Coke and the American Revolution," *Economica* 12 (November 1932): 457–71.

43. John Adams, *Legal Papers of John Adams*, 2: 140, 142.

44. The famous dictum reads as follows: "And it appears in our books, that in many cases, the common law will controul acts of parliament, and sometimes adjudge them to be utterly void: for when an act of parliament is against common right and reason, or repugnant, or impossible to be performed, the common law will controul it and adjudge such act to be void." 8 *Reports* 118a (George Wilson, ed., *The Reports of Sir Edward Coke*, etc. [Dublin, 1793]). For a study of *Bonham's Case* and its place in Coke's overall legal thought, see James R. Stoner, *Common Law and Liberal Theory*, 13–68.

45. John Adams, *Legal Papers of John Adams*, 2: 127–28. Modern scholars today are still disputing Coke's meaning in *Bonham's Case* and its applicability to American

judicial review. One camp sees in *Bonham's Case* the origin of American judicial review: see Corwin, *The 'Higher Law' Origins of American Constitutional Government*, 44–50; Grey, "Origins of the Unwritten Constitution: Fundamental Law in American Revolutionary Thought," 855–56. For the view that Coke was merely issuing a maxim of statutory interpretation, see S. E. Thorne, "Dr. Bonham's Case," *Law Quarterly Review* 54 (1938): 543; "Editor's Note," *Legal Papers of John Adams*, 2: 118. The view that *Bonham's Case* neither invoked a form of judicial review or that it was a precursor to *Marbury v. Madison* has recently been advanced most forcefully by Walter Berns, "Judicial Review and the Rights and Laws of Nature," *The Supreme Court Review: 1982* (Chicago, 1983): 49–83, and Gary L. McDowell, "Coke, Corwin and the Constitution: The 'Higher Law Background' Reconsidered," *Review of Politics* 55 (1993): 393–420. For a view suggesting that Coke was asserting both "a right of strict construction in the courts," and that "the only reason for the existence of this power is to bring the statutes into general conformity with the fundamental law," see R. A. MacKay, "Coke—Parliamentary Sovereignty or the Supremacy of Law?" *Michigan Law Review* 22 (1924): 215–47; Stoner, *Common Law and Liberal Theory*, 59–62.

46. By the "reason" of the common law, Otis did not mean that inner light associated with scholastic natural law, but rather the "artificial" or "legal" reason that custom and precedents had accumulated over time. Otis's constitutional thought is ably discussed in Bailyn, *The Ideological Origins of the American Revolution*, 176–81. For Coke's view of the "reason" of the common law on which Otis based his own understanding, see Stoner, *Common Law and Liberal Theory*, 22–26.

47. For the impact that Otis's speech at the writs of assistance case had on Adams, see his recollections of the case in his autobiography: *Diary and Autobiography*, 3: 276.

48. "Dissertation on the Canon and Feudal Law," *Papers*, 1: 127.

49. "Instructions to Braintree's Representatives," Ibid., 134; "Earl of Clarendon to William Pym," *Papers*, 1: 159.

50. "Argument before Governor Bernard and the Council in Favor of Opening the Courts," *Papers*, 1: 152–53.

51. John Adams, *Legal Papers of John Adams*, 2: 200.

52. See, especially, "On the Independence of the Judges," *Papers*, 1: 292. Having drawn a distinction in the British constitution between that which is legal and that which is constitutional, Adams wrote: "If the King should suffer no parliament to sit for 12 years, by reason of continual prorogations, this would be an unconstitutional exertion of their privilege. Yet the King has power legally to do one, and the commons to do the other."

53. "Earl of Clarendon to William Pym," *Papers*, 1: 164–65 (emphasis added).

54. Ibid., 166.

55. Ibid., 167.

56. "On the Independence of the Judges," *Papers*, 1: 292.

57. "Earl of Clarendon to William Pym," Ibid., 1: 167.

58. Ibid., 169.

59. "Novanglus," Ibid., 314.

60. "Dissertation on the Canon and Feudal Law," Ibid., 127.

61. For a useful study that traces the history of the idea of a written constitution to the first colonial charters, see Benjamin F. Wright, Jr., "The Early History of Written Constitutions in America," in *Essays in History and Political Theory in Honor of Charles Howard McIlwain* (New York, 1936), 344–71.

62. *Diary and Autobiography*, 3: 352.

63. The best general study of this process of constitution-making is Wood, *The Creation of the American Republic*, 259–343.

5. A Guidebook for Lawgivers

1. JA to John Taylor, 15 April 1815, *Works*, 6: 447.

2. James Madison to Thomas Jefferson, 6 June 1787, Robert Rutland, ed., *The Papers of James Madison* (Chicago, 1977), 10: 29–30; Wood, *The Creation of the American Republic*, 567–92.

3. The charge of republican apostasy did not surprise Adams. Just as the first volume of the *Defence* was coming off the press he sensed that he would "be cast out of communion," and he predicted that his treatise would make him "unpopular." JA to Benjamin Franklin, 27 January 1787, John Bigelow, ed., *The Works of Benjamin Franklin* (New York, 1904), 11, 298–99. "Popularity was never my Mistress," he wrote to James Warren, "nor was I ever, or shall I ever be a popular Man. This Book will make me unpopular." JA to James Warren, 9 January 1787, Worthington Chauncey Ford, ed., *Warren–Adams Letters, Being Chiefly a Correspondence among John Adams, Samuel Adams, and James Warren*, 2 vols., (Boston, 1917), 2: 281.

4. Handler, *America and Europe in the Political Thought of John Adams*, 29.

5. Adams himself referred to the *Defence* as a "strange" book. See JA to Richard Cranch, 15 January 1787, *Works*, 1: 432.

6. See Howe, *The Changing Political Thought of John Adams*; Wood, *Creation of the American Republic*.

7. See Haraszti, *The Prophets of Progress*; Handler, *America and Europe in the Political Thought of John Adams*; Appleby, "The New Republican Synthesis and the Changing Political Ideas of John Adams," 578–95.

8. *Works*, 4: 292–93 (emphasis added). As the author of the influential *Thoughts on Government* and as the architect of the Massachusetts Constitution, Adams of course was really referring to his own "reading and reasoning." For evidence that *Thoughts on Government* was used as a constitutional model by several states, see the "Editorial Note" to *Thoughts on Government* in *Papers of John Adams*, ed. Robert J. Taylor et al., 4: 65–73. Also see Wood, *Creation of the American Republic*, 203.

9. Unless I am mistaken, no account of Adams's political thought has ever seriously taken into account his confrontation with Plato, Aristotle, Machiavelli, Bacon, Hobbes, Locke, Montesquieu, or Rousseau. Haraszti's *The Prophets of Progress*, does of course examine his intellectual confrontation with the philosophes.

10. JA to Abigail Adams, 25 December 1786, *Adams Papers*, Reel 369.

11. See JA to Francis Adrian Vanderkemp, 30 January 1800, *Adams Papers*, Reel 120 and JA to Richard Cranch, 15 January 1787, *Works*, 1: 432. To Benjamin Hichborn Adams reported that he had recently "thrown together some hasty speculations on government." See JA to Hichborn, 27 January 1787, *Works*, 9: 551.

12. For the purpose of the present study, I am treating Adams's *Discourses on Davila: A Series of Papers on Political History, by an American Citizen* (1790–91) as the "fourth volume" of the *Defence*. Adams often referred to the *Defence* and the *Davila* essays as his four volumes on government and it was his intention that they be read as a single, unified work. That his intention was such is indicated most explicitly in his correspondence with John Taylor in 1814. Adams, who had just read Taylor's *An Inquiry*

into the Principles and Policy of the Government of the United States (1814), a critical commentary on the *Defence*, was in the process of responding to and correcting Taylor's errors of interpretation when he realized that Taylor had been relying solely on the *Defence*. He then mailed Taylor a copy of the *Davila* essays, which, he said, "you may call the fourth volume of the Defence of the Constitutions of the United States" (*Works*, 10: 96). For supporting evidence that Adams intended the *Defence* and *Davila* to be read as a whole, see *Works*, 6: 482, and Lester Cappon, ed., *Adams–Jefferson Letters*, 2: 356, 357.

13. JA to Thomas Jefferson, 13 July 1813, Cappon, ed., *Adams–Jefferson Letters*, 2: 354–56. Adams's 1813 recollection of events in the mid-1780s is more or less accurate. On February 6, 1787, Jefferson wrote Adams to thank him for having sent a copy of the first volume of the *Defence*, and he reminded his friend that "you told me once you had had thoughts of writing on the subject of hereditary aristocracy." Jefferson hoped that Adams would carry the project "into execution." On 1 March 1787, Adams confirmed having had such a conversation with Jefferson. *Adams–Jefferson Letters*, 2: 170, 176–77.

14. JA to Count Sarsfield, 21 January 1786, *Works*, 8: 370.

15. JA to William Smith, [undated], *Adams Papers*, Reel 188. See also, JA to Thomas Jefferson, 11 September 1786, Cappon, ed., *Adams–Jefferson Letters*, 1: 153; *Diary and Autobiography*, 3: 201–02.

16. JA to William Smith, [undated], *Adams Papers*, Reel 188 (emphasis added).

17. JA to Samuel Perley, 19 June 1809, *Works*, 9: 622–24. Adams attributed the authorship of the Pennsylvania Constitution to Philadelphia radicals, Timothy Matlack, James Cannon, and Thomas Young.

18. *Works*, 4: 299.

19. Ibid., 294.

20. JA to Samuel Perley, 19 June 1809, *Works*, 9: 622–24. The rationale that Adams presents in the Perley letter for having written the *Defence* is supported in other letters. See, for instance, JA to Rev. De Walter, October 1797, *Adams Papers*, Reel 119; JA to F. A. Vanderkemp, 30 January 1800, Ibid., Reel 120; JA to Mercy Otis Warren, 19 August 1807, *Correspondence Between John Adams and Mercy Warren*, Charles F. Adams, ed. (New York, 1972; reprint ed., Boston: *Collections of the Massachusetts Historical Society*, Vol. IV, 5th ser., 1878), 472–73; JA to Thomas Jefferson, 13 July 1813, *Adams–Jefferson Letters*, 2: 354–56. To Richard Rush, son of Benjamin Rush, Adams succinctly summarized his purpose in writing: "As my object in writing was to throw out some Investigations for the consideration of the American people & the great patriots of France, at a time when they were labouring with all their might to tear up the foundations of the Earth & break open the foundations of the great deep." JA to Richard Rush, 11 November 1815, *Adams Papers*, Reel 122.

21. JA to Richard Cranch, 15 January 1787, *Works*, 1: 432; JA to Philip Mazzei, 12 June 1787, Ibid., 9: 552–53.

22. In the opening pages of the second volume, Adams intimated that he could not be entirely forthcoming with his American audience. Indeed, he went so far as to suggest that the *Defence* was written with two levels of readership in mind, and that the text should be read esoterically: The "substance of this sketch," noted Adams, will be taken from Machiavelli, who is "even suspected of sometimes disguising the truth to conceal or mollify its defects." See *Works*, 5: 11. Adams described himself in 1813 as having been a "student of Machiavelli" and advised a young

admirer that when "reading Machiavelli," one "can never know when he is in jest, or in earnest: whether he lies or tells the truth." JA to Francis Adrian Vanderkemp, 9 August 1813 and JA to Richard Rush, 11 August 1813, *Adams Papers*, Reel 95. Adams probably had Rousseau in mind when he spoke of those who "suspected" Machiavelli of writing esoterically. See *The Social Contract*, trans. Maurice Cranston (New York, 1968), Bk. 3, chap. 16: 118.

23. *Works*, 4: 299–300; JA to Richard Price, 20 May 1789, Ibid., 9: 558–59. See also, JA to Thomas Jefferson, 13 July 1813, Cappon, ed., *Adams–Jefferson Letters*, 2: 354–56; JA to Benjamin Hichborn, 27 January 1787, *Works*, 9: 551.

24. JA to Thomas Jefferson, 13 July 1813, Cappon, ed., *Adams–Jefferson Letters*, 2: 354–56; JA to Richard Price, 20 May 1789, *Works*, 9: 558–59; JA to John Jay, 30 November 1787, Ibid., 8: 463; Ibid., 4: 299–300; 4: 302.

25. Henry Knox confided to Mercy Warren that their "respectable and enlightened friend Mr. Adams" had "been a little unfortunate in his title." Knox saw something in the *Defence* that modern historians seem to have missed altogether. He thought that "Mr. Adams's Book" was "not a defence of the constitutions of the United States," but was "rather a sarcasm on them." Knox thought a better title would have been "The Soul of a Free Government." 30 May 1787, *Warren–Adams Letters, Massachusetts Historical Society Collections*, 75 (1925), 2: 294. Another reader thought the "chief *object*" of the second volume "was to point out the *Defects* in the Constitution instead of defending it." Mr. Grady to Mrs. Jeffries, 20 October 1787, *Adams Papers*, Reel 370. John L. Paynter has drawn many of the same conclusions reached here in his "The Rhetorical Design of John Adams's Defence of the Constitutions of . . . America," paper presented at the Southern Political Science Association, Atlanta, Ga., 7 November 1992.

26. Adams, *Works*, 4: 287; JA to John Taylor, 15 April 1814, Ibid., 6: 486–88. "I had only the Massachusetts constitution in view," Adams wrote to Samuel Perley, "and such others as agreed with it in the distribution of the legislative power into three branches, in separating the executive from the legislative power, and the judiciary from both." JA to Samuel Perley, 19 June 1809, Ibid., 9: 622–24.

27. JA to John Trumbull, 23 January 1791, Ibid., 9: 572–73; JA to Mr. Stockdale, 12 May 1793, *Adams Papers*, Reel 116; JA to Thomas Jefferson, 28 October 1787, Cappon, ed., *Adams–Jefferson Letters*, 1: 204. In the years after its publication, the Jeffersonian Party publicly attacked the *Defence* for over a decade. The typical charge accused Adams of criticizing America's Revolutionary constitutions in hopes that they might eventually be replaced with a king and a hereditary senate. The charge of course was absurd. Had the Jeffersonians been honest, they would have said the very same thing about their leader's *Notes on the State of Virginia*. Jefferson's criticism of his own state constitution in the *Notes* was much less restrained than was Adams's critique. With language not disimilar to that used by Adams in the *Defence*, Jefferson described Virginia's Revolutionary constitution as having been formed "when we were new and unexperienced in the science of government. . . . No wonder then that time and trial have discovered very capital defects in it." Jefferson then enumerated six criticisms of the Virginia form of government. The third stated that "The senate is, by its constitution, too homogenous with the house of delegates," and the fourth said that "All the powers of government, legislative, executive, and judiciary, result to the legislative body." In both he suggests that the Virginia constitution was *too* democratic. In the third, the senate is criticized for not adequately representing Virginia's better men: "Being chosen by the same electors, at the same time, and out of the same sub-

jects, the choice falls of course on men of the same description. The purpose of establishing different houses of legislation is to introduce the influence of different interests or different principles. . . . But with us, wealth and wisdom have equal chance for admission into both houses. We do not therefore derive from the separation of our legislature into two houses, those benefits which a proper complication of principles is capable of producing, and those which alone can compensate the evils which may be produced by their dissensions." Not even John Adams said this of the Virginia constitution. In his fourth criticism, Jefferson chastized the Virginia constitution for not separating sufficiently the legislative, executive, and judicial powers. It was in this context that he wrote that "an elective despotism was not the government we fought for." Adrienne Koch and William Peden, eds., *The Life and Selected Writings of Thomas Jefferson* (New York, 1972), 236–44.

28. *Works*, 4: 293; 6: 276, 218.

29. Ibid., 4: 290, 298 (emphasis added), 587; 6: 276–77. In 1787 Adams spoke of the need for America to be on "guard" against the influence of French ideas. It was therefore imperative for the Americans to "complete their constitution of government." JA to John Jay, 30 November 1787, Ibid., 8: 463. By the time he wrote the *Discourses on Davila*, however, Adams hoped that the Americans would complete and perfect their constitutions so as to influence the French. In the *Davila* essays, Adams implored his American audience to "rectify" the imperfections in their constitutional designs, so as not to misguide French constitution makers of 1790 who were then following American "maxims, principles, and example." Ibid., 6: 279. Adams was pleased when Pennsylvania revised its unicameral constitution in 1790, adopting in its place Adams's call for bicameral legislatures. But he feared the example was lost on French constitution makers. "I congratulate you, on the Prospect of a new Constitution for Pensilvania," he wrote to Benjamin Rush. "Poor France," he feared, "will bleed, for too exactly copying your old one." JA to Benjamin Rush, 2 February 1790, Alexander Biddle, ed. *Old Family Letters* (Philadelphia, 1892), 54–55.

30. *Works*, 6: 218; 5: 11; 4: 294; JA to Richard Cranch, 15 January 1787, *Works*, 1: 432; JA to Richard Price, 20 May 1789, *Works*, 9: 559. On 4 February 1787, just as the first volume was coming off the press, Adams wrote to Richard Price explaining his method and reasons for writing: "It is but a humble tho' laborious office to collect together so many opinions and examples but it may point out to my young countrymen the genuine sources of information upon a subject more interesting to them if possible than to the rest of the world." JA to Richard Price, 4 February 1787, *Richard Price and the Ethical Foundations of the American Revolution*, ed. Bernard Peach (Durham, N.C., 1979), 339–40. In the *Discourses on Davila*, the fourth volume of the *Defence*, Adams advised that any defects in the constitutions "be left to the contemplations of our state physicians to discover the causes and the remedy of that '*fever, whereof our power is sick.*'" The fever that threatened the American constitutions was induced, according to Adams, by the infiltration into America of ideas associated with Turgot's dictum that free government is possible only if "all authority" is collected "into one centre." The remedy prescribed by Adams to cure America's constitutional ills was a kind of corrective surgery to restore the "*unum necessarium*" of free government—that being the principle of "three orders, and an effectual balance between them." Without this kind of surgery, Adams's prognosis for the future of the American governments was gloomy. He predicted that they would be "destined to frequent unavoidable revolutions." And if such violent upheavals did not come immediately,

he warned that they would certainly "come in time." (*Works*, 6: 269–70; 4: 299; JA to Philip Mazzei, 12 June 1787, *Works*, 9: 552; 4: 287).

31. *Works*, 4: 292–93.

32. Ibid., 6: 218.

33. JA to James Lloyd, 29 March 1815, *Works*, 10: 148–49. See also JA to John Luzac, 13 December 1781, *Works*, 7: 491. In his *Diary* entry for 26 December 1782, Adams described how the Duke de la Rochefoucault had come to visit one day for the purpose of having him explain "some Passages in the Connecticut Constitution, which were obscure to him." See *Diary and Autobiography*, 3: 100, and 2: 413, where he describes his influence on Spanish reformers.

34. For the important role that Adams played in Dutch revolutionary politics, see Jan Willem Schulte Nordholt, *The Dutch Republic and American Independence*, trans. Herbert H. Rowen (Chapel Hill, N.C., 1982).

35. JA to Thomas Jefferson, 18 July 1818, *Adams–Jefferson Letters*, 2: 527.

36. Ibid.; JA to Francis Dana, 18 April 1781, *Works*, 7: 393.

37. See *Works*, 7: 264–312.

38. JA to Richard Cranch, 15 January 1787, Ibid., 1: 432; JA to Abigail Adams, 14 March 1788, Charles F. Adams, ed., *Letters of John Adams, Addressed to His Wife* (Boston, 1841), 2: 112.

39. Quoted in Jan Willem Schulte Nordholt, *The Dutch Republic and American Independence*, 203.

40. JA to Richard Cranch, 15 January 1787, *Works*, 1: 432.

41. In order to gain public support for his plan of economic and political reform, Charles Alexander de Calonne, the King's Comptroller-General, called for a meeting of the Assembly of Notables, an ancient device last used in 1626. The proposal to convene a meeting of Notables was first broached with Louis XVI in August 1786, but it was not officially called into being until the last day of that year, and only met after some delay on February 22, 1787.

42. JA to Samuel Perley, 14 June 1809, *Works*, 9: 622–24; JA to Alexander B. Johnson, 5 November 1820, *Adams Papers*, Reel 124.

43. The best general history of the political and intellectual climate immediately preceding the French Revolution and the role played by Adams in pre-revolutionary debate is Robert R. Palmer, *The Age of Democratic Revolutions*, especially chapters 9, 14, and 15. On the role that the meeting of the Assembly of Notables had in Adams's decision to write, see also JA to Thomas Jefferson, 13 July 1813, *Adams–Jefferson Letters*, 1: 214–15; JA to James Lloyd, 29 March 1815, *Works*, 10: 149.

44. JA to Lafayette, 12 January 1787, *Adams Papers*, Reel 113; JA to John Jay, 22 September 1787, *Works*, 8: 451; JA to Thomas Jefferson, 10 December 1787, Cappon, ed., *Adams–Jefferson Letters*, 1: 214; Thomas Jefferson to JA, 6 February 1787, Cappon, ed., *Adams-Jefferson Letters*, 1: 170; Lafayette to JA, 12 October 1787, *Works*, 8: 456; JA to Lafayette, 27 October 1787, *Adams Papers*, Reel 113.

45. JA to John Jay, 22 September 1787, *Works*, 8: 451; JA to Lafayette, 12 January 1787, and 27 October 1787, *Adams Papers*, Reel 113; JA to Thomas Jefferson, 10 December 1787, *Adams–Jefferson Letters*, 1: 214–15.

46. JA to John Jay, 23 September 1787, *Works*, 8: 454–55; JA to John Jay, 30 November 1787, *Works*, 8: 463–64; JA to John Jay, 23 September 1787, *Works*, 8: 453 and 30 November 1787, *Works*, 8: 463; JA to Jefferson, 10 December 1787, *Adams–Jefferson Letters*, 1: 214–15.

47. Adams, *Works*, 4: 586–87.

48. See JA to Thomas Boylston Adams, 24 Janurary 1801, *Adams Papers*, Reel 400; JA to Matthew Carey, 21 June 1815, *Adams Papers*, Reel 122; JA to Rev. John De Walter, October 1797, *Adams Papers*, Reel 119.

49. JA to John Jay, 30 November 1787, *Works*, 8: 463–64; JA to Jefferson, 10 December 1787, *Adams–Jefferson Letters*, 1: 214–15; JA to Jefferson, 15 July 1813, Ibid., 357–58.

50. JA to Thomas Boylston Adams, 24 January 1801, *Adams Papers*, Reel 400. As frightened as Adams was by Shays's Rebellion and the meetings of county conventions in 1786, he was nevertheless confident that "any Town Meeting in New England would produce a better Constitution than all the Statesmen and Philosophers in France." (JA to Thomas Boylston Adams, 24 January 1801, *Adams Papers*, Reel 400).

51. He had "shuddered," he later told James Madison, at what had then appeared to be the "inevitable consequences of their theory, of which they made no secret." (JA to James Madison, 22 April 1817, *Works*, 10: 256).

52. "Pray, sir," Adams asked of John Taylor in 1814, "what was the object of my book? . . . This solemn opinion of M. Turgot, is the object of the whole of the three volumes." JA to John Taylor, 15 April 1814, *Works*, 6: 486. After Turgot's death in 1781, Condorcet became the major French defender of Turgot's doctrine of "all authority in one centre." Although the *Davila* essays were generally stimulated by the French Revolution, they were immediately provoked by the publication of Condorcet's *New Haven* letters, a defense of Turgot's position against Adams's criticism in the *Defence*. Condorcet's four letters were published at the end of Philip Mazzei's *Recherches historiques et politiques sur les États Unis de l'Amérique septentrionale* (1788).

6. The Science of Politics

1. JA to John Lloyd, 29 March 1815, *Works*, 10: 148–49. The best study of this subject remains R. R. Palmer, *The Age of Democratic Revolution*. See also, Jacques Godechot, *France and the Atlantic Revolution of the Eighteenth Century, 1770–1799* (New York, 1965).

2. See Henry Steele Commager, *The Empire of Reason: How Europe Imagined and America Realized the Enlightenemnt* (Garden City, N.Y., 1977). In Scotland, home of the most intense eighteenth-century investigations into the moral and poltical sciences, an avalanche of treatises were published, of which only a few can be mentioned: David Hume's *Treatise of Human Nature* (1740), *An Enquiry Concerning the Principles of Morals* (1752), and essays like "The Idea of a Perfect Commonwealth" and "That Politics May be Reduced to a Science" (1740–41); Adam Smith's *Theory of Moral Sentiments* (1759) and *The Wealth of Nations* (1776); Adam Ferguson's *Principles of Moral and Political Science* (1792). In Switzerland, Jean Jacques Burlamaqui published *Principles of Natural and Politic Law* (1747) and Emmerich Vattel the *Law of Nations* (1758). In France, to name just a few: Baron d'Holbach's *Système de la Nature* (1770); the abbé Mably's *Treatise on Legislation* (1776); and Real de Curban's *The Science of Government* (1776). In Italy, Gaetano Filangieri published his *The Science of Legislation* (1784) and Cesare Beccaria published his *Treatise on Crimes and Punishment* (1767).

3. French fascination with the lawgiver of classical antiquity is ably discussed in the following studies: Harold Parker, *The Cult of Antiquity and the French Revolutionaries*

(Chicago, 1937) and Elizabeth Rawson, *The Spartan Tradition in European Thought* (Oxford, 1969).

4. JA to John Lloyd, 30 March 1815, *Works*, 10: 149–50.

5. JA to William Tudor, 14 September 1816, *Adams Papers*, Reel 122.

6. Historians and political theorists have in recent years just begun to uncover the importance and contours of this crucial but hitherto unexplored element in the history of eighteenth-century political thought. Much of this literature has been suggestive, but there has been no exhaustive or systematic study of the subject. The contours of the debate are just now beginning to surface in the scholarly literature. See, for instance: Stefan Collini, Donald Winch, and John Burrow, eds., *That Noble Science of Politics: A Study in Nineteenth-Century Intellectual History* (Cambridge, [Engl.], 1983); Knud Haakonssen, *The Science of the Legislator: The Natural Jurisprudence of David Hume and Adam Smith* (Cambridge [Engl.], 1980); Istvan Hont and Michael Ignatieff, eds. *Wealth and Virtue: The Shaping of Political Economy in the Scottish Enlightenment* (Cambridge [Engl.], 1983); James Farr, "Political Science and the Enlightenment of Enthusiasm," *American Political Science Review* 82 (March 1988): 51–69; Andrew S. Skinner, *A System of Social Science: Papers Relating to Adam Smith* (Oxford, 1979); Donald Winch, *Adam Smith's Politics: An Essay in Historiographic Revision* (Cambridge Mass., 1978); Donald Winch, "Science and the Legislator: Adam Smith and After," *Economic Journal* 93 (September 1983): 501–20.

7. JA to Alexander Jardine, 1 June 1790, *Works*, 9: 567.

8. Adams, *Works*, 4: 283–84. Adams repeated the same theme twenty years later: "The human understanding is very well in the ordinary affairs of life. In architecture, men consider the elements about them: the Earth, the air, the water and the [   ] and construct their houses very well to guard against the dangers and inconveniences of each. . . . but in Government they seem to be destitute of Common Sense. The nature of men and things is laid out of the question. Experiment, which is admitted in all other arts and sciences is totally unheeded in this." JA to John Trumbull, 7 July 1805, *Adams Papers*, Reel 118.

9. JA to A. M. Cerisier, 22 February 1784, *Works*, 9: 522–23.

10. Adams, *Works*, 4: 292–94.

11. "Literary Drafts and Notes," *Adams Papers*, Reel 188.

12. Aristotle, though a great empiricist, is generally not regarded as having employed an experimental method. Indeed, his views on final causation suggest that he was an anti-experimentalist. Some scholars have suggested that Aristotle could not have avoided using some kind of experimental method, particularly in his work in biology and anatomy. It is in this sense, I suspect, that Adams could write that Aristotle shared with Democritus a "taste" for dissecting animals, "in order to discover the Seat of Sensation and the origin of Motion" (*Adams Papers*, Reel 188). See Herbert Butterfield, *The Origins of Modern Science* (Toronto, 1977), 80–83.

13. It should be recalled at this point that Adams said of Machiavelli that he was the first to have "revived the ancient politics" and that the world was much indebted to him for "the revival of reason in matters of government." For a pithy but excellent account of Bacon's scientific method and its relationship to that of the pre-Socratics, see Robert K. Faulkner, *Francis Bacon and the Project of Progress* (Lanham, Md., 1993), 8–9, 265–72.

14. *Adams Papers*, Reel 188.

15. Ibid. See JA to Thomas Jefferson, 28 June 1812, and JA to Thomas Jefferson,

16 July 1814, *Adams–Jefferson Letters,* 2: 308–11, 434–39. See also, JA to Benjamin Rush, 19 September 1806, in Schutz and Adair, eds., *The Spur of Fame: Dialogues of John Adams and Benjamin Rush, 1805–1813,* 65–66. Cf. David Hume, *An Enquiry Concerning the Principles of Morals,* ed. L. A. Selby-Bigge (Oxford, 1902), 174.

16. JA to John Taylor, 15 April 1814, *Works,* 6: 492.

17. See Adams, *Works,* 4: 294–96, 435–45; JA to Samuel Adams, 18 October 1790, *Works,* 4: 415.

18. Ibid., 5: 95 (emphasis added).

19. Francis Bacon, "The Advancement of Learning" in *The Works of Francis Bacon,* 12 vols. ed. J. Spedding, R. L. Ellis, and D. D. Heath (Boston, 1863), 6: 359.

20. Machiavelli, *Discourses on the First Ten Books of Titus Livius* in *The Prince and the Discourses,* ed. Max Lerner (New York, 1950), Greeting; 1: Introduction; bk. 3, chap. 43. The single best commentary on the *Discourses* is Harvey C. Mansfield, Jr., *Machiavelli's New Modes and Orders: A Study of the Discourses on Livy* (Ithaca, N.Y., 1979).

21. Cf. Aristotle, *Politics,* bk. 2, chap. 1; Polybius, *Histories,* bk. 1, chap. 1, sec. 36.

22. Niccolo Machiavelli, *The Prince,* in *The Prince and the Discourses,* chap. 15.

23. Machiavelli, *Discourses,* Introduction.

24. Ibid., bk. 3: chaps. 1, 11.

25. Ibid., bk. 1: chap. 39.

26. Ibid., bk. 2: Introduction.

27. "Wise men say, and not without reason, that whoever wishes to foresee the future must consult the past; for human events ever resemble those of preceding times. This arises from the fact that they are produced by men who have been, and ever will be, animated by the same passions, and thus they must necessarily have the same results" (*Discourses,* 3: chap. 43).

28. On the development of the historical sciences as a part of the empirical study of politics, see Carl Becker, *The Heavenly City of the Eighteenth-Century Philosophers* (New Haven, Conn., 1932); Ernst Cassirer, *The Philosophy of the Enlightenment* (Boston, 1951); Herbert Davis, "The Augustan Conception of History," in *Reason and Imagination: Studies in the History of Ideas, 1600–1800,* ed. J.A. Mazzeo (New York, 1962), 213–29; George H. Nadel, "Philosophy of History Before Historicism," in *The Critical Approach to Science and Philosophy,* ed. Mario Bunge (New York, 1964), 445–70; R. N. Stromberg, "History in the Eighteenth Century," *Journal of the History of Ideas* 12 (1951): 295–304.

29. For an interesting discussion of Machiavelli's influence on Bolingbroke's historical methodology, see Herbert Butterfield, *The Statecraft of Machiavelli* (New York, 1962), 135–65.

30. Henry Saint-John, Lord Viscount Bolingbroke, "Letters on the Study and Use of History," in *The Works of Lord Bolingbroke* (Philadelphia, 1841), 2: 193–94.

31. Ibid., 229–30, 223, 191, 222.

32. That Adams was greatly influenced by Bolingbroke can be little doubted. In his *Autobiography* Adams mentions that when he went to Worcester in 1756 to begin teaching Latin at the local public school, he carried with him "Lord Bolingbroke's Study and Use of History, and his Patriot King." The young Adams then lent his volumes to his teacher, James Putnam, who "was so well pleased with them he Added Bolingbrokes Works to his List, which gave men an Opportunity of reading the Posthumous Works of that Writer in five Volumes. Mr. Burke once asked, who ever read him through? I can answer that I read him through, before the Year 1758 and that

I have read him through at least twice since that time" (Adams, *Diary and Autobiography*, 3: 264). Adams's *Diary* is full of references to Bolingbroke (see Adams, *Diary*, 1: 11, 12, 35, 36, 38, 40, 73, 176, 200; 2: 386; 3: 272). See also, JA to Jefferson, 25 December 1813, *Adams–Jefferson Letters*, 2: 410. The influence is unmistakable.

33. Bolingbroke, "Letters on the Study and Use of History," in *The Works of Lord Bolingbroke*, 2: 229–30. See Alfred Iacuzzi, *John Adams, Scholar* (New York, 1952), 150.

34. *Works*, 6: 232.

35. Bolingbroke, "Letters on the Study and Use of History," 2: 228–29.

36. Ibid.; John E. Paynter, "The Ethics of John Adams: Prolegomenon to a Science of Politics," 97–101.

37. *Works*, 5: 11.

38. Given this methodological standard—the heavy emphasis on experience and history as opposed to rationalism and philosophy—some may wonder why Adams would quote in the *Defence* so approvingly from Plato's *Republic*. The vast bulk of Adams's quotations from Plato are drawn from the eighth and ninth books. It is here that Plato describes the rise and fall of all pure forms of government into their corrupt forms. What impressed Adams was not Plato's unique, noncyclical theory of regime change, but rather his account of the reasons, the underlying causes of this change: "Plato has given us the most accurate detail of the natural vicissitudes of manners and principles, the usual progress of the passions in society, and revolutions of governments into one another" (Ibid., 4: 448).

39. Ibid., 6: 365; 5: 11.

40. JA to Rev. De Walter, October 1797, *Adams Papers*, Reel 119; JA to Francis Adrian Vanderkemp, 20 April 1812, *Adams Papers*, Reel 118.

41. *Works*, 6: 183.

42. "Miscellaneous Notes," *Adams Papers*, Reel 188.

43. Ibid., Reel 118.

44. Ibid., Reel 188.

45. Ibid. Adams's principal teacher on the role of experience in the acquisition of knowledge was John Locke. In his *An Essay Concerning Human Understanding*, for instance, Locke had written: "Let us suppose the mind to be, as we say, white paper, void of all characters, without any ideas; how comes it to be furnished? . . . To this I answer, in one word, from *experience*; in that all our knowledge is founded, and from that it ultimately derives itself" (bk. 2, chap. 1, sec. 2).

46. Haraszti, *John Adams and the Prophets of Progress*, 247.

47. JA to Charles Holt, 4 September 1820, *Works*, 10: 391; JA to John Taylor, 15 April 1814, *Works*, 6: 479.

48. Adams, *Works*, 4: 290; 6: 118. In a useful chapter on "John Adams: Political Scientist as Historian," H. Trevor Colbourn demonstrates how Adams used history as the basis of his political science throughout his entire career. See Colbourn, *The Lamp of Experience*.

49. *Works*, 4: 297. To this point we have only mentioned in passing the influence that David Hume may have had on Adams. In the following passage from *An Enquiry Concerning Human Understanding*, we see the strong similarities between Hume and Adams: "Mankind are so much the same, in all times and places, that history informs us of nothing new or strange in this particular. Its chief use is only to discover the constant and universal principles of human nature, by showing men in all varieties of

circumstances and situations, and furnishing us with materials from which we may form our observations and become acquainted with the regular springs of human action and behaviour. These records of wars, intrigues, factions, and revolutions, are so many collections of experiments, by which the politician or moral philosopher fixes the principles of his science, in the same manner as the physician or natural philosopher becomes acquainted with the nature of plants, minerals, and other external objects, by the experiments which he forms concerning them" (ed. L. A. Selby-Bigge [Oxford, 1902] Sec. 8: Part 1, 83).

50. JA to Richard Price, 19 April 1790, *Works*, 9: 563–64; JA to Francis Adrian Vanderkemp, 27 March 1790, *Adams Papers*, Reel 115.

51. *Works*, 4: 303; "Miscellaneous Notes," *Adams Papers*, Reel 188. See also JA to Jefferson, 25 August 1787, *Adams–Jefferson Letters*, 1: 192.

52. JA to Thomas Jefferson, 25 August 1787, *Adams–Jefferson Letters*, 1: 192; *Works*, 6: 365.

53. *Works*, 6: 205–6.

54. *Works*, 4: 440; 6: 218; JA to John Taylor, 15 April 1814, *Works*, 6: 476–77. The parallel with Hume is again striking: "It is universally acknowledged that there is a great uniformity among the actions of men, in all ages, and that human nature remains still the same, in its principles and operations. The same motives always produce the same actions: The same events follow from the same causes. Ambition, avarice, self-love, vanity, friendship, generosity, public spirit: these passions, mixed in various degrees, and distributed through society, have been, from the beginning of the world, and still are, the source of all the actions and enterprises, which have ever been observed among mankind. Would you know the sentiments, inclinations, and course of life of the Greeks and Romans? Study well the temper and actions of the French and English." (*An Enquiry Concerning Human Understanding*, Sec. 8: Part 1, 83).

55. *Works*, 4: 440; JA to Samuel Adams, 18 October 1790, Ibid., 6: 416.

56. JA to John Taylor, 15 April 1814, *Works*, 6: 481.

57. JA to Thomas Jefferson, 15 July 1813, *Adams–Jefferson Letters*, 2: 357.

7. The Science of History

1. Gordon Wood has described the *Defence* as a "bulky, disordered, conglomeration of political glosses on a single theme" (*Creation of the American Republic*, 568). Peter Shaw found the book absent in "form," "repetitious," inconsistent, and "disordered" (*The Character of John Adams*, 207). J. G. A. Pocock has described the book as "the product of an obsession with disorder so pervasive that it becomes disorderly itself," so much so that Pocock thought Adams "scarcely in control of his materials." " 'The Book Most Misunderstood Since the Bible': John Adams and the Confusion about Aristocracy," paper presented at the Instituto di Studi Nordamericani–Firenze Capitale Europea della Cultura, Florence, Italy, 28–30 November 1987, 13.

2. JA to Thomas Jefferson, 25 August 1787, Cappon, ed., *Adams–Jefferson Letters*, 1: 192. Machiavelli's *History of Florence* (1546), Guicciardini's *Storia d'Italia* (1574), Nerli's *Commentari de' fatti civil occorsi nella cita di Firenze dal 1215 al 1537* (1728) and Varchi's *Storia fiorentina* (1721) are all quoted in the second volume to tell the turbulent story of the Florentine republic. Adams then follows the various histories of Florence with a section entitled "Machiavel's Plan of a Perfect Commonwealth," drawn from the Florentine's little known *Discourse upon the proper Ways and Means of*

reforming the Government of Florence (1519). The history of Siena is next presented through Orlando Malavolti's *Historia . . . de' fatti, e guerre de' Sanesi* (1599), and the political story of Bologna is chronicled in Cherubino Ghirardacci's *Della historia di Bologna* (1605) and Gasparo Bombaci's *Historie memorabili della citt 'a di Bologna* (1666). The histories of various other Italian republics—Pistoia, Cremona, Padua, Mantua, Montepulciano—carry over into the third volume.

3. The difficulties in interpreting the *Defence* are compounded by the fact that approximately three-quarters of volume one, nine-tenths of volume two, and the first half of volume three transcribe multipage quotations borrowed from the writings of classical, medieval, and modern historians and philosophers.

4. *Works*, 4: 293.

5. Ibid., 299.

6. Ibid., 299, 301.

7. Ibid., 301–3.

8. Ibid., 6: 6–131.

9. Ibid., 4: 303.

10. Ibid., 6: 142; 5: 5; 4: 303.

11. Ibid., 4: 304.

12. Ibid., 304.

13. Ibid., 303–10. Originally, sovereignty in San Marino was lodged in a legislative council called an "arengo" representing each household or landed property. But experience quickly revealed that there was "too much confusion in such a multitude of statesmen." The unworkability of the arengo led the people of San Marino to create a new body, something like a senate, the so-called council of sixty, half of which was made up by the local nobility. In time, Adams reports, most authority devolved into this body. In addition to the arengo and council of sixty, the executive power, equal to that of the "old Roman consuls," was lodged in the hands of two "capitaneos." The judicial authority in civil and criminal matters was lodged in the hands of a "commisary," chosen from outside the community in order to avoid "the many alliances, friendships, and intermarriages, as well as the personal feuds and animosities that happen among so small a people." In addition to the primitive separation of powers, the democratic element was checked in additional ways. For instance, the council of sixty, in addition to being limited to half nobles, half plebeians, restricted membership to those older than twenty-five, a vote of two-thirds was required to pass all legislation, "no son" could "sit with his father, and never two from the same family."

14. *Works*, 4: 304, 309.

15. Ibid., 309–10.

16. Ibid., 304.

17. Ibid., 5: 15; 6: 14; 5: 44.

18. Ibid., 6: 95.

19. Ibid., 64.

20. Ibid., 141–42.

21. Ibid., 23, 48, 79, 56.

22. *Works*, 6: 61–62.

23. Ibid., 4: 435, 462. This remarkable statement seems to have been altogether missed by scholars of the American founding period. By those "who framed the American constitutions," Adams was of course referring to himself. When he suggests that the writings of Plato and Polybius were in his mind when he wrote *Thoughts on*

Government and the Massachusetts Constitution, we are introduced to an intellectual world entirely different from the one used by scholars to explain Adams's thought, not to mention that of the founding period in general. As we shall see in the next three chapters, Adams attempted to synthesize ancient and modern thought in a way that brings into question the views of those scholars who see the founding period from the perspective of either classical republicanism or Lockean liberalism. How he reconciled these two traditions is the critical question and is discussed in chapter ten. Although Adams built his political system from the entire tradition of political philosophy, he did rely on some thinkers more than others. For the principles of government, his principal teacher was Locke. On the question of constitutional forms, he was most deeply influenced by the writings of Plato, Aristotle, Polybius, Machiavelli, Harrington, Montesquieu, and Bolingbroke. Contrast with Appleby, "The New Republican Synthesis and the Changing Political Ideas of John Adams," 578–95, who argues that Jean de Lolme's *Constitution de l'Angleterre* was the principal influence on Adams's mature political thought. de Lolme was at best a secondary influence on Adams's thinking.

24. *Works*, 4: 440.

25. Aristotle, *The Politics*, Books 4–5; Polybius, *Histories*, Book 6; Kurt von Fritz, *The Theory of the Mixed Constitution in Antiquity* (New York, 1954; reprint ed., New York, 1975); Zera Fink, *The Classical Republicans: An Essay in the Recovery of a Pattern Thought in Seventeenth-Century England* (Evansville, Ill., 1962). The Polybian categorization of regimes and the related cyclical theory of constitutional change had long been a staple of Adams's political thought. Years before he wrote the *Defence*, he had declared in a 1772 oration delivered at Braintree, that "there are only Three simple Forms of Government": Democracy represented the rule of the of many, aristocracy the rule of a "few, great, rich, wise Men," and monarchy represented the "Rule of one." In addition to the three simple forms of government and their corrupt alternatives, lawgivers might create an "indefinite variety of other Forms of Government, occasioned by different Combinations of the Powers of Society, and different Intermixtures of these Forms of Government, one with another" (Adams, "Notes for an Oration at Braintree, 1772," *Diary and Autobiography*, 2: 57–60).

26. *Works*, 4: 416. Machiavelli is here paraphrasing Polybius, who wrote in the Sixth Book of the *Histories*: "'It is customary, with those who professedly treat this subject, to establish three sorts of government—kingly government, aristocracy, and democracy. . . . It is manifest that the best form of government is that which is compounded of all three. This is founded not only in reason, but also in experience. . . . Six kinds of government must be allowed—kingly government and monarchy, aristocracy and oligarchy, democracy and the government of the multitude'" (*Works*, 4: 435).

27. *Works*, 4: 443, 441.

28. Ibid., 444.

29. For Adams's negative view of Plato see: JA to Thomas Jefferson, 16 July 1814, *Adams–Jefferson Letters*, 2: 437.

30. *Works*, 4: 448.

31. Ibid., 508–9, 448.

32. Ibid., 462–63.

33. Ibid., 469.

34. Ibid.

35. Ibid., 443, 441.

36. Ibid., 4: 416. Adams is quoting here from Book 1, chap. 2 of Machiavelli's *Discourses upon the First Decade of Livy*.

37. *Works*, 4: 474.

38. Ibid., 477, 483, 491, 419, 285.

39. *Works*, 4: 443, 553, 443, 436. The Lycurgan constitution was composed of four distinct bodies: a dual monarchy, a senate, a two-house assembly of the people (one representing the city and one the country), and a five-member council of judicial review called the ephori.

40. *Works*, 4: 443, 551.

41. Ibid., 551–52.

42. Ibid., 553–55.

43. Ibid., 556.

44. Adams's critique of Spartan virtue is discussed in chapter nine.

45. *Works*, 4: 555.

46. Ibid., 469.

8. *The Science of Human Nature*

1. *Works*, 4: 293, 297, 406.

2. Ibid., 6: 365.

3. Ibid., 232.

4. Ibid., 4: 406, 408; 6: 182–83; 4: 406.

5. *Works*, 4: 406.

6. Thomas Hobbes, *Leviathan*, with an Introduction by K. R. Minogue (London, 1973), 49, 88.

7. Ibid., 49.

8. Ibid., 67. See chapters 14 and 15 for Hobbes's discussion of the laws of nature.

9. *Works*, 6: 234.

10. Ibid., 6: 234; 4: 407.

11. Ibid., 6: 114–15.

12. Ibid., 6: 141, 8, 114–15.

13. Ibid., 6: 114–15, 141; 4: 406.

14. Ibid., 6: 234, 232.

15. Ibid., 8, 234.

16. Adams's probable source for the concept of the "spectemur agendo" is, Ovid, *Metamorphoses*, 2, trans. Frank Justus Miller, (Cambridge, Mass., 1984), 236–37.

17. *Works*, 6: 245, 239, 245, 239. Adams would later describe man as a "stareing Animal" (JA to Thomas Jefferson, 16 July 1814, *Adams–Jefferson Letters*, 2: 438).

18. *Works*, 6: 234, 246.

19. Ibid., 233.

20. Ibid., 234, 245 (emphasis added).

21. Ibid., 232, 246, 234.

22. Ibid., 248.

23. Ibid., 246, 237.

24. Ibid., 232–33.

25. Ibid., 239, 248, 241.

26. Ibid., 6: 254, 247.

27. Ibid., 6: 240, 275.

28. Ibid., 246, 249. A classic example of this extraordinary desire for distinction is found in a letter from a young Alexander Hamilton to Edward Stevens: "To confess my weakness, my Ambition is [so] prevalent that I contemn the grov'ling and condition of a Clerk or the like, to which my Fortune &c. condemns me and would willingly risk my life tho' not my Character to exalt my Station. Im confident, Ned that my Youth excludes me from any hopes of immediate Preferment nor do I desire it, but I mean to prepare the way for futurity. Im no Philosopher you see and may be justly said to Build Castles in the Air. My Folly makes me ashamed and beg youll Conceal it, yet Neddy we have seen such Schemes successful when the Projector is Constant I shall Conclude saying I wish there was a War." Alexander Hamilton to Edward Stevens, 11 November 1769, *The Papers of Alexander Hamilton*, ed. Harold C. Syrett et al. (New York, 1961–), 1: 4–5.

29. Adams, *Works*, 6: 248, 245, 249, 239. The Lincoln quotation is from his 1838 "Address Before the Springfield Young Men's Lyceum." See Richard N. Current, ed., *The Political Thought of Abraham Lincoln* (New York, 1967), 19.

30. *Works*, 6: 234, 241, 247, 249.

31. Ibid., 269, 267.

32. Ibid., 269.

33. Ibid., 236, 253, 242, 234–35, 242.

34. Ibid., 242, 253.

35. Ibid., 235; JA to Richard Rush, 5 November 1813, *Adams Papers*, Reel 95; JA to John Taylor, 15 April 1814, *Works*, 6: 452–53; JA to Jefferson, 2 September 1813, *Adams–Jefferson Letters*, 2: 371–72.

36. *Works*, 6: 235, 236.

37. See Alexis de Tocqueville, *Democracy in America*, ed. J. P. Mayer, (Garden City, N.J., 1969), 403–4, 622–23.

38. *Works*, 6: 237–38.

39. Ibid., 238.

40. Ibid., 257.

41. Ibid., 258.

42. JA to Thomas Jefferson, 9 July 1813, *Adams–Jefferson Letters*, 2: 351–52.

43. *Works*, 4: 392.

44. Ibid.; JA to John Taylor, 15 April 1814, *Works*, 6: 453–54. One of the pillars supporting the thesis that Adams's political thought changed over time is grounded, in part, on the idea that he increasingly came to view inequality and aristocracy as necessary instruments of social order. Throughout his life, however, he recognized and supported the argument for natural aristocracy. In 1760 he entered the following thoughts on equality and aristocracy in his literary notebook: "Although there is a moral and political and a natural Equality among Mankind, all being born free and equal, yet there are other Inequalities which are equally natural, Such as Strength, Activity, Industry, Genius, Talents, Virtues, Benevolence ("Literary Notes and Papers," *Adams Papers*, Reel 118).

45. *Works*, 1: 462.

46. Ibid., 6: 285–86.

47. JA to John Taylor, 15 April 1814, *Works*, 6: 451–52, 491–92.

48. Ibid., 272.

49. Ibid., 4: 391–97; In his later years, Adams identified five pillars of aristocracy:

beauty, wealth, birth, genius, and virtue. JA to Thomas Jefferson, 2 September 1813, *Adams–Jefferson Letters*, 2: 371–72.

50. JA to John Taylor, 15 April 1814, *Works*, 6: 451–52, 456, 457, 460.

51. Ibid., 451–52.

52. *Works*, 4: 392.

53. Ibid., 392–93, 396–97.

54. *Works*, 4: 397; 6: 249.

55. *Works*, 4: 397; 6: 260.

56. JA to Thomas Jefferson, 9 July 1813, *Adams–Jefferson Letters*, 2: 352.

57. Ibid., 2 September 1813, 371–72.

58. JA to Richard Rush, 5 November 1813, *Adams Papers*, Reel 95.

9. Republican Government

1. JA to Samuel Adams, 12 September 1790, *Works*, 6: 411–12.

2. Adams, "Thoughts on Government," *Papers*, 4: 86.

3. JA to Mercy Otis Warren, 19 August 1807, *Correspondence between John Adams and Mercy Warren*, 472–73; JA to Samuel Perley, 19 June 1809, *Works*, 9: 624; JA to James Madison, 22 April 1817, *Works*, 10: 256.

4. *Works*, 4: 581.

5. Ibid., 406, 370.

6. Ibid., 398; 5: 25.

7. Ibid., 4: 385; 5: 183 (emphasis added); 6: 165–66; 4: 399, 387; 6: 165, 254; 4: 379. Adams's views on the naturalness of kingship were shared by others of his generation, including Benjamin Franklin who, at the Constitutional Convention in 1787, concluded that "there is a natural inclination in mankind to Kingly government" (Franklin, in *Notes of Debates in the Federal Convention of 1787*, ed. James Madison [Athens, Ohio, 1966]), 53.

8. See *Works*, 6: 64; 4: 392–93.

9. Ibid., 6: 57–58.

10. Ibid., 4: 399, 406–7, 513.

11. Ibid., 399.

12. Ibid., 6: 57–58; 4: 583, 399.

13. Ibid., 6: 54.

14. Ibid., 51; JA to Thomas Jefferson, 15 November 1813, *Adams–Jefferson Letters*, 2: 401.

15. *Works*, 6: 51–52.

16. Ibid.

17. Ibid., 57–59.

18. Ibid., 58–59. That even the theater would be corrupted by democratic politics was largely borne out in the next century. See Carol Nackenoff, *The Fictional Republic: Horatio Alger and American Political Discourse* (New York, 1994), 228–35.

19. *Works*, 6: 58–59, 65.

20. Ibid., 151.

21. Ibid., 68. Compare with *Federalist* No. 10.

22. Ibid., 8, 10.

23. Ibid., 6: 8–9, 110, 8–9, 170, 100, 133. Adams was vehemently opposed to revolutionary and post-revolutionary laws that forced creditors to accept paper money for

loans paid in gold: "The rapid Translation of Property from Hand to Hand, the robbing of Peter to pay Paul distresses me, beyond measure. The Man who lent another an 100 [pounds] in gold four years ago, and is paid now in Paper, cannot purchase with it, a Quarter Part, in Pork, Beef, or Land, of what he could when he lent the Gold." JA to Elbridge Gerry, 6 December 1777, *Papers*, 5: 346–47.

24. Adams, *Works*, 6: 48; 4: 490. Madison had written: "Popular liberty might then have escaped the indelible reproach of decreeing to the same citizens, the hemlock on one day, and statues on the next."

25. *Works*, 6: 48, 89–90, 10, 134; 4: 583; 6: 109.

26. Ibid., 69.

27. Ibid., 5: 288–89, 90; 6: 60 (compare with Aristotle, *The Politics*, 1301a26–37); 4: 410, 400, 411, 415, 585.

28. Ibid., 409–10.

29. Ibid., 5: 452–53.

30. JA to General Lincoln, 19 June 1789, *Adams Papers*, Reel 115; JA to J. H. Tiffany, 31 March 1819, *Works*, 10: 377–78; *Works*, 4: 370–71; 6: 183, 205; JA to John Taylor, 15 April 1814, *Works*, 6: 455; 5: 452–53; 6: 183.

31. JA to John Taylor, 15 April 1814, *Works*, 6: 455; *Works*, 5: 452–53; JA to William Tudor, 28 June 1789, *Adams Papers*, Reel 115; *Works*, 6: 183.

32. JA to J. H. Tiffany, 31 March 1819, *Works*, 10: 377–78; JA to Mercy Otis Warren, 8 August 1807, *Correspondence between John Adams and Mercy Warren*, 432; *Works*, 5: 453. For a brief summary of the varying ways in which the words "republic" and "democracy" were used during the Revolutionary and Founding periods, see Robert W. Shoemaker, "'Democracy' and 'Republic' as Understood in Late Eighteenth-Century America,'" *American Speech*, 41 (1966): 83–95.

33. *Works*, 5: 453; JA to J. H. Tiffany, 31 March 1819, *Works*, 10: 377–78; JA to Roger Sherman, 17 July 1789, *Works*, 6: 428.

34. Baron de Montesquieu, *The Spirit of the Laws*, trans. Thomas Nugent (New York, 1966), 8.

35. *Works*, 5: 453; "Thoughts on Government," *Works*, 4: 194; JA to J. H. Tiffany, 30 April 1819, *Works*, 10: 377–78; JA to Mercy Otis Warren, 20 July 1807, *Correspondence between John Adams and Mercy Warren*, 352–53. Adams's standard for defining a republic is similar to the one used by Alexander Hamilton in *Federalist* No. 6, where he says: "Sparta, Athens, Rome and Carthage were all republics."

36. JA to Mercy Otis Warren, 20 July 1807, *Correspondence between John Adams and Mercy Warren*, 352–53; *Works*, 4: 370–71; 5: 453.

37. *Works*, 4: 370–71.

38. Ibid., 403–5.

39. *Works*, 4: 370–71; 5: 453; 4: 401. See also, 4: 405. This seems to have been Adams's standard for republican government dating back to the Revolution and before: "Society can be governed only by general Rules. Government cannot accomodate itself to every particular Case, as it happens, or to the Circumstances of particular Persons. It must establish general, comprehensive Regulations for Cases and Persons. The only Question is, which general Rule, will accomodate most Cases and most Persons." (JA to James Sullivan, 26 May 1776, *Papers*, 4: 208–12.)

40. *Works*, 4: 402; JA to [Unknown], 10 October 1786, *Adams Papers*, Reel 369; *Works*, 4: 402.

41. *Works*, 5: 453–54. "The Pleasure of Property," Adams wrote in 1772, "arise from

Acquisition more than Possession, from what is to come rather than from what it is." (30 June 1772, *Diary and Autobiography*, 2: 61–62.)

42. In fact, Adams found Madison's definition of a republic in *The Federalist* to be lacking: "The Federalist is a valuable work, and Mr. Madison's part in it as respectable as any other. But his distinction between a republic and a democracy, cannot be justified. A democracy is as really a republic as an oak is a tree, or a temple a building. There are, in strictness of speech and in the soundest technical language, democratical and aristocratical republics, as well as an infinite variety of mixtures of both." JA to J. H. Tiffany, 31 March 1819, *Works*, 10: 377–78. Adams is here referring to Madison's definition of democracy and republic in Federalist No. 10. Madison there distinguished between democracy and a republic in the following way: "From this view of the subject, it may be concluded, that a pure Democracy, by which I mean, a Society, consisting of a small number of citizens, who assemble and administer the Government in Person, can admit of no cure for the mischiefs of faction. . . . A Republic, by which I mean a Government in which the scheme of representation takes place, opens a different prospect, and promises the cure for which we are seeking. . . . The two great points difference between a Democracy and a Republic are, first, the delegation of the Government, in the latter, to a small number of citizens elected by the rest: secondly, the greater number of citizens, and greater sphere of country, over which the latter may be extended." (James Madison, *The Federalist*, ed. Jacob Cooke [New York, 1961], 61–62).

43. *Works*, 6: 8–9.

44. Ibid., 4: 295. This idea of government should be compared with Madison's definition in the tenth *Federalist* essay.

45. The literature on this subject is vast. For a historiographical essay on the subject, see Robert Shalhope, "Toward a Republican Synthesis: The Emergence of an Understanding of Republicanism in American Historiography," *William and Mary Quarterly* 39 (January 1972): 49–80.

46. J. G. A. Pocock, *The Machiavellian Moment*, 526. See also Bruce Miroff, "John Adams: Merit, Fame, and Political Leadership," *Journal of Politics* 48 (1986): 116–32. Joseph Ellis has gone even further in classifying Adams as anti-liberal and as a "classical" republican. Ellis writes: "Adams's vision remained traditional and, as they say, pre-modern or pre-liberal. . . . His ideological orientation was inherently social and collectivistic, driven by the assumption that individual strivings . . . must naturally and necessarily be subordinated to public imperatives if the human potential unleashed by the American Revolution were to achieve its fullest realization." Then, in a breathtaking comparison, Ellis links Adams's political thought to the "socialistic perspective" expounded in Herbert Croly's *The Promise of American Life* and to "the regulatory legislation of the Progressives and the New Deal." See Ellis, *Passionate Sage*, 229, 164.

47. For an excellent attempt to explain the apparent transformation in Adams's understanding of virtue that draws many of the same conclusions, see Robert Webking, *The American Revolution and the Politics of Liberty*, 130–50. See also, Diggins, *The Lost Soul of American Politics*, 69–85.

48. See Aristotle, *Politics*, 1280a 31–1280b 8: "The conclusion which clearly follows is that any polis which is truly so called, and is not merely one in name, must devote itself to the end of encouraging goodness."

49. *Works*, 6: 206–7.

50. Ibid., 206–11.

51. Ibid., 209–11. According to Adams, the ultimate source of the revived idea in eighteenth-century political philosophy of a community of wives and property was Plato: "Nothing can be conceived more destructive of human happiness; more infallibly contrived to transform Men and Women into Brutes, Yahoos, or Daemons than a Community of Wives and Property. Yet, in what, are the Writings of Rousseau and Helvetius wiser than those of Plato? 'The Man who first fenced a Tobacco Yard, and said this is mine ought instantly to have been put to death' says Rousseau. 'The Man who first pronounced the barbarous Word 'Dieu,' ought to have been immediately destroyed,' says Diderot. . . . In short Philosophers antient and modern appear to me as Mad as Hindoos, Mahomitans and Christians." (JA to Thomas Jefferson, 16 July 1814, *Adams–Jefferson Letters*, 2: 435–38.)

52. *Works*, 6: 219.

53. See Herbert Storing, *What the Anti-Federalists Were For* (Chicago, 1981).

54. *Works*, 4: 556–57, 287; 6: 96.

55. Ibid., 97, 99, 61, 95 96.

56. Ibid., 5: 289.

57. For the French fascination with the ancient republics, see Parker, *The Cult of Antiquity and the French Revolutionaries: A Study in the Development of the Revolutionary Spirit* (Chicago, 1937), and Storing's *What the Anti-Federalists Were For* for the influence of the classical models in America.

58. *Works*, 6: 555, 554.

59. Ibid., 4: 554, 555 (emphasis added).

60. Ibid., 555 (emphasis added); 6: 95. "There are no people on earth so ambitious as the people of America," Adams wrote in 1811. "The reason is," he said "because the lowest can aspire as freely as the highest. The highest offices are as fair objects to the tradesman or farmer as to the lawyer, the priest, physician, or merchant." JA to Josiah Quincy, 18 February 1811, *Works*, 9: 633.

61. Aristotle, *Politics*, 1280a30–40.

62. *Works*, 4: 470.

63. Ibid., 6: 94, 102, 219. Even in 1776, at the very time when historians claim that Adams was attempting to restore the virtue associated with the ancient republics, he was arguing that it "is the *Form* of Government which gives the decisive Colour to the Manners of the People, more than any other Thing." (JA to Mercy Otis Warren, 8 January 1776, *Papers*, 3: 397–98 [emphasis added].)

64. Samuel Adams to JA, 4 October 1790 and JA to Samuel Adams, 18 October 1790, *Works*, 6: 412–13 and 414–15; Ibid., 4: 557–58; 6: 96. Ultimately, the teaching of virtue to children was for Adams the responsibility of parents. John and Abigail took fewer responsibilities more seriously: "It should be your care, therefore, and mine, to elevate the minds of our children and exalt their courage; to accelerate and animate their industry and activity; to excite in them an habitual contempt of meanness, abhorrence of injustice and inhumanity, and an ambition to excel in every capacity, faculty, and virtue. If we suffer their minds to grovel and creep in infancy, they will grovel all their lives. But their bodies must be hardened, as well as their souls exalted. Without strength and activity and vigor of body, the brightest mental excellencies will be eclipsed and obscured." (JA to Abigail Adams, 29 October 1775, *Adams Family Correspondence*, 1: 317–18.)

65. *Works*, 4: 526. Adams's understanding of the relationship between commerce

and virtue anticipates Tocqueville's more famous description of the American character in the early republic: "The doctrine of self-interest rightly understood does not inspire great sacrifices, but everyday it prompts some small ones; by itself it cannot make a man virtuous, but its discipline shapes a lot of orderly, temperate, moderate, careful, and self-controlled citizens. If it does not lead the will directly to virtue, it establishes habits which unconsciously turn it that way." Alexis de Tocqueville, *Democracy in America,* ed. J.P. Mayer (Garden City, N.Y., 1969), 527.

66. *Works,* 5: 289.

67. Ibid., 5: 289; 6: 109; 5: 289.

10. The Principles of Government

1. JA to Alexander Jardine, 1 June 1790, *Works,* 9: 567–58; "Thoughts on Government," *Papers,* 4: 86.

2. *Works,* 4: 284.

3. See Pierre Manent, *An Intellectual History of Liberalism* (Princeton, N.J., 1994), 62.

4. See, for instance: W. B. Gwyn, *The Meaning of the Separation of Powers* (New Orleans, 1965), 116; Wood, *The Creation of the American Republic,* 577.

5. Francis G. Wilson, "The Mixed Constitution and the Separation of Powers, *Southwestern Social Science Quarterly* 15 (1934–35): 14–28; Martin Diamond, "The Separation of Powers and the Mixed Regime," in *As Far as Republican Principles Will Admit,* ed. William A. Schambra (Washington, D.C., 1992), 58–67; Gwyn, *The Meaning of the Separation of Powers,* 26–27; M. J. C. Vile, *Constitutionalism and the Separation of Powers* (Oxford, 1967), 33–34, 98.

6. Aristotle, *Politics,* 1266a5, 1290b20–1291b12.

7. As Aristotle put it: "The regime is an arrangement of a city with respect to its offices, particularly the one that has authority over all matters. For what has authority in the city is everywhere the governing body, and the governing body *is* the regime." *Politics,* 1278b8–12.

8. Harry V. Jaffa, "Aristotle," in *The History of Political Philosophy,* eds. Leo Strauss and Joseph Cropsey (Chicago, 1963), 64–125; Carnes Lord, "Aristotle, Ibid., 4th ed., 118–54; Harvey C. Mansfield, *Taming the Prince: The Ambivalence of the Modern Executive* (Baltimore, 1989), 45–72.

9. Aristotle's mixed regime is, therefore, not to be confused with the modern doctrine of the separation of powers. In the Aristotelian polity, there was no division or separation of power.

10. At the beginning of the *Second Treatise,* Locke explains how he will address this problem: "To understand political power right, and derive it from its original, we must consider what state all men are naturally in, and that is, a *state of perfect freedom* to order their actions, and dispose of their possessions and persons, as they think fit, within the bounds of the law of nature, without asking leave, or depending upon the will of any other man." *Second Treatise of Government,* ed. Richard Cox (Arlington Heights, Ill., 1982), 3.

11. Montesquieu, *The Spirit of the Laws,* 150, 152, 161, 160.

12. Adams, "The Report of a Constitution or Form of Government for the Commonwealth of Massachusetts," *Papers,* 8: 238, 237.

13. *Works,* 6: 116; 4: 308–9; 6: 116, 4: 359.

14. *Works*, 6: 116 (emphasis added). See also *Works*, 7: 117, 118.

15. Adams did not say nor did he mean to say that the people should only participate "directly as a constituent element of the society in one part of the government." This is the view of Wood, *Creation of the American Republic*, 585. Wood's argument rests almost entirely on one word, in one sentence of one Adams letter. In 1790 Adams had written the following to his cousin Samuel Adams: "Whenever I use the word republic with approbation, I mean a government in which the people have collectively, or by representation, an essential share in the sovereignty." JA to Samuel Adams, 18 October 1790, *Works*, 6: 415. Samuel Adams responded to his cousin with a slap on the wrist: "Is not the *whole* sovereignty, my friend, essentially in the people? Is not government designed for the welfare and happiness of all the people? and is it not the uncontrollable, essential right of the people to amend and alter, or annul their constitution and frame a new one, whenever they shall think it will better promote their own welfare and happiness to do it? That the sovereignty resides in the people, is a political doctrine which I have never heard an American politician seriously deny." Samuel Adams to JA, 20 November 1790, *Works*, 6: 421. That the ever combatative John Adams did not respond to his cousin's criticism suggests that he recognized his error.

16. John Paynter has summarized perfectly Adams's position: "The people must *constitute* government; they need not actually *run* government." "John Adams: On the Principles of a Political Science," *Political Science Reviewer*, 42.

17. *Works*, 6: 118, 171–72, 130–31, 116–17.

18. "Thoughts on Government," *Papers*, 4: 87–88.

19. JA to Joseph Hawley, 25 August 1776, *Papers*, 4: 496–97; "Thoughts on Government," *Papers*, 4: 87–88.

20. JA to James Sullivan, 26 May 1776, *Papers*, 4: 208–12.

21. Ibid.

22. After criticizing Aristotle's position, Adams then quoted from several places in Book 4 of *The Politics* where Aristotle defined the best polity as that which was governed by the middling element, precisely that class of people that he had later excluded from the polity in Book 7.

23. *Works*, 5: 456–57.

24. See the "Novanglus" essays in *Papers*, 2: 238.

25. *Works*, 4: 579.

26. JA to Richard Henry Lee, 15 November 1775, *Papers*, 3: 307–8; "Thoughts on Government," *Papers*, 4: 87–88; *Works*, 6: 171.

27. Adams's construction of an independent executive was well ahead of other Revolutionary constitution-makers in 1780. A large majority of the first state constitutions empowered the legislature to elect the chief executive, and no state constitution gave its executive an absolute veto. As it turned out, neither did Massachusetts. The Massachusetts Convention later amended this provision, giving the governor a partial veto. Adams's independent and energetic executive provided the model for the Federal Constitution of 1787. On Adams and the executive power, see Ryerson, "'Like a Hare before the Hunters': John Adams and the Idea of Republican Monarchy," 16–29.

28. *Works*, 6: 171–72.

29. "The Report of a Constitution or Form of Government for the Commonwealth of Massachusetts," *Papers*, 8: 251–52.

30. "Thoughts on Government," *Papers*, 4: 91; "The Report of a Constitution or Form of Government for the Commonwealth of Massachusetts," *Papers*, 8: 256–57.

31. *Works*, 4: 406.

32. See Wood, *The Creation of the American Republic*, 575; Paul K. Conkin, *Self-Evident Truths* (Bloomington, Ind., 1974), 151; Richard, *The Founders and the Classics*, 132.

33. *Works*, 6: 44; 4: 381 (emphasis added).

34. "Notes for an Oration at Braintree, 1772," *Diary and Autobiography*, 2: 57–60.

35. JA to Thomas Jefferson, 9 July 1813, *Adams–Jefferson Letters*, 2: 352; *Works*, 4: 397; 6: 246; 4: 414.

36. *Works*, 6: 280.

37. Ibid., 4: 406.

38. *Works*, 6: 521; JA to Thomas Jefferson, 9 October 1787, *Adams–Jefferson Letters*, 1: 202–3.

39. *Works*, 6: 8 (emphasis added); 4: 462; 6: 208. See also 4: 406; 5: 473.

40. Ibid., 6: 284; 4: 354–55, 548; 6: 57, 200; 4: 462; 6: 10, 341.

41. "A constitution in which the people reserve to themselves the absolute control of their purses, one essential branch of the legislature, and the inquest of grievances and state crimes," Adams wrote, "will always produce patriotism, bravery, simplicity, and science." *Works*, 5: 290.

42. Ibid., 4: 290–91, 444–45. On the need to "ostracize the natural aristocracy," see also *Works*, 4: 398, 414.

43. Ibid., 6: 396; 4: 473, 585.

44. Ibid., 462, 390; Harazsti, *John Adams and the Prophets of Progress*, 219; *Works*, 6: 157–58, 152–53; 4: 377; 6: 277; 4: 413.

45. *Works*, 6: 246, 109.

46. Ibid., 6: 246, 248.

47. Ibid., 6: 104–5, 243, 241.

48. Ibid., 6: 241, 242, 250.

49. Ibid., 6: 13, 183–84; JA to John Jebb, 21 August 1785, *Works*, 9: 533; 6: 183–84.

50. JA to John Jebb, 21 August and 10 September 1785, *Works*, 9: 535, 542; 6: 183–84.

51. *Works*, 6: 249–50.

52. Ibid., 6: 104–5, 76, 159, 106, 77.

53. Bruce Miroff, "John Adams: Merit, Fame, and Political Leadership," 125.

54. *Works*, 6: 249, 104–5, 256.

55. Ibid., 6: 243–44, 104–5, 243–44.

11. The Art of Political Architecture

1. *Works*, 4: 291–92.

2. John Adams to Richard Price, 19 April 1790, *Works*, 9: 565; Ibid., 4: 293–94; JA to Benjamin Rush, February 1790, *Old Family Letters*, 52–53; JA to Benjamin Rush, 8 February 1789, Ibid., 31–32. Rousseau's estimation of the legislator is not dissimilar to Adams's: In *The Social Contract* he wrote that the "Legislator is an extraordinary man in the State in all respects. If he should be so by his genius, he is no less so by his function." *On the Social Contract, with the Geneva Manuscript and Political Economy*, trans. Judith R. Masters and ed. Roger D. Masters (New York, 1978), 68.

3. *Works*, 4: 587–88.

4. JA to Henry Marchont, 20 March 1790, *Adams Papers*, Reel 115.

5. JA to Richard Rush, 14 May 1821, *Works*, 10: 397; JA to James Warren, 20 April 1776, *Papers*, 4: 132; "U" to the Boston Gazette [5 September 1763]—"On Private Revenge," *Papers*, 1: 86; JA to Abigail Adams, 12 May 1780, *Adams Family Correspondence*, 3: 342.

6. JA to Benjamin Rush, 5 July 1789, *Old Family Letters*, 41–43.

7. JA to John Quincy Adams, 20 March 1816, *Adams Papers*, Reel 122.

8. *Works*, 4: 551; Adams to Elbridge Gerry, 2 May 1785, *Adams Papers*, Reel 364.

9. *Diary and Autobiography*, 1: 195; "Notes for an Oration at Braintree," Spring 1772, *Diary and Autobiography*, 2: 56–60.

10. See Rousseau's *Social Contract*, Bk. 2, chap. 7, and Montesquieu's *The Spirit of the Laws*, Book 29.

11. Condorcet, *Lettres d'un bourgeois de New Heaven*, 69.

12. Aristotle, *Politics*, 1289b1–14.

13. See *Works*, 4: 295.

14. Solon's views on constitutional construction are described in Plutarch, *The Lives of the Noble Grecians and Romans*, trans. John Dryden (New York, n.d.), 97–116. The Aristotelian art of lawgiving is best seen in Book 4, chap. 1 of *Politics*; Montesquieu's understanding of the Lawgiver is found in *The Spirit of the Laws*, chap. 29.

15. JA to Richard Henry Lee, 15 November 1775, *Papers*, 3: 307; JA to Horatio Gates, 23 March 1776, Ibid., 4: 59–60; JA to Patrick Henry, 3 June 1776, Ibid., 4: 234–35; JA to Benjamin Rush, 14 March 1809, *The Spur of Fame: Dialogues of John Adams and Benjamin Rush, 1805–1813*, 113. Adams's views on the art of political architecture and the role of constitutional architects may be usefully contrasted with those of the Abbé Sieyès. In his influential pamphlet *What is the Third Estate?*, Sieyès encouraged his Lawgiver to apply shock therapy when needed: "Everywhere I go, I meet those persons who in their moderation would like to break up the truth or proclaim it bit by bit. . . . It is false to assume that if the truth is divided and fragmented, the bits and pieces can thereby be fed the more easily into the mind. Not at all! Usually what is required is a powerful jolt." Sieyès blurred the distinction between philosophy and statesmanship; he thought the lawgiver, unlike the politician who is constrained by interests, should first be a philosopher who would study society "as though it were an ordinary machine" and who would open and map "the road" for this social machine, directing it "to its very end." But to achieve this end, Sieyès's philosopher-lawgiver was advised to root out all "errors" that block his advance. "To make progress," the lawgiver must "destroy" all errors of the past "without pity." Emmanuel Joseph Sieyès, *What is the Third Estate?*, trans. M. Blondel (London, 1963), 167, 168, 120, 171.

16. *Works*, 4: 300.

17. JA to James Sullivan, 26 May 1776, *Papers*, 4: 208–12; *Works*, 4: 380.

18. "Thoughts on Government," *Works*, 4: 195; JA to Horatio Gates, 23 March 1776, *Papers*, 4: 59–60; JA to Francis Dana, 16 August 1776, Ibid., 4: 466; JA to Abigail Adams, 14 April 1776, *Adams Family Correspondence*, 1: 381; JA to Elbridge Gerry, *Papers*, 3: 3, 26.

19. JA to Patrick Henry, 3 June 1776, *Papers*, 4: 234–35; "Thoughts on Government," *Works*, 4: 197 (emphasis added).

20. JA to Francis Dana, 16 August 1776, *Papers*, 4: 466; JA to Abigail Adams, 10 July 1776, *Adams Family Correspondence*, 2: 42–43. On his devotion to the right of the people to choose whatever form of government they please, see also JA to Patrick

Henry, 3 June 1776, *Papers*, 4: 234–35. Adams was entirely consistent on this point. Although he greatly disapproved of the Pennsylvania's unicameral constitution, he supported the right of the people to construct any form of republican government they deemed appropriate for their happiness: "You will see by the same Papers too, that the Writers here in Opposition to the Constitution of Pensilvania, are making a factious use of my Name and Lucubrations. Much against my Will, I assure you, for altho I am no Admirer of the Form of this Government, yet I think it is agreable to the Body of the People, and if they please themselves they will please me." (JA to Abigail Adams, 4 June 1777, *Adams Family Correspondence*, 2: 255).

21. Robert Brown, *Middle Class Democracy and the Revolution in Massachusetts* (Ithaca, N.Y., 1955), 393–96.

22. See the editor's Introduction to the Massachusetts Constitution in Taylor et al., eds. *Papers of John Adams*, 8: 231–32.

23. JA to Elbridge Gerry, 4 November 1779, *Papers*, 8: 276.

24. Ibid.; JA to Edmé Genet, 29 February 1780, *Papers*, 8: 379.

25. Plutarch, *Lives of the Noble Grecians and Romans*, 105.

26. Appleby, "The New Republican Synthesis and the Changing Political Ideas of John Adams," 578–95; Handler, *America and Europe in the Political Thought of John Adams*, 70.

27. *Works*, 4: 284–85.

28. Ibid., 6: 95, 94.

29. Ibid., 3: 449–50.

30. JA to James Lloyd, 30 March 1815, *Works*, 10: 149–50; JA to Abigail Adams, 4 December 1796, *Letters . . . Addressed to His Wife*, 2: 232–33.

31. *Works*, 4: 288.

32. Ibid., 297, 283–84.

33. JA to John Taylor, 15 April 1814, *Works*, 6: 490; JA to John Jay, 23 September 1787, *Works*, 8: 454. Revolutionary though he was, Adams was not a messianic revolutionary. In 1782 he indicated to Lafayette his views on the prospect of European revolutions: "I am not . . . an enthusiast who wishes to overturn empires and monarchies for the sake of introducing republican forms of government, and, therefore, I am no king-killer, king-hater, or king-despiser." JA to Lafayette, 21 May 1782, *Works*, 7: 593.

34. *Works*, 4: 284.

35. JA to Mercy Otis Warren, 11 July 1807, *Correspondence between John Adams and Mercy Warren*, 324.

36. "The Earl of Clarendon to William Pym," 27 January 1766, *Papers*, 1: 167.

37. *Works*, 4: 358–59, 468, 556.

38. JA to Samuel Perley, 19 June 1809, *Works*, 9: 622. Two years earlier, Adams told Mercy Otis Warren that he thought the limited and mixed monarchy of England to be "the only government which could preserve civil, political, or religious liberty, or even the semblance of it, in any of the great populous, commercial opulent, luxurious, and corrupted nations of Europe." JA to Mercy Warren, 11 July 1807, *Correspondence between John Adams and Mercy Warren*, 325.

39. *Works*, 4: 556.

40. Ibid., 308–9, 428, 359.

41. Ibid., 5: 488; 4: 493, 380, 358–59, 434, 382. In his autobiography, Adams provides yet further evidence that his theory of constitutional construction and its relation to the British form of government did not substantially change in the years

between the Revolution and his writing the *Defence*. Recalling an inquiry in June 1775 from John Rutledge while the two were serving in the Continental Congress on how to design and construct constitutions, Adams made clear what he meant when he spoke favorably of the English constitution: "Mr. Rutledge asked me my Opinion of a proper form of Government for a State. I answered him that any form, that our People would consent to institute would be better than none. Even if they placed all Power in a House of Representatives, and they should appoint Governors and Judges: but I hoped they would be wiser, and preserve the English Constitution in its *Spirit* and Substance, as far as the Circumstances of this Country required or would Admit. *That no hereditary Powers ever had existed in America, nor would they or ought they to be introduced or proposed.* But that I hoped the three Branches of a Legislature would be *preserved*, an Executive, independent of the Senate or Council and the House and above all things the Independence of the Judges [italics added]."

Several months later, Adams was barraged by questions from other members of the Congress on how to construct revolutionary governments. He told those who asked (as he would in the *Defence*) that the best models to imitate were their old colonial charters. "But what Plan of a Government, would you advise? A Plan as nearly resembling the Governments under which We were born and have lived as the Circumstances of the Country will admit. Kings We never had among Us, Nobles We never had. Nothing hereditary ever existed in the Country: Nor will the Country require or admit of any such Thing: but Governors, and Councils We have always had as Well as Representatives. A Legislature in three Branches ought to be preserved, and independent Judges" (*Diary and Autobiography*, 3: 354).

In his correspondence with John Taylor of Caroline, Adams addressed directly the charge that the *Defence* had been intended to promote the English constitution, with its hereditary House of Lords, as the best model for America: "It is true that, in my apology, I expressed in strong terms my admiration of the English constitution; but I meant no more of it than was to the purpose of my argument; that is, the division and union of powers in our American constitutions, which were, indeed, so far, imitations of it. My argument had no more to do with hereditary descent than it had with the Church or the Bank of England." JA to John Taylor, 15 April 1814, *Works*, 6: 489.

42. *Works*, 4: 359.

43. Ibid., 493, 440.

44. Ibid., 359. Adams's views on the changing nature of American society and its relationship to constitutional construction and revision are compared with those of James Madison, Charles Pinckney, Alexander Hamilton, and Gouverneur Morris in the conclusion to this work. See chapter twelve of the present work.

45. In addressing Mercy Warren's charge of monarchism, Adams enunciated his strongest opinion against the libel: "So far from manifesting a partiality for monarchy, I have always uniformly declared to my friends, whenever the subject has been seriously started in conversation, that if the people of America would unanimously confer on me the power of instituting a government for them, as the Athenian did on Solon, and the Lacedaemonians on Lycurgus, and I knew beforehand that they would quietly submit to whatever plan I should propose, I would not recommend to them either an hereditary king or an hereditary nobility, because I did not in my conscience believe it would be for their happiness, security, or prosperity." (JA to Mercy Otis Warrren, 11 July 1807, *Correspondence between John Adams and Mercy Warren*, 325–26).

12. Posterity Must Judge

1. Quoted in Ellis, *Passionate Sage*, 113. For a selection of the eulogies offered around the country, see *A Selection of Eulogies, Pronounced in the Several States in Honor of Those Illustrious Patriots and Statesmen, John Adams and Thomas Jefferson* (Hartford, Conn., 1826).

2. *The Papers of Daniel Webster: Speeches and Formal Writings*, ed. Charles M. Wiltse (Hanover, N.H., 1986), 1: 239, 241, 271.

3. See Wood, *The Creation of the American Republic*, 567–92. In recent years, however, the importance and relevance of Adams's political thought has received favorable notice from Diggins, *The Lost Soul of American Politics*, 69–85; Lerner, *The Thinking Revolutionary*, 16–29; Ellis, *Passionate Sage: The Character and Legacy of John Adams;* and from J. David Greenstone, *The Lincoln Persuasion: Remaking American Liberalism* (Princeton, N.J., 1993), 71–118.

4. Benjamin Rush to JA, 2 July 1788, *Letters of Benjamin Rush*, Lyman Butterfield, ed. (Princeton, N.J., 1951), 1: 468–69; Henry Knox to Mercy Warren, 30 May 1787, quoted in John P. Kaminski and Gaspare J. Saladino, eds. *The Documentary History of the Ratification of the Constitution* (16 vols. to date; Madison, Wis., 1981), 13: 83; Tench Coxe to John Brown Cutting, 19 May 1787, quoted in Kaminski and Saladino, eds., *The Documentary History of the Ratification of the Constitution*, 16: 83; Joel Barlow to JA, 14 June 1787, *Adams Papers*, Reel 370; Joseph Willard to JA, 1 September 1787, Ibid.; Ezra Stiles to JA, 1 August 1788, Ibid., Reel 371.

5. David Ramsey to JA, 20 September 1787, *Adams Papers*, Reel 370; Silvanus Bourne to JA, 17 January 1790, Ibid., Reel 373; John Trumbull to JA, 5 June 1790, Ibid., Reel 373; Thomas Brand Hollis to JA, 15 October 1787, Ibid., Reel 370.

6. Henry Knox to Mercy Warren, 30 May 1787, Kaminski and Saladino, eds., *The Documentary History of the Ratification of the Constitution*, 16: 83; Richard Cranch to JA, 24 May 1787, *Adams Papers*, Reel 370; Richard Henry Lee to JA, 3 September 1787, Ibid.; Thomas Pinckney to JA, 10 July 1787, *Works*, 8: 443.

7. Tench Coxe to John Brown Cutting, 19 May 1787, quoted in Kaminski and Saladino, eds., *The Documentary History of the Ratification of the Constitution*, 16: 83; "Sidney," Philadelphia *Independent Gazetteer*, 6 June 1787, Ibid., 88; Benjamin Rush to Richard Price, 2 June 1787, Ibid., 83; William White to JA, 1 August 1787, *Adams Papers*, Reel 370; "Centinel" quoted in *The Anti-Federalist: Writings by the Opponents of the Constitution*, ed. Herbert J. Storing (Chicago, 1981), 15; "Address of John Humble," in *The Complete Anti-Federalist*. 7 vols. Ed. Herbert J. Storing (Chicago, 1981), 3: 89.

8. Benjamin Franklin to JA, 18 May 1787, quoted in Charles Warren, *The Making of the Constitution* (Boston, 1937), 157; William R. Davie to James Iredell, 30 May 1787, quoted in Kaminski and Saladino, eds., *The Documentary History of the Ratification of the Constitution*, 16: 84; John Jay to JA, 4 and 25 July, 16 October 1787, *Adams Papers*, Reel 370.

9. James Madison to Thomas Jefferson, 6 June 1787, *The Papers of James Madison*, ed. Robert Rutland (Chicago, 1977), 10: 29–30; Francis Adrian Vanderkemp to JA, 7 January 1790, *Papers*, Reel 373. Madison's letter is often quoted by scholars attempting to demonstrate the anomalous character of the *Defence*. Unfortunately, too often they quote Madison's criticism without quoting his praise for the book. See Wood, *Creation of the American Republic*, 582, and Jack N. Rakove, *Original Meanings: Politics and Ideas in the Making of the Constitution* (New York, 1996), 24.

10. Reverend James Madison to James Madison, 11 June 1787, *The Papers of James Madison*, ed. William T. Hutchinson et al., 17 vols. (Chicago, 1962–), 10: 44–46.

11. [John Stevens], *Observations on Government, Including Some Animadversions on Mr. Adams's Defence of the Constitutions of Government of the United States of America: and on Mr. De Lolme's Constitution of England* (New York, 1787), 3–4, 46–47, 24. So fantastic were Stevens's claims that Adams might very well have wondered if this New Jersey "farmer" had actually read, let alone comprehended, the entirety of his book.

12. John Taylor, *An Inquiry into the Principles and Policy of the Government of the United States* (Indianapolis, 1969, first published 1814), 3–4.

13. Ibid., 3–4, 26, 79, 92, 104; *Works*, 6: 461–62.

14. Richard Price to JA, 8 February 1787, *Works*, 6: 220; 5 March 1789, *Adams Papers*, reel 37. Price even recognized *A Defence* in his 1787 essay on *The Evidence for a Future Period of Improvement in the State of Mankind*. He there described the subject of government and the question of constitutional forms as the most important subject for philosophers. Though he thought the science of government in need of some improvement, he recommended that readers turn to Adams's books on government for "much assistance in this inquiry." D. O. Thomas, ed., *Richard Price: Political Writings* (Cambridge, 1992), 164.

15. A. M. Cerisier to JA, 29 May 1787, *Adams Papers*, Reel 370; Alexander Jardine to JA, 26 May 1789, Ibid., Reel 372; Joseph Priestley, *Familiar Letters Addressed to the Inhabitants of the Town of Birmingham* (Birmingham 1790), Letter 8; Cooper quoted in Richard Rush to JA, 3 November 1815, *Adams Papers*, Reel 427.

16. John Trumbull to JA, 5 June 1790, *Adams Papers*, Reel 373; Trophime Gérard, marquis de Lally-Tollendal, *Moniteur Universel*, 19 August 1789, also in *Rapport de M. le Comte de Lally-Tollendal*, 22–24, quoted in Lewis Rosenthal, *America and France: The Influence of the United States on France in the 18th Century* (New York, 1882), 196–200; Lally-Tollendal, *Mémoire de M. le comte de Lally-Tollendal, ou Seconde lettre à ses Commettans* (Paris, 1790), 136, quoted in Joyce Appleby, "America as a Model for the Radical French Reformers of 1789," *William and Mary Quarterly*, 28 (April 1971), 283; JA to Abigail Adams, 2 March 1793, in Charles F. Adams, ed., *Letters of John Adams, Addressed to His Wife* (Boston, 1841), 2: 128; "Extract from the Speech of Boissy D'Anglais, on delivering the reported plan of the New Constitution of France, in 1795," appended to [William Loughton Smith], *The Pretensions of Thomas Jefferson to the Presidency Examined; and the Charges Against John Adams Refuted* (October 1796), Evans Imprints 32212. For biographical sketches of Lally-Tollendal and Boissy d'Anglais, see Samuel F. Scott and Barry Rothans, eds., *Historical Dictionary of the French Revolution, 1789–1799* (Westport, Conn., 1985), 538–39, 101–3. The *Defence* did have its critics in France as well. See C. Bradley Thompson, "John Adams and the Coming of the French Revolution," *Journal of the Early Republic* 16 (fall 1996): 361–87 and "The American Founding and the French Revolution," in *The Legacy of the French Revolution*, eds. Ralph C. Hancock and L. Gary Lambert (Lanham, Md., 1996), 109–50.

17. See Wood, *The Creation of the American Republic*, 580, 584.

18. James Madison, *Notes of the Debates in the Federal Convention of 1787*, with an Introduction by Adrienne Koch [Athens, Ohio, 1966], 135. One gets a fuller sense of Hamilton's reasoning from his notes for the June 18 speech. See Henry C. Lodge, ed., *The Works of Alexander Hamilton*, 12 vols. (New York, 1904), 1: 374–75, 352.

19. Madison, *Notes of the Debates in the Federal Convention of 1787*, 181–87.

20. Ibid., 193–95, 403–4. For a penetrating account of Madison's views on the

senate in the Constitutional Convention, see Paul Eidelberg, *The Philosophy of the American Constitution: A Reinterpretation of the Intentions of the Founding Fathers* (New York, 1968), 137–65.

21. Jacob E. Cooke, ed., *The Federalist,* 58.

22. Madison, *Notes of the Debates in the Federal Convention of 1787,* 193–95.

23. Ibid., 233–35.

24. Wood, *The Creation of the American Republic,* 569.

25. This episode is usefully recounted in Stanley Elkins and Eric McKitrick, *The Age of Federalism* (New York, 1993), 46–50. For Adams's preferred presidential title, see JA to William Tudor, 28 June 1789, *Adams Papers,* Reel 115; JA to Benjamin Rush, 24 July 1789, *Old Family Letters,* 1: 44–47. Also see John Howe's account in *The Changing Political Thought of John Adams,* 176–82, and that of James Hutson, "John Adams's Titles Campaign," *New England Quarterly* 41 (1968): 34–41.

26. JA to Benjamin Rush, 24 July 1789, *Old Family Letters,* 1: 44–47. See also JA to Benjamin Rush, 5 July 1789, Ibid., 42.

27. *Works,* 6: 246, 109.

28. JA to Benjamin Rush, 5 July 1789, *Old Family Letters,* 1: 41–43; JA to Benjamin Rush, 28 July 1789, Ibid., 47–51; JA to William Tudor, 28 June 1789, *Adams Papers,* Reel 115; *Works,* 6: 246.

29. JA to Benjamin Rush, 24 July 1789, *Old Family Letters,* 1: 44–47.

30. James Madison to Thomas Jefferson, 23 May 1789, *Papers of James Madison,* 12: 182–83; Thomas Jefferson to James Madison, 29 July 1789, Ibid., 315.

31. *Works,* 6: 232, 269, 273, 276, 252.

32. Ibid., 276.

33. Ibid., 227.

34. Thomas Jefferson to George Washington, 8 May 1791, *Papers of Thomas Jefferson,* 20: 291–92; Thomas Jefferson to James Monroe, 10 July 1789, Ibid., 296–98; Thomas Jefferson to Thomas Paine, 29 July 1789, Ibid., 308–9; Thomas Jefferson to Benjamin Vaughan, 11 May 1791, Ibid., 391; Thomas Jefferson to JA, 30 August 1791, Ibid., 310–12.

35. John Quincy Adams, "Publicola," quoted in *The Selected Writings of John and John Quincy Adams,* ed. Koch and Peden, 227.

36. The best account of the ideological fallout following the *Rights of Man* controversy is Banning, *The Jeffersonian Persuasion,* 93–100, 155–60.

37. On Jefferson's role in suppressing the French translation and publication of Adams's *Defence,* see Joyce Appleby, "The Jefferson-Adams Rupture and the First French Translation of John Adams' *Defence,*" *American Historical Review,* 73 (April 1967), 1084–91, and Thompson, "John Adams and the Coming of the French Revolution," 361–87. In summer of 1793, Jefferson frantically appealed to James Madison to respond to Alexander Hamilton's anti-French "Pacificus" essays. "For god's sake, my dear Sir," Jefferson implored, "take up your pen, select the most striking heresies, and cut them to pieces in the face of the public." (Thomas Jefferson to James Madison, 7 July 1793, *Papers of Thomas Jefferson,* 26: 444. During the public controversy surrounding the founding of Freneau's *National Gazette,* Jefferson was once again less than honest in explaining his role in the matter to George Washington. Julian Boyd, editor of the Jefferson *Papers,* was forced to conclude that Jefferson was thoroughly disingenuous in explaining to the President the role that he had played in founding and sponsoring a newspaper that was hostile to the administration. See Julian Boyd,

"Editor's Note," Ibid., 20: 724–25, 753. Jefferson's use of the press to further his political aims is ably discussed in Frank Mott, *Jefferson and the Press* (Baton Rouge, La., 1943).

38. JA to Thomas Jefferson, 29 July 1791, *Papers of Thomas Jefferson*, 20: 305–7. In a thinly veiled reference to Adams, Jefferson told Philip Mazzei in 1796 that it "would give you a fever were I to name to you the apostates who have gone over to these heresies [monarchy and aristocracy], men who were Samsons in the field and Solomons in the council, but who have had their heads shorn by the harlot England." Right up until the end of his life, Jefferson insisted on repeating his indictment. In 1825, he asked William Short if it was possible to "read Mr. Adams's defence of the American Constitutions without seeing that he was a monarchist?" (Thomas Jefferson to Philip Mazzei, 24 April 1796, in *The Writings of Thomas Jefferson*, ed. Andrew A. Lipscomb and Albert Ellery Bergh (Washington, D.C., 1903), 9: 335–37; Thomas Jefferson to William Short, 8 January 1825, Ibid., 16: 93). See also, Thomas Jefferson to William Short, 28 July 1791, *Papers of Thomas Jefferson*, 20: 692–93; Thomas Jefferson to Lewis Littlepage, 29 July 1791, Ibid., 703.

39. "Editor's Note," *Papers of Thomas Jefferson*, 20: 289; James Monroe to Thomas Jefferson, 25 July 1791, ibid., 303–5; "Catullus, No. 3" [Alexander Hamilton], *Papers of Alexander Hamilton*, ed. Harold C. Syrett (New York, 1967), 12: 501–4.

40. JA to Thomas Jefferson, 29 July 1791, *Adams–Jefferson Letters*, 249; JA to Abigail Adams, 8 January 1793, *Adams Papers*, Reel 376.

41. Charles Holt to JA, 27 August 1820, Ibid., Reel 450.

42. JA to Thomas Jefferson, 13 July 1813, *Adams–Jefferson Letters*, 2: 356.

43. JA to Elbridge Gerry, 6 December 1777, *Papers*, 5: 346–47; JA to John Quincy Adams, 16 May 1815, *Adams Papers*, Reel 122.

BIBLIOGRAPHY

Primary Sources

Adams, Charles Francis, ed. *Correspondence between John Adams and Mercy Warren*. New York: Arno Press, 1972.

Adams, John. *The Works of John Adams*. Edited by Charles Francis Adams. 10 vols. Boston, 1850–56; reprint ed., Freeport, New York: Books for Libraries Press, 1969.

———. *Adams Family Correspondence*. Edited by L. H. Butterfield et al. 4 vols. Cambridge, Mass.: Harvard University Press, 1963.

———. *Diary and Autobiography of John Adams*. Edited by L. H. Butterfield. 4 vols. Cambridge, Mass.: Harvard University Press, 1962.

———. *The Earliest Diary of John Adams*. Edited by L. H. Butterfield. Cambridge, Mass.: Harvard University Press, 1966.

———. *Legal Papers of John Adams*. Edited by Kinvin L. Wroth and Hiller B. Zobel. 3 vols. Cambridge, Mass.: Harvard University Press, 1965.

———. *Papers of John Adams*. Edited by Robert J. Taylor et al. 10 vols. (to date) Cambridge, Mass.: Harvard University Press, 1977.

Boston Public Library. *Catalogue of the John Adams Library in the Public Library of the City of Boston*. Boston: The Trustees, 1917.

Cappon, Lester J., ed. *The Adams-Jefferson Letters: The Complete Correspondence Between Thomas Jefferson and Abigail and John Adams*. 2 vols. New York: Simon and Schuster, 1971.

Correspondence between the Hon. John Adams . . . and the Late Wm. Cunningham, Esq. Boston: Truce & Greene, 1823.

Ford, C. Worthington, ed. *Statesman and Friend: Correspondence of John Adams and Benjamin Waterhouse, 1784–1822*. Boston: 1927.

Peek, George A., ed. *The Political Writings of John Adams: Representative Selections*. Indianapolis: Bobbs-Merrill, 1954.

Schutz, John A., and Douglass Adair, eds. *The Spur of Fame: Dialogues of John Adams and Benjamin Rush, 1805–1813*. San Marino, Calif.: The Huntington Library, 1966.

Warren–Adams Letters: Being Chiefly a Correspondence among John Adams, Samuel Adams, and James Warren. Boston: Massachusetts Historical Society, 1917–25.

Books

Adams, Randolph G. *Political Ideas of the American Revolution: Britannic-American Contributions to the Problem of Imperial Organization, 1765–1775*. New York: Barnes & Noble, 1958.

Adair, Douglass. *Fame and the Founding Fathers*. Edited by Edmund P. Willis. Bethlehem, Pa.: Moravian College, 1967.

Arendt, Hannah. *On Revolution*. New York: Viking Press, 1963.

Bailyn, Bernard. *The Ideological Origins of the American Revolution*. Cambridge, Mass.: Harvard University Press, 1967.

Banning, Lance. *The Jeffersonian Persuasion: Evolution of a Party Ideology*. Ithaca, N.Y.: Cornell University Press, 1978.

Burleigh, Anne Husted. *John Adams*. New Rochelle, N.Y.: Arlington House, 1969.

Chinard, Gilbert. *Honest John Adams*. Boston: Little, Brown, 1933.

Cohen, I. Bernard. *Science and the Founding Fathers: Science in the Political Thought of Thomas Jefferson, Benjamin Franklin, John Adams and James Madison*. New York: W. W. Norton, 1995.

Colbourn, Trevor. *The Lamp of Experience: Whig History and the Intellectual Origins of the American Revolution*. New York: Norton, 1965.

Conkin, Paul. *Puritans and Pragmatists: Eight Eminent American Thinkers*. New York: Dodd, Mead, 1968.

Dakin, Douglas. *Turgot and the Ancien Regime in France*. London: 1939.

Dauer, Manning. *The Adams Federalists*. Baltimore: Johns Hopkins Press, 1953.

Diggins, John P. *The Lost Soul of American Politics: Virtue, Self-Interest, and the Foundations of Liberalism*. New York: Basic Books, 1984.

Elkins, Stanley and McKitrick, Eric. *The Age of Federalism*. New York: Oxford University Press, 1993.

Ellis, Joseph J. *Passionate Sage: The Character and Legacy of John Adams*. New York: W. W. Norton, 1993.

Ferling, John. *John Adams: A Life*. Knoxville: University of Tennessee Press, 1992.

Gebhardt, Jürgen. *Americanism: Revolutionary Order and Societal Self-Interpretation in the American Republic*. Translated by Ruth Hein. Baton Rouge: Louisiana State University, 1993.

Greene, Jack P. *Peripheries and Center: Constitutional Development in the Extended Polities of the British Empire and the United States, 1607–1788*. Athens: University of Georgia Press, 1986.

Greenstone, J. David. *The Lincoln Persuasion: Remaking American Liberalism*. Princeton, N.J.: Princeton University Press, 1993.

Handler, Edward. *America and Europe in the Political Thought of John Adams*. Cambridge, Mass.: Harvard University Press, 1964.

Haraszti, Zoltan. *John Adams and the Prophets of Progress*. New York: Grosset & Dunlap, 1964.

Howe, John R., Jr. *The Changing Political Thought of John Adams*. Princeton, N.J.: Princeton University Press, 1966.

Hutson, James. *John Adams and the Diplomacy of the American Revolution*. Lexington: University of Kentucky Press, 1980.

Huyler, Jerome. *Locke in America: The Moral Philosophy of the Founding Era*. Lawrence: University Press of Kansas, 1995.

Iacuzzi, Alfred. *John Adams, Scholar*. New York: S.F. Vanni, 1952.

Kettner, James H. *The Development of American Citizenship, 1608–1870*. Chapel Hill: University of North Carolina Press, 1978.

Knollenberg, Bernard. *Origin of the American Revolution: 1759–1766*. New York: Free Press, 1965.

Koch, Adrienne. *Adams and Jefferson: "Posterity Must Judge."* Chicago: Rand McNally, 1963.

Kurtz, Stephen G. *The Presidency of John Adams: The Collapse of Federalism, 1795–1800*. New York: A. S. Barnes, 1961.

Lerner, Ralph. *The Thinking Revolutionary: Principle and Practice in the New Republic*. Ithaca, N.Y.: Cornell University Press, 1987.

Manent, Pierre. *An Intellectual History of Liberalism*. Princeton, N.J.: Princeton University Press, 1994.

Mansfield, Harvey C. *Taming the Prince: The Ambivalence of the Modern Executive*. Baltimore: Johns Hopkins University Press, 1989.

May, Henry F. *The Enlightenment in America*. New York: Oxford University Press, 1976.

Mayer, David N. *The Constitutional Thought of Thomas Jefferson*. Charlottesville: University Press of Virginia, 1994.

McIlwain, Charles H. *The American Revolution: A Constitutional Interpretation*. New York: Macmillan, 1924.

McWilliams, Wilson Carey. *The Idea of Fraternity in America*. Berkeley: University of California Press, 1973.

Nordholt, Jan Willem Schulte. *The Dutch Republic and American Independence*. Translated by Herbert R. Rowen. Chapel Hill: University of North Carolina Press, 1982.

O'Brien, Conor Cruise. *The Long Affair: Thomas Jefferson and the French Revolution, 1785–1800*. Chicago: University of Chicago Press, 1996.

Palmer, Robert R. *The Age of Democratic Revolution: The Challenge*. Princeton, N.J.: Princeton University Press, 1959.

Pangle, Thomas L. *The Spirit of Modern Republicanism: The Moral Vision of the American Founders and the Philosophy of Locke*. Chicago: University of Chicago Press, 1988.

Peterson, Merrill D. *Adams and Jefferson: A Revolutionary Dialogue*. New York: Oxford University Press, 1976.

Pocock, J. G. A. *The Machiavellian Moment; Florentine Political Thought and the Atlantic Republican Tradition*. Princeton, N.J.: Princeton University Press, 1975.

Shaw, Peter. *The Character of John Adams*. New York: W.W. Norton, 1976.

Smith, Page. *John Adams*. 2 vols. New York: Doubleday, 1962.

Stoner, James R. *Common Law and Liberal Theory: Coke, Hobbes, and the Origins of American Constitutionalism*. Lawrence: University Press of Kansas, 1992.

Vile, M. J. C. *Constitutionalism and the Separation of Powers*. Oxford: Oxford University Press, 1967.

Walsh, Correa M. *The Political Science of John Adams: A Study in the Theory of Mixed Government and the Bicameral System*. Free Port, N.Y.: Books for Libraries Press, 1915, 1969.

Webking, Robert H. *The American Revolution and the Politics of Liberty*. Baton Rouge: Louisiana State University Press, 1988.

Wood, Gordon S. *The Creation of the American Republic*. New York: W. W. Norton & Company, 1969.

Zuckert, Michael. *Natural Rights and the New Republicanism*. Princeton, N.J.: Princeton University Press, 1994.

Articles

Appleby, Joyce. "The Jefferson-Adams Rupture and the First French Translation of John Adams' *Defence*." *American Historical Review*, 73 (1967): 1084–91.

————. "The New Republican Synthesis and the Changing Political Ideas of John Adams." *American Quarterly* 25 (1973): 578–95.

Bailyn, Bernard. "Butterfield's Adams: Notes for a Sketch." *William and Mary Quarterly* 3rd Ser., 19 (1962): 239–56.

Breen, Timothy. "John Adams' Fight against Innovation in the New England Constitution: 1776." *New England Quarterly* 40 (1967): 501–20.

Cooke, J. W. "John Adams on Liberty and Equality." *Enlightenment Essays* 8 (1977): 53–63.

Dauer, Manning. "The Political Economy of John Adams." *Political Science Quarterly* 56 (1941): 545–72.

Dorfman, Joseph. "The Regal Republic of John Adams." *Political Science Quarterly* 59 (June 1941): 227–41.

Evans, William B. "John Adams's Opinion of Benjamin Franklin." *Pennsylvania Magazine of History and Biography* 92 (1968): 220–38.

Farrell, James M. "John Adams's Autobiography: The Ciceronian Paradigm and the Quest for Fame." *New England Quarterly* 62 (December 1989): 505–28.

Fielding, Howard Ioan. "John Adams: Puritan, Deist, Humanist." *Journal of Religion* 20 (January 1940): 33–46.

Grinnell, Frank Washburn. "John Winthrop and the Constitutional Thinking of John Adams." *Massachusetts Historical Society, Proceedings* 63 (1929–1930): 90–119.

Gummere, Richard M. "The Classical Politics of John Adams." *Boston Public Library Quarterly* 9 (1957): 167–82.

Harazsti, Zoltan. "John Adams Flays a Philosophe: Annotations on Condorcet's Progress of the Human Mind." *William and Mary Quarterly* 3rd ser., 7 (1950): 223–54.

Knollenberg, Bernhard. "John Dickinson vs. John Adams: 1774–1776." *American Philosophical Society, Proceedings* 107 (1963): 138–44.

————. "John Adams, Knox, and Washington." *American Antiquarian Society, Proceedings* 56 (1946): 207–38.

Morgan, Edmund S. "John Adams and the Puritan Tradition." *New England Quarterly* 34 (December 1961): 518–29.

Morison, Samuel E. "Struggle Over the Adoption of the Constitution of Massachusetts, 1780." *Massachusetts Historical Society, Proceedings* 50 (1917): 353–411.

Morse, Anson D. "The Politics of John Adams." *American Historical Review* 4 (January 1899): 292–312.

Paynter, John L. "The Ethics of John Adams: Prolegomenon to a Science of Politics." Ph.D. Diss., University of Chicago, 1974.

————. "John Adams: On the Principles of Political Science." *Political Science Reviewer* 6 (1976): 34–72.

Porter, J. M. and Farnell, Stewart. "John Adams and American Constitutionalism." *American Journal of Jurisprudence* 21 (1976): 20–33.

Robathan, Dorothy M. "John Adams and the Classics." *New England Quarterly* 19 (March 1946): 91–98.

Rossiter, Clinton. "The Legacy of John Adams." *Yale Review* 46 (June 1957): 528–50.

Silbey, John E. "Richard Henry Lee, John Adams, and the Virginia Constitution of 1776." *Virginia Magazine of History and Biography* 84 (October 1976): 387–400.

Taylor, Robert J. "Construction of the Massachusetts Constitution." *American Antiquarian Society, Proceedings* 90 (1980): 317–46.

Thompson, C. Bradley. "John Adams's Machiavellian Moment." *Review of Politics* 57 (summer 1995): 389–417.

———. "John Adams and the Coming of the French Revolution." *Journal of the Early American Republic* 16 (fall 1996): 361–87.

———. "The American Founding and the French Revolution." In *The Legacy of the French Revolution,* ed. Ralph C. Hancock and L. Gary Lambert (Lanham, Md.: Rowman and Littlefield, 1996), 109–50.

Warren, Charles. "John Adams and American Constitutions." *Massachusetts Law Quarterly* 12 (1917): 66–82.

INDEX